EXERCISE, AGING, AND HEALTH

EXERCISE, AGING, AND HEALTH:
Overcoming Barriers to an Active Old Age

Sandra O'Brien Cousins

USA	Publishing Office:	Taylor & Francis
		325 Chestnut Street, Suite 800
		Philadelphia, PA 19106
		Tel: (215) 625-8900
		Fax: (215) 625-2940
	Distribution Center:	Taylor & Francis
		1900 Frost Road, Suite 101
		Bristol, PA 19007-1598
		Tel: (215) 785-5800
		Fax: (215) 785-5515
UK		Taylor & Francis Ltd.
		1 Gunpowder Square
		London EC4A 3DE
		Tel: 0171 583 0490
		Fax: 0171 583 0581

EXERCISE, AGING, AND HEALTH: Overcoming Barriers to an Active Old Age

1 2 3 4 5 6 7 8 9 0   E B E B   9 0 9 8

This book was set in Times Roman.

A CIP catalog record for this book is available from the British Library.
∞ The paper in this publication meets the requirements of the ANSI Standard Z39.48-1984 (Permanence of Paper)

Library of Congress Cataloging-in-Publication Data

O'Brien Cousins, Sandra.
   Exercise, aging, and health: overcoming barriers to an active old age / by Sandra O'Brien Cousins.
     p.   cm.
   Includes bibliographical references and index.

    1. Aged—Health and hygiene.   2. Exercise for the aged.
I. Title.
RA564.8.O27   1997
613.7'0446—dc21

                                      97-37825
                                         CIP

ISBN 1-56032-413-9 (case)
ISBN 1-56032-414-7 (paper)

I dedicate this book to my mother, Gladys Hartley.
Although my work has situated me almost a thousand miles away,
she has been the single most influential person in my life. In recent years,
her own aging, health, and challenges to keep physically active have been
thought-provoking. With my encouragement to keep active,
my mother does her best to maintain her health. Still there are many
disruptions to her physical activity with illness, aches, and pains.

I want to thank her for her courage to sit through my doctoral defense as
I was grilled by some of the brightest minds at the University of British Columbia.
Although scientists have learned many things about the important contribution
of exercise to better aging and health, my mother's experiences continue
to temper my confidence that we will ever really know the solutions
for the many barriers which challenge the participation of aging adults.

Contents

PART TWO   TOWARD A THEORY OF OLDER ADULT EXERCISE MOTIVATION

Preface

In 1985, Dr. Ernst Jokl gave a keynote speech at the Physical Activity, Aging, and Sport Conference at West Point Military Academy. I was intrigued by something he said.

> Play bestows and conveys the attitudes of youth. An old person who plays turns young. A young person who cannot play turns old.

The importance of physical recreation at all life stages is a concept that many exercise scientists endorse, but the lifelong significance of physical activity, exercise, and sport has as yet to be publicly accepted. Dr. Jokl's speech started me thinking about the role of physical activity in healthy aging.

Shortly after this conference, I began to teach fitness classes to adults ages 50 to 75. Many of the participants were truly unfit, and, among the women, some could not do even one modified push-up or sit-up. Others in the group demonstrated excellent physical abilities—physical fitness and skills that compared favorably to adults 30 to 50 years younger. Within a few months, the unfit were significantly fitter, and the already fit had started taking up new physical challenges, namely, gymnastics!

This was an intriguing phenomenon: elderly women venturing beyond the challenges of physical fitness, forging new skills in a young girls' sport, and then enjoying their efforts in public performances. There was a visible enthusiasm to test their physical limits and the commitment to learning skills was obvious. Why were these women so eager now?

The research literature is replete with evidence about the increasing biological, psychological, and social heterogeneity that accompanies aging; it seems that human variability is no better demonstrated than in the exercise patterns and physical fitness of aging adults, some of whom have become functionally frail while others appear to counter aging declines with high levels of physical activity. Such visible evidence of these different outcomes for people led me to wonder why older people do what they do. Which of the many biological, social, and psychological forces are operating to create such diverse lifestyles and disparate health outcomes by late life?

The fitness class developed into a performing gymnastics team that trains at the University of Alberta. Since May of 1986, the twenty-five women and men on "the

U of Agers team" have been seen on national television broadcasts on a number of occasions. They are the documentary centerpiece of the National Film Board's (1990) "Age Is No Barrier." They have appeared frequently on CBC's "The Best Years" and are regularly solicited to perform at major events across Canada and the United States. These older adults have become a remarkable social phenomenon mainly because the general public has so underestimated the physical capabilities and interests of older adults. This narrow social perspective, which finds elderly athleticism incongruous, drives the sociological and psychological aspects of my research.

Never before has society been better able to offer leadership, supportive technology, and diverse opportunities for the physical education and recreation of aging adults. While a minority of elderly are ready for, and engaging in, vigorous forms of physical activity, the majority of older adults do not appear to be interested. My curiosity about what leads to highly active versus highly sedentary living in older adulthood has helped to bring my research into focus.

The challenge of aging better lies before all of us. Clearly, aging processes cannot be halted by any intervention known to us today. Still, with many circumstances beyond our control, there is much that individuals can do to alter their lifestyle, longevity, and end-of-life health outcomes. Scientific evidence suggests that it is never too late to take some action for the betterment of health. With this book, I hope to strengthen the awareness about the magnitude of the positive outcomes that can be expected from increasing the activity levels of the older half of the population. In addition, I am hopeful this book will act as a useful resource to the many health professionals who have become aware of the important role they are now expected to play in community health promotion.

The gradual reduction of physical activity as one gets older seems to be a natural and normal phenomenon. Yet being sedentary exposes individuals to high risk of early death and disability. While the social, psychological, and biological benefits of regular exercise at all ages are becoming better known, most adults are still compromising their health by getting insufficient exercise.

Why so many elderly surrender their bodies to the ravages of a sedentary lifestyle warrants investigation and explanation. Finding answers to this question has challenged my research program since the mid-1980s and challenges me still.

This book is original work that will be of interest to academics in the fields of gerontology, physical and health education, health promotion, sport psychology, health psychology, and social sciences. The text is aimed at medical practitioners, health professionals, physical educators, gerontologists, and new scholars and students. The general objective of this book is twofold: 1) to summarize the research findings regarding the known contribution that regular physical activity makes toward healthy or successful aging, and 2) to examine how social, cognitive, biological, and contextual forces over the life course influence activity patterns.

My first goal is to consolidate the scientific evidence about the significant benefits of exercise for the aging adult. Since the evidence is scattered among dozens of journals of various disciplines, my hope is that Part One will facilitate the reader's confidence that regular exercise is an important survival resource for older adults. As one looks at the range and depth of benefits, and acknowledges the potency of some of the most basic human movements to human health—such as walking or stretching—it is tempting to consider that exercise is the "best medicine" for many of the ills of old age.

My objective in Part One is to lay out this powerful evidence and contrast it with the known risks of physical activity so that readers can judge for themselves. My hope is that, in my lifetime, physicians will routinely inquire about and prescribe increased physical activity prior to advocating medication, especially for those patients exhibiting symptoms of hypokinetic disease. Toward this end, Chapter 8 is aimed at providing some guidelines to older people and assisting professionals on the kinds of physical movements that they can do during their daily living to "use it" and not "lose it."

Part Two is aimed at the reader who is interested in the theoretical explanations for older adult activity behavior. Part Two explores needed and promising explanations for older people's reluctance to reap the benefits of regular physical activity. The section begins with an overview of the main theories used in explaining the health and activity behavior of adults. The contextual setting or given life situation and circumstances of an individual that affect their exercise involvement is then discussed, followed by a chapter on the cognitive beliefs that facilitate active living in older people. The goal of Part Two is to explore and provide evidence for the contextual and cognitive features associated with healthy levels of physical activity involvement. The section will be of interest to scholars from various disciplines because support is provided for a multidisciplinary perspective or composite theoretical model of late-life exercise prediction. The multidisciplinary perspective, while challenging for scientists, coincides with North American calls for more collaborative research.

Part One, titled *Living Longer and Aging Better*, includes eight chapters. The opening chapter introduces the social problem of normal aging facing many industrialized countries, which are forecast to be headed for an "aging explosion" in the coming decades. The explosion in itself is not the problem, but rather the proposed impact that so many elderly people who are aging poorly will make on an already overburdened health care system. Chapter 1 gives an overview of the social and personal impact of sedentary lifestyles. Gender is a central issue because women are less physically active than men at all ages. This single lifestyle difference may be an important explanation for the more prevalent health and aging problems of women. Chapter 1 acknowledges that the role of active or inactive living is complicated by poverty, lack of opportunity, social stigmas, and internalized beliefs about the risks of physical exertion for older people.

Chapter 2 presents demographic and historical information on today's elderly cohort. Each generation has unique experiences and historical features that help to make that cohort unique. Reviewing the historical context helps to set the stage for understanding the physical activity and sport patterns of today's elderly. The primary context is North American with a focus on adults born in the 1920s or earlier.

Chapter 3 examines past and present activity patterns of today's elderly adults. The chapter takes a historical look at the varying opportunities for physical activity in the early lives of today's elderly adults. The historical perspective helps to explain why so few seniors are not involved in the sporting life in their older years. In the second part of the chapter, the current activity patterns of older North Americans are addressed, followed by a look at the tools for physical activity assessment. Although the tools for assessment are still rather crude, the data is consistent in finding that older adults are still the most sedentary segment of the population according to a number of large North American studies.

Chapter 4 addresses the actual risks of late-life exercise involvement. Inactive people are known to exaggerate the risks associated with being more active and to underestimate the benefits. This section discusses both perceived and known risk in older adult exercise. New findings in older adults perceptions of risk for exercise are presented.

Chapter 5 presents a brief summary of the benefits of late-life exercise. Hundreds of intervention studies across a number of disciplines provide strong support that "exercise is the best medicine" for avoiding many of the ills of advanced aging. The chapter reviews the convincing scientific evidence about the many biological, social, and psychological benefits of physical activity for older people. Information is presented that the health-promoting features of exercise are currently not being adequately employed by the most influential health care providers—physicians. The chapter concludes with a discussion of the political economy of traditional medical practice.

A trail-blazing case study of the rewards and tribulations facing both an elderly individual and her exercise supervisor is presented in Chapter 7. A true story is presented that demonstrates the potential of seriously impaired elderly to adopt physical activity and still exhibit reversals leading to better quality of life and greater independence. The exercise program and personal progress of a woman in her early eighties are provided as an example that exercise must be professionally guided to suit the needs of the frail individual. The other value to this case study is its testimony to the effort and costs of such undertakings. Reversing the downward spiral is time intensive, laborious, and possibly short-lived.

In Chapter 8, exercise survival skills for a healthy old age are presented. This final chapter of Part One proposes the essential movement ingredients of a health-promoting exercise program for the oldest life stage. The focus is on the basic movements needed to maintain mobility and strength.

Part Two, titled *Toward a Theory of Older Adult Exercise Motivation,* examines explanations for older adult exercise and presents useful theoretical approaches to understand late-life exercise behavior. Two main theoretical perspectives that have been used to predict health behaviors in adults are: 1) attitude and expectancy models and 2) socialization and ecological models. The theoretical perspectives reviewed in Chapter 9 are: Social Cognitive Theory (Bandura), the Health Belief Model (Rosenstock), Theory of Planned Behavior (Fishbein & Ajzen), Protection-Motivation Theory (Weinstein), and Health Locus of Control Theory (Wallston).

Chapter 10 examines the role of personal attributes and social context as situational forces affecting individual behavior. Social epidemiology and socialization theory are introduced as perspectives that attend to the personal characteristics and life circumstances of an individual. Ten characteristics are reviewed for their known relationship to physical activity involvement: age, health, gender, cultural background, educational level, childhood experiences, financial status, employment, marital status, and family size.

Chapter 11 presents in-depth cognitive explanations for late-life physical activity. In psychology, many theorists take the perspective that the individual is the controlling aspect of behavior. Although the individual confronts social forces that may shape their values and beliefs, ultimately the individual's motivation, and the way they experience their world, lead to predictable patterns of behavior. Social Cognitive Theory is the main focus of the chapter because this broadly applied behavioral theory has already met with good success in the explanation of older adult physical activity. Two key components explaining late-life exercise are social reinforcement to be physically active and self-efficacy, the belief that one has the ability to succeed at the physical task required.

Chapter 12 presents a synthesis of theory. Composite models to understand and explain the diverse determinants for participation in physical activity and exercise in the elderly are relatively undeveloped. Motivational theories that have had some success are now being reconceptualized and, in some cases, combined for further strength in prediction. Three main theoretical perspectives—Social Cognitive Theory, Socialization Theory, and Health Locus of Control Theory—provide important elements for the construction of a composite model of exercise behavior. In this chapter, the composite model is proposed and tested on women over age 70.

Chapter 13 represents an original self-talk model for understanding the cognitive barriers of exercise motivation. A 10-stage "exit" model aims to capture key components of a simulated decision-making process.

Chapter 14 acknowledges the challenges facing the research community and identifies unanswered questions. Key among these challenges is subject recruitment and response bias. The complexity of interpreting the effects of a basic construct such as health is addressed. The chapter acknowledges that the lack of attention to the domestic work patterns of women must be addressed, and gender issues from childhood on continue to hinder the ability of women to mobilize themselves in enjoyable forms of physical activity.

Implications for future health and social policy are the theme of Chapter 15. Social support for a more physically active lifestyle may be the most powerful source of motivation for people over the age of 70. Because social support and encouragement are modifiable, favorable intervention strategies can be developed. Families, close friends, and physicians appear to be the main players in the immediate social network of older people. At a societal level, stereotypes about aging people, about gender roles, and about limited physical potential as one gets older may act as insidious barriers to more active living in the elderly. The chapter concludes with some speculation about the future of aging cohorts with consideration for the current activity levels of today's children.

Acknowledgments

Writing a manuscript of this magnitude comes at a price. I am grateful to my children, Catherine and Kristina O'Brien, who waited and watched Mommy working on her dissertation for five years, and then wondered, watched, and waited as this book was being composed. They both have provided patience and understanding beyond their years.

David Cousins, my husband and resident computer expert, was the "wind beneath my wings." As head coach for all four of our home computers, David has empowered me to learn a variety of software programs. He stresses a critical thinking perspective, one which I am sure has made more effective the way I do my work.

My first drafts of the materials in this book were written during the 1992 Summer Olympic Games in Barcelona and the U.S. men's basketball team were so talented they were soon dubbed, "the dream team." That description is also suited to the quality of my doctoral supervisory committee: Patricia Vertinsky, Ph.D.; Doug Willms, Ph.D.; and Kjell Rubenson, Ph.D. Not only are all three stellar in their areas of expertise, but they all were able to capitalize on each other's strengths and work together as a graduate student's "dream team." I thank them for their carefully thought out advice along the way.

I wish to acknowledge Art C. Burgess, Ph.D., former director of Campus Fitness and Lifestyle at the University of Alberta, contemporary Master's athlete, and sincere colleague. Art gave me the first opportunity to teach seniors' fitness, has been my mentor in gerontology since 1985, and cowrote the remarkable case study presented in Chapter 7.

Wonita Janzen, M.Sc., co-researched and cowrote Chapter 6. Although our study represents very preliminary work in the area of motivation and active living among older adults, Wonita used excellent judgment in carrying out the research plan. Gratitude is extended to the Strathcona Seniors Centre, and the Society for the Retired and Semi-Retired, both of which supported this study with dozens of volunteers. The directors of those agencies, Jeff Allen and Walter Coombs, enthusiastically facilitated the on-site focus groups.

Funding for this work was provided by Central Research Funds and the Social Sciences and Humanities Research Council of Canada (SSHRCC). Indeed, three-year program funding by SSHRCC made the writing of this manuscript possible.

I am indebted to the women and men of the U of Agers gymnastics team and the 327 women who gave their valuable time to be a part of my dissertation research. I often wonder if these individuals fully appreciate their contribution to the growing field of knowledge regarding older adult activity patterns over the life course, and their enhancement of our understanding of the determinants of late-life exercise.

Part One

Living Longer and Aging Better

EXPLORING THE ISSUES

In order to effectively implement older adult exercise systems, it is necessary to first garner an understanding of the history of both the incidence of and beliefs regarding exercise among this population. In addition, the facts about the benefits of exercise must be realized, and the perceptions of older adults explored.

Chapters 1 and 2 explore the social and personal impact of sedentary lifestyles, and present demographic information which paints a historic background of today's elderly population. Chapters 3 and 4 provide a look at past and present activity patterns, and present new information regarding perceived and actual risks of older adult exercise. Chapter 5 includes a summary of the benefits of exercise for this population. Chapter 6 further examines barriers to an active old age, and Chapter 7 presents an inspiring case study which illustrates the positive effects of physical activity among older adults. Finally, Chapter 8 introduces specific exercise skills that focus on the maintenance of mobility and strength.

Chapter 1

Aging Poorly with Sedentary Living

TYPES OF AGING

Differences in the way individuals age have intrigued scientists for years. The contemporary search for perpetual health and immortality has failed to find any "fountain of youth," but we know that people do age with remarkable variation (Nelson & Dannefer, 1992). The range of aging possibilities is probably best seen in people's unique day-to-day lifestyle behaviors and the effects of these behaviors over the life span. Individual experiences of aging depend on the interrelationships among biology, behavior, and the environment. Together these factors place a person at some point on "The Health Continuum" (Figure 1.1).

The health continuum represents the range of an individual's possibilities for health from premature morbidity and death to optimal fitness and health (Teague, 1987). Considering that individual behavior has an impact (positive or negative) on one's health, the purpose of the health spectrum is to have people realize that they can move "away" from the illness side of the spectrum toward optimal wellness. The health continuum concept views health with the complexity that it deserves, and serves to counter the notion that health is a discrete entity that you have or do not have. Rather, the health continuum depicts the idea that, with knowledge, motivation, and personal action, one can distance oneself from some diseases by taking up positive behaviors directed at health promotion.

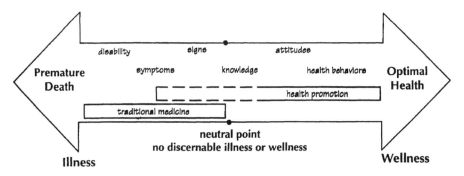

Figure 1.1 The health continuum. Reprinted with permission by Michael L. Teague, 1995. In Teague, M. L. (1992). *Health promotion: Achieving high-level wellness in the later years* (p. xiii). Indianapolis, IN: Benchmark Press, Inc.

For at least three decades, gerontologists have suggested there are two ways of growing old: "usual" aging and "successful" aging (Butler, 1988; Dermody, Saxon, & Sheer, 1986; Havighurst, 1963; Meusel, 1991; Nowlin, 1985; Palmore, 1989; Rowe & Kahn, 1987). In recent decades, increased longevity has illuminated the problems of "usual" aging, clarified and differentiated between normal and abnormal aging, and compelled societies to "rethink how we age" (Prado, 1986). Evidence is rapidly accumulating that regular and moderate forms of physical activity are a health benefit for adults, fostering opportunities for improved survival and life quality and more successful aging (O'Brien & Vertinsky, 1991; Stewart & King, 1991).

Although knowledge about how to age better is improving, population disability levels are climbing because of the relative aging and inactivity of the population (Verbrugge, 1994). In a chapter in *Aging and Quality of Life* (Abeles, Gift, & Ory, 1994), Verbrugge writes a section titled, "Prevention of Disability." She outlines the classic triumvirate of prevention strategies, which include primary prevention (efforts to avert the onset of pathology), secondary prevention (early detection and management of pathology), and tertiary prevention (reduction of disease impact). Recent research reported in person by Stephen Blair (from the Cooper Institute in Dallas) shows that when controlling for all other possible explanations, the best predictor for full physical function and avoidance of disability in one's later years is physical fitness (Blair, lecture at the University of Alberta, November, 1995).

Habitual exercise has major implications for the quality, if not the quantity, of life. Enough scientific support exists to suggest that moderate and frequent exercise may be the "best preventive medicine" for old age. Regular exercise is prescribed by the Centers for Disease Control and Prevention and the American College of Sports Medicine (Pate et al., 1995), first to prevent premature aging (Spirduso, 1986), and second, to prevent premature disease by controlling hypertension, heart disease, bowel and breast cancer, the immune response, osteoporosis, obesity, arthritis, diabetes, insomnia, and depression (see Chapter 5 for a complete review of benefits). Exercise scientists are beginning to understand the significant role exercise can play in controlling aging decline and delaying mortality (Blair, Kohl, III, Paffenbarger, Clark, Cooper, & Gibbons, 1989; Donahue, Abbott, Reed, & Yano, 1988; Grand, Grosclaude, Bocquet, Pous, & Albarede, 1990; Kaplan, Seeman, Cohen, Knudsen, & Guralnik, 1987; Linstead, Tonstad, & Kuzma, 1991; Rakowski & Mor, 1992).

Physiologists estimate that up to half of what we currently know as usual aging is a phenomenon of disuse (Berger, 1989; Bortz, 1982; DeVries, 1970, 1975; DeVries & Adams, 1972; Smith, 1981)—disuse that predisposes more women than men to experiences of hypokinetic disease (Abdellah, 1985; Butler, 1968; Heckler, 1984; Ostrow, 1989; Verbrugge, 1990b; Vertinsky, 1991). Olshansky, Carnes, and Cassel (1993) noted that women in western societies can expect to live 25 percent of their lives disabled, while men will experience physical limitations for the latter 20 percent of the life span. Government health promotion programs are examples of conspicuous public health campaigns addressing the issue of unfit aging in Canada—an issue targeting women, who appear to have the most to gain from increased participation in physical activity.

WHY EXERCISE? WHY BOTHER?

Several thousand scientific studies from various health disciplines have, in over 200 scientific journals, documented the broad benefits of physical activity for older adults (O'Brien Cousins & Horne, in press). When all of the evidence is consolidated, there is abundant support for the idea that elderly individuals can positively affect their mobility, endurance, strength, and balance by, first, reversing the circulatory and neurological deficits they have acquired through sedentary living (MacRae, 1989; Spirduso, 1986), and, second, by elevating their functional capacities to the level of adults decades younger than themselves (Dummer, Clarke, Vaccaro, Vander Velden, Goldfarb, & Sockler, 1985; Fiatarone, Marks, Ryan, Meredith, Lipsita, & Evans, 1990).

The known health advantages for individuals who maintain an active lifestyle are so profound that sedentary living is now considered to be a costly "public health burden" (McGinnis, 1992). For example, Dr. William Foege, former Director of the Centers for Disease Control and Prevention (CDC), has suggested that physical activity has a potency comparable to immunization in repressing disease. The Heart and Stroke Foundations in both Canada and the United States have identified physical *inactivity* as the fourth major modifiable risk factor for cardiovascular disease, along with smoking, high blood pressure, and high blood cholesterol. In support of these statements, the Alberta Centre for Well-Being (1995) reported that individuals climbing 36 or more flights of stairs per week had a 28 percent lower relative risk of death from cardiovascular disease than sedentary individuals.

Research indicates that an active lifestyle decreases a person's risk of many other chronic diseases including hypertension, stroke, cancer, non-insulin dependent diabetes, osteoporosis, osteoarthritis and depression.

Furthermore, physical activity is known to be more than just a preventive and controlling measure; at certain intensities, sustained activity is health-promoting and can lead to a "high-level wellness" (Teague, 1992). Exercise elevates cognitive and physical function to levels which can guarantee more years of independent living (Health & Welfare Canada, 1989; Spirduso, & MacRae, 1991). Regular physical activity places controls on aging decline which, in "usual" aging, contributes to physiological losses of about one percent per year in most body systems (DeVries, 1979). Active living reduces age decline to 0.5%.

A consensus is forming that the health of most adults, including the able elderly, can best be promoted by the start of a walking program at 40 percent to 75 percent of one's maximal heart rate (MHR = 220 − age) (Bouchard, Shephard, Stephens, Sutton, & McPherson, 1990). Older adults should be informed that three 10-minute walks have about the same impact as one 30-minute walk (Blair, Kohl, Gordon, & Paffenbarger, 1992). Benefits exist for frail elderly too. Adults in nursing homes and lodges should be encouraged to walk at any pace they can for as long as they can (Gueldner & Spradley, 1988). Following Blair et al.'s advice, several walks a day may be just as health-promoting as one bigger walk for the physically frail older person.

THE MATTER OF BEING NORTH AMERICAN

Just under half (48%) of all adults are classified as being involved in "high" levels of activity on the index of leisure-time physical activity. "High" leisure-time physical activity is generally defined as a minimum of 15 to 30 minutes of exercise, three times a week (Stephens & Craig, 1990). But compared to rising activity levels in Finland and Germany, the involvement of North American adults in vigorous exercise is low and in visible decline since 1980 (Figure 1.2). Although almost 25 percent of sedentary North American adults have taken up moderate levels of leisure-time physical activity since 1981, about 40 percent of the general population is still considered sedentary (Pate et al., 1995; Stephens & Caspersen, 1994), and most of these are aging adults.

THE MATTER OF BEING OLDER

Daily exercise decreases with age through middle adulthood and then increases temporarily after people reach the retirement years (Stephens & Craig, 1990). Even after age 70, there is still a significant gradient in activity level with every passing year, even when health is taken into account (O'Brien Cousins, 1993). This age gradient is clear in the seven-day exercise level of Vancouver women (Figure 1.3). Cohort age differences are also significant for late-life movement confidence, and also for beliefs of physician support for exercise (Figure 1.4). This suggests that chronological age is a powerful force that is somehow linked to physical activity level, movement confidence, and encouragement by society for older people to live their lives actively.

The *Health Promotion Survey* points out that the Canadians most likely to engage in daily exercise in their leisure time are men ages 65 and older (Stephens & Craig, 1990). However, the proportion who never exercise at all is also greater among older adults. Of interest is the finding that older adults, more than younger adults, feel that they get as much as exercise as they need.

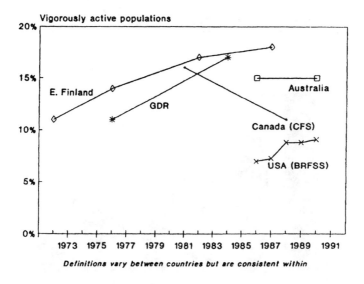

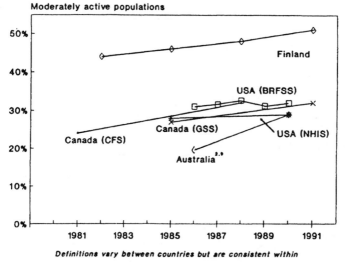

Figure 1.2 Temporal trends in leisure-time physical activity. Reprinted with permission from T. Stephens and C. J. Caspersen. (1994). The demography of physical activity. In C. Bouchard, R. J. Shephard, & T. Stephens (eds.), *Physical activity fitness, and health* (p. 207).

THE MATTER OF BEING FEMALE

Until recently, little attention has been given to the mechanisms of women's aging, health, and activity patterns. Frail elderly women, especially, have been virtually invisible in feminist, sociological, and gerontological literature (Evers, 1985; Vertinsky, 1994). By many accounts, most women can expect to live to the ripe age of 80 years

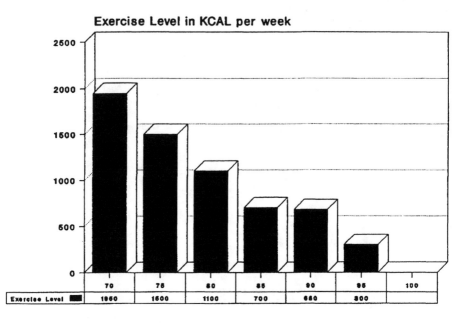

Figure 1.3 Exercise in the past week for Vancouver women over age 70.

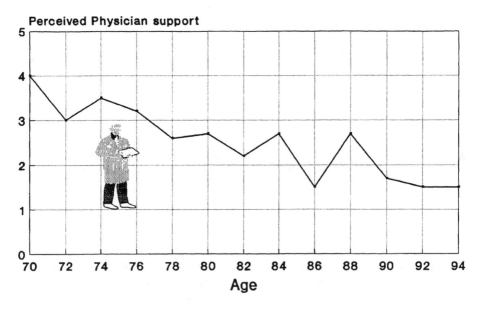

Figure 1.4 Perceptions of physician support for exercise by age.

or better, but they are not likely to age very "successfully" (Lewin & Olsen, 1985; Posner, 1980; Quinlan, 1988; Vebrugge, 1990a, 1990b; Verbrugge & Wingard, 1987).

In the eight extra years that women live, on average, compared to their male counterparts, too many of them endure poor mental health (Grau, 1988), over one-third are frail and physically limited (Charette, 1988), and almost one-quarter of women over age 65 use sleeping pills (Health & Welfare Canada, 1989). Medical and social researchers have begun examining various lifestyle habits and social roles of aging women and, among other findings, have discovered the one factor that is most likely to exacerbate the emotional and physical difficulties of very aged women is their inadequate leisure-time exercise—often a lifelong deficiency of vigorous and strength-promoting sport and physical activity (Biddle & Smith, 1992; Verbrugge, 1990a; Vertinsky, 1991; Work, 1989).

As women age, they tend to slow down and, for many, up to 55 percent of their minimally muscled body mass can be infiltrated with fat (Young, Blondin, Tensuan, & Fryer, 1963). Significant declines in strength, endurance, and aerobic fitness are apparent even by middle-age (Alexander, Ready, & Fougere-Mailey, 1985; Cinque, 1990). Although much of the early research focused on men's aging and the physiology of age decline, Lee (1991) has reviewed the exercise intervention studies pertaining to middle-aged and older women and concluded that "older women have the potential to benefit from exercise to much the same degree as men." Yet rarely are older women found participating in the more vigorous forms of sport and recreation (Cauley, LaPorte, Black-Sandler, Schramm, & Kriska, 1987).

Indeed, among older women, such activity is almost nonexistent except for the 12 percent who over a four-week period undertake from time to time a walk of two miles or more. (Abrams, 1988).

Health promoters are concerned, not only about older women, but about much younger females too. A combination of vigorous strength and aerobic exercise, started early in life, is an effective strategy for the prevention of osteoporosis (Gutin & Kasper, 1992). Yet only 24 percent of girls ages 15 to 19 could achieve the recommended levels of aerobic fitness on a recent fitness survey (Stephens & Craig, 1990). Other research has found that 20 percent of Canadian children are considered obese and that 80 percent to 85 percent of those children remain obese as adults.

Despite public awareness of the benefits of exercise at every life stage, as yet, females are less active in their leisure-time than their male counterparts (Stephens, Craig, & Ferris, 1986). According to the Health Promotion Survey in Canada (Stephens & Caspersen, 1994), females are significantly less physically active than males at ages 20 to 24 and again at ages 65 and older, years during which older men increase their activity levels. Table 1.1 summarizes national data indicating that women sustain active leisure for shorter intervals than men; for adults 65 and older, 43 percent of men and only 29 percent of women will endure 30 minutes or more of leisure-time physical activity (Stephens & Craig, 1990). Both men and women tend to become progressively less active as they get older (Alexander, Ready, & Fougere-Mailey, 1985).

Table 1.1   Leisure Time Physical Activity by Age and Gender

	Duration	
	15–30 minutes	**>30 minutes**
Percent of men participating		
Ages 15–19	16	78
Ages 20–24	12	77
Ages 25–44	18	55
Ages 45–64	17	42
Ages 65 and older	18	43
Percent of women participating		
Ages 15–19	34	58
Ages 20–24	27	53
Ages 25–44	26	55
Ages 45–64	23	38
Ages 65 and older	24	29

Source: Adapted with permission from T. Stephens (1992). Leisure time physical activity (chp. 10). In *Health Promotion Survey*. Ottawa, ON: Ministry of Supply & Social Services.

By late life, only a small minority are active enough to benefit their health and well-being (Blair, Brill, & Kohl, 1989; Lee, 1991; Stephens & Craig, 1990; Teague & Hunnicutt, 1989). Statistics Canada (1990) reports that only 10 percent of women over the age of 45 are considered to be "active" compared with one in three males. In the United States, only one percent of adult women regularly performed more than one vigorous activity (Sallis et al., 1985).

What are the explanations for the lifelong differences in the activity patterns of men and women? Contemporary research is exploring the possibility that women simply do not have equity with males in terms of dispensable leisure time. The caregiver role played by the majority of adult women, while buffering them with strong social supports, is perhaps demanding enough of their time to deplete their free time and energy for personal pursuits. The advantages and disadvantages of women's diverse social roles are not well understood, however, and there is evidence that raising children may actually encourage greater involvement in physical activity for some women (Branigan & O'Brien Cousins, 1995), while acting as a barrier to physical activity for other women (O'Brien Cousins & Keating, 1995).

While "doctor's orders" might activate up to 25 percent of women, almost 60 percent of older women have said that "nothing would persuade them to increase their physical activity" (Shephard, 1986c). Of interest is the fact that where other health behaviors are concerned, women generally exhibit better life habits than men; physical activity is the *only* positive health behavior that is pursued by men more than women (Stephens & White, 1985; Stephens & Craig, 1990). While public health campaigns about the risk of heart disease have spurred many men into joining health-promoting exercise programs (Davidson & Sedgewick, 1978), the mere act of raising the issue of heart disease may have frightened away aging women.

If there are persuasive reasons to mobilize aging women to engage in more physical activity, they might be "figure improvement" (Davidson & Sedgewick, 1978) and stress reduction (Duda & Tappe, 1989). "Feeling better" and "looking better" are important reasons why older people have been physically active in the past (Canada Fitness Survey, 1983). But this reasoning is problematic. Almost half of people over age 45 are at risk of health problems resulting from obesity—a group that could most benefit from participating in increased physical activity but that also places itself at risk by doing so. The individuals who are more inclined to be active are already leaner and healthier, and, thus, the people who least need to increase activity levels are the most likely to do so (Dishman, 1990; Sallis, Haskell, Wood, Fortman, Rogers, Blair, & Paffenbarger, 1985; Stephens & Craig, 1990).

About 50 percent of active women over age 65 say they exercise in public places and are more likely than men to be in supervised activity settings (Stephens & Craig, 1990). Possibly concerned about their health and safety, most women prefer to exercise in groups under expert leadership. Thus, in order to participate, older women must first be able to afford to pay for this leadership. In contrast, many men prefer unguided activities, although they often seek out and enjoy the company of others in informal exercise and sport settings. Many active men can be found in golf, master's swim and hockey programs, and in running clubs where they pay annual membership fees but do not have to pay for instruction every time they participate.

The female propensity for public participation does pose a problem for bigger and older women. Recent research has found that overweight women perceive social disapproval for their shape and body size; unfortunately they also perceive disapproval and experience embarrassment in the exercise setting where they also anticipate some social support for participating (Bain, Wilson, & Chaikland, 1989). Evidently, older women who are active are already somewhat comfortable with their physique in public settings; heavier women who most want to look and feel better as they age, are unfortunately less likely to participate in, or adhere to, the kinds of programs that can help them succeed.

But female health is more important than female appearance. Yet few women appear to be exercising for health reasons. Public information, with unexplainable cause, has conditioned society to believe that heart disease is a male issue. Although more women than men die each year of heart disease (U.S. Department of Health and Human Services, 1994a; Statistics Canada, 1990), women's health risks from sedentary living and fatty food choices have not been a focus of major heart health campaigns like the Mr. Fit trials in the United States (Nachitall & Nachitall, 1990). While women's spines and abdomens "take a tremendous beating in pregnancy and childbirth" (Davidson & Sedgewick, 1978), "older women who perform aerobic exercise for the sake of improved health are generally viewed somewhat suspiciously." Without sufficient exercise, older women will continue to exhibit a level of muscle weakness that places them in a category of "functionally disabled" (Branch & Jette, 1984; Work, 1989).

Social scientists have argued convincingly that women have merely learned their social roles well; sedentary living may be partly the outcome of a lifelong experience of female disempowerment and learned helplessness (Fedorak & Griffin, 1986; Myers

& Huddy, 1985; Schulz, 1980; Zinberg & Kaufman, 1963). Others point to women's chronic stress with poverty (Labonte & Penfold, 1981), their commitment to caregiving for others (Robinson, 1988; Thomas, 1990), and persisting fatigue with "daily hassles" (Mishler, Amarasingham, Osherson, Hauser, Waxler, & Liem, 1981; Spacapan & Oskamp, 1989).

Too many aging individuals apparently live up to the "self-fulfilling prophecy" of social expectation that labels older people in general, and women in particular, as less physically competent (Kuypers & Bengston, 1973). Evers (1985) proposed that elderly women, more than men, continue to live at home with disabilities because "women are simply expected to be able to put up with limiting disabilities to a greater extent than are men."

Indeed it is a paradox that one of the main reasons given in surveys of elderly women for not being more physically active is their declining health and the perception that they are "too old," while at the same time scientific research demonstrates more and more that one of the certain benefits of physical activity is health improvement. It is a further paradox that, while women have proven more durable than men from a physiological standpoint, they have done so in a culture that has, until recently, encouraged them to take on the characteristics of aging too readily (Vertinsky, 1991).

Elderly women, suggest some critics, impose more on the health care system, collect social security benefits and receive government assistance longer than men, and are most at risk of living out their last decade of life with severely diminished capacities (Statistics Canada, 1990). These phenomena concern officials of government and health care systems (Eriksson, Mellstrom, & Svanborg, 1987), especially since older women are the fastest growing segment of the population. Women who reach the age of 90 outnumber their male counterparts by almost three to one (Statistics Canada, 1990).

THE HETEROGENEITY OF OLDER PEOPLE

There are, however, examples of remarkably athletic elderly women with limited resources who have not shied away from vigorous involvements with their own serious and sometimes multiple health conditions (Drinkwater, 1988; Dummer, Clarke, Vaccaro, Vander Velden, Goldfarb, & Sockler, 1985; Gandee, Campbell, Knierim, Cosky, Leslie, Ziegler, & Snodgrass, 1989; National Film Board of Canada, 1990; Starischka & Bohmer, 1986; Wilmore, Miller, & Pollock, 1974). While some females at all ages do enjoy a highly active lifestyle, insufficient participation, especially in vigorous play and sport, is more characteristic of the female life course from adolescence on (Vertinsky, 1992), and serves to highlight the heterogeneity of this social group. This heterogeneity is aptly described by Eric Pfeiffer:

> In my considerable contacts with elderly persons, both clinically and socially, I have run into not only the lonely and the despaired and disabled elderly. I have also met some very, very exciting older people. Older people who were intellectually and socially stimulating and exciting, who were physically active and who obviously seemed to have made a

successful adaptation to their growing years. Yet as I observed one after another aging person with whom I came in contact, there did seem to emerge a set of common characteristics for all or almost all of these persons. It struck me as though the successfully aging person was someone who somewhere along the way had decided to stay in training. He or she had decided to stay in training physically, intellectually and emotionally, and socially (1973).

This holistic view of human aging accounts for physical, intellectual, emotional, and social developments and provokes the conception of biopsychosocial models that could better guide research, have clinical utility, and provide more comprehensive understanding (Engel, 1980; Levy, Derogatis, Gallagher, & Gatz, 1980). McPherson (1986) advocates the interdisciplinary approach in aging and sport research:

> . . . there could very well be greater levels of explanation achieved concerning aging phenomena and the elderly if sport scientists from different disciplines were to pool their expertise. Specifically, greater attention needs to be directed to possible interactions among social, psychological, biological and physiological variables (1986a).

SUMMARY

This chapter has explored the paradox that those aging people whose well-being could best benefit from regular exercise, may often be the least likely to engage in it. The fact that there is a strong gradient in age, the fact that North American adults are far less active than those of other northern hemisphere nations, and the fact that females are generally less active than males—all suggest that certain barriers may be operating, barriers that may be related to people's internalized belief systems and predispositions related to gender's influence on life experience, or barriers that may be a matter of physical and social environment and personal circumstance. As evidence mounts regarding the significant health-promoting role of exercise in mental, social, and physical well-being, social scientists ask, "Why are so few older people taking advantage of the 'best medicine?'"

Working toward an answer to that question, Chapter 2 examines the unique characteristics of the population cohort born near the turn of the 20th century. The chapter examines the social, scientific, political, and economic forces, that have influenced that generation, which might help us to explain why some older adults are leading fully active lives, while others have retired with the main goal of enjoying a well-deserved rest.

A Demographic Profile of Adults
Born Before 1921

Each generation is accompanied by contextual features that help make that cohort unique. Reviewing these features may aid understanding of the physical activity and sports patterns of today's older adults in North America. Although life circumstances do not remain stable over the life span, the prospects for raising the quality of aging will improve with knowledge of how past and present circumstances create barriers or opportunities for exercise involvement.

This chapter presents a demographic profile of today's elderly, namely those born before 1921. It addresses the following topics: size of the aging population, life expectancy, marital status, work and retirement status, financial status, family size, education, health and lifestyle behavior, morbidity levels, population health, health care utilization, physical limitations, living arrangements, and transportation.

OUR AGING SOCIETY

Health United States 1993 reports that between 1980 and 1991 the elderly population in the United States grew more rapidly than other age groups (National Center for Health Statistics, 1994). By 1991, over 3 million Americans were over age 85, a growth rate of 41 percent. In the 75- to 84-year-old group, a growth of 33 percent led to a population of 10.3 million by 1991. In comparison, the total U.S. population

**Table 2.1   Resident Population, According to Age:
United States, Selected Years 1950–1991 (in thousands)**

Description	U.S. pop. total	55–64	65–74	75–84	85+
All persons:					
1950	150,697	13,370	8,340	3,278	577
1970	203,212	18,590	12,435	6,119	1,511
1991	252,177	21,005	18,279	10,314	3,160

Source: Table reprinted from U.S. Department of Health and Human Services, National Center for Health Statistics. (1994a). *Health United States 1993.* Rockville, MD: U.S. Government Printing Office.

increased by 11 percent to over 252 million. When all Americans ages 55 and over were counted in 1991, the total exceeded 53 million, or 21 percent of the U.S. population (Table 2.1). In the 85 and over age group in 1991, 795,000 were male compared to over 2 million women of the same ages. The veteran population also grew to 27 million in 1992 with 30 percent of the veterans aged 65 or over compared with only 11 percent in 1980 (National Center for Health Statistics, 1994).

Life Expectancy

In 1991, overall American life expectancy at birth reached a record high of 75.5 years. Still, this was lower than life expectancy in Japan; American males had a shorter life span by 4.4 years, American women had lives 3.6 years shorter than those of Japanese women. Life expectancy at age 65 in the United States was also shorter than in Japan by 1.4 years for men and 1.7 years for women. Life expectancy was at its highest level ever in 1991 for white females (79.6 years), black females (73.8), and white males (72.9). In 1991, life expectancy for black males (64.6) was slightly higher than in the previous three years, but was lower than the high of 65.3 years attained in 1984. Added to the impact of longevity on social aging, the U.S. fertility rate declined by 2 percent to 69.6 live births per 1,000 women ages 15 to 44 years.

Canadian society is aging in a similar pattern to the United States. Canadians are also living longer than ever before—in 1987, women had a life expectancy of 79.7 years; men's life expectancy was 73.1 years. The most elderly age groups are growing faster than any other age groups. Between 1981 and 1991, the proportion of Canadians aged 75 and over grew by 22 percent and the proportion aged 85 and over increased by 31 percent. In 1991, there were 94,000 seniors aged 90 or over, and 3,700 Canadians ages 100 or more. A projected estimate for the United States would suggest that centenary Americans could easily number over 37,000.

Canadian women over the age of 65 began to outnumber men of the same age in 1961 (Stone & Fletcher, 1980). By 1980, women aged 85 and older outnumbered their male peers by two to one and by age 90, by almost three to one (Statistics Canada, 1984). Projections suggest that by the year 2001, women aged 80 and over will outnumber men at a rate of 218 to 100—or better than two to one (Novak, 1993).

In the moderate west coast climate of Vancouver, there are proportionally more older women in the 65 and over population than are found in British Columbia or in Canada as an average. Women over the age of 65 in Vancouver now represent about 60 percent of the total population of seniors.

Marital Status

Forty-two percent of women and nine percent of men 65 years or older are widowed. After age 85, 82 percent of women are widowed (National Advisory Council on Aging [NACA], 1993, *No. 2*). Few widowed women can expect to remarry, although most widowed men remarry quite quickly. *Women in Canada* (Statistics Canada, 1990) reported that the most significant group of people living alone are females ages 65 and over. Thus by late life, the majority of women are without partners and many are without adequate pensions: a predicament with serious economic implications for their quality of life and life choices.

Work and Retirement Status

Labor force participation after age 65 has been decreasing since 1981 (NACA, 1993, *No. 16*) even though only about one-third of people ages 15 and over supported the policy of mandatory retirement in 1989. In addition, 10 percent of retirees report that lack of employment is a problem. As many as 60 percent intend to retire on or before age 65. After age 55, the percentage of men in the work force drops to about 60 percent and the figure for employed women rises to about 35 percent.

Financial Status

Between 1980 and 1991, the number of low-income Canadian seniors dropped from 731,000 to 590,000 (*Seniors Info Exchange*, 1993). Almost two-thirds of senior citizens lived in their own homes, and 67 percent of senior retirees owned homes. Of these, 90 percent have paid off their mortgages. Sixteen percent of men and five percent of women ages 65 to 69 were still in the labor force. In 1991, six percent of seniors had a personal income of over $40,000; of these, 10 percent were men and two percent were women.

Nearly 20 percent of older Canadians—mainly women—are poor. In 1991, 47 percent of women and 14 percent of men ages 65 and over had a personal income of less than $10,000 per year. Yet 82 percent of all seniors felt that their current income and investments satisfied their needs adequately or very well.

The statistics on the financial status of older women are shocking. In Canada, 60 percent of *all* women over age 65 are regarded as poor, and 80 percent of these poorer women are widows. The National Advisory Council on Aging (NACA) (1993) reports that 43 percent of seniors received the Guaranteed Income Supplement (GIS) in 1990, meaning that almost half of Canada's seniors need to supplement a marginal monthly income. Among women ages 90 or older, 70 percent received some GIS (NACA, 1993).

Government programs are the main and increasingly important source of income for seniors. (NACA, 1993, *No. 4*).

The traditional social roles of men and women have meant that marriage has usually provided a woman a degree of financial security, at least while her spouse was alive. But being widowed, living alone, and living with minimal finances are predictable outcomes for the majority of elderly women. Housing represents 29 percent of the expenses of female seniors compared to 16 percent of the expenses of the total population (NACA, 1991). In British Columbia, 56 percent of female seniors live in detached family homes and another 33 percent live in their own apartments. Even when mortgages have been paid off, property taxes and house repairs can be a major financial burden to an older woman living on her own. Even those women who procured satisfactory employment in their younger years earned the lower wages of women throughout the 20th century, leaving them fewer resources to last longer lives. Thus poverty often accompanies women's aging. Yet despite such limited finances, less than five percent of women over age 65 report any current employment income (Statistics Canada, 1986).

In 1981, the average income of British Columbia females ages 65 to 69 was $8,478 at the same time same-age males earned double that amount, $16,802. In 1988, the average annual income of families headed by a person ages 65 and older was $37,462, but only $16,316 for singles ages 65 and over (NACA, 1991).

The high poverty rates among older females, no doubt, have some degree of impact on their nutrition, leisure activity choices, and general health. Limited financial resources place extra stress on the older woman, and ultimately limits her available solutions to health problems that accompany aging.

Family Size

Family size is a possible contributing factor in the financial and health burden of today's elderly. Women born at the turn of the 20th century tended to raise larger families than women do today. The U.S. Bureau of the Census (1975) reported there were 2.7 children for each ever-married women in the years 1920 to 1924. Although many North American women at the turn of the century remained single and up to 20 percent of all women were childless between 1910 to 1920, 11 percent to 16 percent of all women ages 15 to 44 years gave birth in any single year (U.S. Bureau of the Census, 1975).

Education

In the mid-1980s, only about 27 percent of Canadians ages 65 and older had graduated from high school or a post-secondary educational institution (NACA, 1993). By the year 2006, the proportion of seniors with at least a high school diploma will approach 40 percent. Based on current estimates of their educational attainment, almost 40 percent of Canadian seniors have deficient literary skills. Only a few percent of all seniors enroll in continuing education, but as many as 20 percent of seniors who have taken post-secondary courses enroll. Projected growth in adult education in Canada is expected to rise dramatically over the next two decades. In the past 10 to 15 years, participation in Elderhostel multiplied fivefold, and retirement educational activities have increased 60 times (NACA, 1993, *No. 17*).

The Canada Fitness Survey states that "by most definitions of active leisure, there is a direct relationship between amount of education and the probability of being active" (Stephens & Craig, 1990).

Recognition of a relationship between education and economic development and of the subsequent improvement of personal and social life thus provides a further economic argument for a radical change in the organization of education, because education, economic development, and improved quality of life are intimately connected (Cropley, 1977).

Lack of education is related to poorer health, physical limitations, and less happiness. People who have less than a secondary-school education are less likely to have plans to improve their health than those with higher level education. About 50 percent of adults over the age of 70 have less than a ninth grade education, and less than 5 percent received a university degree (Statistics Canada, 1984). In the 65 and over age group, 34 percent of those with just an elementary education report fair to poor health, compared to 7 percent of those with post-secondary education (Health & Welfare Canada, 1989).

Having a higher education does not guarantee women the same financial status as males. For example, women ages 65 to 74 with university degrees had an average annual income of $14,500, half that of the same age and qualified male income of $27,900. Women with some university education had an annual income at the same level as males who had a less than ninth grade education (about $9,000).

These data suggest that education may not be a good proxy variable for socioeconomic status of women. Rather, higher education may be important to examine as a factor lending skills for information seeking about health knowledge, as well as extending opportunities to female students to participate in active recreation and sport further into their adult years.

Healthy Lifestyle Behavior

In a recent health survey, about two-thirds of seniors rated their health as good, very good, or excellent for their age (NACA, 1993), and more than half of all seniors reported having done something in the past year to improve their health. Seniors generally did not skip breakfast. All but eight percent claimed that they were either pretty happy or very happy. Data have shown that 99 percent of people over age 60 would like to have sex if a willing partner was available.

Television viewing and reading are two activities enjoyed by seniors. Men and women over age 60 watched 33 and 36 hours, respectively, of television per week in 1988 (NACA, 1993). This is about 10 hours more than men and women ages 18 to 59. Seniors are less likely than other adult groups to spend money on recreational equipment and associated services (including skis, golf clubs, home exercise equipment, hobby materials, computers, and camping equipment) than other adults. They also tend to spend more money on spectator entertainment and sports than on their personal participation in activities (NACA, 1993).

About 51 percent of seniors report daily or frequent exercise; 36 percent say they never exercise (NACA, 1993). Seniors are half as likely to smoke as persons under age 55 (19 percent versus 37 percent), and seniors are less likely to consume alcohol than persons under age 55 (61 percent versus 87 percent).

Morbidity Status

Approximately 80 percent of persons ages 65 and older report one or more chronic conditions, yet only 20 percent claim this disrupts their everyday activities (NACA, 1993). Common health problems for seniors are arthritis-rheumatism (55%), hypertension (39%), and respiratory difficulties (24%).

Between 1980 and 1991 the age-adjusted death rate attributed to heart disease declined 27 percent (*Health United States*, 1993). Still, Asian-Americans have about a 50 percent reduced risk of heart disease compared to other Americans, and Blacks have a 42 percent greater mortality from heart disease than Whites. Between 1971 and 1986, coronary heart disease declined in Canada 30 percent for males over age 65 and 35 percent for females over age 65 (NACA, 1993).

Stroke, the third leading cause of death in the United States, declined 34 percent between 1980 and 1991, maintaining the downward trend of the 1970s. Hypertension also declined for both men and women to a low of 23 percent from 39 percent in the late 1970s. For each race or ethnic subgroup, the prevalence of hypertension was higher for males. Similarly, mean serum total cholesterol level for adults 20 to 74 years of age declined from 220 mg/dL to 205 mg/dL over the same time period. However, despite these good trends, overweight as a health indicator increased for all population subgroups from 25 percent to 33 percent with more women than men classified as overweight.

During the same time frame, lung cancer increased a dramatic 41 percent to 47 percent for black women and white women (USDHHS, 1994c). Lung cancer increased 8 percent for black men and white male lung cancer rates stabilized. Chronic obstructive pulmonary disease (COPD), the fourth leading cause of death, increased almost 80 percent for females, increased 24 percent for black males, and was stable for white males.

Population Health

About 90 percent of North American adults across all ages perceive their health to be good, very good, or excellent (Health & Welfare Canada, 1989). However, by age 70, almost 30 percent rate their health as fair to poor, and almost 40 percent report one or more physical limitations (Figure 2.1). On the positive side, life stress is perceived to diminish after age 50 and perceived overweight peaks in the 50s and then declines somewhat.

Older women rate their health less positively than men. Only 17 percent of women over age 65 rate their health as excellent compared to 24 percent of men; 29 percent

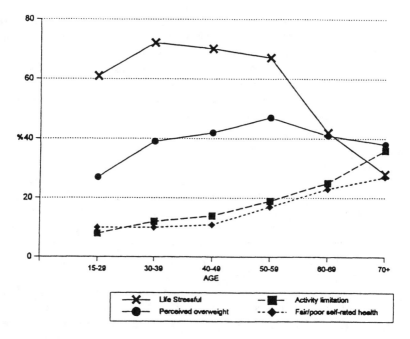

Figure 2.1 Selected health status indicators, by age, age 15 and over, Canada, 1990. Reprinted with permission from Health Canada. Age-related differences (chp. 18, p. 249). In M. J. Penning & N .L. Chappell (Eds.), Health Promotion Survey 1990.

of older women rate their health as poor compared to 24 percent of men; 37 percent of women report activity limitations compared to 31 percent of men; 32 percent of older women say life is fairly or very stressful compared to 27 percent of men; and 9 percent of older women say they are not too happy compared to 6 percent of men (Health & Welfare Canada, 1989).

People living at a low socioeconomic level and the elderly were two groups less likely to report good health. Not only was reported health poorer in these groups but plans to improve health were less common. Seniors in the upper-middle income category are more than twice as likely (59 percent) to rate their health as excellent as are those in the financially very poor category (28 percent) (*Sources*, 1991).

Health Care Utilization

Older people use medical care services heavily, and rising health care costs are a major concern in both the United States and Canada. However, health care expenditures are inflating at rates that exceed what would be expected even for two aging societies.

In 1991 health spending in the United States accounted for a larger share of gross domestic product (GDP) than in any other major industrialized country and the gap has continued to widen since 1985 (USDHHS, 1994c). The United States currently spends about 14 percent of its GDP on health care, and the publicly funded health care system in Canada consumes about 10 percent of that country's GDP. In comparison, Japan's population by some standards has the best health in the world, and spends only six to seven percent of its GDP on health (Evans, Barer & Marmor, 1995). One explanation for Japan's superior health despite modest spending is that the economy has had a recent period of growth and the disparity in income among Japanese workers is minimal. The connection between health disparity and wealth disparity is acknowledged in much of the contemporary population health literature (Evans, Barer, & Marmor, 1995).

The average Canadian visited a physician five times a year, persons between the ages of 65 and 74 made 7.4 visits, and those over 75 made 8.2 visits (Schick, 1986). In comparison, U.S. seniors ages 65 to 74 averaged 9.2 physician contacts for males and 10.1 contacts for females. Americans over age 75 averaged about 12 physician visits per year with no differences observed between men and women.

In the United States in 1980, the average amount per hospital inpatient per day was $298 compared to $1,113 in 1991. The average number of days per hospital stay was 8.7 per patient discharge. About 1.4 million American men over age 85 were enrolled in Medicare in 1991 compared to 2.5 million same-age women. Of these 849,000 men ages 85 and over and 896,000 women of the same ages received medical service accounting for $4,471 and $4,203 annually per male and female enrollee, respectively. Functional problems rise after the age of 80 and this is the point where need for support systems greatly increases (Stone & Frenken, 1988).

Physical Limitations

In 1992, 45 percent of non-institutionalized Americans ages 75 and over reported some limitation of activity as a result of chronic conditions (USDHHS, 1994c). Activity limitations were 10 percent greater among women than men and 20 percent greater for black elderly than for white elderly.

The Health and Activity Limitation Survey (Statistics Canada, 1988) uses the World Health Organization's (WHO) definition of disability, which is

". . . any restriction or lack (resulting from an impairment) of ability to perform an activity in the manner or within the range considered normal for a human being." (Statistics Canada, 1988).

In this survey, disabled persons were defined as those who indicated some difficulty in performing any of 17 activities, such as, "Do you have any trouble walking up and down stairs?" or, "Are you limited in the kind or amount of activity you can do because of a long-term emotional, psychological, or mental health condition?" Older Canadians rated their health quite positively considering that about 30 percent of them reported activity limitations (Figure 2.1), and 6 percent of these limitations were considered severe (Health & Welfare, Canada, 1989). In 1987, there were 494,340 disabled males over the age of 65 compared to 727,655 disabled older women (Statistics Canada, 1988).

Living Arrangements

Adults ages 55 and over are less likely to move than the general population (14 percent compared to 31 percent) and 75 percent said they would prefer to stay in their own homes as long as possible (NACA, 1993). Although 20 percent of older adults indicated that they would consider cashing in home equity to pay for in-home care to postpone the need to be institutionalized, in general, housing problems were experienced by only 9 percent of retired seniors (NACA, 1993). Seniors represent almost half the occupants of social housing, rent-supplement units, and residential rehabilitation units. Over half of rent-subsidized apartments were home to adults ages 55 and over. In 1990, over one-third of all women ages 75 and older lived in subsidized housing (NACA, 1993, *No. 14*).

The proportion of women ages 65 and over living in non-family private households is more than double that of men, and far more older women (34 percent) than older men (14 percent) are living alone. Just less than one-third of seniors rent their dwellings (NACA, 1993, *No. 13*), but among women over age 80, almost half are renters. Eighty percent of families headed by a senior own their own homes; 72 percent of them are mortgage-free. Far more elderly men (73 percent) ages 65 and older are found living in a private household with their spouse (43 percent) (NACA, 1993).

About 55 percent of Americans confined to nursing homes suffer from chronic mental conditions or senility (Schick, 1986). Although the number of seniors living in institutions increased from 1981 to 1991, the percentage of the senior population living in institutions actually decreased from 8 percent to 6.4 percent (NACA, 1993, *No. 12*). Of all the seniors residing in Canadian institutions, 72 percent were women.

Similarly, in the United States, women comprise 75 percent of all nursing home residents ages 65 and over (United Nations, 1990), and yet families are still the single largest resource for the long-term care of older relatives. Popular perception is that the majority of informal caregivers are women, and many appear to be mid-life women who are caring for older relatives as well as children. Meta-analysis recently conducted on gender differences in caregiving contradicts this finding (Miller & Cafasso, 1992), but in the majority of studies documented, most caregivers were women with female children claiming caregiver roles in 79 percent of the cases (Miller, 1990).

The family unit as caregiving resource for the elderly appears to be in jeopardy. In Canada, Fletcher and Stone (1982) claimed that the increasing incidence of childlessness or one-child families, the increasing rate of divorce, the high rate of mobility among young adults, and recent increases in the labor force participation of women, all point to the probability that an elderly person in the future will have less access to family support than present and previous generations of older persons. This means that middle-aged adults need to be maintaining their strength and mobility in order to live out their remaining years with dignity and independence.

Transportation

In 1990, 25 percent of seniors reported having problems with transportation. Between 25 percent and 30 percent of small-town seniors do not drive a car and very few small towns have public transportation services such as buses or taxis. Among senior couples, 87 percent own a car; 63 percent of unattached men own a car compared to 33 percent of unattached women (NACA, 1993). About 70 percent of Canadians ages 55 and over are licensed to drive; in any given year about 3 percent to 5 percent of them are involved in a motor vehicle collision.

Accident statistics indicate that people ages 60 and above are more likely than younger drivers to be involved in collisions and to suffer serious or fatal injuries as a result. (NACA, 1993, *No. 15*)

In addition to driving vehicles, 67 percent of senior couples also use public transportation. As many as 78 percent of unattached women and 65 percent of unattached men use public transportation.

SUMMARY

This demographic profile of North American adults born around the beginning of the 20th century portrays a cohort that, in many ways, is pioneering the full aging experience. Never before have so many people survived to old age, and thus this generation considers health to be one of its strengths. Clearly, however, the problems faced by Canada and the United States are similar and reflect the fact that people are living longer than ever before; quality of life issues such as dying with dignity, creating housing for seniors that permits varying degrees of care at affordable rates, providing safe driving standards for the elderly that accommodate their range in ability, developing transportation systems considerate of the needs of older people, promoting health care that gives more research attention to chronic disease and to the health issues of aging women—all are quite new challenges. As the 21st century arrives, the time to resolve these issues is at hand. Part of this resolution of these issues may be found in more active living patterns.

In preparation for that prospect, Chapter 3 examines activity patterns in both a historical and contemporary context. Physical activity is defined and the challenges of assessing and increasing older adult levels of exercise are presented.

Activity Patterns—Past and Present

PHYSICAL ACTIVITY AT THE TURN OF THE CENTURY

As We at Tennis Played
He tossed her ball this way and that,
And shrieked whene'er it strayed;
She wore a most coquettish hat—
As we at tennis played.

No creature was to me so dear
As that same little maid;
I trembled now 'twixt hope and fear,
As we at tennis played.

My foolish heart went pit-a-pat,
And all its chances weighed;
I whispered something 'neath that hat,
As we at tennis played.

The sweet reply came low and clear
Beneath that hat's broad shade;
We've fixed the day for just a year
Since we at tennis played.

—Edith Sessions Tupper, 1888, *Outing*, 12

What people do in their leisure time and what people do in their work time says much about the culture and the historical context of their society. Older people's beliefs and behaviors in North America are founded on their earlier individual life experiences and are shaped by larger political and historical forces. This chapter contains three major sections—first is a historical portrait of physical activity at the turn of the century; second, an examination of the contemporary physical activity patterns of older people, and third, an exploration of the validity and reliability of activity measurement.

At the turn of the century, coeducational sports such as tennis, golf, and skating provided acceptable settings for men and women to socialize. However, social incentives and public support for participating in more serious forms of exercise and sport have historically been more available to males (Csizma, Wittig, & Schurr, 1988; Greendorfer, 1983). In 1888, Kennedy Childs excused himself for aiming his article in *Outing*, titled, "Training for Cycle Competitions," exclusively at men by stating:

> This recreation is recruited in the main from the ranks of our more youthful manhood (for the purpose of this article the writer will, forgetful of his past flattery of the fair sex, assume its practice by the lords of creation only).

To achieve road-riding condition, the cyclist was given specific directions to visit the track twice each day for a period of one month to six weeks prior to the date of the competition, and to ride steadily a few miles, gradually building up distance. The athletic reader would have imagined himself a thoroughbred upon reading:

> Great care must be taken that a capable rubber-down should thoroughly handle the man on his return to the dressing tent; all perspiration should be fully removed, and a gentle rub follow. This in turn should be succeeded by a plentiful application of rum, alcohol, or Pond's Extract.

While competitive cycling was prohibited for women, female cyclists faced social risks by simply riding publicly. The physical dangers of bicycling were real for American women who occasionally encountered a boy who would ram a stick into the back wheel as they rode by. Helena Swanwick (1854–1939) of England described in 1891 how she and her husband "took to bicycling" especially when "the dropped frame adapted it to the skirted sex" (Murray, 1982). There was only one other woman in her part of Manchester who took to bicycling that year, and she reported that she "was frowned on by some of the college ladies, until the royal ladies took to riding round a London Park, and I was suddenly in fashion." Manchester was a mill town, and boisterous mill-hands would play dangerous pranks on the lady cyclist by linking arms across the road to upset her:

> The only way to cope with this was to avoid looking at them and, putting down my head, charge full tilt, when they would scatter. In London, bus drivers were not above flicking me with the whip, and cabmen thought it fun to converge upon me from behind. I was pulled off by my skirt in a Notting Hill slum, and felt a bit scared till a bright idea struck me. I said to the loutish lad who had seized my handle-bar, "I say, they seem rather a

rough lot here. I wonder whether you would kindly help me out?" He instantly clutched my arm with his other hand, and bustling along with great dignity, shouted, "Nah, then! Mike room for the lidy, can'tcher?" He saw me through, and helped me to re-mount with the recommendation, "Cut awy nah, quick!" And I did. My long skirt was a nuisance and even a danger. It is an unpleasant experience to be hurled on to stone setts (paving stones) and find that one's skirt has been so tightly wound round the pedal that one cannot even get up enough to unwind it. But I never had the courage to ride in breeches except at night. Then, oh then, I sang with jubilation. . . (Murray, 1982).

As concerns mounted for the deplorable state of public health in early turn-of-the-century North America, the meaning of physical culture as sport began to change to accommodate health appeal and mass participation. The message was that individual health could be achieved and preserved by daily exercise. *Cosmopolitan* provided a glimpse on how physical culture had been defined in the United States prior to 1900:

> In the past, physical culture has been much misunderstood and maligned. It was connected with prize-fighting, weight-lifting, acrobatic and athletic performances exclusively. The man who was able to develop the most monstrous muscles was supposed to be the best representative of its benefits (MacFadden, 1903).

In the new-century view, exercise or physical culture was "for everyday man and woman who wishes to get all out of life that Nature intended—who wishes to really live, wide awake, alert and pulsating with the delight of being" (MacFadden, 1903). One cannot help but be surprised by how familiar these early 1900s health announcements sound to us at the end of the very same century! For example, both male and female readers were encouraged to take up outdoor exercise like walking, which was extolled as simple, natural, and wholesome and "by far the most valuable exercise"—one that alone could lead to vigorous health. Walking was to be done in an upright posture, not "moping along," but, instead, with the shoulders down and the trunk and abdomen relaxed for breathing. Running was also advocated for "lung power" and "purer blood," providing the activity was taken up gradually. Over years of practice, running up to five miles was proposed to require "no extraordinary exertion."

MacFadden's article on health and exercise was accompanied by ink print illustrations of men and women doing exercises. The men are mainly holding dumbbells "for developing the shoulders" and the women demonstrate support and flexibility positions "to enlarge the hips and create a long waistline."

In 1913, Dr. W.A. Evans from Chicago pointed to the deplorable physical state of U.S. school children, and cited the fact that one million of them had spinal curvature, flat foot, or some other remediable deformity. In his article on "Human Efficiency" in the March issue of *The Public Health Journal* (1913), Dr. Evans highlighted how overexerting as well as sedentary occupational activities could negatively affect health:

> The soldier who is exposed to the elements and forced to take long marches is not more in need of mechanical perfection and physical fitness than the bookkeeper who sits at his desk or the sewing girl who directs the course of the needle.

He further commented on the beneficial role of physical activity in deterring old age through avoiding "less lung freedom, less room for lung expansion, less air, less oxygen, poorer blood, less general resistance, [and] early actual aging of the body."

In contrast to today's concerns for older adult safety in exercise situations, back then there was not much concern for the older exerciser; instead, concern for physical harm seemed to reside with the young male athlete. The October issue of *The Public Health Journal* of 1913 included a piece, apparently excerpted from *The Sanitary Record*, about "freak athletics" titled, "Athletics Gone Mad." The article began with praise for the social development of older adult physical activity:

> We rejoice in the growth of all rational recreation, and there is no more cheerful sight than to pass through the cricket fields, tennis courts, croquet lawns and bowling greens and see thousands enjoying themselves on a Saturday afternoon. The best feature of such a visit is the revelation that middle-aged and even elderly people may find pastimes in which change and healthful recreation are combined.

But the main point of the article was to "utter a warning over the development of strenuous athletics among young people—we mean those scarcely in their teens." The article noted that it is the height of folly to have boys run five or six miles in a marathon race that would "exceed their physical powers and possibly work for their permanent injury." The recommended distance of "100 yards or even race of a mile might be entertained." What is interesting about this article is that it may reflect the conservative tone held by some health professionals of the day. The boys who were the very target of this concern for "overtaxing their strength" are the same males who are among the older male population today. What are older people to think about late-life exercise if they have been told that running was a physical strain on their bodies at the age of 16?

Despite the early-century social movement advancing the health benefits of physical culture, there were clear directives that differentiated the exercises appropriate for males and females. The 1909 Toronto Board of Education's *The Syllabus of Physical Exercises for the Public Elementary School* portrays females demonstrating a number of static postures in the gym. In the same syllabus, boys are depicted climbing ropes, and in more dynamic situations showing active movement and strength (Board of Education, 1909). Adding to this lack of curricular support for girls to be as vigorously active and skillful as boys have been medical notions of female fragility (Vertinsky, 1988a, 1988b), and social devaluation and invisibility (Gee & Kimball, 1987), notions that still haunt the portrayals of females in sport today. A letter to the editor of *The Edmonton Journal*, published on July 31, 1995, refers to a story and picture about a baseball summer camp for kids:

> The boys are shown in action sequences which clearly show that they have the skills to play the game. Then there is a picture of a girl who is shown trying to catch a ball, glove extended, head turned, eyes closed. She's obviously afraid of the ball. Since this photo is the only one of a female, it reinforces the stereotype about girls/women in sports—that they cannot really play and should not be taken seriously. How often have we heard men

and boys put down females with phrases, "You throw like a girl," or "You run like a sissy" (Karen & Jerry Clarke)

Sport socialization research describes a clear picture of the gender differences among turn-of-the-century, middle-class people engaging in the more vigorous forms of exercise (Lucas & Smith, 1978; Morrow, Keyes, Simpson, Cosentino, & Lappage, 1989; Verbrugge, 1990a). One conspicuous limitation for women was the heavy, multi-layered, and cumbersome skirts and dresses worn by females of all ages, which added to their physical burden (Bolotin, 1980, 1987; Heisch, 1988; McCrone, 1988). The corset was not only uncomfortable, it deformed the ribs, and caused abdominal organs to be displaced permanently. The wasp-waist corset bound the lower rib cage so tightly and restricted breathing so seriously that women easily fainted. Judged by their clothing alone, women of this generation were not meant to be physically adept, but were rather socially designed to be physically limited and helpless.

As significant as fashion in dictating the physical abilities and activities of girls and women was their socialization for a particular feminine role—a socialization that involved their role (current or eventual) as mother and caregiver to the family (McPherson, Curtis, & Loy, 1989). Tomboy style of play was considered by many to be rude and vulgar (Guttman, 1988). The need to give birth to children was of great import in the "new world"—a fact that allowed medical authority to have a crucial role in prescribing appropriate behaviors and activities for females. Early adolescence was the focus of most concern, for this was the stage of maximum female growth for sexual maturation. All physical energies had to be conserved for the critical development of reproductive maturity (Vertinsky, 1990). The complex physiology of women seemed to overtax the understanding of an all-male medical profession; rather than encouraging outdoor play and exercise for females, physicians prescribed the even more restrictive "rest-cure" for those women who were having physical or psychological difficulties. Vertinsky (1987) has explored how "long-standing propositions about women's capacity for sport and strenuous exercise developed in response to late 19th century physicians' interpretations of biological theories about menstruation." Vertinsky describes how menstruation was seen as "an eternal wound" that necessitated the exclusion of women from vigorous and competitive sports and from any physical exertion that the medical experts considered overtaxing.

Until quite recently, for example, the International Olympic Committee believed that sports training and competition were detrimental to proper reproductive functioning in women and used these beliefs to circumscribe female participation in certain sports (Vertinsky, 1987).

The end of the 19th century has been pointed to by feminist historians as a time when tensions between men and women regarding intellectual and physical capabilities were particularly high. Feminists "expressed a growing desire to control their own bodies and reproductive lives by pursuing health and wholeness" (Vertinsky, 1989). One advocate of an emancipated womanhood was Charlotte Perkins Gilman, who through her prolific writing and her personal struggles for fulfillment, has been identified as a major intellectual force in turn-of-the-century America. At the time, males at all ages were universally judged to be better physical specimens than females—a phenomenon, noted by Gilman, that seems to have been rooted in their more permissive and physically aggressive play patterns in childhood. Gilman (1911) claimed that "the play instinct is common to girls and boys alike; and endures in some measure throughout life," but explained that men had the advantage in sport:

> In games of skill we have a different showing. Most of these are developed by and form men; but when they are allowed, women take part in them with interest and success. In card games, in chess, checkers and the like, in croquet and tennis, they play, and play well if well-trained. Where they fall short in so many games, and so are wholly excluded from others, is not lack for human capacity, but for the lack of masculinity. Most games are male (Gilman, 1911).

Tolerance for aggressive behavior, even fighting, was the social context for boys and men, but for girls, the label of "tomboy" with the flushed look of "bicycle face" (Heisch, 1988) was probably only a small part of the larger socio-environmental forces limiting the physical opportunities and leisure time choices of females (Dishman & Dunn, 1988; Espenshade, 1969; Gilman, 1911). Once into the mothering role, a woman would have scant time and energy to take on sportive or other recreative activity outside the context of her family (Gee, 1986a, 1986b; Gee & Kimball, 1987). Although acknowledging economic conditions as a limiting factor in everyone's recreation time, Gilman suggested that although most men had surplus energy and enjoyed better health, women were "restrict[ed] to one set of occupations, and over-tax[ed] their energies with mother-work and housework combined" (1911).

Deterrents to women to be as strong, as fast, and as physically able as the average male were operating in the early 20th century and undermined many young females' motivations to be physically competent and able-bodied in strenuous undertakings. Negative reactions from the female body to this narrow social role and its negative impacts on female mental health were explained at the time as further evidence of the inferiority of women. For those women who did ignore society's expectations, competencies were acquired in skilled activities, which no doubt enhanced their physical well-being, but that took a social, if not psychological toll, on their self-esteem as they stepped outside conventional female roles.

Just over one hundred years ago, young women were admonished for their reckless attempts to learn how to ride bicycles (Lucas & Smith, 1978), yet by the mid-1890s, a number of city women were riding bicycles for transportation and pleasure (Harmond, 1984). Even though they were chastised for some activities, demanding forms of dance such as ballet training and tap dancing were encouraged for females. Social types of dance were highly popular with both men and women and "marathon" dancing was in vogue. Others developed interest in tennis (Danzig, 1928; Heathcote, 1894), swimming, (Shea, 1986), golf (Nickerson, 1987), basketball (Smith, 1984), and figure skating (Cruikshank, 1921).

A dialectic concerning the roles of women according to their social class is perhaps part of the cultural answer in explaining the heterogeneity in physical activity that accompanies women's aging. In the early decades of the 20th century, upper-class women were beginning to experience the sport club scene in golf and tennis. While middle-class women were still being socialized into more passive roles than males, necessity required that working-class women add their physical toughness, endurance, and sweat to the physical labor of men.

There are some historical accounts and women still alive to tell us that, by necessity or choice, they did not assume the passive role that society presented to them. Although middle- and upper-class women were socially constrained in the working world, there were many women who had to labor intensively to survive. Photographic evidence exists that show many immigrant women were tied together as "horse teams" on the prairies, pulling ploughs when oxen were not available (Bolotin, 1987). Hundreds of women combed the fields, literally on their hands and knees, at harvest time. Thousands of rural women, mostly immigrants, were taking up intense and difficult work carving out a pioneer existence and building homesteads in western North America. For many prairie and farming women, the physical challenge and skill of horseback riding and rounding up cattle were simply part of life along with beating back prairie fires with water bucket brigades and wet potato sacks (O'Brien Cousins & Vertinsky, 1995).

Recreation was also available to some women. Historical displays in the sports arenas of Western North America show us that women's hockey teams were prevalent in the 1920s and enjoyed a certain degree of status in being photographed and publicly acknowledged in the same way as the men's teams. Many of our elderly people today were physically involved in city life and/or pioneer life at a level that would have increased their personal skills, knowledge, and interest in the physical capabilities of the human body.

Such early opportunities to participate in skilled exercise may have offered some men and women a level of mastery and customary activity that could last a lifetime. The extent to which regular sports pursuits and habitual activity can be sustained over the life course, or can be reinstated later in life, is a subject requiring more study. Godin, Valois, Shephard, and Desharnais (1987) examined, among other factors, the influence of past exercise behavior on subsequent exercise behavior. They found that exercise involvement weeks and months later was predicted by immediate past behavior. The important role of activity "habit" was highlighted in this study and Godin and colleagues concluded that if a person had never engaged in a particular behavior, future involvement would be unlikely. Among older women, current exercisers often reported that they were tomboys as young girls (O'Brien Cousins, 1997b). Little research has attended to the possibility that the physical competencies acquired in childhood may last a lifetime. Self-reported efficacy for physical skill in childhood has been found to correlate ($r = .44$, $p < .001$), with late-life efficacy ratings for fitness types of exercise in women over age 70 (O'Brien Cousins, 1997b). Multiple regression analysis indicated that movement confidence as a child was a significant predictor of late-life weekly physical activity ($b = .27$, $p < .001$) even when controlling for health, age, and cultural background. The study provided preliminary evidence that late-life involvement and efficacy for healthy forms of exercise may have origins in girlhood competencies over six decades earlier.

PRESENT ACTIVITY PATTERNS OF OLDER ADULTS

Temporal Changes in Physical Activity Patterns

The national obsession with personal fitness and wellness may have started as a fad, but it has quickly worked its way into the foundations of a myriad of professions and businesses. From food products and clothing to medicine and science, the promotion of sports and fitness now makes up part of the very fabric of our society (Aldana & Stone, 1991).

Some improvement in adult physical activity is evident in recent decades. A study on 31,663 Arizona adults, ages 16 to 88, surveyed exercise habits between 1986 to 1989. The sample were users of a health-care package of the CIGNA Healthplan of Arizona. Fourteen activities most frequently cited in surveys were examined specifically for number of involvements per week and the duration of each involvement. The demographic data gathered at the same time showed that the Arizona adults closely matched those of national surveys. The conclusion from this study was that more adults were getting more regular vigorous physical activity than at any other time in the previous two decades. As many as 61 percent indicated they exercised regularly and 72 percent of males over age 65 said they exercised regularly. The lowest participation, 53%, was found among American minorities, which included all races except white, black, and Hispanic.

Walking was the most popular activity in the Arizona study. Slightly more than 44 percent of all adults surveyed indicated that they walked for exercise at least once a week. Among both sexes, the percentage of walkers increased with age, peaking at 55 percent for adults over age 65. When comparing slow walking (20 minutes per mile) to fast walking (15 minutes per mile), more people were found to be walking in the slow category (34%) than the fast (24%). Females were more likely to be fast walkers than were men, with 45 percent of women walking fast compared to 24 percent of men. In all age groups, females had almost double the percentage of fast walkers.

At its peak in 1982, jogging was popular with only 14 percent of Americans (Figure 3.1). It has dropped off rapidly in subsequent years, especially with the increasing age of the participating adults. Only about 4 percent to 5 percent of adults over age 45 were runners or joggers. Three times as many females as males (5.5%) were doing aerobics (17%), but only 9 percent of women over age 45 did aerobics for exercise. Aldana and Stone (1991) noted that although 61 percent reported they got "some type of regular exercise" many did not appear to get enough exercise to reap health benefits.

Despite this negative finding, the numbers of Americans walking has doubled in the past 10 years. And walking is the *only* activity that people tend to do more of as they get older (Figure 3.2). Training with weights became more popular after 1980 (Figure 3.3), with women increasing participation from .8 percent in 1975 to 7.0 percent in 1989, an 800-percent increase. Cycling and swimming seem to have plateaued and calisthenics may even be on the decline.

Physical activity patterns are a socially dynamic phenomenon requiring regular

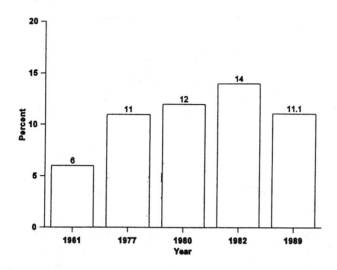

Figure 3.1 Percentage of Americans who run or jog for exercise. Reprinted with permission from Aldana, S. G. & Stone, W. J. (1991). Changing physical activity preferences of American adults. *Journal of Physical Education, Recreation & Dance, 62*(4), 67–71, 76.

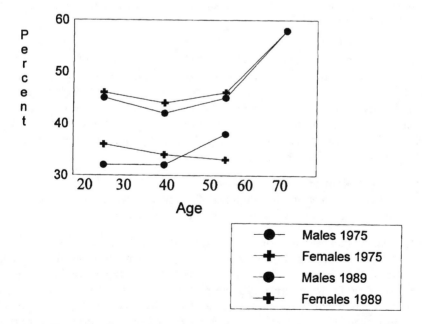

Figure 3.2 Percentage of males and females who walk, 1975 and 1989. Reprinted with permission from Aldana, S. G., & Stone, W. J. (1991). Changing physical activity preferences of American adults. *Journal of Physical Education, Recreation & Dance, 62*(4), 67–71, 76.

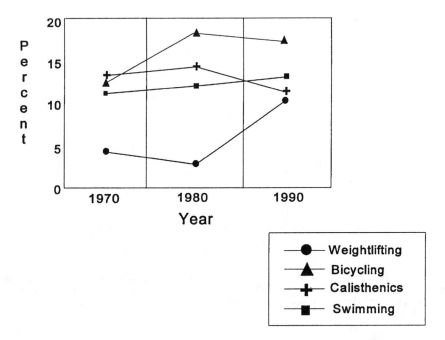

Figure 3.3 Percentage of adults in bicycling, swimming, weight-training, and calisthenics over the past 14 years. Reprinted with permission from Aldana, S. G., & Stone, W. J. (1991). Changing physical activity preferences of American adults. *Journal of Physical Education, Recreation & Dance, 62*(4), 67–71, 76.

monitoring. However, attempts to identify the activity patterns of older adults precisely continues to be a challenge. Inconsistent findings are blamed on differences found among seniors who live in different geographic settings and who possess unique cultural traits to consider. In addition, inconsistencies arise because there have been dynamic shifts in participation trends over even a period of a few years. Moreover, there are different methods used to define and quantify physical activity. Definitions of "active" include:

- total amount of energy expended
- frequency, intensity, and duration of physical activity
- amount and consistency of time devoted to active leisure

Energy expenditure estimates (in kilocalories) based on *leisure time physical activity* (LTPA) are generally widely accepted; typically a seven-day recall format such as that described in Chapter 8 is one way to estimate this energy expenditure. However, some people prefer to examine only the number of hours of exercise per week, or estimate the number of sweat episodes associated with activity in the past four months, or document the level of intensity at which the older person is capable of performing. For example, vigorous leisure time activity has been the focus of most research by its very definition:

. . . by exercise, we mean vigorous activities such as aerobics, jogging, racquet sports, team sports, dance classes, or *brisk* walking. (Stephens, 1992)

In Canada, two leisure time physical activity statistics have been used in long-term studies between 1981 and 1988. "Energy expenditure" on physical activity greater than 3+ KKD (kilocalories per kilogram of body weight per day) was one measure; the second measure was "time" spent on physical activity (3 or more hours per week for 9 or more months of the year). For energy expenditure, the general population ages 15 and older increased from 24 percent (1981) to 31 percent (1989). For the 65 and over population, the improvement was 27 percent to 42 percent for men, and 17 percent to 23 percent for women. In terms of time spent, more of the general population was active in 1989—from 57 percent to 79 percent. The activity improvement was 59 percent to 75 percent for men, and 54 percent to 69 percent for women for those 65 and older. The lower figures for energy expenditure suggest that Canadians may be putting in the time, but they are not choosing activities that give them the best health benefits for the time spent. However, choosing more vigorous activities may require more expert supervision and add risk for older people. Requiring older people to do more demanding forms of exercise may be a problem since the majority (80%) of older adults prefer "casual" activities.

Between 1981 and 1988, Canadian physical activity participation increased in most activities with the exception of jogging (Stephens & Craig, 1990). These increases were found in all age and social groups, except for males and females ages 20 to 24, they actually declined 11 percent and 10 percent, respectively. Men ages 65 and older increased their leisure time exercise by 15 percent and females of the same ages increased activity by 6 percent. But for older people, such a narrow focus on only the most vigorous forms of activity excludes the majority of seniors who are moderately or mildly active. For example, in *Canada's Fitness Survey*, 52 percent of women ages 65 and older were active less than three times weekly compared to 41 percent of men. Also alarming are the statistics that 31 percent of males and 36 percent of females were "inactive" by this definition. The General Social Survey (1987) warned that with a vigorous classification, only 6.5 percent of women ages 65 and over would be identified as "active."

The Campbell's Survey (Stephens & Craig, 1990) notes that there is a general decline in participation as people get older, but, since 1981, adults of all ages, and notably older adults, have made significant efforts to become more physically active. In the 1990 Health Promotion Survey, a clear majority of adults (58%) felt that they exercised less than they should. When asked if anything was stopping them from exercising more, the only significant barriers were a lack of time (34%) and a lack of self-discipline or energy (34%). These comments are surprising coming from a cohort that has developed a reputation for discipline and hard work, and whose members admittedly have more discretionary time in retirement!

Of the 42 percent of adults who reported increasing their LTPA in 1987, a majority (59 percent) claimed they did so because of increased knowledge of the risks of remaining sedentary. Having the example of others, the support of family and friends, and facing changes in social values or a new life situation were also important supports in helping people become more active. Interestingly, health promotion messages seem to be increasing the activity levels of the people who are already active.

> Those who reported increases are much more likely to be active currently at a high rather than a moderate level (68% versus 22%), suggesting that much of the reported change has been from moderate to high intensity, rather than from sedentary to a moderately active lifestyle. (Stephens, 1992)

In the *1990 Health Promotion Survey*, high-level exercisers are those who report vigorous leisure time activity of at least 15 minutes at least three times per week. Table 3.1 represents an index to assist in understanding how both frequency (days per week) and duration (minutes of exercise) have been combined to define low, moderate, and high levels of exercise that do not take into account the level of intensity (Stephens, 1992). According to this index, an ideal level of exercise for adults would range from periods longer than 30 minutes for 5 to 7 days a week, to periods of 15 to 30 minutes 3 to 4 days a week.

An interesting feature of Figure 3.4 is the indication that high LTPA is held quite steady for women after age 25, although men's takes a dramatic drop until age 65 when it bounces back somewhat. Using the index in Table 3.1 as a guide, Stephens (1992) has estimated that men age 65 and older are more active than all other age and gender groups older than 25 (Figure 3.4). One conclusion from this finding is that older men apparently find ways after retirement to maintain or even increase their levels of activity. Another possibility is that middle-age men, some of whom have already encountered heart problems or lung cancer, are deceased by age 65, and that leaves a healthier group of men contributing activity statistics in the 65 and over group. Probably both explanations apply.

Table 3.2 provides data on the usual duration of LTPA in Canadians 15 years of age or older by age and sex. Looking at the far right column, which represents the percentage of people reporting exercise lasting more than 30 minutes, one can see that compared to women, more men reported longer durations of exercise. In the 65 and over category, 43 percent of men and 29 percent of women reported exercising more than 30 minutes per session.

The *1988 Campbell's Survey on Well-Being* was a longitudinal follow-up study of the 1981 Canada Fitness Survey (Stephens & Craig, 1990) that provided a detailed

Table 3.1   Leisure-Time Physical Index Defined

	Usual duration of activity		
Average frequency	>30 Minutes	15–30 Minutes	<15 Minutes
Daily	HIGH	HIGH	MOD
5–6 times per week	HIGH	HIGH	MOD
3–4 times per week	HIGH	HIGH	MOD
1–2 times per week	MOD	MOD	LOW
Less than once per week	LOW	LOW	LOW
Never, don't know	LOW	LOW	LOW

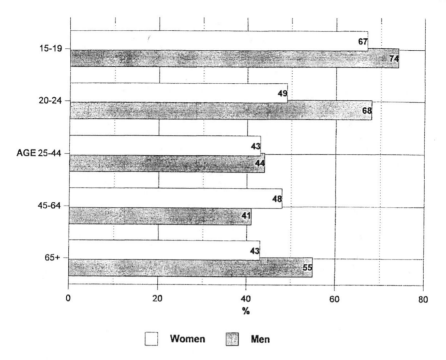

Figure 3.4 High leisure time physical activity index, by age and sex, ages 15 and over, Canada, 1990.

portrait of the physical recreation habits, physical fitness, and health status of 4,000 adults. The survey investigated changes in patterns of recreation and fitness, demographic profiles of people at various activity levels, health outcomes of physical activity, and relationships between activity level and motivation. "Active" was defined as "doing activities at least once weekly in the three months prior to the survey" (Stephens, 1992). Highlights of this survey were:

- One-third of individuals ages 10 and over were classified as "active" in their leisure time
- 43 percent were considered to be "inactive"
- 25 percent were moderately active
- Males were more active at every age group

There was a general decline in activity with age that reversed for men at age 65.

The *Campbell's Survey on the Well-Being of Canadians* reported that 50 percent of men and 30 percent of women over the age of 65 were participating in regular aerobic activity for at least 30 minutes every other day (Stephens & Craig, 1990). Males spent about equal amounts of time on physical recreation, but males were far more active when *intensity* was part of the definition. The physical recreation activities that had the largest number of participants were walking (77% of all-age women),

Table 3.2   Usual Duration of Leisure-Time Physical
Activity, by Age and Sex, Age 15+

	Duration (%)	
	15–30 Minutes	>30 Minutes
Total	22	48
Men	17	55
Women	26	42
Age group		
15–19	25	68
Men	16	78
Women	34	58
20–24	20	65
Men	12	77
Women	27	53
25–44	23	50
Men	18	55
Women	26	55
45–64	20	40
Men	17	42
Women	23	38
65+	21	35
Men	18	43
Women	24	29

gardening (55% of all-age women), and swimming (48% of all-age women). With increasing age, the number of adults walking and gardening increased, but the number who were cycling, swimming, and dancing decreased. The common features of activities on the increase were that they were low-cost, had flexible scheduling, and were convenient. Homemakers and clerical/sales employees were among the groups least likely to be active in scheduled activities and more likely to be active in casual activities. The activity level of retirees was second only to students (Stephens, 1990).

CURRENT PATTERNS OF PHYSICAL ACTIVITY

In *Healthy People 2000*, the U.S. Department of Health and Human Services (1994b) reported that in meeting each of its 12 physical activity and fitness objectives for 1990, the record of progress has been mixed. Only one goal—availability of work site fitness programs for 20 percent of companies with 50 to 99 employees and 35 percent of companies with 100 to 249 employees—has been exceeded. Four other population targets show progress: fewer deaths due to coronary heart disease, increased moderate physical activity, reductions in sedentary living among people 65 years and over and among people with disabilities, and increases in muscular strength, endurance, and flexibility.

However, the findings indicate that current rates of participation in physical activity in the United States generally fall far below the 1990 objectives. The level of activity is considered to be comparable to Australia, but is less than the activity rates of Canadians (Dishman, 1990).

One target is to increase clinician counseling about physical activity from 30 percent to 50 percent of all sedentary patients. Family practitioners are credited for counseling 19 percent of their sedentary patients, and assisting in the formulation of an exercise plan with 18 percent. Internists apparently are the closest to the target goal, reporting inquiry about exercise habits of 40 percent of sedentary patients and assisting in the exercise planning of 25 percent of their patients.

Health: United States, 1993 (USDHHS, 1994c) reported on health status, health resources and expenditures, and the prevalence of negative health behaviors such as smoking, but unfortunately it did not report on exercise among the health promotion behaviors it covered. Other population estimates indicate that 30 percent to 60 percent of North Americans engage in no leisure time physical activity; only 10 percent of Americans and 25 percent of Canadians are regularly and vigorously active (Dishman, 1990). Dishman (1990) noted that drop-out rates from supervised exercise programs have remained at about 40 percent to 50 percent over the last 20 years, and this finding holds for Scandinavia, the United States, and Canada.

Data collected in 1991 on Vancouver women, average age 77, indicated that about 10 percent were in a highly active exercise-level category above 3,000 kilo-calories a week (O'Brien Cousins, 1995c, 1993). Another 25 percent were at an "ideal" exercise level of 1,500 to 3,000 kcal/week. Together, these two categories made up about one-third of the sample. Another one-third of the women were basically seden-tary because they were reporting activity levels of less than 500 kcal/week. The final one-third were somewhat active, but likely not active enough to obtain many health benefits (Figure 3.5).

Although activity levels seem to be generally on the rise since 1981, Stephens (1988) warned that many adults are unsure of how much exercise is appropriate. Most epidemiological literature acknowledges an age-related decline in participation, with women exhibiting less activity and less physical fitness at every age group ranking

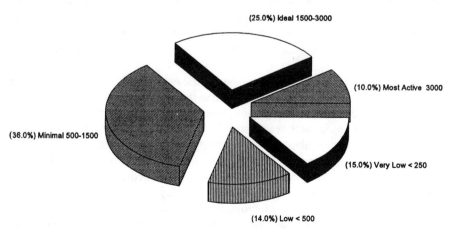

Figure 3.5 Exercise status in the past week for Vancouver women over age 70.

(Alexander, Ready, & Fougere-Mailey, 1985; Shephard, 1997). Post-adolescent girls demonstrated a greater decline in fitness than did women in any other age group; the next most critical period in terms of physical fitness decline is considered to be ages 40 to 49 (Alexander, Ready, & Fougere–Mailey, 1985).

Over 1,200 women across six Canadian regions were interviewed in the 1985 General Social Survey where active physical exercise was defined as "exercise which made one perspire or breathe more heavily than normal" (General Social Survey, 1987). From this survey it was estimated that only 27 percent of the adult female Canadian population over the age of 15 was active enough to anticipate health benefits that included additional years of life. The survey noted that physical activity declined sharply after age 24, and again after age 44. In addition, among adults over age 65, almost 40 percent were identified as sedentary. Only 14 percent of the 65 and over women in this survey were in the "active" category, but 36 percent were in the "sedentary" category.

Other studies show that older women are inadequately active. The report *Changing Times: Women and Physical Activity* (Fitness and Amateur Sport: Women's Program, 1984) reported that 53 percent of Canadian females over age 60 were active in their leisure time (an average of at least three hours per week over nine months of the year). About 21 percent of the women were moderately active and 24 percent were sedentary. Only 39 percent of the women studied achieved the recommended level of cardiovascular fitness. Therefore, the agency concluded that, "women need to increase the intensity of their participation." More alarming findings are found in *Women in Canada: A Statistical Report* (1990) using data from the 1985 General Social Survey conducted a few years earlier. This report classified only 6.3 percent of Canadian women over age 65 as "active."

MEASUREMENT OF PHYSICAL ACTIVITY

Habitual on-the-job physical activity is so rare in contemporary society that occupational energy expenditure is not likely to be a factor in future fitness. The historical interest in the idea that habitual occupational activity protects against coronary heart disease waned in the 1960s when occupational activity levels were universally declining as a result of technological advancement (Yasin, Alderson, Marr, Pattison, & Morris, 1967).

Contemporary research began to emphasize the expenditure of energy apart from work activity. This section summarizes evidence that most self-report measures about exercise provide adequate scientific utility. Self-report has become the measure of choice by epidemiologists and health educators because a researcher can acquire a vast amount of information about physical activity patterns with relatively little inconvenience to subjects, and with little time and expense (Baranowski, 1988; Godin, Jobin, & Bouillon, 1986). Since the complexity of detailed survey methods about activity patterns was thought to undermine the accuracy of the data (Buskirk, Harris, Mendes, & Skinner, 1971; Reiff, Montoye, Remington, Napier, Metzner, & Epstein, 1967), there was an appeal for uniformity and brevity among assessment instruments (Wilson, Paffenbarger, Morris, & Havlik, 1986).

Several studies have demonstrated significant relationships between self-reported physical activity and epidemiological variables with simple activity questions about strenuous activities. For example, the question, "Do you regularly engage in strenuous exercise or hard physical labor?", was a better predictor of HDL cholesterol levels in the blood than was direct fitness measurement on the treadmill (Haskell, Taylor, Wood, Schrott, & Heiss, 1980). With the question, "Considering a seven-day period (a week), during your leisure time, how often do you engage in any regular activity long enough to work up a sweat (heart beats rapidly)?", Godin and Shephard (1985) obtained a correlation of $r = .35$ with a direct estimate of aerobic fitness (VO$_2$ max).

Despite these crude and varied tools, a relatively consistent pattern has been demonstrated between increased physical activity and reduced risk of coronary heart disease, osteoporosis, and non-insulin-dependent diabetes (LaPorte, Montoye, & Casperson, 1985).

Simple self-ranking into categories of "little or no physical activity," "occasional physical activity," and "regular physical activity at least three times per week" have been found to predict percentage of body fat as seen in Table 3.3 (Horowitz, Blackburn, Edington, & Berlin, 1987).

Sallis and colleagues (1985) assessed specific vigorous activities by asking subjects, "For at least the last three months, which of the following activities have you performed regularly?" Subjects then chose up to five of the listed activities for a score of 0 to 5. In women, physical activity was significantly related to high education ($r = 0.141$, $p < .0001$), managerial occupation ($r = 0.112$, $p < .002$), and nonmarried status ($r = 0.140$, $p < .0004$) (Sallis, Haskell, Wood, Fortman, Rogers, Blair, & Paffenbarger, 1985).

In their study, Siconolfi, Lasater, Snow and Carleton (1985) strongly advocated:

> . . . that brevity, low cost, and physical activity estimates are all well served by the very simple question, "At least once a week, do you engage in any regular activity similar to brisk walking, jogging, bicycling etc. long enough to work up a sweat?" Then if the answer is yes, "how many times per week?"

This question correlated $r = .46$ with *direct* measures of maximal oxygen uptake (Siconolfi, Lasater, Snow, & Carleton, 1985).

A measure of caloric expenditure based on the type and duration of activities in the past week was designed by Paffenbarger, Wing, and Hyde (1978) to assess exercise levels in male college alumni. This instrument was used with 59 older women

Table 3.3   Body Fat and Aerobic Fitness Differences among Exercisers and Non-Exercisers

	Percent body fat	Aerobic fitness VO$_2$ max ml/kg/min
Exercisers	20.9	41.3
Non-exercisers	27.6	30.9

ages 45 to 74 (mean = 61.1) in two trials one year apart (LaPorte, Black-Sandler, Cauley, Link, Bayles, & Marks, 1983). The one-year test-retest reliability was $r = .73$ ($p < .05$). Other relationships were of interest; estimated kilocalories correlated with blocks walked ($r = .42$, $p < .05$), stairs climbed ($r = .54$, $p < .05$), and sweat episodes per week ($r = .46$, $p < .05$).

Unfortunately, no single standardized measure of exercise behavior is universally supported; there is still a vigorous search for a powerful but simple survey instrument. LaPorte, Montoye, and Caspersen (1985) summed this problem up best:

> More than 30 different methods have been used to assess physical activity. These methods can be grouped into seven major categories: calorimetry, job classification, survey procedures, physiological markers, behavioral observation, mechanical and electric monitors, and dietary measures. No single instrument fulfills the criteria of being valid, reliable, and practical while at the same time not affecting behavior. The instruments that are very precise tend to be impractical on a population basis. Surveys are the most practical approach in large-scale studies, although little is known about their reliability and validity. (p. 132)

Reliability of Self-Reported Exercise

In general, the reliability of self-reported exercise status is quite good in adults of all ages ($r > .70$), especially if the exercise is intense (LaPorte, Black-Sandler, Cauley, Link, Bayles, & Marks, 1983; LaPorte, Montoye, & Caspersen, 1985) or sweat-inducing (Kohl, Blair, Paffenbarger, Macera, & Kronenfeld, 1988). Baecke, Burema, and Frijters (1982) factor-analyzed 29 items about habitual physical activity on a young, adult, Dutch population. Thirteen items were retained in three indices of physical activity: (1) a work index, (2) a sport index, and (3) a leisure time activity index. The three-month test-retest reliabilities for these indices were $r = .80$, $r = .90$, and $r = .74$, respectively.

A two-week test-retest reliability study on 163 males and 143 females ages 18 to 65 years was conducted by Godin and Shephard (1985). A simple two-part leisure time questionnaire requested this self-report information:

1   Considering a seven-day period (a week), how many times on the average do you do the following kinds of exercise for more than 15 minutes during your free time? (Write in each circle the appropriate number).
    a) strenuous exercise (Heart beats rapidly)   ( )
    b) moderate exercise (not exhausting)   ( )
    c) mild exercise (minimal effort)   ( )
2   Considering a seven-day period (a week), during your leisure time, how often do you engage in any regular activity long enough to work up a sweat? (Heart beats rapidly).
    a) often   ( )
    b) sometimes   ( )
    c) never/rarely   ( )

Two-week test-retest reliability coefficients were, respectively, 0.94, 0.46, 0.48, and 0.80 for self-reports of strenuous, moderate, light, and sweat-inducing exercise.

Cauley, LaPorte, Black-Sandler, Schramm, and Kriska (1987) compared five methods of assessing physical activity in 255 white, post-menopausal women: (1) the Paffenbarger survey estimating weekly kilocalories expended; (2) a modified Paffenbarger survey focused only on sports activities; (3) the LSI or Large-Scale Integrated Activity Monitor, an electronic recorder with a mercury sensor for movement; (4) the Baeke survey, developed in the Netherlands, to assess occupational and leisure time activity; and (5) caloric intake from food records. Large intra-individual variation was found in day-to-day caloric assessments and in the body movements counted by the LSI Activity Monitor. The modified Paffenbarger (sport-assessment) index failed, since only one-third of the women had had any sport activity to report. The Baeke leisure time index—but not its work or sport index—was predictive of the number of blocks walked. The best assessment tool was Paffenbarger's composite Physical Activity Index estimating weekly kilocalories with a reliability coefficient of .73 four weeks later, and .73 one year later. Paffenbarger's index also demonstrated concurrent validity through its significant association with the electronic monitor of .33 ($p < .01$).

Sallis and colleagues (1985) reported test-retest data on 2,126 men and women, ages 20 to 74. The correlation between the two weekly reports of the number of vigorous activities was .83 ($p < 0.0001$). For moderate activities, the correlation was $r = 0.75$ ($p < 0.0001$). This kind of reproducibility and stability in human self-reporting is certainly satisfactory for research purposes.

A lifestyle assessment tool administered by a microcomputer examined reliability of reporting among 117 outpatients 18 to 80 years of age with a mean age of 37 years (Skinner, Palmer, Sanchez-Craig, & McIntosh, 1987). Physical exercise in reported days per week was 2.5 days at Time 1 and 2.6 days at Time 2 ($r = .82$).

In a study by Gross, Sallis, Buono, Roby, and Nelson (1990), 21 trained interviewers demonstrated test-retest reliability (with a seven-day recall instrument administered on separate occasions) of .99; inter-rater reliability of the same individual on the same day was .86. Gross and colleagues concluded that novice individuals can be taught to reliably conduct and score the Seven-Day Physical Activity Recall Interview (Gross, Sallis, Buono, Roby, & Nelson, 1990).

Validity of Self-Reported Exercise

A measuring tool should have predictive validity, concurrent validity, and construct validity if it is to serve a variety of measurement purposes (Chen, Calderone, & Pellarin, 1987). Criterion or predictive validity is the degree to which the measuring instrument can predict a criterion. Concurrent validity is the degree to which two or more comparable measuring instruments agree in measuring the same underlying concept. Construct validity is the degree to which the results of the measurement support hypothesized relationships or differences in individuals or groups.

The lack of detailed information on exercise habits is, ironically, partially a result of the large number of positive relationships found from early studies that used only gross estimates of exercise status (Sallis et al., 1985). Despite the simple activity measures used in large epidemiological studies, strong relationships were still obtained in explaining general health, specific disease, mortality rate, and fitness performance. Thus, there appears to be support for criterion or predictive validity of self-reported exercise status.

A wide variety of studies have acknowledged, and even apologized for, the crudeness of their physical activity measures. Nevertheless, research is unhindered in finding significant relationships of self-reported physical activity: with caloric intake (Alderson & Yasin, 1966); with smaller body fat skinfolds (Epstein, Wing, & Thompson, 1978); with aerobic fitness (Godin & Shephard, 1985; Haskell, 1984; Horowitz, Blackburn, Edington, & Berlin, 1987); with daily activity diaries (Taylor, Coffey, Berra, Iaffaldano, Casey, & Haskell, 1984); with self-motivation to persevere (Dishman & Ickes, 1981); with heart attack risk (Paffenbarger & Hale, 1975; Paffenbarger, Wing, & Hyde, 1978); with improved levels of HDL blood cholesterol; with physical health status (Belloc & Breslow, 1972); and with longevity (Paffenbarger, Hyde, Wing, & Hsied, 1986; Powell, Thompson, Caspersen, & Kendrick, 1987).

There are few concurrent validity studies. LaPorte's research team (1983) compared a movement-activated mercury sensor (LSI Activity Monitor) and the seven-day recall survey of Paffenbarger, Wing, and Hyde (1978) in assessing the physical activity of older women. After finding a small concurrent validity coefficient of $2r = .23$ they reported:

> The LSI activity monitoring and Paffenbarger survey were both effective, reliable measures of physical activity. However, they appeared to measure somewhat different aspects of physical activity. The LSI measured physical activity associated with movement, whereas the surveys measured the intensity component of energy expenditure. The research indicated that it is important to evaluate the characteristics of the activity of interest in order to select a physical activity tool for assessing activity patterns in older women (LaPorte et al., 1983).

Baranowski (1988) reviewed prominent epidemiological studies that assessed self-reported physical activity. He came to four conclusions:

1 The same instrument assessing patterns of habitual activity, when applied to the same group of people, has reasonably high reliability coefficients.
2 The same instrument applied to the same group of people in different time periods produces modest correlations.
3 When two different instruments are applied to the same group of people, at the same time, the correlations are modest to nonexistent.
4 The correlation with external criteria are modest to nonexistent.

When statistically significant correlations are obtained, this is evidence for validity. Since the measures are supposed to be measures of differing phenomena, and links between measures are primarily theoretical, it is impossible to say how high these coefficients should be (Baranowski, 1988).

Even establishing high validity in objective, mechanical instruments measuring activity is a challenge. LaPorte, Kuller, and Kupper (1979) obtained a correlation of $r = .69$ between trunk movements as recorded on the motor activity monitor and energy expenditure over two days. Siconolfi, Lasater, Snow, and Carleton (1985) noted the obvious face validity of Paffenbarger's Physical Activity Index Questionnaire, assessing frequency of sports and recreational activity, city blocks walked, and flights of stairs climbed. Using this index for a sample of male college alumni data, and expressing activity involvement in kilocalories per week, Paffenbarger and colleagues (1978) found greater first heart attack risk with low adult physical activity patterns. Finding this relationship provided criterion validity for Paffenbarger's instrument.

Washburn and Montoye (1986) noted that "adequate validation of physical activity questionnaires has not been done because of the difficulty in obtaining an acceptable criterion [or outcome] measure." Consequently there have been mixed results in demonstrating the reliability and validity of the seven-day recall inventory. Researchers are warned, therefore, that there are variations between studies in measuring subject characteristics, the definition of physical activity, and most seriously, the wording, design, and types of criterion measured in the seven-day recall inventory.

Such variation in the seven-day recall instrument has undermined the demonstrated validity of this instrument in at least one study. Kohl, Blair, Paffenbarger, Macera, & Kronenfeld (1988) set out to validate self-reported physical activity (seven-day recall) in a mail survey with an objective measure of physical fitness (maximal treadmill test). Even though their research paper claimed that the seven-day activity recall method of assessment "appeared to be ineffective in measuring exercise behavior in this mail survey," a number of problems appeared to have undermined the statistical relationship between reported activity level and physical fitness. First, physical fitness was assessed over a four-month period, and activity level was assessed over seven days. This differential time frame reference may explain the lack of association. Second, both measures were admittedly imperfect, and each added a significant amount of non-identified error. Third, a strong genetic component was known to be involved in the individual performance of aerobic fitness (Dishman & Ickes, 1981). Fourth, individuals varied on the intensity of their weekly exercise—some exercised intensively for short periods, others exercised at low to moderate levels for several hours per week. The latter group may not have been exercising intensively enough to elevate their aerobic fitness, and this became another source of error. Despite these difficulties, Kohl and colleagues (1988) claimed "physical fitness" was a poor choice for a criterion variable and concluded "these results indicate that exercise behavior can be accurately estimated in large populations by using simple questions in a mail survey."

Support for the Seven-Day Recall In spite of the equivocal findings, the seven-day recall form for leisure time activity assessment gathered research support. Blair and colleagues (1985) found adequate precision and have demonstrated concurrent validity with related questions on physical activity and job classification (Blair et al., 1985); an exercise and control group reported significantly different activity levels at the three-month mark ($p < .05$), six-month mark ($p < .01$), and 12-month mark ($p < .004$). After six months of participation in an exercise program, an individual's reported exercise was significantly correlated with maximum oxygen uptake ($r = 0.33$; $p < .05$) and body fat ($r = -0.50$; $p < .01$).

The seven-day recall format is useful for older adult research because it does not appear to surpass the recall memory of most individuals and does not create too great a respondent burden (Blair, 1984). A one-year "recall" of the Leisure Time Physical Activities Questionnaire was used with middle-age men. This instrument was conducted by interview and validated against physical work capacity (Taylor, Jacobs, Schucker, Kinedsen, Leon, & Debacker, 1978). But the one-year recall may be too onerous for older people to complete with any accuracy. The seven-day recall has the advantage of brevity and detail. It has been used in a number of important studies and appears to have scientific merit in terms of reliability and validity (Blair, Haskell, Ho, Paffenbarger, Vranizan, Farquhar, & Wood, 1985).

Taylor, Coffey, Berra, Iaffaldano, Casey, & Haskell (1984) compared seven days of recalled activity (in an interview) to two other activity measures: (1) a seven-day daily activity log, and (2) an electronic movement detector (Vitalog). These researchers found that recalled seven-day activity somewhat underestimated diary logs of activity, but found overall that "a seven-day recall significantly agrees with daily self-report of physical activity and directly measured physical activity" (Taylor et al., 1984). It was concluded that:

> . . . a seven-day activity recall accurately reflects mean kcal/day expenditure, with conditioning activities being the best recalled. (Taylor et al., 1984)

Furthermore, age-appropriate, gender-appropriate, and activity-prompted styles of survey information are considered important in reducing report error in research with the elderly (Cauley, LaPorte, Black-Sandler, Schramm, & Kriska, 1987; Washburn, Jette, & Janney, 1990). Baranowski (1988) suggested that the self-report accuracy of physical activity might be increased using memory-enhancing procedures such as listed activities. Washburn, Jette, and Janney (1990) reported that their questionnaire underestimated light and moderate standing work for elderly men and women ages 65 to 91 years. They concluded that, "the activity most likely to be engaged in by older people is the type that is most inaccurately assessed by questionnaire." Error rate has been found to increase, however, in individuals with less education and less income, and those with very high activity levels. More important was the finding that strenuous activities are reported with more accuracy though mild activities can be underestimated by over two hours per day.

The recall accuracy of older people is critical to activity assessment. Ridley, Bachrach, and Dawson (1979) examined recall ability of females ages 66 to 76. Recall of fertility history over the life course revealed a "high and invariant level of recall ability" with over 90 percent accuracy to 15 items asked. Reliability was highest for subject matter that was factual more than attitudinal. Re-tests conducted three weeks later ranged from 44 percent to over 90 percent accuracy.

Readers who wish to try assessing their physical activity in the past week can read Chapter 8, which contains a two-page physical assessment for older people. The format is a seven-day inventory called The Older Adult Exercise Status Inventory. The procedure for assessment is described in detail.

SUMMARY

The present chapter has explored the patterns of physical activity in adults—both past and present. The historical record documents medical warnings about the dangers and risks of physical culture, especially strenuous competitive sport for young men, and exerting exercise for females. Today's older adults were the very young people who were the target of these warnings. The current physical activity choices and commitments of older people are generally lacking, although evidence has been provided in the present chapter for the improving involvement of older men. Even though many older women are spending a good deal of their leisure time on some kind of physical activity, only a minority are choosing activities vigorous enough to really promote their biological health. Data has also been presented in this chapter demonstrating that habits, vigor, and competencies formed in one's youth may be significant contributing factors, and the historical record shows that older men had more opportunities in their youth to obtain these skills and habits than did their female counterparts.

Before hearing about senior's current understandings concerning what is appropriate activity for them now that they are older, two chapters are coming up which provide information about the "real" or known risks and benefits of late-life exercise. Chapter 4 presents information on the known risks regarding physical activity and sport participation for older adults. Chapter 5 identifies the known benefits, and it will be clear to the reader by Chapter 6, that the beliefs that older people have concerning physical activity are the key to their behavior.

The deficient activity patterns of adults of all ages, and the particular reluctance of women to participate in more vigorous activities, suggests that the benefits of involvement in progressive and moderate exercise are not well known or are of little consequence to the average citizen. The risks of exertion or overexertion may appear to be too great although the benefits are not well understood. On the contrary, the reality is that the known benefits of regular exercise are almost too long to list. Moreover, the known risks of adult participation are negligible, even among very old people.

sudden death are almost universally a male phenomenon (Ragosta, Crabtree, Sturner, & Thompson, 1984).

Risk judgments may be influenced by the memory of past events and the imagination of future events. Slovic (1986) claimed that simply reminding people that exercise prevents cardiovascular disease may alert them to their personal vulnerability to heart attack and thereby further encourage even more cautious behavior.

Because correcting misperceptions about suffering personal harm in the exercise setting is perhaps the central issue in promoting late-life exercise, this chapter examines what is known about actual risk. In the following section, five types of risk are presented as potential outcomes of late-life exercise: (1) risk of heart attack or sudden death; (2) exercise and sport injury; (3) risks of falls and consequent injury; (4) risk of overexertion and exhaustion; and (5) risks of provoking ill-health.

THE RISK OF SUDDEN DEATH

Contrary to popular belief, serious complications in supervised exercise programs are rare, even among heart-diseased patients. In 1986, Van Camp and Peterson documented one fatality per 750,000 patient hours of supervised exercise, and nine cardiac arrests per million patient hours of exercise—a mortality figure no different than that which would be expected in non-exercising patients in this age group. Indeed, active older adults may be particularly advantaged, because aerobic exercise, acting as a prevention activity, can provide older adults with early detection of disease, with warning signs and symptoms and deficiency in the cardiovascular system (Gottlieb & Gerstenblith, 1988). Undiagnosed disease processes are more likely to be detected in activity settings where all body systems need to be performing optimally.

In sedentary adults, symptoms of heart disease often go unnoticed until it is too late. Ironically, cardiac risk assessment ("stress" test) more often occurs *after* heart disease is diagnosed; such testing is considered to be an essential protocol in identifying what is normally "silent ischemia" (Smith, 1988). Ironically, the only people who can get a free fitness test are those who are already diseased! Unfortunately, for health-conscious individuals who could benefit from the knowledge that their active lifestyles have indeed prevented heart disease, such high-stress tests are usually reserved for those who have already encountered non-silent ischemia (angina)—the very people most at risk from running nonstop on an inclined treadmill. In such a risky setting, a cardiac specialist and supporting technicians must be present to monitor heart rate on an electrocardiograph (ECG). During such tests, submaximal and maximal exercise stress assessment permits a differentiation of changes in heart rhythm, heart rate, systolic blood pressure, and ECG manifestations if myocardial ischemia is present (Bruce & McDonough, 1969). In a diseased older adult, this procedure is a more costly undertaking than if the situation involved a preventive approach—a healthy older person who simply wanted to know how aerobically fit he or she was. In the latter example, a certified fitness appraiser and assistant would be needed rather than an attending cardiac physician. This is the same irony alluded to by P.O. Astrand in several of his lectures: "The people who most need medical clearance by their physician are not those who want to be physically active, but those who plan to be sedentary."

There is no medical evidence that physical activity—even strenuous exercise—is harmful to the healthy cardiovascular system. However it is true that a person with serious structural cardiovascular disease, even if asymptomatic, is at an increased risk for sudden death during vigorous forms of physical activity. Therefore, supervised and graded exercise for these individuals becomes mandatory (Van Camp, 1988).

Van Camp and Petersen (1986) obtained data from 167 randomly selected cardiac rehabilitation programs via mailed questionnaires reporting on over 50,000 cardiac patients and over 2 million hours of exercise between 1980 and 1984. Twenty-one cardiac arrests (18 in which the patient was successfully resuscitated and three fatal) and eight nonfatal myocardial infarctions were reported. The 1.3 fatalities per 784,0000 patient-hours of exercise was considered to be a normal mortality rate. The findings suggested that supervised programming along with heart-rate monitoring provided low-risk, or no-risk, exercise opportunities for cardiac patients.

Ewart and Taylor (1985) claimed that the biggest barrier to recovery in individuals experiencing a cardiac event is an unrealistic fear arising from inaccurate self-perceptions about one's physical abilities. Nearly half of the men under 70 years of age who survive three weeks after a myocardial infarction are physically capable of resuming their normal activities within 12 weeks of the acute event. But many of these men become physically overly cautious and a few become overzealous and are apt to exercise too strenuously. Ewart and Taylor made a case for the role of self-efficacy assessments to identify two types of adults who are most at risk: (1) individuals who lack confidence in their ability to participate and (2) those who were once athletic and are overconfident in their self-perceived ability to quickly resume high-intensity levels.

Not all physical activity may be protective of heart disease. Some activities may actually add stress to the older body. For example, McKelvie (1986) claimed there is no medical evidence that marathon-type running protects one from coronary heart disease; rather, participating in extreme endurance events, especially in middle to old age, may place people with unknown problems at increased risk. People add to their own risk by ignoring symptoms of vague or definite chest, arm, or shoulder pain during activity—warning signs that should be immediately addressed to reap the benefits of early detection.

As the age of the population increases, progressively larger numbers of older adults will be affected by serious pathologies that would contraindicate their vigorous exercise involvement. In such cases, a reconditioning program at a heart rate of 100 to 120 beats per minute provides an effective stimulus for senior citizens, meaning that for older individuals new to exercise, "walking, recreational swimming, dancing, lawn bowling, and even chair exercises have training value" (Shephard, 1986a). Shephard summarized the available evidence by stating:

> Given the strong probability that moderate, progressive activity improves the quality of life, such findings are no reason to prohibit physical activity in an asymptomatic senior citizen (1986a).

For those older people with known medical conditions, professionally supervised exercise programs are recommended.

KNOWN RISK OF INJURY IN THE ELDERLY

The potential for injury is often raised as a concern when older adults engage in the more adventurous or exerting forms of physical activity. In reality, sport injuries affect less than 5 percent of the over 65 age group (Stephens & Craig, 1990). However, such a low risk quotient may be a reflection of the low sport participation rates of elderly people. Kallinen and Allen (1994) claimed that injury outcomes are very much tied to the type of sport and its movement requirements. For example, tennis participation tends to lead to risk of leg injury (Feit & Berenter, 1993). Even if the risk of musculoskeletal injury were to be high among athletic seniors, it would most likely be in sport activities requiring intense training for competition. Musculoskeletal injury is less likely to exist at less intense, noncompetitive activity levels.

Aerobic exercise and more vigorous forms of physical activity have been the main focus of injury research. Injury which occurs during stretching and strengthening activities needs more attention. Furthermore, researchers need to attend to the unique characteristics and needs of the individuals participating. Activities which are contraindicated for one group may not be contraindicated for another.

There is some evidence that risk of injury may also increase in programs that have regimented and high levels of repetitions of a series of exercises. When a program is heavily structured and externally paced by fast music or an overzealous instructor, it is not enjoyable, and this may be a sign that people are being pushed to perform beyond their capacity. Koplan, Siscovick, and Goldbaum (1985) suggested that the potential for exercise injury is linked to the specific characteristics of the type of activity (intensity, duration, and frequency) as well as the attributes of the participant and the exercise environment. In this respect, incidence information is sparse on the actual risks of exercise to specific individuals in specific situations. Kavanagh and Shephard (1978) found that in the early months of geriatric exercise programs, about 50 percent of the participants had suffered muscular injury. Yet, a ten-week, five-days-a-week aerobic program of brisk walking and jogging elicited not a single injury in sedentary middle-age women according to Johannessen, Holly, Lui, and Amsterdam (1986). These and other programs need to be compared to find out which characteristics of each program and its leadership are likely to lead seniors into higher risk of injury.

Footwear as a potential factor leading to injuries has not been adequately examined (Ting, 1991). Runners may be particularly vulnerable to inadequate foot protection and cushioning against leg strike impact. Individuals who are out of shape should take heed to start out at very short distances and at a slow self-pace. It makes intuitive sense that physical deficiencies derived from sedentary living can lead to hypokinetic injury, but it is also true that people do put themselves at risk of injury in certain forms of physical activities. Low-impact, shorter-distance, and submaximal efforts such as walking are recommended in several studies to reap the benefits of physical activity with minimal risk of injury.

In summary, there is a paucity of data with which to objectify and quantify specific injury risk. Adding to the problem of insufficient short- and long-term data are inadequate definitions. Comparisons across programs require standard definitions of injury, matched characteristics of participants, description of the nonparticipants (or drop-outs), and equated exercise interventions such as type, intensity, duration, frequency, and so on (Koplan, Siscovick, & Goldbaum, 1985). Without comparable longitudinal and randomized cohort studies, generating new knowledge about the safest forms of exercise may be difficult. In summary, the literature advises the pursuit of self-paced, moderate exercise in a variety of physical activities allowing for adequate recovery, and this makes good sense until more is known about incidence relationships (Bruce, 1984; Munnings, 1988; O'Brien Cousins & Burgess, 1992).

Risk of Falls

Falls are the leading cause of accidental death among seniors, and the cost of caring for fallers with injury is approaching $1 billion a year (Canada). A 1988 study in British Columbia indicated that people over age 65 requiring hospital care after a fall had an average stay of 16 to 25 days at a cost of about $300 per day (*University of Victoria Centre on Aging Newsletter*, January, 1993). The costs are profound because the magnitude of the problem is profound.

> "It would be hard to find an Alberta family who hasn't been affected by the problem and worry of a senior's fall since 30 percent and 50 percent of seniors have at least one fall per year" (Robson, Capital Health Authority, 1995).

Tinetti, Speechly, and Ginter (1988) and Speechly and Tinetti (1991) noted that seniors tend to have at least one fall per year. To date, most research on falls has focused on the frail, institutionalized senior. Ellie Robson, working with the Edmonton Board of Health, conducted pilot research in the winter of 1993–1994 and found that 30 percent of seniors did not think that falls had causes, 30 percent did not know how frequently seniors fall, most seniors thought all falls resulted in serious injury, and almost every senior in the study had no idea of who to talk to about their fear of falling.

Early research concerning community-dwelling older adults falls first appeared in the work of Droller (1955). Falls research reappeared in the later 1970s, with interest increasing substantially in the past decade. Compared to other known risk factors, falling is a significant problem for older people who are moving about. Women are two to three times more likely to fall than men (Cook, Exton-Smith, Brocklehurst, & Lemper-Barber, 1982) with correspondingly higher institutionalization rates (Prudham & Evans 1981). Each year, one in five aged women suffers an injury requiring medical attention and women's injury rate surpasses that of elderly men. Robson (1995) noted that the reasons why women fall more often and have more injuries are not clear; exercise researchers hypothesize that the inadequate activity patterns of women undermine their muscle and bone strength, limit their joint flexibility, sap their endurance, and retard their neuromuscular mechanisms for balance so that they react too slowly and too late to prevent falls. Others argue that the breaking of the brittle bones of women is the cause, rather than the outcome, of many falls for women.

Estimates of the frequency of falls in independent-living older adults suggest with some consistency that about one-third fall each year (Tinetti, Speechly, & Ginter, 1988; Campbell, Spears, Borrie, & Fitzgerald, 1988, 1989, 1990). Estimates regarding injury from these falls suggest that about seven percent of fallers encounter a serious injury as a result. Speechly and Tinetti (1991) studied community seniors in three categories: (1) vigorous, (2) transitional, and (3) frail seniors. Their findings showed a low incidence of falls and injury as a gradient in favor of the vigorous adults (17% fallers, 6% injury rate). People who were judged to be in transition or in the frail category experienced the most falls (32% and 52%, respectively), and a greater proportion of injuries (11% and 22%, respectively). Moreover, there were differences found in *how* people fell according to these three categories. Speechly and Tinetti (1991) found that the vigorous subjects tended to fall while away from home, on stairs, in the presence of environmental hazards, or during displacement activities, while the frail fell at home and during routine non-displacing daily activities.

Some scientists suggest that the very act of being ambulatory puts people at risk of injury (namely fall injury) even though others blamed lack of exercise for falls injuries (Svanstrom, 1990). Hornbrook, Wingfield, and Stevens (1991) provided evidence that the environment had a major role to play in 45 percent of all falls. Early research on the environment looked only at the immediate home environment, but recent research has broadened this focus. Reinsch and colleagues (1992) found that falls of healthy seniors occurred mostly outside the home and a sizable number (16%) also occurred in transition areas such as entrances, garages, patios, and gardens. About 32 percent were falls in the home.

In the mid-1990s, Dr. Elaine Gallagher of the University of Victoria directed a study called, "Head over Heels" Falls Intervention Trials (F.I.T.). She reported that 50 percent of falls occurred in the house or yard, with the bedroom being the most common location in the home. Behavioral risk factors such as inattention and hazardous activities (such as climbing a ladder) were to blame for 28 percent and 30 percent of falls, respectively.

The causes of seniors' falls are multifactorial. What is not known is how frequently older people fall during formal or informal exercise activity.

Risk of Overexertion or Exhaustion

"In those callings that require great physical qualifications, old age is decisive" (de Beauvoir, *The Coming of Age*, 1972).

One has to be realistic about the aging process and admit that physical declines are part of the natural aging process no matter how heroic one is in terms of disciplined participation in fitness activity. With even the most ambitious older adult, declining activity levels are likely to accompany old age if one "sinks into physical weariness, general fatigue, and indifference" (de Beauvoir, 1972, p. 404). Fatigue is a qualitative feeling, but appears to have a genuine role in guiding people as to the amount of energy they are willing to expend on an activity.

Exercise is a complex, time-consuming, and high-effort behavior—one that requires self-confidence, energy, and persistent motivation. Even though sedentary adults may be lacking in these very qualities, active adults hold positive expectations about the value of exercise in their lives, believing it to provide adequate compensation for the effort involved. In contrast, sedentary adults lack these experiences and the accompanying rewards; they may conceive of exercise as leading mainly to discomfort and fatigue—negative outcomes that act as barriers to their participation. Beliefs that exercise is overly strenuous and uncomfortable will override the knowledge that physical activity has health-promoting benefits.

Since the 1960s, exercise scientists have devoted considerable attention to a self-rated cue of effort called *perceived exertion* (Borg, 1970; Mihevic, 1991). Early research found that older people rated exercise tasks as requiring more physical effort than did younger people (Bar-Or, 1994). However, only recently have prospective beliefs about exertion been applied to exercise as a psychological barrier. Steinhardt and Carrier (1989) reported that both college students and employed adults claimed that "effort" in physical activity was a significant barrier to their participation. Indeed, "the major defining property of motivation is the level of effort mobilized and sustained in a pursuit" (Bandura & Cervone, 1986), and competent individuals who are self-dissatisfied with their level of performance are known to heighten their efforts (Bandura, 1989). Such efforts may be lacking in older people, in part because they may feel less competent, and in part because 70 percent of adults ages 80 and over are satisfied that they are already doing the right amount of physical activity for their age (Statistics Canada, 1992). Planned exercise may be perceived to be unnecessary and excessive, if not dangerous, and thus the motivation to be an active older adult is undermined.

The issue is not how justified, valid, or "real" beliefs about overexertion may be, but, rather, how people conceive of exercise, a very important guide to future involvement. Referring to exercise motivation, Rejeski (1981) stated,

> Quite frankly, from the standpoint of understanding participant behavior, knowing what people think they are doing may be well more important than knowing what they are doing.

Research suggests that exertion ratings increase with advancing age (Monahan, 1988) and decrease with positive affect and self-efficacy for exercise (McAuley & Courneya, 1992). Sallis (1994) reported that "one of the main influences on enjoyment is the amount of exertion required by the activity." Perceptions of high levels of exertion or of overexertion may be particularly salient for older women contemplating personal involvement in strength training activities, simply because well-defined gender roles in the early 20th century permitted them to describe (and avoid) high-exertion tasks as "men's work." Currently, older women may view the more athletic forms of physical activity not only as socially inappropriate for them, but as biologically dangerous in view of their life experience, age, and social learning. Even in contemporary times, Monahan (1988) noted that medical debates on women and exercise (i.e., aerobic dance injury) can be used by females to justify their passive activity choices.

In a study among women over age 70, sedentary patterns of daily living were associated with heightened perceptions of the effort required to engage in fitness activities such as walking, stretching, cycling, aquatic exercise, and strength exercises such as curl-ups and push-ups (O'Brien Cousins, 1993). Of the six contemplated fitness activities, women rated curl-ups, push-ups, and aquatic exercise the most exerting. Because brisk walking for 15 minutes was rated the lowest in exertion level, walking at a comfortable pace may be the most promising exercise for mobilizing large numbers of sedentary older women. The study found further that expectations regarding physical exertion were linked significantly to one's self-efficacy for fitness activity and to beliefs about risk outcomes arising from exercise (O'Brien Cousins, 1996).

These findings supported those of McAuley and Courneya (1992) who found that in middle-age adults, those individuals who had lower ratings of perceived exertion while engaging in stationary cycling exercise were mainly the same adults who subjectively rated their efficacy for cycling to be very high. What does this mean? The significance of this finding is that the older adults who most need to change their sedentary lifestyle may be encountering a cognitive barrier that is more obstructive than that of their very old age and their actual health difficulties. Rather than viewing fitness activity as a resource through which they might moderate the aging decline, negotiate improved strength, improve joint mobility, and increase aerobic fitness, many older people conceive of such involvement as exerting enough to be a possible threat to their enjoyment of life and well-being. Because little is known about all the possible negative outcomes that older people might project for exercise involvement, further research is needed to determine if worry about overexertion is acting as the main barrier to late-life exercise.

In the applied setting, this means that exercise programs geared toward the sedentary adult must be initially low-skill and low-intensity so that people contemplating their involvement will perceive a nonthreatening environment at the "getting started" stage. Exercise leaders who are professionally certified and trained to lead enjoyable and self-paced older adults programs will have a better chance of sustaining participation over enough weeks to allow the physical, social, and psychological benefits to be realized.

Risk of Provoking Ill Health

Older women are more often ill and experience more days of bed disability than men. Older women also are twice as likely as men to have arthritis, and 13 percent of elderly women are limited by arthritis in their daily activities (Haug, Ford, & Sheafor, 1985). While exercise is often considered to be risky for arthritic adults, in fact, Burckhardt (1988) has reported that active recreation pursuits are particularly important to women *with arthritis*. She noted that, among arthritic women over 70 years old, poorer quality of life and dissatisfaction with active recreation were significant problems. Gentle movements are now considered essential for managing the symptoms and pain of arthritis. Moreover, exercising joints vigorously does not lead to osteoarthritis as is often suspected. The long-term effects of exercise, such as causal relationships to osteoarthritis, simply do not exist in the scientific literature. However, we know that the bones of elderly women are more vulnerable to fracture because they are smaller and more porous, and though exercise certainly helps maintain bone strength, activity itself is an inherent risk.

Musculoskeletal fatigue, soreness, joint stiffness, and delayed recovery are particular risks for those who are unaccustomed to exercise and who do not initiate exercise in very gradual and low-intensity stages (Kasper, 1990). The first experience with an exercise program for an older adult women may turn out to be a painful experience, and one that women soon learn to avoid.

SUMMARY

This chapter provides support to the contention that the known risks of exercise participation appear to be almost insignificant. Older adult concerns for being involved in health-promoting forms of physical activity may involve beliefs about mortal trauma, sport injury, injury from falling, overexertion leading to exhaustion, and the possibility of provoking future illness. Added to the already overly cautious behavior of many older people is that of zealous but inexperienced leaders who often err on the side of precaution. For this reason, the facts about the minimal risks of exercise involvement in late life may not be readily available to the public. Although more research is required to clarify how risk expectancies form, health educators need to develop innovative ways to inform the elderly public about the very low risk of progressive exercise, and about the many benefits of engaging in regular exercise such as daily walking. The time has come to talk about the risks of being sedentary, instead of the risks of being active. In the following chapter, the known benefits of late-life exercise are presented.

Chapter 5

Benefits of Exercise Participation

Because of all that has been learned in the past 20 years about the positive health outcomes of regular physical activity, the United States government in 1990 established national objectives aimed at reducing sedentary lifestyles and increasing moderate daily physical activity among older people. Physical activity and fitness are the priority components of the report, *Healthy People 2000: National Health Promotion and Disease Prevention Objectives* (Public Health Service, 1990). In fact, of 22 listed health promotion themes in *Healthy People 2000*, increasing physical activity is number one.

In 1995, with the impetus of Prime Minister Jean Chrétien, Canada began a major health promotion initiative, inclusive of health care reform, called the *National Forum on Health*. This federal study, which was aimed at designing a cost-effective and evidence-based health system for Canadians, followed a series of less ambitious programs produced by smaller federal agencies. For example, in Canada in the 1980s and early 1990s, the Secretariat for Fitness of the Third Age published *Issues of a Fit Third Age* to advocate, inform, and unite efforts toward activating seniors. Fitness Canada produced *Move through the Years: A Blueprint for Action* (n.d.) to outline a national framework for promoting more active lifestyles throughout the life span. Internationally, the World Health Organization (WHO) has often advocated increased levels of physical activity including in their publication, *Health of the Elderly: A Concern for All* (1992).

With the worldwide push to improve the health situation of aging adults, physical activity has taken center stage as the targeted behavior most likely to alter health. Dr. William Foege, former director of the Centers for Disease Control and Prevention (CDC), claiming that physical activity has the capability to provide the control that we have been seeking in curbing chronic disease, compared the revolutionary health potential of more active lifestyles to that of mass immunization (McGinnis, 1992). Without this health revolution, sedentary living will continue to be an unnecessary "public health burden" (McGinnis, 1992). Therefore, "health, in its broadest sense, is the topic of central interest and is the primary reason for most research on physical activity" (Kohl, Blair, Paffenbarger, Macera, & Kronenfeld, 1988).

Evidence has accumulated in recent years that physical mobility has become a survival need for the elderly, and that society must change its attitudes toward older people, especially older women, and their physical capabilities and requirements (Milde, 1988). An array of studies from a number of disciplines provides support for a long list of biopsychosocial benefits from involvement in physical activity: reduced chronic disease, increased longevity, and improved physical and mental health, as well as independence and improved quality of life in very old age (O'Brien & Vertinsky, 1991). Inactive people run a 1.5 to 2.4 times higher risk of developing coronary heart disease—a risk that starts decreasing when physical activity of even a low-to-moderate level is performed regularly (Canadian Fitness and Lifestyle Research Institute, 1995). Aerobic forms of physical activity help to reduce the risk of developing Type-II diabetes, and colorectal and other cancers, and help prevent back problems, osteoporosis, and obesity.

A comprehensive literature review conducted by a research team at the University of Alberta indicated that since 1990, over 1,500 scientific studies have been published that positively link short- and long-term physical activity to important health benefits (CFLRI, 1995). Thirty-eight positive health outcomes were identified ranging from symptom management for Alzheimer's disease patients to pain control in osteoarthritis. In that report, six major positive health outcomes were identified: (1) the slowing of many forms of physical decline by up to 50 percent; (2) improving prospects for increasing social networks through active living; (3) enhancement of various cognitive and neurological functions of the brain; (4) early detection of disease; (5) more rapid recovery following a bout of serious illness; and (6) the probability that the immune system will function at a more optimal level thereby maximizing protection against many serious ailments.

Although most prominent physical activity researchers recommend at least 30 minutes of exercise each day, policy makers have come to realize that this prescription is not likely to recruit adults who are already inactive, precisely because it sounds so demanding.

Researchers have found, however, that there is a continuum of benefits starting with even low-intensity activities. Perhaps the more important objective is to mobilize people who are normally sedentary, so that healthy activity habits are formed. Daily involvement in moderate-intensity activities such as brisk walking, cycling, or swimming, or physical tasks such as home repair, cleaning, painting, or gardening are advocated by the CFLRI (1995). Its recommendation is for a minimum energy expenditure of 200 calories per day, which would be the equivalent of a two- to three-mile walk. Many seniors appear to be well aware of some of these health benefits; 30 percent of older men and women with heart disease identified lack of exercise as a personal lifestyle problem (Clark et al., 1992).

Not only do seniors want to stay healthy to avoid institutionalization, but they also seek opportunities to enhance their lives with social involvement and personal growth (British Columbia Task Force on Issues of Concern to Seniors, 1989). However, recent research has indicated that implementing health promotion programs for older people will not be easy. Increasing opportunities for older employees may have an insignificant impact on increasing their exercise behavior, even when the employees have good intentions to become more active. For example, after one year of health promotion activities such as participation in walking groups, one-to-one counseling, and work site exercise programs, Sharpe and O'Connell (1992) failed to find any increase in the overall exercise participation of university faculty and staff. At the start of the study (baseline), predictors of intention to exercise were level of education, gender, self-efficacy, outcome expectancies, perceived barriers, and exercise frequency. However, at the end of the study, only exercise level at baseline was predictive of current exercise level. Thus, community-based, or work-based initiatives, may not succeed in promoting physical activity if older adults have not been previously active or are not convinced of the personal benefits of exercise, or, if other life circumstances interfere with their intentions to exercise.

Researchers have developed an astonishing profile of those elderly who are physically active. The physically active older adult is likely to be one or two decades younger physiologically than their sedentary contemporaries (Drinkwater, 1988). Moreover, they cut the effects of the age decline in half—that is, in many biological functions, the 1 percent decline per year is reduced to a 0.5 decline per year. Over many decades, this slower rate of aging becomes significant and it is not uncommon to find Master's athletes in their 70s who can match performances of sedentary 20-year-old individuals (Vaccaro, Dummer, & Clarke, 1981). With superior training, facilities, equipment, and coaching, a few older people have even exceeded their own young adult peak performances (Shea, 1986).

Such feats are easy to understand when put in the context of earlier involvement. Isobel Bleasdell Saumier Cunningham of Ajax, Ontario is a case in point. At the age of 81, she was the world record holder for the Master's (80 and up) 100-meter sprint. When asked how she came to be a world record sprinter at that age, she replied, "Well, I was world record holder in 1937." In that year she was coholder of the world indoor record for the 50-yard dash (6 seconds). Few people are aware of her achievements because World War II stopped all Olympic competitions for the next eight years (1940, 1944). By that time, Isobel Bleasdell had gone on with her life, and never did make her world debut until much later.

In between her early and late-life stints as world record holder, Isobel was a mother, not a runner. Raising four children, teaching art and math in Montreal high schools, and maintaining a household consumed her middle-age energy. Yet her athletic abilities and motivation transcended mid-life and allowed her to take up running again by 1975 at age 61. Although she is not running at the same speed she did decades ago, Isobel is still in a league of her own. Today she travels a world master's athletic circuit from Finland to Japan with many other older adults who are also extending the "prime of their life" to include old age. Just like them, Isobel looks 61, not 81, and runs as if she is 41.

TWO TYPES OF BENEFITS

Available evidence suggests that older people can acquire two types of benefits from regular participation in physical activity. First, either immediately or within a very short time, people can expect to feel changes in physical, social, and emotional well-being. Individuals can increase their physical mobility and overcome a certain amount of stiffness right away. The aches and pains of muscles and joints often subside or improve during a gentle movement program.

In addition to a reduction of the mechanical tension in the body, social and psychological benefits can be noticed immediately. People who are physically active enjoy better health and well-being and exude a happy disposition. They are often gregarious and tell jokes. Exercise participants are already laughing and in good spirit before they even get moving. Moreover, exercise settings offer a support network to bolster one's commitment to stick with it, and the exercise leaders are often providers of health information which enhances the knowledge and positive attitudes of participants. Many older people report that "feeling better" is the main reason they participate, and "feeling better" may be experienced within minutes.

Second, a host of biological survival advantages accrue over a longer period of time. Within months or years, older people can anticipate long-term benefits such as prolonged good health, resistance to illness, optimization of self-care and functional independence, reduced mortality risk, and an overall improvement in their quality of life. Regular physical exercise is generally considered to be the "best medicine" (Jokl, 1985) because it is inexpensive, has no side effects, can be shared with others, and is health-promoting as well as disease-preventing.

Table 5.1 outlines some of the health outcomes that have been scientifically documented for adults over age 50 (O'Brien Cousins, 1993). Although some studies have found no significant changes with exercise, further analysis reveals that inadequacies in the intensity of exercise, the duration of the training program, or the type of exercise chosen are often the explanation. Overall, the evidence favors sustained aerobic activity at moderate to vigorous levels for optimal psychological and physiological impact. However, frail adults, or those who are at very advanced age (80 years and older), appear to be able to make significant gains in functional status starting with gentle mobility programs. Even adults in their 90s can improve their muscle strength at a rate comparable to younger adults (Fiatarone et al., 1994).

Short-Term Benefits

Many health and fitness benefits of participation in regular exercise are felt immediately by the older adult. For example, those who are new to physical activity have often reported "feeling better" right away (*Fitness and Aging*, 1982; *Feel Better*, &

Table 5.1 The Known Benefits of Exercise

Health benefit	Scientific sources
Delayed mortality from all causes	Blair et al., 1989; Bokovoy & Blair, 1994; Grand et al., 1990; Kaplan et al., 1987; Karvonen, Klemola, Virkajarvi, & Kellonen, 1974; Koiso & Ohsawa, 1992; Linstead, Tonstad, & Kuzma, 1991; Paffenbarger & Hale, 1975; Paffenbarger, Wing, & Hyde, 1978; Paffenbarger, Wing, Hyde, & Hsied, 1986; Quinn et al., 1990; Rakowski & Mor, 1992; Rehm, Fichter, & Elton, 1993; Sandvik et al., 1993
Aerobic fitness, increased maximum oxygen uptake	Barry et al., 1966; Blumenthal, Emery, Madden, et al., 1991; Buskirk & Hodson 1987; Coggan et al., 1990; DeVries, 1970; Foster, Hume, Byrnes, Dickinson, & Chatfield, 1989; Hagberg et al., 1989; Hopkins, Murrah, Hoeger, & Rhodes, 1990; Johannessen, Holly, Lui, & Amsterdam, 1986; Kasch et al., 1990; Kilbom, 1971; Kohrt et al., 1992; Spina et al., 1993; Suominen, Heikkinen, & Parkatti, 1977; Tonino & Driscoll, 1988
Management and control of chronic obstructive pulmonary disease	Atkins, Kaplan, Timons, Reinsch, & Lofback, 1984; O'Donnell, Webb, & McGuire, 1993; Swerts et al., 1990; Toshima, Kaplan, & Ries, 1990; Weaver & Narsavage, 1992; Webster, 1988
Prevention and control of heart disease	Barnard, 1991; Marti et al., 1989; Morey et al., 1989; Nieman et al., 1993; Puggaard, Pedersen, Sandager, & Klitgaard, 1994; Singh et al., 1993; Takeshima et al., 1993; Sedgwick, Taplin, Davidson, & Thomas, 1988; Sidney & Shephard, 1978; Upton, Hagan, Rosentswieg, & Gettman, 1983
Control of obesity, cholesterol, body composition	Aronow & Ahn, 1994; Blumenthal et al., 1989; Butterworth et al., 1993; Danielson, Cauley, & Rohay, 1993; Evans & Meredith, 1989; Gardner & Poehlman, 1993; Kohrt, Malley, Dalsky, & Holloszy, 1992; Kohrt, Obert, & Holloszy, 1992; Nieman et al., 1993; Rantanen et al., 1994; Schaberg, Ballard, McKeown, & Zinkgraf, 1990; Shephard, 1986b; Sidney, Shephard, & Harrison, 1977; Upton, Hagan, Rosenswieg, & Gettman, 1983; Webb, Poehlman, & Tonino, 1993; Whitehurst & Menendez, 1991
Therapeutic value for arthritis	Ellert, 1985; Harcom, Lampman, Banwell, & Castor, 1985; Konradsen et al., 1990; Lewis, 1984; Minor & Brown, 1993; Minor, Hewett, Webel, Anderson, & Kay, 1989; Peterson et al., 1993; Stenstrom, 1994
Incidence of cancer, heightened immune response	Fiatarone, Morley et al., 1989; Gerhardsson et al., 1990; Levi, LaVecchia, Negri, & Franceschi, 1993; Mellemgaard, Engholm, Mclaughlin, & Olsen, 1994; Pukkala, Poskiparta, Apter, & Vihko, 1993; Satariano, Ragheb, Branch, & Swanson, 1990; Shephard, 1992; Shu et al., 1993; Slattery et al., 1990; Sturgeon et al., 1993; Vetter & Lewis, 1992

(*Table continues on next page*)

Table 5.1   The Known Benefits of Exercise (*Continued*)

Health benefit	Scientific sources
Bone health and prevention of osteoporosis	Beverly, Rider, Evans, & Smith, 1987; Block, Smith, Freidlander, & Genant, 1989; Blumenthal et al., 1989; Greendale, Hirsch, & Hahn, 1993; Hatori et al., 1993; Krall & Dawson-Hughes, 1994; Lau et al., 1992; Martin & Notelvitz, 1993; Nelson et al., 1991; Oyster, Morton, & Linnell, 1984; Rikli & McManis, 1990; Rutherford & Jones, 1992; Sidney, Shephard, & Harrison, 1977; Smith, Reddan, & Smith, 1981; Snow-Harter, 1987; Sorock et al., 1986; Suominen, & Rahkila, 1991
Social support for and encouragement of exerrcise	Andrew et al., 1981; Dishman, 1986; Gray, 1987; Hauge, 1973; McPherson, 1982; Perusse, LeBlanc, & Bouchard, 1988; Powell, Spain, Christenson, & Mollenkamp, 1986; Snyder & Spreitzer, 1973; Spreitzer & Snyder, 1983; Stephens & Craig, 1990; Wechsler, Levine, Idelson, Rohman, & Taylor, 1983
Control of hypertension	Adams & de Vries, 1973; Barry, Daly, Pruett, et al., 1966; Ehsani et al., 1991; Emes, 1979; Hamdorf, Withers, Penhall, & Haslam, 1992; Kasch et al., 1990; Richardson & Rosenberg, 1989; Sedgwick, Taplin, Davidson, & Thomas, 1988; Shephard, Corey, & Cox, 1982; Spina et al., 1993; Vaccaro, Ostrove, Vandervelden, Goldfarb, & Clarke, 1984; Weber, Barnard, & Roy, 1983
Control and management of diabetes	Barnard, Ugianskis, Martin, & Inkeles, 1992; Cantu, 1982; Durak, 1989; Kahn et al., 1990; Kirwan et al., 1993; Kohl, Gordon, Villegras, & Blair, 1992; Page et al., 1993; Rooney, 1993; Rogers, 1989; Schneider et al., 1992; Shephard, 1984; Wallberg-Henriksson, 1989; Weber, Barnard, & Roy, 1983; Williams, 1987
Improved function in Activities of Daily Living	Avlund et al., 1994; Borchelt & Steinhagen-Thiesen, 1992; Duffy & MacDonald, 1990; Kaplan, Strawbridge, Camacho, & Cohen, 1993; LaCroix et al., 1993; McMurdo, & Rennie, 1993; O'Hagan, Smith & Pileggi, 1994
Cognitive processing speed	Baylor & Spirduso, 1988; Blumenthal et al., 1991; Borchelt & Steinhagen-Thiesen, 1992; Chodzko-Zajlko, 1991; Chodzko-Zajko et al., 1992; Christenson & MacKinnon, 1993; Clarkson-Smith & Hartley, 1990; Cockburn, Smith, & Wade, 1990; Dustman et al., 1990; Dustman, Ruhling, Russell et al., 1984; Emery, 1991; Hawkins, Kramer, & Capaldi, 1992; Lord & Castell, 1994; McMurdo & Rennie, 1994; Molloy et al., 1988; Powell, 1974; Rogers, Meyer, & Mortel, 1990; Shay & Roth, 1992; Stacey, Kozma, & Stones, 1985; Stones & Dawe, 1993; Stones & Kozma, 1988, 1989
Alzheimer's disease and dementia	Clark, Wade, Massey, & Van Dyke, 1975; Friedman & Tappen, 1991; Meddaugh, 1987; Powell, 1974; Stamford, Hambacher, & Fallica, 1974
Reaction time	Bashore, 1989; Bashore et al., 1988; Baylor & Spirduso, 1988; Clarkson, 1978; Clarkson-Smith & Hartley, 1989; Del Rey, 1982;

Table 5.1 The Known Benefits of Exercise (*Continued*)

Health benefit	Scientific sources
Reaction time (*Cont.*)	Era, Jokela, & Heikkinen, 1986; Hart, 1986; Hassmen, Ceci, & Backman, 1992; Kerr & Normand, 1992; Kroll & Clarkson, 1978; Lord & Castell, 1994; Lord, Caplan, & Ward, 1993; Lupinacci, Rikli, Jones, & Ross, 1993; McMurdo & Rennie, 1994; Normand, Kerr ,& Metivier, 1987; Panton et al., 1990; Puggaard et al., 1994; Rikli & Edwards, 1991; Spirduso, 1975, 1980; Spirduso & Clifford, 1978; Stones & Kozma, 1988; Voorips et al., 1993
Balance	Binder et al., 1994; Brown & Holloszy, 1991; Buchner et al., 1993; Duncan et al., 1993; Emes, 1979; Hopkins, Murrah, Hoeger, & Rhodes, 1990; Hu & Woollacott, 1994, Study 1 and 2; Lichenstein, Shields, Shiavi, & Burger, 1989; Lord, Caplan, & Ward, 1993; MacRae, Feltner, & Reinsch, 1994 (balance not improved); McMurdo & Rennie, 1993; Puggaard et al., 1994; Rikli & Edwards, 1991; Sauvage et al., 1992; Voorips et al., 1993; Weiner et al., 1993
Falls prevention	Arfken et al., 1994; Connell, 1993; Fleming & Pendergast, 1993; Hornbrook et al., 1991; MacRae, Feltner, & Reinsch, 1994; Nevitt, Cummings, & Hudes, 1991; O'Loughlin, Robitaille, Boivin, & Suissa, 1993; Reinsch, MacRae, Lachenbruch, & Tobis, 1992; Topper, Maki, & Holliday, 1993
Positive self-concept, improved body image, and control of depression	Bolla-Wilson & Bleeker, 1989; Hallinen & Schuler, 1993; King, Taylor, Haskell, & DeBusk, 1989; Mittleman, Crawford, Holliday, Gutman, & Bhaktan, 1989; Perri & Templar, 1984–85; Sidney & Shephard, 1976; Tucker & Mortell, 1993
Joint mobility	Blumenthal et al., 1989; Brown & Holloszy, 1991; Duncan et al., 1993; Frekany & Leslie, 1975; Hopkins et al., 1990; Karl, 1982; Misner et al., 1992; Morey, Cowper, Feussner, et al., 1989; Rikli & Edwards, 1991; Voorips et al., 1993
Muscular strength	Avlund et al., 1994; Brown & Holloszy, 1991; Era et al., 1994; Fiatarone et al., 1994; Gueldner & Spradley, 1988; Heislein, Harris & Jette, 1994; McMurdo & Rennie, 1994; Meredith et al., 1989; Peterson et al., 1991; Pyka, Lindenberger, Charette, & Marcus, 1994; Rikli & Edwards, 1991; Shephard, 1978; Sinaki & Grubbs, 1989; Work, 1989

1980). Such feelings included the perception of doing something good for oneself (Dowell, Bolter, Flett, & Kammann, 1988) as well as a sense of achievement (Lutter, Merrick, Steffen, Jones, & Slavin, 1985). Participants entering supervised programs generally find themselves in a social group with others their age, and the potential then exists to expand their social network of support.

Exercising individuals demonstrated higher levels of self-efficacy (Atkins, Kaplan,

Reinsch, & Lofback, 1984; Hogan & Santomier, 1984), internal locus of control (Perri Templer, 1984–85), and a sense of life control (Rodin, 1986). No less important to psychological health is the opportunity created by exercise to socialize, play and have fun with peers, form new friendships, and develop a community spirit with other older people (Eckert, 1986; Langlie, 1977; Wakat & Odom, 1982).

Social support and interaction are thought to be among the most important factors in adherence and enjoyment in activity programs, although research is lacking on older adults (Lee & Markides, 1990; Wakat & Odom, 1982). New evidence suggests that insufficient encouragement for late-life exercise is a key barrier to participation among older women (O'Brien Cousins, 1995a). Physician approval for being active in old age is important as is family support and having peers who are active. Motivation for late-life exercise is enhanced by having encouragement from even one individual. However, almost 40 percent of older women surveyed said that they were unsure if their physician would approve of exercise for them, and another 25 percent were sure that their physician would disapprove. Recollection of childhood encouragement for physical activity was a significant predictor of late-life encouragement for exercise, suggesting that "childhood encouragement perhaps provided women with the confidence to seek out the support they need to be active in their older years" (O'Brien Cousins, 1995a). Women who need incentives and companionship for more active lifestyles may find these most readily in the exercise setting itself.

Not all physical activity settings are supportive, however. For example, a quite strenuous seniors' 100-day cycling tour under the scientific scrutiny of Mittleman, Crawford, Holliday, Gutman, and Bhaktan (1989) proved instead to be a test of the social relations of older adults with six of the 33 cyclists dropping out only one week before the conclusion of the tour. Negative feelings toward others and social intolerance were cited as reasons. More study is needed to determine the social benefits and social risks of physical activities in a variety of contexts.

A number of psychological, social, and biological parameters have been positively linked to short-term exercise participation. Possibly among the most important outcome of physical activity is stress reduction (DeVries, 1975) because coping with stress is linked to other benefits such as better sleep (Griffin & Trinder, 1978; Osis, 1986), muscle relaxation (Berger, 1989), positive mood states (Bolla-Wilson & Bleeker, 1989; Monahan, 1986), improved self-image (Paige, 1987) and self-concept (Perri & Templer, 1984–85). Overall, exercise appears to act as a buffer in many stress-illness relationships (Eichner, 1987; Eisdorfer & Wilkie, 1977), possibly through biochemical interactions linking mind and body (Haug, Ford, & Sheafor, 1985). For example, increased levels of beta-endorphins accompanying high-intensity exercise may explain elevated mood, positive coping, and feelings of relaxation in some individuals (DeVries, 1981). However, only a few individuals are likely to exercise at this level of intensity.

Preliminary work on the impact of exercise on cognitive function is exciting. Temporary improvements in cognitive function related to short-term memory in normal older people have been found (Emery, 1994; Hawkins, Kramer, & Capaldi, 1992), but caregivers of family members with Alzheimer's disease may be able to expect symptom management and less wandering (Bonner & O'Brien Cousins, 1996).

Possibly the most significant short-term benefits for adults of any age is the potential to gain same-day improvement in joint mobility (O'Brien Cousins & Burgess, 1992). Mobilizing and lubricating major joints of the body through a variety of stretching and relaxation regimes seems to have great therapeutic merit by contributing to better motor control and dynamic balance (Manchester et al., 1989). However, joint mobilization, on its own, has not been researched for its potential in easing the psychological strain of everyday living.

Long-Term Benefits

The broader health benefits of regular physical activity can be realized months or years later (Suominen, Heikkinen, & Parkatti, 1977). Bortz (1980) claimed that there is no medicine that can compete with the range of pathology for which exercise has been prescribed—obesity, depression, diabetes, arthritis, hypertension, coronary heart disease, menstrual cramps, migraine, smoking cessation, and many other conditions.

Even the brain adapts favorably to regular involvement in physical activity. Rikli and Edwards (1991) found significant improvements in motor function and cognitive processing speed continuing throughout a three-year period of exercise in older women, even though declines were evident in a non-exercising control group. This finding is typical of other studies whereby nonexercising (control) groups showed declines over the course of a longitudinal study, exercising intervention groups tend to completely or partially retard the downward age decline (Dustman, Emmerson, & Shearer, 1990).

Added to the rapidly accumulating mortality data is an extensive list of long-term benefits from exercise such as postponement of cardiac diagnoses; reduced mortality risk through mediating factors such as effective weight control and not smoking lower blood pressure; lowered cholesterol levels; reduced risk of colon cancer; and increased aerobic fitness.

The most tantalizing prospect is the ultimate extension of life and several studies have supported the prospect of reduced mortality stemming from regular participation in physical activity (Table 5.1). Reuben, Siu, and Kimpau (1992) found that measures of physical performance can predict mortality over a two-year period. Rakowski and Mor (1992) reported that less activity/exercise was associated with a higher risk of mortality for each of four questions relating to activity compared to their peers, having a regular exercise routine, getting enough exercise, and days walking a mile per week. For individuals with one or more impairments in the activities of daily living, walking was associated with lower mortality.

Some have argued that the prospects for life extension are effectively very small (Waterbor, Cole, Delzell, & Andjelkovich, 1988) and others have claimed that life span outcomes are affected more by genetics (Johnson, 1988), environment (Bourliere, 1973), and cultural factors (Waldron, 1976). An early animal study revealed a possible age threshold for mortality benefits; strenuous exercise initiated in older rats was found to actually reduce their survival rates (Edington, Cosmas, & McCafferty, 1972). Another criticism came from Palmore (1989) who reviewed the exercise/longevity evidence and suggested that healthy people who have lower mortality rates are naturally inclined to be more active; hence, reduced mortality may just be an association with healthier individuals who self-select for physical activity. Studies that randomly select people from a population, and randomly assign seniors to either the exercise or control group, are considered superior as they provide control for self-selection bias. Few such controlled studies exist, but longitudinal epidemiological studies that statistically control for all kinds of bias support both quality and quantity of life outcomes (Bokovoy & Blair, 1994; Rehm, Fichter, & Elton, 1993; Sandvik et al., 1993).

Other researchers argue that physical activity promotes health and longevity by countering negative body attributes such as obesity. For example, a nine- to twelve-month exercise program of walking and/or jogging at 80 percent of maximal heart rate improved fat distribution patterns in 60- to 70-year-old men and women (Kohrt, Obert, & Holloszy, 1992). Older adults lost 3 percent to 4 percent of their body weight over the course of the intervention, all of the weight lost was fat weight, and, furthermore, the fat loss occurred in the trunk area indicating "a preferential loss of fat from the central regions of the body." This study provided evidence that one mechanism by which exercise operates to reduce risk of disease may be the control of abdominal obesity.

There is evidence that physically fit elderly adults experience less profound declines in cognitive performance over the long-term than do their less-fit contemporaries (Chodzko-Zajko, 1991). Sustained aerobic exercise, more than a basic calisthenics program, appears to be important in enhancing the cognitive skills of older adults. Although research supports short-term neurophysiological improvements in measures of memory, intelligence, and cognitive speed (Stacey, Kozma, & Stones, 1985), a non-aerobic three-month exercise program was ineffective in elevating neuropsychological attributes in elderly institutionalized women (Molloy, Delaquerriere Richardson, & Crilly, 1988). Thus, although the level of intensity of an exercise program matters, whether the program is conducted at home or in a supervised setting does not (Miller, Haskell, Berra, & DeBusk, 1984).

Other significant findings accompanying exercise participation include quicker reaction time (Baylor & Spirduso, 1988), improved joint flexibility (Rikli & Edwards, 1991), muscular strength and endurance (Rikli & Edwards, 1991), increased muscle mass (Meredith et al., 1989), and the retardation of osteoporosis (Oyster, Morton, & Linnell, 1984), or even increased bone mineralization (Rikli & McManis, 1990) after only weeks of exercise (Beverly, Rider, Evans, & Smith, 1987). Bone health and osteoporosis prevention is a major benefit, especially for aging women. A balanced program of nutrition, exercise, and stress reduction appeared to benefit all postmenopausal women (Davidson, 1986). A study of 3,110 retired Florida residents, average age 73, concluded that walking one mile at least three times per week offered protection from bone fractures (Sorock, Bush, Golden, Fried, Breur, & Hale, 1986). Peterson and associates (1991) found that 59 healthy women, ages 36 to 67, increased muscular strength over 12 months, but not bone mass.

Not all aerobic studies, however, provide the expected advantage in very old age. In women averaging over 80 years of age, active women were walking briskly over 100 minutes per week, while an inactive group was averaging only 5 minutes of walking per week. Exercise histories showed that the active group had followed their present exercise program of walking for an average of 28 years. These differences in activity level did not translate into statistical differences in aerobic fitness in old-old age, a finding that is counter to most findings, but explained by inadequate sample sizes (Nieman, Pover, Segebartt, Arabatzis, Johnson, & Dietrich, 1990). Indeed, the active women had higher aerobic capacities, less body fat, and lower perceived exertion—but in samples so small that statistical significance was not reached. In other studies on cardiovascular responses with small sample sizes, the exercise effects have been powerful enough to obtain 30 percent increases in aerobic capacity (Seals et al., 1984). In sum, most studies find that physical conditioning has significant positive effects on the older adult. Even adults suffering from osteoarthritis and rheumatoid arthritis can obtain important improvement in aerobic capacity, walking time, depression, anxiety, and increased habitual activity after only 12 weeks of walking or aquatic exercise program (Minor, Hewett, Webel, Anderson, & Kay, 1989).

Researchers are exploring the possibility that exercise might prevent falls by improving balance, but so far, the findings are not consistent. Binder and colleagues (1994) used a one-hour exercise class three times a week for six weeks, and obtained significant improvements in balance scores even at one-year of follow-up. Hu and Woollacott (1994) used a randomized control design with 12 subjects ages 65 to 90 in each group. They used a multisensory platform for training and assessing balance, eyes open and closed, and reported significant balance improvements after 10 days which were retained up to one month later.

However, a prospective study attempted to reduce falls and injury in the elderly using stand-up exercises from sitting in a chair, and step-ups onto a six-inch-high stool (Reinsch, MacRae, Lachenbruch, & Tobis, 1992). The researchers concluded that the exercise program had some merit, but was too light in intensity and regularity to reduce falls significantly.

Many of the activities that seem to appeal to the interests of women are also lacking in adequate intensity. While old-timer hockey, golf, volleyball, and slow-pitch are attracting large numbers of middle-age and older men, skilled pursuits and team sport activities do not seem to be favored by many older women; rather, individual, musical, expressive, socially cooperative, and self-paced activities are more popular community programs for older women (e.g., tai chi, yoga, line dancing, aquacise). Although men team up for golf or old-timers baseball and hockey, or jog in small packs on back roads, older women seem to prefer the companionship available in supervised and noncompetitive programs close to home. An important activity that is fitness-enhancing, age-appropriate, suitable to both men and women, and self-paced is walking. Not surprisingly, walking is the most popular form of exercise with older adults (*Fitness and Aging*, 1982; O'Brien Cousins, 1993).

CONCLUSION

Despite the enormous list of benefits just outlined, the declining involvement in physical activity as people get older suggests that there must be significant barriers that undermine their participation. The fact that older women are rarely seen in vigorous activities such as running and team sports suggests that older people, and in particular

Chapter 6

Older Adult Beliefs About Exercise

Sandra O'Brien Cousins and Wonita Janzen

Over their life courses, people exhibit increasing individual diversity so that by late life, individual biological and genetic variations are obvious. This increased variation over time is called heterogeneity; older people are more different than alike. Added to biological variation are behaviors originating from a lifetime of socialization, unique events, cultural impact, and individual choices and philosophies (Nelson & Dannefer, 1992). Thus older adulthood appears to express itself as a dichotomy in life approaches: some people view late life as a stage of physical precaution and conservation (O'Brien Cousins & Burgess, 1992). Others view their maturity as a time to expend energy and resources and seek adventure, enrichment, and adult development (O'Brien & Conger, 1988). Assuredly, these contrasting life philosophies are likely to lead to differences in life goals, lifestyle preferences, motivation, and health outcomes. This chapter explores the variability that may be seen in the kindred beliefs of older people regarding exercise. A qualitative study is presented that elucidates some of the perceptions that might act as barriers or incentives to more active living and ultimately better aging and health.

Among the explanations for older people's inclination to favor more sedentary pastimes is the notion that people are poorly informed about the many benefits of regular exercise and how serious the risks of being sedentary are. In March 1994, a report was published indicating that only 18 percent of Albertans associated active living with health and physical activity (*Active Living*, 1994). About 18 percent did not know what active living was, suggesting that knowledge is indeed lacking for older adults on the lifestyle behaviors that can lead them to enjoy better health and life quality. Although 70 percent of the people surveyed acknowledged the benefits of daily physical activity, Albertans over age 50 were significantly less convinced. The belief in such benefits was highest at the high school graduate level and above, and lowest among older individuals and people who didn't complete high school. The 50 and over age group was least likely to see health benefits.

Although national health promotion campaigns such as *Healthy People 2000* in the United States (USDHHS, 1994b) and *ParticipACTION* in Canada have been clear signals that to "choose health" is an official ideology. Lack of personally meaningful health information could be one reason older people do not take advantage of more active living. When asked about the importance of exercise for health, aging adults are aware, at least in a general way, that "exercise is good for you." But despite a general public awareness, from middle age on, aging adults and especially older women continue to be among the most sedentary adults in North American society (*General Social Survey*, 1987; Novak, 1994).

Another probable determinant of sedentary behavior as people get older is declining health. As the human body ages, the immune system declines in vitality and acute or chronic forms of health difficulties arise (Shephard, 1992). Although illness can cause prolonged bed rest at any age, chronic illness accompanying advanced age is viewed as a more permanent vice. There is some evidence to support the idea that poor health in older people can impact negatively and more permanently on late-life physical activity level (O'Brien Cousins, 1993). However, the health–activity link is not a simple one, at least in women. Older women who disclosed that they were taking four or more prescription medications reported weekly activity levels on a par with the most healthy and most active women in the same study. Thus, failing health may be the cue acting as an *incentive* or a *barrier* to active living in this age group. This finding needs to be confirmed in other research, but raises the possibility that declining health is a complicating force for motivation and not necessarily the major barrier to participation. Two major determinants that do have strong theoretical support are 1) insufficient feelings of capability and experience to succeed or participate (self-efficacy); and 2) inadequate encouragement or downright disapproval from physicians, family members, and close friends (O'Brien Cousins, 1994).

Advancing our knowledge of ways to motivate and activate aging adults requires theoretical direction. Explanations are needed for how cognitive processes and lay exercise beliefs of aging adults are formed and how these processes translate into behavioral action. To date, a number of theories of human behavior have received serious consideration. At the 1993 Gerontological Society of American Conference in New Orleans, a sociologist presented a scientific poster titled, "Exercise: It adds life to our years, so why don't more people do it?" (Brooks, 1993). This research provided theoretical support for both continuity theory and disengagement theory. Two forms of continuity were found among 199 men, average age of 70. Continuity theory was supported because 32 percent of the men claimed they had simply maintained an active lifestyle all life long. In addition, another 17 percent of the men had maintained a habitually sedentary lifestyle. Brooks interpreted the findings on life continuity to mean that "efforts to promote exercise should begin prior to old age." In support of the disengagement perspective, 55 percent of the men reported experiencing social pressure to avoid strenuous activities. An important point Brooks stressed was that more elderly would likely continue or even begin exercise in late life if such fears about exercise could be modified or prevented from forming in the first place.

THEORETICAL SUPPORT

Most people think of exercise as a health behavior. Assuming that is true for the most part, the Health Belief Model (HBM) of Rosenstock, Strecher, and Becker (1988) provided guidance for several important theoretical determinants for exercise behavior. Health behavior is defined by Rosenstock's team as, "any activity undertaken by a person who believes him/herself to be healthy for the purpose of preventing disease." The original HBM proposed by Rosenstock (1974) and Becker (1974) hypothesized health-related behavior required 1) the existence of sufficient motivation (or health concern) to make health issues salient; 2) a belief that one is susceptible to a serious health condition; and 3) a belief that a particular health action would be beneficial in reducing the perceived threat. Thus one interpretation of this theory is that people who feel susceptible to health difficulties are more likely to be motivated to take up exercise as a health behavior.

The Health Belief Model is based on the assumption that people weigh the estimated benefits of a health behavior against the estimated risks and costs. These perceived risks and benefits are probably heavily reliant on personal experience and the lay knowledge developed through socialization (see Chapter 10). Where such personal experience is lacking, socialization forces may be even stronger guides to action. Thus, taking up a sport-like lifestyle in one's older years may be a formidable task for those who have little mastery or direct experience. Without such experiences, feelings of ability may be lacking. Also firsthand knowledge of the benefits is needed to offset negative environmental cues such as a sedentary spouse, inactive friends, and a noncommittal physician. Under such conditions, the potential outcomes of involvement may seem more negative than positive.

In various reports, the notion of overexertion as a barrier to exercise has been exposed (Bar-Or, 1994; Ewart et al., 1986b; Goforth & James, 1985; Monahan, 1986; Winborn, Meyers, & Mulling, 1988). Given that women are often excused from trying more strenuous tasks, it is not surprising that older women are doing far less vigorous activities than men their age (Stephens, Craig, & Ferris, 1986). Even so, exercise is a complex, time-consuming, and high-effort behavior—one that requires self-confidence, encouragement, and persistent motivation. Although sedentary adults may lack these very qualities, active adults develop certain positive expectations about the value of exercise in their lives that is adequate compensation for the effort involved. In contrast, sedentary adults lack these experiences and the accompanying rewards; at best they may conceive of exercise as leading to discomfort and fatigue; at worst they may harbor fears about injury, overexertion, heart attack, or even sudden death. So even though the health benefits of physical activity are widely accepted, several researchers have claimed that older people feel particularly vulnerable to injury or exaggerate personal risks in physical activity settings (Calnan & Johnson, 1985; Heitmann, 1982; Siscovick, LaPorte, & Newman, 1985). A key belief, which is poorly understood, could well be the negative expectancy that exercise is overly strenuous and uncomfortable and the known benefits are diminished in the face of such objectionable outcomes. Moreover, the negative expectancies associated with exercise may be viewed with more certainty than the positive expectancies that have yet to be experienced.

The formation of beliefs about coming to harm in certain situations or activities may be usefully linked to precaution motivation and self-protection theory, a relative of the HBM (Weinstein, 1984, 1988). Self-protection theory has received little attention compared to new theoretical developments with regard to stages of change theory which focuses on motivational readiness for exercise (Marcus, Rakowski, Simkin, & Taylor, 1992). This is unfortunate in that Weinstein was an early advocate of stages of decision making, and used actual discourse to elaborate on the self-talk that people might use to make decisions about health actions. His framework could be helpful to get at the deep-seated beliefs that seem to be operating for many older adults who, despite knowing about the benefits of active lifestyles, despite contemplating plans to become more active, and despite short-lived attempts to get their bodies moving, still fail to carry out health-promoting involvement in late-life exercise.

Weinstein (1988) is perhaps a dark horse in the theoretical thicket as he claims that health behavior decisions are not as tidy as theorists might infer. He used a "messy desk" analogy to illustrate how people deal with health issues—the papers (health issues) on top of the pile being the ones likely to get any attention. He claimed that as intentions to do various things pile up, people fail to sort out their behavioral needs in terms of highest to lowest priority. Thus, he claimed, health behavior will always be a challenge to explain because so much of what people do is random and haphazard.

Bandura's Social Cognitive Theory (SCT) may hold the most promise for understanding older adult exercise behavior, at least from a cognitive determinants point of view (Dzewaltowski, 1989b). In particular, four cognitive constructs of Bandura's model of human behavior appear to be relevant to exercise behavior: self-efficacy; outcome expectations; motive, goals, or incentives; and social/environmental cues (Bandura, 1977a, 1986). Self-efficacy, or the belief that one is capable of undertaking the action under consideration, has, to date, received the most research attention among exercise psychologists. Without the belief that one is capable of doing the required activity, the action is not likely to be attempted. Virtually no attention has been paid to *outcome expectation*, an individual's belief about the likely consequences of performing a behavior, even though expectancy about future outcomes is the driving cognitive framework behind SCT. For theoretical support, the issue is not how justified, valid, or "real" the belief may be, but rather that the belief exists as it is, and it is a very important guide to future behavior. Referring to exercise motivation, Rejeski (1981) stated:

> Quite frankly, from the standpoint of understanding participant behavior, knowing what people *think* they are doing may well be more important than knowing *what* they are doing. (p. 305)

Social scientists do not understand mechanisms underlying the formation of cognitive beliefs. What is known is that currently physically active older adults perceive far more benefits and far less risk in physical activity settings than do adults whose lives are more sedentary (O'Brien Cousins, 1996b). Moreover, many older people are unable or unwilling to identify *any* risks or benefits of late-life physical activity in open-ended survey responses. Efficacy to exercise and beliefs about the outcomes of their participation, although conceptually distinct, are strongly related statistically. In the O'Brien Cousins study of 327 women over the age of 70, perceived risks associated with six fitness activities were highly correlated ($r = -.657$, $p < .0001$) with self-efficacy ratings for the same six activities. That is, older women who rated their level of feelings about being at personal risk as being high, tended to be among the same women who lacked confidence in their ability to take part in that activity. Perceived risk explained 40 percent of the variability in older women's ratings of efficacy for late-life exercise. An in-depth examination of benefit and risk perceptions therefore appears to be fundamental to our understanding older people's expectancies about the possible outcomes arising from engagement in moderately strenuous physical activity.

The research described in the following discussion attempted to identify older adult beliefs about exercise and specifically their expectations for personal harm. The general objective of this research study was to explore the lay beliefs among older adults that could be acting as cognitive incentives and/or barriers to the adoption of more active lifestyles. The more specific goal of this study was to assist professionals in identifying key psychological elements which are most fruitful for community intervention.

The research aimed to answer several questions: What do adults over age 65 think are the reasons why some people become quite sedentary as they get older? What do seniors think are the benefits of exercise for older adults? What do they think are the turn-offs or barriers to exercise? What kinds of support do older people think would be helpful in getting people more physically active? Until the specific beliefs and attitudes of the elderly toward exercise are more clearly defined, health professionals and government policymakers will continue to be frustrated in effectively directing society toward healthier ways of aging.

Gender differences were anticipated because the unique socialization of men and women over the life course was hypothesized to alter their outcome expectations for exercise. The years after age 65 offer a rich reservoir of untapped information; this was the primary life stage of interest.

COLLECTING INFORMATION ON OLDER ADULT PHYSICAL ACTIVITY

Both quantitative and qualitative methods were used to gather information from seniors about their participation in and beliefs concerning physical activities. Initially, two large community-based seniors' organizations were contacted regarding the nature of the study and their permission was sought to conduct surveys and focus group interviews at their facilities. Meetings were held with the directors of the organizations and the study was explained in detail.

The nature and objective of the study was explained as follows:

This research concerns adults ages 65 and older and their beliefs about the role of physical activity in their current lifestyle. We are mainly concerned with their beliefs about the value of activity in their leisure time. Governments and health agencies are saying that many older people should be more physically active. We are wondering what seniors think of this idea. If it's so good for you, why aren't more seniors choosing physical activity for part of their leisure time?

In addition we explained why the study was needed:

Seniors are the experts about why they do the things they do. Adults form beliefs about things after years of learning and experience. Yet seniors do not often have the opportunity to inform others about these experiences. We want to know about older people's life experiences with physical activity and how those experiences have formed their beliefs about late-life physical activity. We are especially interested in talking to older people who are not particularly physically active right now.

After approval by an ethics review panel and by the directors, arrangements were made for the researchers to attend large social gatherings to distribute recruitment surveys. The one-page surveys were used to explain the study and to gather brief information about each senior. The profile forms, which were filled out on-site with assistance as needed, provided information on gender, years of formal education, marital status, type of residence, retirement status, financial status, subjective health (self-rating from poor to excellent), and objective health (number of current prescription medications). In addition, open-ended questions were included that allowed seniors to list the kinds of activities they engaged in during leisure time, and to report any activities that they would like to pursue but which they are not involved with currently. A standardized question used by Godin & Shephard (1985) to assess physical activity over the life course was included along with a question about their belief whether "physical activity is harmful or beneficial as people get older." Respondents could answer ( ) harmful, ( ) not sure, or ( ) beneficial.

THE ELDERLY PARTICIPANTS

Profile forms were completed by 102 women and 29 men from the two Edmonton organizations. Six forms were too incomplete to be useful. The 125 profile forms were sorted by gender, age, and activity level, creating smaller, strategic samples for the focus group study. During December, seniors were contacted who were over 65 years of age and who generally indicated that they were not very active, or indicated that they thought physical activity might be harmful for them. These seniors were asked to participate in a two-hour focus group to discuss physical activities in greater detail. The target was to meet with six to eight seniors per group. Focus groups were established separately for men and women because perceptions of risk and benefit could differ for the genders and these differences needed to be fully represented.

In total, four groups were established, one group of men and one group of women for each of the two seniors organizations. These groups will be referred to as Men #1, Men #2, Women #1, and Women #2. From these surveys, 22 women and 23 men were telephoned and asked to participate in the two focus groups. Six of the women and 11 of the men were not able or willing to participate in the focus groups. Two of the men could not be reached by phone. Nine of the women and four of the men who agreed to participate either cancelled or did not show up for the groups on the scheduled day. Thus, the total sample consisted of 13 seniors: Women #1, 3 participants; Women #2, 4 participants; Men #1, 3 participants; and Men #2, 3 participants.

The groups were smaller than anticipated because of extremely bitter winter weather (−23 to −27 degrees Celsius), miscellaneous cancellations, and no-shows. Recruiting men for the focus groups was difficult because so few had been contacted through the surveys. As a result of the difficulty in finding participants for the focus groups, we decided to include some seniors who had indicated on the surveys that they were somewhat active in physical activity.

The focus groups were held at each of the two society buildings in quiet boardroom settings with a large table and a number of chairs. Participants were greeted at the door of the meeting, introduced to others, and given a name card to place in front of them. When everyone had arrived, the nature of a focus group—to assemble ideas about a particular topic—was explained. Further explanation was available in the introduction of the consent forms, which were distributed at this time for providing consent:

". . . to be involved in a focus group aimed at identifying some of the beliefs that older people hold about physical activity in their older years. I understand that there are no incorrect responses and everyone's opinions and ideas are valued. I understand that the discussion will last no more than 90 minutes and that I do not have to respond to all of the questions which may be asked. I may withdraw from the focus groups at any time without prejudice to myself. The details of the study have been explained to me. I understand the nature of the study and I have had the opportunity to ask questions."

The focus group interviews were semi-structured, guided by a series of general statements and questions. After obtaining permission to audiotape the meeting, the interview proceeded approximately as follows:

- We'd like to understand why more older people are not as active as they could be . . . what do you think are some of the reasons that many older people grow to be quite sedentary?
- Are there any benefits to being physically active in your older years?
- Does anyone here think about negative things that could happen to older people who are exercising? Do you think exercise can cause harm to older people's health?
- In what situations are these harmful things more likely to happen? Do you ever think or worry about your heart, for example, when you are doing something strenuous?
- How do people know about these possible risks about being active?
- In this next section of questions, we will discuss the kinds of incentives and support that older people may need to become active or maintain activity. If

you are already physically active, you might want to comment on the kinds of things that have helped you to stay active. But first, I'd like to hear from those of you who are not that active right now about the assistance that you would need to become more active . . . for example, would you do more activity if your doctor advised it?
- If you knew that you would live two years longer with the same, or better quality of life, providing you walked 20 minutes everyday, would you do it?
- In other words, what does it take to get people more active? Is there any incentive or motivation that would help you to get started? Who do you need to help you, and what could they do to help?

The core of the discussion was on possible negative outcomes of physical activity participation. Near the end of the time allotted for each focus group, four posters measuring 12 inches by 18 inches were exhibited. These illustrated six to eight possible negative and positive outcomes in three categories (identified by seniors in previous research) to see if the seniors could think of any omissions (see Figure 6.1). At the conclusion of the meeting, the participants were thanked for their involvement. A few months later, the directors of the societies were thanked formally by letter, and given a two-page report summarizing the key findings.

ANALYZING THE DIALOGUE OF OLDER ADULTS

The data was transcribed from audiotape to typed manuscript on a part-time basis and took several months. A total of 116 pages of single-spaced transcript dialogue was produced. Content analysis was used to look for patterns of positive and negative outcome beliefs that might prevent seniors' participation in physical activities. Previous discussions with seniors and older adult fitness professionals suggested that there may be three types of benefits and risks:

- physical benefits versus health risks
- social benefits versus social risks
- cognitive benefits versus psychological risks

In addition, a fourth category called "other" was used to capture miscellaneous extrinsic barriers created by the environment (e.g., bad weather, no transportation) and the nature of the activity (e.g., needing a partner to square dance). These cognitive themes were used as starting strategies to analyze the data. A fourth category called "other concerns" was added for beliefs that were acting as barriers but which did not fit the four themes:

- perceived benefits
- perceived physical risks
- psychological concerns
- perceived social risks
- "other" barriers to physical activity

POSSIBLE PERCEIVED BENEFITS

No benefits
Feeling better
Moving better
Looking better
Delaying some diseases
Meeting people
Change of scenery
Living longer

POSSIBLE HEALTH CONCERNS

No physical concerns
Falling with injury
Overexerting myself
Muscle soreness
Aggravating joint pain
Angina or heart attack
Weakening my resistance

POSSIBLE SOCIAL CONCERNS

No social concerns
Less time for friends
No companionship
Disapproval by family
Disapproval by doctor
No appropriate attire or equipment
Not sure what to do
Not fitting in

POSSIBLE PSYCHOLOGICAL CONCERNS

No psychological concerns
A waste of my time
Quitting part-way through
Disappointing performance
Feeling foolish or embarrassed
Afraid to start
Feeling a failure

Figure 6.1   Poster lists of possible benefits and risks of exercise for older adults.

Using colored felt markers, relevant statements were identified. Both researchers reviewed the transcripts this way, and used the margins of the transcripts to identify one or more themes. For example the comment, "feeling foolish" was placed in the psychological concerns category.

Five charts were produced that identified the page number on which dialogue pertaining to that theme could be found (Tables 6.1–6.4). The charts are *not* meant to quantify the beliefs, but rather as a checklist that there is some support, or none, for the belief. The number of pages with dialogue are not a good indication of the *quantity* of dialogue because some respondents provided long and rich explanations of their understanding and experiences. Some longer sections of dialogue happen to fall on one page, although other sections of dialogue happen to overlap on the next page. Thus the charts were mainly useful in effectively locating supportive dialogue for the process of synthesis and write-up. Furthermore, they tell us where there is more support and less support for certain beliefs about late-life exercise.

THE BELIEFS OF OLDER ADULTS REGARDING PHYSICAL ACTIVITY

Sample Description

The profiles of the 125 participants ages 53 to 96 are seen in Table 6.6. The sample represented a range of health experiences with 23 percent of the adults saying their health was fair or poor, although 20 percent rated their health as excellent. Objective

Table 6.1   Thematic Chart Identifying Number of Instances of Dialogue about Benefits

Perceived benefits	Men #1	Women #1	Men #2	Women #2
No benefit I can think of	0	1	0	0
Feeling better, happier mood, less stress, less pain	2	4	2	1
Moving better, less stiff, more energy, strengthen back	1	1	0	1
Looking better, lose weight	2	1	1	1
Avoid/delay disease, improve health and fitness	0	1	0	1
Fresh air	0	0	0	0
Meeting people, seeing active role models	1	3	1	1
Change of scenery, getting out of the house, keeps life interesting	1	2	2	0
Living longer	1	0	0	0
New additions				
Enjoyment, accomplishment, doing what you've always been good at	5	0	2	3
Quality of life, functional independence, use it or lose it	1	1	1	0
Thinking better, mental sharpness	1	0	1	1
Gets me where I have to go, cheap transportation	0	2	0	0
Exercises the dog too	0	1	0	0

Table 6.2 Thematic Chart Identifying the Number of Instances of Dialogue about Physical Risks

Physical risks	Men #1	Women #1	Men #2	Women #2
Slips, falls, injury	1	3	1	1
Overexerting oneself	1	2	1	3
Aggravating joint pain, arthritis, bad back	1	2	0	5
Muscle soreness, stiff the next day	0	0	1	1
Angina or heart attack	1	0	1	1 (for men)
Weaken body resistance, fatigue, get too cold	1	0	3	0
New additions				
Physically unable, health problems, "I just can't do it anymore"	5	6	4	6
Breathlessness	1	0	0	0
Overweight	1	0	0	0
Physical discomfort (e.g., chlorine in eyes); can't stop in deep water	1	0	0	1
I am a smoker	0	0	5	0
Breathing fumes, traffic	0	0	1	0

health varied from 0 medications to as many as 7 medications. Two-thirds of the sample claimed that they were currently engaged in physical activity.

Outcome Beliefs

The main objective of this research study was to explore the outcome beliefs among older adults that could be acting as cognitive barriers to the adoption of more active lifestyles. Because, the HBM states that people weigh the benefits of an action against the costs or risks, the intent was to examine both types of beliefs. However, beliefs about benefits became a more minor aspect of this study, as the participants spent much of their time talking about the barriers. By keeping the dialogue of men and women separate, gender differences were examined.

Beliefs about Benefits   Support was found in this study for seven of the eight items on the original list of benefits. The only benefit of exercise that was not identified in this group of adults was getting fresh air. Much discussion revolved around "getting out," but *fresh air* in Edmonton in mid-winter was likely to conjure up images of cold air that was too fresh.

Some of the adults in this study were very knowledgeable about physical activity from direct experience. Articulation of the benefits of active individuals was more detailed.

Table 6.3   Thematic Chart Identifying the Number of Instances of Dialogue about Psychological Concerns

Psychological concerns	Men #1	Women #1	Men #2	Women #2
A waste of my time, better things to do, it's boring, ties up my schedule, no interest	3	1	1	2
Quitting part-way through, too difficult	1	0	0	1
Disappointing performance, can't do what I used to do, or like to do	0	1	0	2
Feeling foolish, embarrassment	1	4	1	3
I am afraid to start being controlled, scheduled, organized, told what to do	3	0	0	2
Feeling inadequate to others, feeling a failure, can't keep up	2	3	2	7
New additions				
Turn-off labels, negative connotations of words like "exercise," "swimming"	4	0	0	1
Low self-esteem, negative self-perception, too lonely, depressed	0	1	3	5
No motivation, commitment, lazy, no incentive, why bother? Easier to stay at home	2	0	0	0
Information overload, too many health messages; exercise is a lower priority	1	0	0	0
Negative attitude about exercise, a mental block, dislike exercise, resistant feeling, no pleasure, no enjoyment	9	3	4	2
No reason to exercise, feel fine, it's not in my hands, live one day at a time	1	0	2	0

V: (referring to a swimming pool) . . . you can walk in the water, uh, and it doesn't hurt your knees. You feel buoyant with the water and you can walk and you get excellent exercise.

L: . . . it is really enjoyable to go out and cross-country ski when it is brisk. It's really nice because what's out there is . . .

V: See, I do the exercises to help me grow older, cause if I don't do them I won't be around (laughs).

J: This mention of gardening, though. Don't play that down, that's hard work. I garden every summer and I really enjoy it. But that is probably, almost the toughest exercise you can get is gardening.

Concern for controlling weight and shape with exercise is expressed as a need for women. Women's weight is expressed as having "a tummy" and the weight appears to more a concern for their appearance than for their health.

V: Well, here's a good example. The other day, in the very cold weather, my wife got out her old fur coat, a good warm one, and she said "V___, it shrunk" (laughs). I said well,

Table 6.4 Thematic Chart Identifying the Number of Instances of Dialogue about Social Risk

Social risks	Men #1	Women #1	Men #2	Women #2
Too busy, takes time from friends, socializing, mental activities	1	1	2	0
No companionship, no partner, no support	1	5	2	4
Disapproval, discouragement by family, friends, or spouse	0	1	3	1
Disapproval by doctor, nurses	0	1	1	1
Need appropriate footwear, sports gear, equipment, swimsuit	1	1	0	0
Not sure what to do, self-conscious, lack knowledge, not keeping up, I'm a klutz, I've had bad experiences in the past	5	0	2	4
Not fitting in, feel uncomfortable, rejected, don't feel wanted	0	1	2	0
New additions				
Messes up my appearance, hair gets wet, changing is a nuisance	1	1	0	1

having been in the dry-cleaning industry for many, many years, I've heard this time and time again. "You shrunk it." And there is great incentive, uh, not only for females, is to, uh, your appearance. And I think, for the ladies particularly, they hate to put on weight, and yet they just, uh, don't have the incentive or whatever it takes to go and do the exercises to, uh, because it obviously keeps your body in better shape.

Five benefits were added to the original list. These were 1) enjoyment, accomplishment, doing what you've always been good at; 2) improving quality of life,

Table 6.5 Thematic Chart Identifying the Number of Instances of Dialogue about "Other" Concerns

"Other" concerns	Men #1	Women #1	Men #2	Women #2
Inconvenience of activity, nuisance of changing, checking coats, lockers	2	4	0	1
Bad weather	6	2	3	3
No prior experience, why start now?	6	0	0	0
Afraid to go out, concern for personal safety	1	2	1	0
Getting muscle-bound (female)	0	1	0	0
Too expensive, can't afford it	1	1	0	0
No transportation	0	2	0	0
Inappropriate seniors activities in the community (Spa Lady)	0	1	0	0

E: I think (inhale), "what if I slip and fall?" And, you know, think of all kinds of calamities that might happen.

M: I hear a lot of people today saying, "I love to walk but I don't dare go out because its icy. If I slip and fall and break something. . . ." But even jogging is, now they say, is hard on the spine. Brisk walking is much better.

Concern for angina or heart attack as a negative health outcome to participating in physical activity was expressed by women and men for men.

M: (female) It's men who die of heart attacks after they shovel snow.

P: (male) . . . overexerting myself, I think of that because I don't want to get a chest pain or a heart attack. I think of that.

When the responses of the participants were compared with the original list of negative health outcomes compiled by the researchers, there was some support for every category, but six new health themes were added: Just can't do it anymore, breathlessness, overweight, physical discomfort, habitual smoking, and breathing traffic fumes (Table 6.2). With regard to his breathless experience in swimming lengths at a local pool, one man commented,

V: I find that I get halfway along and I want to stop. I get out of breath and want to put my feet down. But if you're in the deep end you can't do that. You gotta get back to the other end.

In addition to one man who said sitting on his exercise bike was really uncomfortable, a woman who tried swimming also experienced physical discomfort:

J: I have a swimming pool right there and I used to go every morning, but then they had so much stuff (chlorine) in there that it bothered my eyes.

One group of men kept returning to the evils of smoking as an antagonist to physical activity.

P: (male) I wish I had better knees, I wish I didn't smoke, and I, I look at myself and I says "gee, I was able to quit drinking." But I haven't been able to quit smoking. And I know it's not, I know it's destroying myself.

In general, the men and women in the focus groups expressed less concern with negative outcomes from participating in physical activity, but gave more examples of health problems that prevented them from participating. They viewed health as a deterrent to physical activity as opposed to an outcome of activity. Many of these older people did not even contemplate more active living; they could not conceive of doing it because of their current state of health. Therefore the alternatives of active living for them were not explored, they saw no value or benefit in physical activity for them, health problems had stolen their ability, there was no need to summon support from others to help them keep at it or get started, and they felt helpless to correct the state of their health.

Psychological Concerns   Of all the concerns, the seniors in this study were most vocal about psychological barriers to late-life physical activity as can be seen in Table 6.3. Support for the original six concerns were found, and the seniors seemed to express more psychological deterrents to participating in physical activities than possible negative expectancies as outcomes of participating.

Boredom while exercising was mentioned frequently as a key reason not to be more physically active. Watching television or getting company while you exercise were two suggested ways to eliminate boredom.

> **V:** And I say to my wife, well you know, "go down to the bike" and she doesn't get down to do it. Oh, the odd time. But, uh, because it's boring. It's boring if you're not watching t.v.

> **H:** I feel better for doing it (t.v. exercise show) but it's sorta boring because I'm by myself doing it.

Feeling foolish or being embarrassed was reported in the women's groups in particular. One example of feeling foolish was felt by a woman when her dog died and she felt funny going walking without the dog. Another woman, referred to her love of gardening, and then her friend's love for golf. She tried golfing with her and,

> **H:** I find it sort of silly, walking around, hit, pound the heck out of a ball that never did anything to you.

> **E:** Foolish and embarrassed when I was doing yoga. I had a terrible time getting up off the floor. Another little gal I knew, she could just jump up [off the floor after sitting] and I, that was one of the reasons I quit.

> **H:** I know a couple of friends who are telling me that I'm foolish to do exercises because I'm going to get muscle-bound.

> **P:** (male) You see, feeling, feeling foolish, or embarrassed, that's rejection.

The women's groups also voiced many concerns about feeling inadequate to others, and used inferior social comparisons to justify why they withdrew from physical activity settings.

> **J:** My sister is a year younger than me but she can do everything. Acrobatics, all this dance, she was a dancer. Well, I tried and "no you don't do it that way." I was always put down in everything I did. She had to be the top dog. And she was the top dog.

The seniors in this study added six more psychological components to this theme: turnoffs such as the words themselves, low self-esteem as a result of being retired, no incentive to be bothered, information overload, mental blocks and resistance, and not feeling susceptible to, or in control of health problems. Negative connotations associated with words like "exercise" and "swimming" were considered to be big turnoffs for many older people. To get some friends in swimming, one man just asked them to "come down to the pool." If he mentioned the word "swim" they would not come. These seniors inferred that some people were not as knowledgeable about benefits simply because they tuned out when information was made available to them.

L: The word "exercise" just shies them right off.

J: To some degree, that turns people off organized sports.

J: People just resist. They'll listen to any rumour but you give them some good, factual information and really they slough it off.

But the words that were turnoffs for some were not turnoffs for others.

M: Swimming wouldn't bother me at all, because I swim well. Skating wouldn't bother me, other than I have no desire to be out in the cold. But as far as exercise, uh, no. (How is skating or swimming different from exercise?) It's fun, it's fun, it's fun.

Discussion on negative attitudes, mental blocks, laziness, and lack of commitment were bountiful, especially among new retirees.

L: When they retire they figure, "Well, this is what I've been waiting all my life for, is to become retired." And they talked themselves into saying, "Well this is when you don't do anything. I, uh, don't have to get up in the morning."

L: Well, I haven't done it all my life, why do I have to do it now?

The men felt that losing the freedom that they had earned at retirement was at risk:

J: It's partly the routine of course. A lot of people, I think, are afraid of exercising, that they don't want to get into a routine that each day you . . . ride a bike or you do something, yah, they just feel . . . that it's a routine.

Along with other negative outcomes such as disappointing performance, and afraid to start, was the idea of feeling a failure. Some of the women, and several men emphasized that a low self-esteem or negative self-perception may be an important factor. For the men, low sense of self seemed to mean low sense of value for oneself rather than low sense of physical ability or low value for exercise.

P: I find that one of the biggest problems in older people is low self-esteem . . . they're reluctant to go out and get involved because they don't think they are good enough to get involved.

M: My husband seems to be withdrawing more and more all the time. I find it harder and harder to get him out. . . .

For the women, negative self-perception came from previous negative experiences with their earlier involvement with sports activity

M: Mine is all psychological as far as, not only that but, uh, it's a terrible thing to blame your dislike of physical activity, on the fact that when I was 12, 13, 14 and in high

school and the tallest, uh, the tallest person in the class, . . . I always had to be the first
one to do any activity and I am a klutz . . . and I had three girl cousins who went through
the same city high school . . . and they were the stars on the basketball team, they were all
members of the sports club. And, of course we had the same phys ed teacher and then she
would say "and what's wrong with you?" It's just, you know how we avoid the things
that make us look stupid or that we can't do.

One new concern that arose numerous times with regard to motivation had to do
with seeing little point in expending energy on exercise. They have heard good and
bad things about exercise—that some activities may be harmful to them, aren't worth
the bother, and "they figure they don't need it."

> **V:** I think that's one of the biggest barriers is I just can't be bothered doing it.
>
> **J:** It doesn't take much to think "aw what's the bother!" It's just not worth bothering.
>
> **L:** . . . when we're swimming, the wife and I, we, uh, swim twice a week and we . . . it's
> not carved in stone but we'll say "We're going to!" And then you don't say "Oh well,
> maybe I won't." We say Tuesday is our day to swim, and Friday too. And we do it. But
> it's very easy to say "I don't think I'll bother. It's too cold [outside]."

Part of the meaning of "bother" may have something to do with lack of energy or
perceived effort required. The energy may be lacking because there is no incentive,
goal, or value attached to being more physically active.

> **P:** I'm just not able to motivate myself to get physically active . . . I just can't get the
> energy.
>
> **V:** But incentive is important . . . I get up in the morning, three mornings a week and
> watch Canada AM while I'm bicycling . . . but my wife doesn't have the incentive to get
> on and she really needs exercise more than I do.
>
> **M:** And it's also to get over that first barrier of, I suppose, inertia, if I was polite, laziness
> if I was talking about myself.

Many seniors' health was apparently fine without much activity; they think "it's going
to be somebody else" who will have health difficulties, they see no reason to go to the
trouble of risking all that effort for no guarantees, and there are always exceptions.

> **J:** There are people still, lots of them you know, who go around and say "well, so-and-so
> never exercised in his life and he lived to be 90." So what's the point?
>
> **V:** Uh, then, other people you know that exercise diligently, and then something comes
> along, something strikes them like cancer or something, and they're gone at a young age.
> So a lot of people say, uh, "if it's going to be, it's going to be."

Women's longevity accompanying perceived inactivity seems to cause confusion as
to the real value of being active.

> **J:** Well they (women) outlive us by quite a few years regardless of whether they exercise
> or not.

V: But I, I was just thinking of another friend of mine, uh, who's in good condition, she never exercises. She couldn't be bothered. And I think that's another thing when you talk about exercising. "Who needs exercise? I get enough exercise just walking around the house, going shopping, and doing these things" . . . um, and they live a long time.

Even though the benefits of exercise were accepted, people didn't think it was relevant to them given they had so few years left to live.

P: I think about the future. I sometimes think, aw gees, I've only got 10 years to go if I do this or if I do that. I live life one day at a time as a rule. The past is there. I can change myself for the present, but I find it difficult to prepare myself for the future because it is so, uh, it's not 20 or 30 and 40 years now like it was when I was 20, 30 or 40. I don't read the obituary. The simple reason is that I see too many ages that are younger than mine and I don't think of death.

SOCIAL CONCERNS

Both the men and women mentioned possible negative social outcomes to physical activity participation, however the women commented more often on social concerns than the men. Although some felt that being busy with other activities, the prominent concern was lack of companionship to do physical activity.

H: I've started doing the exercises with Cynthia Kereluk on t.v. . . . and feel better for doing it, but it's sort boring because I'm by myself, doing it, you know.

J: I think the first barrier would be to have somebody to go with.

Two women lamented the loss of their husbands, who were also their dance partners.

E: We went (dancing) Monday night, and we went Friday night to round dancing, Saturday night to square dancing and uh, I was really, really active and so was he. But you see, when he went (died) I didn't really have a partner, so I didn't go. Well, you go and you sit there and you hope that somebody's husband is going to ask you to square dance.

H: I went with other couples but it's not fun. I still have my costume and everything, but, you know . . . That's why I'm less active now.

These two women tried to maintain their dance involvement after their husbands died, but found that "with the men at a premium," they did not feel welcome there.

E: I remember when I first went and a lady said to me, "I'll let you dance with my husband but, you know, we have to watch these widows."

The psychological resistance can be in the social setting too, and no one wins. For example, one woman described how she got her husband to go walking.

H: There's no way he's going to go for a walk and I say "well let's just go. Let's start and we're going to go two blocks." So we'd walk a block and he'd say we gotta go back. And

I'd say "why?" "Well," he said, "because that will be two blocks." And I said, "No, I meant two blocks there and two blocks back." "Well, then you conned me because that's four blocks." You see (laughs). He'd rather sit on the back porch and smoke a cigarette and watch the world go by.

A second woman had a similar story about walking as a couple:

> **E:** Mine, too, mine too. We'd go round and round the crescent and I says to Ron "the crescent, you go half way." "Well I'm going the rest of the way, dear" and away he'd go, he'd just go home.

Companionship may be a larger concern for women who outlive their husbands or female walking companions. Because older women are more likely to be afflicted with chronic diseases, few of their friends may be active themselves, and therefore not very supportive.

Disapproval by family and friends was experienced by these seniors.

> **H:** (female) I know a couple of friends who are telling me that I'm foolish to do exercises because I'm going to get muscle-bound.
>
> **P:** . . . a lot of people have families that don't approve of them going out at all . . . and the family is usually the biggest problem they have. Um. You'll have a daughter who will say "well it looks stupid if you do this."

Not being sure of what to do, and not fitting in were two other concerns of the seniors. Part of this concern comes with a lack of previous experience or skill development with an activity.

> **V:** But when you're 65 and you start to learn to play golf I think it's very difficult.
>
> **J:** . . . if we hadn't played tennis when we were in our 20s say, or 30s, chances are you wouldn't start playing tennis now.
>
> **M:** People have a reluctance to get involved in something that they've never been involved in before.
>
> **E:** (referring to square dancing) But it's the attitude of some of the women when you go in, when you're another woman. Then men are at a premium, but let another woman walk in and "hmm, gee, not another woman." I know I never went back again.

Other Concerns   The seniors in the focus groups also expressed a number of concerns not part of the above three categories (Table 6.5). The category of "other" concerns included barriers that were mainly extrinsic to the individual. Again, many of these items seemed to be barriers in contemplating activity rather than as barriers perceived as consequences of participation.

Even though the seniors attending the focus groups came despite harsh temperatures near −25 degrees Celsius, weather was a large concern for many of these seniors.

> **H:** For six months of the year the weather is, uh, a factor . . . it's very difficult to walk because a lot of people don't shovel their walks and it's slippery, so you have to be careful.

V: . . . A lot of them won't take their cars out because the roads are bad in the residential districts.

D: Imagine anybody with crutches or a cane in, in January, or in a wheelchair in Edmonton. It's just almost an impossibility to get out of the house.

Some of the men and women commented on the inconvenience of participating in physical activities, the cost involved in some activities, and the lack of transportation to facilities:

V: (referring to swimming) Uh, it's just the fuss of getting in and locking up your clothes and getting out, and then some people have trouble with their hair getting wet.

H: (referring to winter exercise) If you want to go to the mall to walk, uh, you know, there's no place to hang your coat up. You can't leave your coat in the car because you have to walk (some distance) to the mall. So, if you walk, I mean, walk at a fairly good clip, you get warm.

H: (referring to a sports facility) She can't afford to pay the $2.75 it costs to go there, you know.

E: (referring to a house-bound friend) So, like a lot of other older people don't care or they no longer can drive.

Some of the seniors thought that a deterrent to late-life physical activity participation was a lack of natural ability for sports and not finding sports enjoyable.

V: Some people just don't get into sports because they, they're not athletic.

E: Some people don't like walks.

D: (My wife) tried running but she didn't like it.

A concern for their own personal safety when going out to activities was also expressed by some of the men and women in the groups.

V: (referring to swimming) And at the university they scare you about, about the security of the lockers . . . it scares you.

P: And, yah, I live downtown. I don't like going out at night-time because I don't feel secure, don't feel safe. Especially in winter.

H: One fear I have about going out at night-time, even in the car, is either getting mugged or robbed . . . I feel quite unsafe. Especially after my husband died. I'm getting braver now, but um, it's, uh, at night-time it's a fear, you know.

Some of the seniors suggested that busy schedules of many seniors may prevent them from setting aside time for physical activities.

J: (Seniors) are very involved in volunteer work so some of them that may, you think are inactive, and I suppose in sports they may be inactive, but they may still be doing quite a lot in volunteer work.

The issue of being active in sedentary activities raises an interesting point. What is meant by activity? Do older people who are busy doing various sedentary activities think they are active? For example one woman speaks of her weekly involvements:

> **E:** Of course, where I live, there's more chance for mental activity, if you want to call it that, because we play, um, whist Monday night, cribbage Tuesday night, and there's shuffleboard Thursday and bingo Friday. Well I don't go down to bingo because, for one thing I want to see on television is the Royal Canadian Air Farce and it comes on at seven so . . .

The confusion is pinpointed by one of the active men who describes bridge as an "inactive activity" and another woman who knows a friend who is "active at bridge." The definition of activity, although broad in reality, seems to have a meaning all its own among older adults. You are physically active if you get out of your home, and you are physically active if you are a volunteer in your community, and you are physically active if you are busy all day long.

Some physical activities in the community are not appropriate for seniors.

> **H:** If you join an aerobics class for example, and you're my age then you should have your head examined . . . that's why I went into a place called . . . Spa Lady or something like that, and, you know, I got some 18-year-old who's telling me to jump on the spot and the music is making the windows shatter, and I know that's not for me.

One of the men thought that information from professionals and organizations regarding physical activity was contradictory and perhaps too much for seniors to remember and understand. The following comments from an older adult come close to representing the "messy desk" and haphazardness of human activity based on Weinstein's (1988) notion of competing responsibilities.

> **J:** With some people, this whole matter may be a matter of overload. I mean, we do emphasize nutrition, we emphasize exercise, we emphasize preventing obesity, we emphasize don't smoke, we emphasize so many things. I think people start to think, "aw, heck, there's too many things involved here."

In discussing health behaviors in general, such as eating, drinking, smoking an so on, one woman talked about maintaining some "sinful pleasures" that added to her happiness.

> **H:** You can't take everything away from a person. You have to have something that, uh, gives you pleasure.

THE IMPORTANCE OF QUALITATIVE RESEARCH
FOR UNDERSTANDING BENEFITS

This study was conducted on a convenience sample of 125 Alberta seniors who were members of one of two Edmonton societies for seniors. However, in the midst of winter, a small group of 13 men and women became the target of our attention for more in-depth study. The small size of the focus groups has some redeeming features: there was an intimate atmosphere that afforded us more time to hear from each individual. In addition, the seniors who did participate were diverse in health, life experience, and current activity level. The quality of the data gathered in this study was likely enhanced rather than undermined by the size of the sample.

The purpose of this study was to learn about older people's beliefs about physical activity and how these beliefs are informed by past or present circumstances. The study was specifically aimed at perceptions about personal outcomes (benefits and risks) in exercise settings. In addition to providing us with a rich understanding of their lay beliefs and the contextual formation of those beliefs, the study garners support for the theoretical construct of *outcome expectancy*. Clearly, in making cognitive judgements about whether to take up or sustain involvement in late life exercise, older people do consider some of the benefits and risks. Active older adults appear to be highly aware of the benefits, and articulate consternation that some other older people have little interest in doing anything physical with their free time. The less active seniors spend little time articulating the specific benefits of exercise for them, and rather prefer to discuss in depth the reasons why they are not as active as other people.

Focus group interviews permitted a good deal of information to be gathered on a variety of these beliefs, and support was acquired for categorizing the negative beliefs into four categories. Moreover, the qualitative data from this study confirmed most all of the specific beliefs that had been identified in earlier work: beliefs about coming to physical harm; beliefs about experiencing negative social outcomes; beliefs regarding negative psychological consequences; and, other beliefs related to the environment or nature of the activity. The first three categories seem to capture the range of intrinsic concerns that older people hold for late-life exercise whereas the fourth category of "other concerns" seemed to be barriers external to the person.

Beliefs that acted as main barriers to late-life exercise were mainly psychological with mental blocks, negative attitudes, feeling foolish, and feeling inferior to other participants all acting to undermine older adult exercise. Most of the participants claimed that there were some things they could not do in their later years, but few attempted to explain why they could not. Sedentary living was not blamed for any physical deficiencies; all physical faults were accepted as inevitable consequences of aging. Even with the hefty list of psychological reasons that make it difficult to be active in old age, authentic health problems acted as major deterrents to physical activity involvement. However, none of the men or women expressed serious ailments— arthritis and being overweight were the main health limitations. Breathlessness, physical discomfort in the activity, and not being able to stop smoking were other barriers.

IMPORTANT BARRIERS TO OVERCOME

Seniors participating in this study provided unique conceptions of the problem of motivation and a different conception of activity. For example, there was some consensus among the men that low self-esteem or self-respect would undermine one's motivation to be active and doing something good for oneself. Some of the men agreed that this basic self-respect is often affected by retirement. Mandatory retirement is viewed by them to mean that they are officially no longer useful to society. This perspective has not been theoretically addressed in the exercise adherence literature. Although numerous studies have demonstrated that sedentary living is associated with low self-esteem, the assumption has been that inactivity, not retirement, is the cause. More research should attend to the possibility that individuals who retire successfully self-select into more active lifestyles although people who experience a more traumatic retirement tend to avoid and even resist activity opportunities.

The comment "why bother?" was voiced several times by members of this group of seniors. The group of older adults most resistive to late-life activity are convinced that there is no point to being involved at such a late stage. A few things may help them understand why they should bother. First, immediate benefits can be felt in reducing painful joints and in improving flexibility. The body will not ache as much, and if programmers are creative, some activities can be really fun. A favourite activity of a veteran's home is batting a large ball tethered from the ceiling. The men are very frail looking sitting in the wheelchair circle, but once they have their bats, watch out! People will immediately feel better too, and usually feel energized not fatigued. Perhaps the tact to take is to promote "feeling better" rather than being healthier as the route to motivating older people.

The other issue that needs to be clarified with older people is that both men and women need to be physically active even if women live longer. Women need balanced exercise to maintain bone and muscle strength to withstand their extra longevity. The men need to be active to keep their cardiovascular system in good shape to delay the onset of cardiovascular disease. Public perception is that more men die of heart disease each year, but that is not true if you look at *U.S. Department of Health and Human Services 1994*. Men die sooner, but more women actually die on an annual basis. The women who die each year of heart disease are simply somewhat older. These myths suggest that the heart disease findings disseminated in the media reflects a strong gender-bias among the research community; more balanced public funding of such research and gender balance in public education is still a serious issue.

Embedded in the dialogue of some of the participants of this study is the notion that an older adult is active if they are engaged in community work, are busy doing many things, and get out of the house regularly. More research is needed to confirm that seniors are satisfied with themselves if they are "active" by this definition. If so, then program planners and health professionals will have to take the time to differentiate the health costs of spending long winter months playing bridge, bingo, whist, reading, and watching television day in and day out. The social and personal costs of sedentary recreation need to be better understood.

Weinstein (1984, 1988) claims that current theoretical models ignore the fact that single threats to health can be met with multiple actions (heart disease controlled by diet, exercise, stress management) and that people are often faced with multiple threats to their health simultaneously. Added to these multiple threats in people's daily lives are other responsibilities that compete for their time, energy, and material resources.

Chapter 7

Reversing the Downward Spiral

Art C. Burgess and Sandra O'Brien Cousins

In the past 20 years, scientific evidence has been accumulating that vigorous forms of physical activity of sufficient regularity, intensity, and duration are a significant preventive measure against a host of diseases associated with aging. More recent evidence suggests that even mild forms of activity have merit in preventing hypokinetic disease, particularly in the elderly. Evidence is rapidly accumulating that the activation of elderly people provides them with considerable advantages such as increased likelihood of maintaining full independent living through health and functional benefits (Barry, Rich, & Carlson, 1993).

The merits of trying to maintain or initiate physical activity during times of severe health difficulties have not been addressed in the exercise psychology or physiology literature at any age. Moreover, the prospect of developing an exercise program appropriate for an elderly individual who is already encountering chronic, multiple, and serious health complications poses a challenge even for the most seasoned exercise professional or sports medical practitioner.

A trail-blazing case study of the rewards and tribulations facing both an elderly individual and an exercise supervisor are offered in this chapter. A true story is presented that demonstrates the potential of seriously impaired elderly to adopt physical activity and make reversals leading to better quality of life and greater independence. The exercise program and personal progress are provided as an example to demonstrate that, ideally, exercise must be customized to suit the needs of a frail individual. The value of the case study is evident in acknowledging the potential of ill elderly to make reversals, but is also a testimony to the costs of such undertakings. Transformations from frail to fit are time-intensive, laborious, and possibly short-lived.

THE CHALLENGE OF MAINTAINING MOVEMENT IN FRAIL POPULATIONS

A 99-year-old, Akhba Suleman, stated, "It is better to move without purpose than to sit still. . . ." (*The New York Times*, December 26, 1971). Almost a quarter of a century later, inactivity is a serious public health hazard of the same magnitude as smoking, hypertension, and high cholesterol, all of which lead to heart problems and early disability with advancing age (Olshansky, Carnes, & Cassel, 1993; Pemberton & McSwegin, 1993). The population most at risk are the frail elderly since their mature age and health status leaves them little room to compromise their physical and emotional health.

What Is Appropriate Exercise for Frail People?

Some contemporary researchers advocate that gentle movement in the very aged may be the most important element leading to daily survival (Gueldner & Spradley, 1988; O'Brien & Vertinsky, 1991). Without daily movement, those who still live independently are at risk of losing that very ability because of muscle wasting and generalized weakness, poor endurance, stiffening of joints, and impaired gait and balance. Many physiological changes and pathologies predispose the oldest old to extreme frailness and frequent falls. Most physicians are untrained and reluctant to prescribe physical activity as a solution since the risks seem to outweigh the benefits. Even if an older individual attempts to get moving anyway, professionals can err in a number of ways: 1) they may be ignorant of the real physical and psychological needs of the individual and fail to adapt the program accordingly; 2) they may not account for the unique abilities of each individual and therefore assume that all abilities of the frail individual are minimal; and 3) they may be overcautious and exercise ambulatory elderly in a chair—or provide so many warnings about risk that the older individual is afraid to do anything on their own. Therefore,

> . . . therapeutic nihilism on the part of the clinician may lead to lowered expectations of recovery and an inappropriately timid approach to rehabilitation after stroke in the oldest old (Fiatarone & Evans, 1990).

More recent research highlights the enormous capabilities of aged, frail, and untrained adults to handle the more strenuous forms of training. Moreover, Fiatarone and Evans (1990) noted that the oldest age groups may stand more to gain than any other group from the clinical application of exercise physiology. However, they suggested that "much more research is needed to determine the safety, efficacy, and specificity of the exercise prescription in the oldest old" (1990).

Following up on their own advice, Fiatarone's team (1994) conducted exercise and nutrition supplement programs to determine which treatment would best counter the problems of frailty in adults averaging 87 years. The nutrition supplement program that attempted to control for frailty caused by undernutrition consisted of a 240-ml liquid supply of 360 kcal of 69 percent carbohydrate, 23 percent fat, and 17 percent soya-based protein designed to augment caloric intake by about 20 percent.

Subjects assigned to exercise training underwent a regimen of progressive resistance training of the hip and knee extensors three days per week for 10 weeks. For each muscle group, the resistance was set at 80 percent of one repetition maximum (RM) or the maximum that could be lifted fully one time only. The training sessions lasted for 45 minutes and were separated by a one-day rest. Each repetition lasted 6 to 9 seconds, with a one- to two-second rest between repetitions and a two-minute rest between the three sets of eight lifts. The control groups took a nutrition placebo and did no resistance training but did do other activities such as walking and chair exercises.

Their findings indicate that "high-intensity strength training exercise was a feasible and effective means of counteracting muscle weakness and physical frailty in very elderly people" since the average improvement in strength was 113 percent. At the same time that the exercisers were gaining strength, the control (inactive) group showed slight declines in their muscle force and showed atrophy in muscle mass. In summary, they found that "multinutrient supplementation without concomitant exercise does not reduce muscle weakness or physical frailty." In fact the nutritional supplement program had no effect on any of the main outcome variables.

A joint research team from Tufts University and Harvard Medical School asked if high-intensity strength training exercises in postmenopausal women could alter multiple risk factors for osteoporotic fractures (Nelson, Fiatarone, Morgani, Trice, Greenberg, & Evans, 1994). Using a randomized control trial, they exercised 20 women who were between 50 and 70 years of age two days per week for 52 weeks. The other half of the sample acted as a control group. The high-intensity resistance training was targeted at several muscle groups at 80 percent RM: hip extension, knee extension, and lateral pull-down exercises, back extension and abdominal flexion.

After one year of the study, total body bone mineral content of the femoral neck and lumbar spine was preserved in the strength-trained women, while bone mineral content decreased in the controls. Muscle mass, muscle strength, and balance in walking backward also increased in the exercising women and declined in the control group, leaving little doubt that muscle training does strengthen bones. A more serious outcome of their research was the finding that bone mineral content declined measurably on an ongoing and annual basis without adequate levels of physical activity. Older people who did not exercise regularly and adequately appeared to be giving in much too readily to Mother Nature's invitation to accelerated aging.

The following is the story of the rehabilitation of a seriously debilitated elderly woman. We describe what turned out to be an experimental program of exercise loading and supervision. We document the triumphs and setbacks. We delineate an emerging methodology of working with and motivating an older person who had "one foot in the grave." The chapter sets forth some operating principles for training frail elderly people. In addition, we extend an invitation to physicians and geriatricians to create partnerships with those physical educators who have training and certification in older adult fitness.

Background

Art C. Burgess, Ph.D., has been a physical educator for over 40 years, directing the Campus Fitness and Lifestyle programs at the University of Alberta since 1977. Now in his sixties, he has personally experienced a double hip replacement, is diabetic, and wears a pacemaker. He is *far* from an invalid however, as his hundreds of exercise followers will attest. In an average week, Dr. Burgess leads 6 hours of exercise classes and 4 hours of ice skating activities for people of all ages. In addition, he and his wife, Dorothy, are ice dancers and enjoy folk and ballroom dancing, and master's gymnastics. His innovative fitness programs have obtained national interest, particularly his physical activity program for adults over age 55 called *Project Alive and Well*. Hundreds of older adults have been regulars at his classes. Art Burgess has rarely felt challenged in the exercise setting . . . until the day when Mrs. E. approached him for help.

Mrs. E. was 79. She had been a writer and radio broadcaster almost all her adult life. A hard-driving compulsive woman who lived on the edge of deadlines, she was bounded by pressure and seemed to thrive on it. After turning 70 in 1982, she began to experience health problems associated with that lifestyle. Obesity, high blood pressure, arthritis, and general debilitation from years of sedentary living took its toll. She began to experience arthritis in her right knee, which increasingly restricted her ability to get about. After two years of continually increasing pain, she consulted an orthopaedic surgeon to have a knee prothesis put in place. This was not to be. Before she could be given an appointment for surgery, she suffered a serious coronary attack and was treated with triple bypass surgery. After that operation, her life slowed down markedly. She stopped writing and looked for rehabilitation. Her search took her to Dr. Burgess who agreed to meet with Mrs. E. to determine where she could be involved in his program.

The Initial Condition of Mrs. E.

It took all her physical stamina just to get herself to the office of Dr. Burgess. Her gait was slow and unsteady as was her movement just to change body position. She relied heavily on a cane to get anywhere. She had little appetite and complained of having great difficulty in sleeping.

Even in the normal course of a conversation, Mrs. E. seemed out of breath. She took large gasps through her mouth as nasal breathing did not seem to satisfy her needs. She was markedly over-fat and demonstrated elevated blood pressures—180/110 at best. Moreover, she reported that she was taking a large daily intake of prescription drugs.

Mrs. E. was suffering from osteoarthritis in the right shoulder, which had restricted mobility in that joint to about 40 percent of normal range. She also had osteoarthritis in both knees with the right knee showing visible swelling. Circulatory insufficiency was evident in the lower left leg resulting from the surgical use of leg vessels for the bypass.

Psychologically, Mrs. E. had problems too. As a former radio broadcaster of some renown, Mrs. E. had been a competitive, compulsive, and impatient personality, akin to a "type A." However, these traits were somewhat masked by her advanced age and diminished energy. Added to her problems were uncharacteristic traits of depression, apprehension, and loss of self-esteem. Mrs. E. was a bundle of misery and in her despair was taking what many people would consider an extreme, if not futile, attempt to create a remedy for herself. She viewed her current health problems to be permanent unless she could find some extraordinary assistance; she could not see how she would get any better than this unless Dr. Burgess had some advice.

It was clear at once that she was not ready to participate in the group exercise classes, so Dr. Burgess agreed to work individually with her until she was fit enough to join in the group fitness program. Unknown to both of them was the fact that the health promotion of Mrs. E. would take another two years.

THE OPENING STRATEGY

After the first interview, an effort was made to get some medical clearance for the client to exercise. Beyond the indication that she could exercise regularly, her physician gave no specific direction or guidelines. The client was insistent that she proceed with training despite this lack of information. Recognizing the experimental nature of the situation, it was decided to proceed in a limited way and to monitor heart rate and respiration rate closely. Training sessions were very tentative at first. As training proceeded, further contacts were made with the primary physician, but with no further response.

Bearing in mind her physician's general approval of exercise that brought no specifications with it, the task was to attempt to define an appropriate exercise intensity. A starting point was defined as what Mrs. E. was capable of with no distress. Because she was walking about 200 meters up a slight incline to get from her car to the exercise facility, this became her first operational performance and the basis of the aerobic segment of her training.

Mrs. E's first involvement was in stretching exercise so that a sound warm-up would be established early in her repertoire as a necessary preliminary to training. There were a number of benefits to this approach. First, flexibility gains are immediate, and observable thus providing an immediate indicator of a level of success that was motivating. Second, flexibility is highly specific to the joint being mobilized and this was an asset when certain joints had to be avoided due to inflammation and pain.

Even with the omission of the occasional painful joint, the static and passive stretching regimen was challenging. Eight areas of the body were targeted each day (see illustrations). Stretches were held at a point subjectively defined "as below the pain threshold" for 15 to 20 seconds. In the interest of relaxing the muscles under stretch, a concerted effort was made to maintain regular and easy breathing throughout the stretch. At the end of each stretch, she was encouraged to shake out the area affected by the stretch and then move to an entirely different joint. The practice of rotating the area under stretch, from legs to shoulders, to wrist to trunk with as little delay as possible was a strategy used to sustain and build a warm-up effect. Along the way, conversation and laughter were a very effective part of the program.

The program for Mrs. E. targeted mobility in eight muscle/joint regions. The specific stretches are identified in the following section along with description of the procedure.

JOINT ACTION	MUSCLE GROUP	DESCRIPTION
Wrist	Forearm Muscles	With arms extended, pull one hand toward you to feel a position of stretch. Stretch the other hand, and then repeat the exercise.
Shoulder	Deltoid muscle Pectoralis major Latissimus dorsi	Clasp hands behind your back and flex the knees slightly. Bend forward as far as possible keeping your head above your hips.
		Intertwine fingers, palms facing outward, and stretch arms straight forward until stretch is felt in the back of the hands, wrists, and arms. Raise arms above your head momentarily.

JOINT ACTION	MUSCLE GROUP	DESCRIPTION
Ankle	Calf region: Soleous muscle Achilles tendon	Feet flat on the floor, legs straight, lean against a sturdy object or wall. The toes are facing directly forward, and the hips are also pressing forward so that the stretch is felt behind the lower leg at the calf. Don't arch your back.
Hip, back of legs	Hamstring	Using a sturdy object and muscles to support your balance, lean back on your heels by bending at the hips. The stretch should be felt at the back of the legs from hips to ankles.
Hip, front of legs	Gluteal and quadriceps area	Place one leg on a stool or low step at a distance of a few feet away from the rear leg. Keep both feet facing forward while you shift weight forward onto a bent knee. Stretch may be felt at the muscle above the flexed knee and at the front of the hip and behind the calf area of the rear leg.

JOINT ACTION	MUSCLE GROUP	DESCRIPTION
Hip, front of legs	Gluteal and quadriceps area	Using a sturdy support, swing one leg gently backward 10 or 12 times until you feel more limber. Repeat on the other leg.
Lateral spine	External oblique muscles (trunk)	Stand tall with feet apart as you bend sideward. Keep the body aligned as you slide one hand down the leg to a point of stretch. Hold 15 to 20 seconds and do the other side.
Elbow/Shoulder	Triceps	Stand in a comfortable position and reach behind the back with both hands. Bring the thumbs together as high up the back as possible.

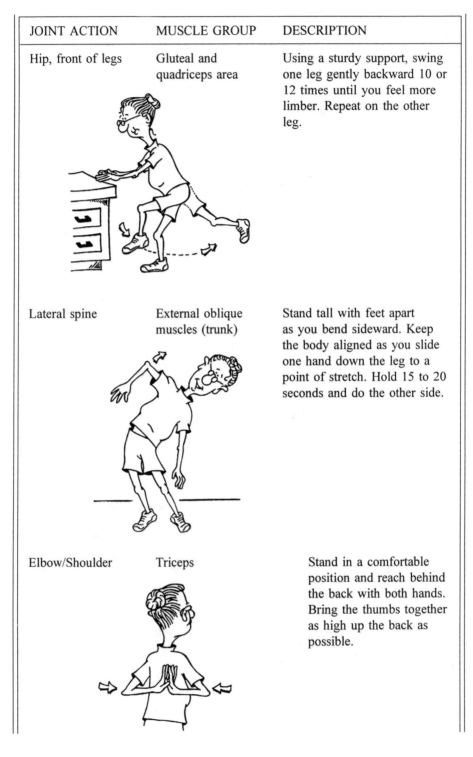

JOINT ACTION	MUSCLE GROUP	DESCRIPTION
Lower body	All leg joints	For strength and good posture, knee bends are done with a straight back, slow movement, and feet flat on the floor. Only go halfway down while you breath out and relax. Repeat about 5 times.

Over a few sessions, the initial stretching routine was expanded to include 8 to 10 minutes of mild locomotion designed to increase heart, respiration rate, and ambulatory skill (such as walking with variations such as changing stride length and rolling the foot heel to toe). This was followed by sub-maximal aerobic walking (with a heart rate (HR) of 108 beats per minute [BPM]), which was then followed by the eight stretches held for 15 to 20 seconds each. The general workout plan consisted of the warm-up stretches, aerobic walking program, aerobic cool-down, active stretching in combination with muscle strength and endurance exercises, and a general cool-down. The plan was followed for 56 training sessions over a 20-week period, three days per week starting in December 1991.

Recognizing that the trainer had a full load of other professional responsibilities, it was decided early in the training that whenever possible, Mrs. E. would be encouraged to take responsibility for her own training. Thus empowered, the client could train alone or at home whenever circumstances prevented a supervised workout.

From the outset, Dr. Burgess insisted that Mrs. E. to take control of the decisions regarding the exercise session. Mrs. E. was invited to decide for herself what the loading would be. For example, when they engaged in partner walking, Burgess took pains never to take the lead from Mrs. E. She established the pace and slowed down or stopped as needed. Similarly, intensity levels were never imposed on the exercise portion of the program. Rather, a discussion ensued as to what the day's load would be compared to other day's training. The intent was to provide as many loopholes for honorable withdrawal as possible. The whole process was laced with good humor, which seemed useful for Mrs. E. in de-escalating the sense of being pressured to perform and gave her opportunity for legitimate withdrawal on those occasions when she felt distressed.

Perhaps the greatest strategy developed by the trainer was the capacity to direct, but not load, and to praise, but not judge. The whole experience of training was characterized by an existentialism that demonstrated continually the value of just being there. Exercise loads that increased, or decreased, or were forgotten entirely, were not nearly as important as the act of showing up and being positive. Mrs. E. would say, "I'm not perfect, but I'm here."

Training Protocol

Several operating principles guided the training. These principles were important for various reasons—safety, motivation, empowerment, self-esteem, and the independence of the older participant.

1   Client control or empowerment
    The client was fully in control of the training. The trainer adopted a consultative stance in which he was advising, suggesting, encouraging, but never controlling.

2   The "show-up" principle
    From the start, it was agreed that Mrs. E would show up for training in any condition short of serious illness. Whether any training occurred after showing up was another matter. The intent was to instill a sense of urgency about maintaining continuity. "Above all, don't miss." Maintaining continuity in the face of difficulty was thought to engender a sense of personal control and efficacy. In retrospect it is of interest to note that training on those difficult days was often close to optimal.

3   Principle of gradualism
    In contrast to traditional fitness prescription, early efforts were made to determine operational work loads as opposed to upper limits. The upper limit was treated as hypothetical. The intent was to perform submaximally, systematically, and consistently.

4   Basic principles of training and conditioning
    • Adequate warm-up
      Various gentle moves were selected. These were performed without stopping but with frequent changes from muscle group to muscle group in order to achieve an adequate warm-up effect without undue fatigue. The warm-up usually occupied 10 minutes.
    • Overload
    Counseled by Dr. Burgess, Mrs. E. selected submaximal loads, which were repeated several times. As training progressed, she was asked to consider accepting one or two more repetitions of given exercise or slightly extending the distance covered in her walking. The strategy was to subdivide her maximum performance at a given task and to repeat fractions of it throughout the workout. For example, her estimated maximum of single leg tucks was 12 with each leg. In the course of a workout, she would perform 8, 6, and 4 repetitions of the exercise—an accumulation of 18 repetitions, which was 50 percent more than her original maximum.

- Rest

  "A change is as good as a rest" had application here. The intention was to maintain a submaximal loading throughout the training period. Focusing too long on any one body part would have been too tiring and would have caused discouragement. The variety of exercises seemed to be helpful in cognitively distracting Mrs. E. from what fatigue she experienced. In a very real way, Mrs. E. was impressed with the variety of movements so that she ended her workout perspiring and exhilarated. All this was conducted through a barrage of conversation to keep spirits up and to discourage comparisons and complaints. At the start of training the intensity was so low, that training occurred every day, five days a week. As the loading increased, the frequency was lowered to three training sessions a week (M/W/F), thus creating four resting days. However, some informal weekend activity was encouraged. This often was gardening in season, or active housework.

- Progression

  Keeping in mind the day to day variability of the Mrs. E.'s energy level, the intent was to help her gradually increase the number of repetitions, the intensity of performance, the length of training, and the devotion of difficulty of the individual exercises.

- Challenge

  An atmosphere of challenge was created so that Mrs. E. always felt that there was more to do *when she chose to do it*. The trainer would challenge her at strategic moments by saying: "Would you like to. . . ?", or "Do you think you could. . .?"

5   Safety, above all

All exercise tasks were determined through consultation between client and trainer. In the absence of clear medical guidelines, safety hinged on the rapport and communication between these two.

- Breathing

  Conscious control of breathing to avoid a valsalva effect was a continuing concern. All exertions were accompanied with a concerted exhalation in order to keep the glottis open. Nevertheless, Mrs. E. would become so engrossed in exercising that she would frequently hold her breath. This was a continuing concern. On the other hand, the active control of breathing might have led to a hyperventilation—this was an early concern. But in fact, hyperventilation never occurred. All exercise tasks had a counterpoint of conversation with the assumption that as long as Mrs. E. could converse, she was in a comfortable zone of aerobic training.

- Warmth

  The client was encouraged to dress warmly in the cold sub-zero weather and to wear a track suit and leg warmers while training. She tended to overheat once indoors, so training was conducted on the balcony of a ice hockey rink.

- Anatomically correct movements
  Avoidance was made of straight-legged forward bends of the trunk, deep circumduction of head, straight-legged sit-ups, ballistic movements in general, and high impact landings or locomotions.
- Maintenance and development of movement repertoire
  Because this woman was previously near obese and subsequently experienced substantial weight loss (due to health problems), there was concern that she would have to relearn previously learned patterns. More likely, the lifelong abstinence from vigorous physical activity left her with limited repertoire of movements. Indeed, early in the training, it became evident that she had lost her ability to move herself around. Movements such as getting down onto a gym mat from standing erect, sitting on the mat and changing position to lying prone or supine, or changing from prone to supine were very difficult. It was as though she had forgotten the sequence of moves. Movement changes from standing or sitting (in a chair) were familiar enough from her daily activities. Other position changes, however, were awkward and confused—looking as if they had been forgotten. One of the tasks was to relearn these position changes.

  This relearning took the form of rehearsing a movement sequence. After viewing a demonstration, Mrs. E. would perform the sequence with corrective feedback. After 48 lessons of supervised practice, Mrs. E. acquired the sequence along with the physical strength to execute the position changes with confidence.

  To foster her motor development, each training session included variations of locomotions such as walking on toes, walking flat footed, walking on heels, and, finally, walking on a gymnastic balance beam set 6 inches from the floor.

6 Challenge—"Be the Best You Can Be"
The client had to learn a basic truth about exercise for the elderly. All physical performances are relative, but within this relativity is the possibility for excellence —relative excellence. It recognizes that on a given day one may be "up" or may be "down." That these natural variations occur is immaterial to the reality of training and doing the best possible at that particular moment. In short, how you are, is how you are. "Try your best" was the advice for Mrs. E.

7 Respect for performance variability
From past experience, Dr. Burgess recognized the value of adapting each day's involvement to the varying needs of the individual. He recognized that this older woman was a unique person needing variable teaching styles and customized guidance. This principle of acknowledging variability in physical performance within an older individual, and between older adults, has important implications for exercise leaders and counsellors. For example, the day-to-day variability of an older adult can be noticeable and frustrating at times (O'Brien Cousins & Burgess, 1992).

Mrs. E. was the subject of considerable variation in general health, which was influenced by emotional and psychological considerations. Physically, there were no constants beyond her persistent participation. As a widowed older woman of 25 years duration, it was clear that she felt very much alone. Her family were living abroad and her closest son was a few thousand miles away. Her extensive circle of friends did not appear to be as attentive as in the years previous to her illness. Her work life, which had occupied her time fully, was over. The combination of these factors seriously affected her morale. Her efforts to meet expectations of friends for home entertainment, visits by grandchildren, all conspired to drain her energy. Nevertheless, Mrs. E. was devoted to the exercise program and rarely missed a training session.

In addition, some respiratory deficiency continued to appear. She would often arrive for training quite short of breath. This predicament was met with a concerted effort to help her get her breathing under control and to integrate active breathing into all exercises. We resolved this problem by making concerted breathing integral to all movements so that she felt in control. Walking was started with 3 deep exhaling breaths. Certainly this procedure assisted in combatting breathlessness but on certain days she arrived breathless and remained so. All performances would then be scaled back to what she could handle.

Mrs. E suffered from ischemic pain in the leg that had been used to supply vessels for her bypass operation. Additionally, the other leg, which had been surgically entered for the bypass, would also pain her. On a good day, she would walk 200 meters before stopping. She would then lie on a bench and raise the aching leg for two minutes. Interestingly, after 600 to 800 meters of walking, this condition would disappear to her continuing surprise and delight. On a bad day, walking would be shortened to 100 m. intervals followed by "legs-up." On these bad days, her total distance for a workout was generally 400 meters or less.

THE REINVENTION OF MRS. E.

The first 12 months of training had a profound effect on Mrs. E. Although she still remained an elderly lady with a triple bypass, she experienced a marked rehabilitation that went beyond what was available to her in the health care setting. At her first training session, she arrived with her large cane. Comforted by the presence and assistance of a personal trainer, she immediately abandoned this cane while training. This pleased her immensely. Now four years later, the cane has yet to reappear.

Her pronounced limp was gradually reduced over the next 22 sessions. The swollen right knee became less enlarged and was more the size of her left knee joint. Her stair climbing ability improved so that she could mount 12 stairs unaided. Her stair-descending ability still required a hold on the banister, but was performed with relative ease on her own. From day to day, her self-assessed blood pressure results varied but were always high (180/90).

Some improvement occurred in the active mobility of the right shoulder, which had been restricted to 40 degrees above horizontal in both vertical and lateral movements. Although some decrepitus occurred at the extremes of the range of movement, persistent activity at each session gradually improved the joint and associated tissues so that the arm could be activated to 15 degrees short of the vertical, and 5 degrees under the lateral position. Moreover, an absence of serious pain in this undertaking was an incentive in itself.

Walking distances progressively increased as well. After 56 sessions, she was able to walk 600 to 800 meters with brief interruptions for pulse monitoring at 150 meter intervals. Heart rates taken by wrist palpitation were 108 beats per minute (range was 103 to 113 bpm; 73–80 percent of maximum heart rate [MHR] at the conclusion of the walk). In the immediate post-walk period, heart rates of 114 were customary and on one occasion a 120 bpm (85% MHR) was recorded with no apparent distress. A 600-meter walk took Mrs. E about 2:30 minutes at this point.

Breathlessness was a concern at the outset of this project, and continued to be a concern. Mrs. E. was a mouth-breather and tended to hold her breath when her concentration was required or extra effort was anticipated. Efforts to have her breathing better controlled produced some improvement, but in the preoccupation of the moment, sometimes would be forgotten resulting in breathlessness.

Ischemic pain in both calf muscles also continued to be limiting factor in training loads. As soon as circulatory insufficiency in the legs appeared as evidenced by pain in the muscles (claudication), Mrs. E. was urged to ventilate more fully and more frequently. This seemed to alleviate the pain for a few minutes. Throughout the walk, she would stop at intervals and would elevate the leg on a support for about 2 minutes to assist in the shunting of blood back to the heart. After a few weeks of this, a shoulder stretching routine was designed that could accompany the leg resting routine. This caused considerable satisfaction from the perspective of spending the time efficiently.

At the 56th training session, her pace of walking had increased from intermittent (with regular stops), to a continuous pace of 1.1 meters per second. Notable too was the observation that her ischemic leg pain seemed to respond to the warm-up effect so that after about 4 minutes of walking exercise, the pain diminished markedly. This occurrence was a constant source of delight to Mrs. E. and proved to be a strong motivator. It was a tangible evidence of the ability of her muscles to compensate for muscle ischemia.

Each training session involved various position changes with an emphasis on learning an organized set of movements that helped her get to a specific position and back to a starting position. The physical effort of moving an elderly body around prevented much practice of this. Therefore each change of position was planned and cued up before execution. Over time, movements became easier; a certain sureness or confidence developed. Because most of these transition movements are a complex of agility, strength, learning, and confidence, it is difficult to credit any individual component as improving more than others. The general effect was increased efficiency of movement and a noticeable leap in confidence.

At the 30th training session, Mrs. E. was introduced to a low gymnastics balance beam. At 6 inches above the floor surface, and with one hand held for support, she traveled the beam pausing to take a breath before dismounting to the side. By week 56, she was walking the beam cautiously and assisted by a mere finger touch for reassurance. She could walk forward, pause, walk backwards a few steps, stop, and then continue on to her dismount.

The balance beam was more an expression of competence and general body control than any other exercise. However, too little time was spent on the beam for large scale improvements to occur. Rather, the activity could be construed to be reducing the likelihood of experiencing a fall. The challenge was real, the task intriguing, and the likelihood of success was high. As a motivator, this activity was powerful and far outweighed the small extra risk incurred.

At the outset, Mrs. E. was timorous but anxious to take some action about her declining vitality. It was significant to observe the return her confidence as her fitness improved. Early in her program she would sit passively in the training office, waiting for her trainer to arrive for the workout. Later in the program, as her physical condition improved, she would pace around impatiently until she could pointedly tease him for tardiness.

After the bypass operation, Mrs. E. had largely disengaged from her extensive social life. After several months of training, and as her vitality improved, she began to accept social engagements again and even to entertain guests in her own home. Flashes of her earlier assertiveness appeared in her conversation. She seemed to have recaptured important elements of herself and began to manifest personality traits common to her younger years. The training was transforming Mrs. E.

DISCUSSION

Enhancing prospects for independence among frail elderly may lead to economic benefits for society at large (Pelletier, 1993). Strained health care budgets simply cannot afford to shelter older people who have gotten out of the habit of moving for themselves, or have been weakened by recent illness. Active forms of recreation in the community setting appear to be necessary to promote the physical abilities of older adults once hospital discharge has occurred and rehabilitation has terminated. Although some would doubt the ability of frail older people to commit to exercise as a survival resource, some elderly women in their 90s are known to be listening to their medical directives and following a daily exercise regime, on their own bed at home, if necessary (O'Brien Cousins & Vertinsky, 1995).

Armed with more information about the enormous benefits of late-life exercise, elderly people and supportive health professionals may try to solve or reduce late-life health problems with increased physical activity. Besides the recovery of Mrs. E., other evidence exists to support of the notion that older people with health problems become motivated enough to take up exercise. For example, a recent study found that women over the age of 70 who were taking four or more medications were as physically active as women who reported no medication and excellent health (O'Brien Cousins, 1993). This finding suggests that people who encounter multiple health problems feel susceptible enough to an early demise that they may turn to exercise to try to gain better control over their health and longevity. Once physical activity takes place, these individuals may then recognize the significant personal benefits to be acquired.

Clearly older people who are discharged from hospital into the community setting are not fully healed. They are discharged when risks of serious complications are passed, but there is still a long road of recovery ahead. Full recovery, let alone the advancement of fitness and health of individuals, has traditionally been beyond the scope of current medical care. Unless an infinite period of physical therapy is prescribed, the older adult can normally expect to stay this course of inadequate recovery alone. At present there is no referral system in place to promote the fitness status of older people within their communities. Furthermore, it is not clear that the medical community is prepared to provide the encouragement or formal exercise prescription that would ensure reconditioning in the community setting.

Many older adults claim that they do not know if their primary care physician holds an opinion regarding physical activity in late life (Branigan & O'Brien Cousins, 1995). Because so few physicians enquire about the exercise habits and preferences of their older clients, it is not surprising that this omission and apparent disinterest is construed by older people as an indicator of the irrelevance of exercise as an important health behavior. When active seniors mention their physical activities to their doctor, they are usually encouraged to continue doing whatever they are doing. Apparently physicians generally understand the benefits of exercise, and thus the explanation for their lack of direct involvement must be that they have too little office time to deal with it, or they feel ill-equipped to counsel or prescribe for exercise. However, medical practitioners may need to be more aware 1) of the important role they play in providing advocacy and prescription for safe forms of physical activity, and 2) that some elderly are likely to resort to unmanaged and unprescribed exercise if they sense a lack of direction and or knowledge by the supervising physician. A community directory of older adult exercise programs can be easily assembled and maintained in the waiting rooms of physicians (Johnston, 1997). Instead of nurse-managed activity, active recreation and physical activity in communities may be the most cost-effective and socially empowering course of action. Thus the issue arising from the health promotion perspective, is how much involvement in health promotion are geriatric care providers required to undertake? Does walking really have to be a "nurse-managed" activity? These issues were raised when the opportunity arose to support the health improvement needs of an 80-year-old sedentary woman who called on a fitness professional for assistance.

Although the merits of regular exercise are now well-identified for older adults, little attention has been paid to the risks and challenges facing the elderly who are experiencing multiple and serious health difficulties. Do the benefits still outweigh the risks? This chapter highlights the situation of a woman in her 80th year as an example of the mutual challenges facing medical practitioners, community health promotion professionals, and seniors themselves. After five years of active living, interspersed with several relapses, Mrs. E. was still far ahead of where she was at the start of her training. Now deceased, Mrs. E. continued her training and enjoyed a high quality of life to her final days.

Such an undertaking requires an enormous time commitment and expertise on the part of the exercise supervisor. Further, current health systems do not provide financial support to assist the physical activity professional who is willing to oversee the fitness activities of the frail individual.

On the positive side, short-term outcomes suggest that a regular, gentle movement program is not only possible and helpful to the continued mobility of the frail elderly adult, but that physical movement is key to independence and the survival of the spirit. When health care professionals withdraw support and interest for daily activity in the elderly, all hope of recovery and healing may be lost.

SUMMARY

This case study reviews one methodology for progressive training of a frail older woman. In 18 months, Mrs. E. progressed from slow walking 200 meters with a cane to striding 1000 meters with several stops to deal with leg pain. She improved her flexibility. Her balance and agility was substantially improved—to the point where she could walk a 20-foot-long low-level gymnastics balance beam.

Her progress through the training was not steady. She improved in fits and starts. After the study period reported here, she regressed when she became ill, but returned to train after three months away and soon recaptured her previous training highs. The reality for Mrs. E. was that her exercise continued to cycle between illness and healing, rest and exercise. Most important in this process was the reemergence of her original self. The shock of her heart attack and the accumulated debilitation reduced her to a timorous elderly woman. As she became more fit, the younger Mrs. E. emerged. Through exercise, Mrs. E. reinvented herself.

This chapter highlights the challenges facing us all as we get older and provides an example of the importance of collaborative efforts between physicians and exercise practitioners. The case study presented here illustrates some of the strategies that may be useful in assisting motivated, independent, but frail, older adults. The issue that remains is not whether such interventions are feasible and beneficial; the question is whether such expertise can be made available to the frail public in the current health care economy, and whether many of today's elderly will exhibit the courage and commitment to undertake such enormous responsibility for their own health and well-being.

Chapter 8

Survival Skills for Independent Living

PHYSICAL ACTIVITY: A SURVIVAL RESOURCE

Consensus has formed that some exercise is better than none, and the more physical activity the better. "Every U.S. adult should accumulate 30 minutes or more of moderate-intensity physical activity on most, preferable all, days of the week" (Pate et al., 1995). The U.S. Surgeon General reported that 1996 was "a national call to action" that invited even active adults to "pick up the pace" (U.S. Department of Health and Human Services, 1996). The key to survival in old age appears to be *regular* physical activity—not just for quantity of life, but also for quality of life.

Death rates in sedentary individuals are approximately twice as high as those of physically active persons (Mummery, 1995). For example, individuals climbing 36 or more flights of stairs in the normal course of a week had a 28 percent lower relative risk of death from cardiovascular disease than individuals not using stairs. Some scientists believe that a 30-minute walk per day is just as effective to health even if it is broken up into three ten-minute walks (Blair, Kohl, Gordon, & Paffenbarger, 1992). Other researchers favor an uninterrupted aerobic effort. Blair and colleagues (1989) have suggested that a brisk 30- to 60-minute walk every day can achieve adequate fitness to delay all-cause mortality.

In terms of quality of life, the evidence is rapidly accumulating that moderate levels of physical activity moderates the effects of stress, enhances other healthy behaviors such as choosing foods with good nutrition, reduces or eliminates the need for medications, tends to replace alcoholism as a coping behavior, and leads to more positive behaviors in other areas of life (O'Brien Cousins & Vertinsky, 1995).

Such positive health effects are not only advantageous to the individual but also are predicted to have a substantial impact on medical treatment costs. A doubling in the percentage of North Americans who were physically active in 1981 would have led to a yearly reduction of about $350 million in Canada and several billion dollars in the United States for the treatment costs of ischemic heart disease alone (*CAHPER Journal*, 1994). A retrospective longitudinal study by Shephard and Montelpare (1988) found a significant relationship between physical activity at age 50 and current level of disability as a senior citizen. A gradient of activity level was found with the most active adults reporting no disability and progressively lower levels of physical activity were linked to minor and institutionalized levels of disability.

The health promotion evidence for exercise is so strong that the Heart and Stroke Foundations in both Canada and the United States have recently added physical *inactivity* as a major modifiable risk factor as severe as smoking, high blood pressure, and high cholesterol (Olshansky, Carnes, & Cassel, 1993; Pemberton & McSwegin, 1993). In terms of social significance, sedentary living may be an even more important risk factor than smoking since almost twice the population (60% vs. 30%) are inadequately active versus smoking. An inactive lifestyle increases a person's risk of many other chronic ailments including hypertension, high cholesterol, stroke, cancer, diabetes, osteoporosis, osteoarthritis, and depression (U.S. Department of Health and Human Services, 1996). An active lifestyle is so essential to health that one can imagine a day may come when casual stretching and conditioning exercise becomes in vogue in the very public places where smoking is now banned.

The goals of this chapter are to:

- Provide a comprehensive tool for assessing weekly physical activity.
- Identify a number of strategies for obtaining a more active lifestyle.
- Identify who needs supervised exercise.
- Comment on "contraindicated" exercises.
- Present the fundamental movement needs of the aging body, and movements that can be done safely without supervision.

ASSESSING PHYSICAL ACTIVITY

Physical activity can be considered to be fitness and health-enhancing if the Frequency, Intensity, Type of Exercise, and Time (duration) is adequate. These four exercise attributes are easily recalled as F.I.T.T. The recommended *exercise prescription* for adults is 20 to 30 minutes of exercise, at least three days per week (Orban, 1994). However, there is much debate on having a standard prescription especially for older adults. There is general consensus that a weekly energy expenditure of 2,000 kcal on leisure time physical activity is required for men for a positive influence on all-cause mortality (Paffenbarger, Hyde, Wing, & Hsied, 1986). For older people, and women in particular, little is known about the optimal frequency, intensity, or duration that would lead them to reap significant health benefits. If one is to accomplish

2,000 kcal in leisure time physical activity in a one week period, one must do a volume of 650 kcal of work in 30 minutes or less. This is simply an impossible goal for the majority of older adults (Orban, 1994). Other scientists advocate a daily walk, up to one hour, at about 50 percent of maximum walking speed as valuable to health risk reduction (Bouchard, Shephard, & Stephens, 1994). Other locomotor activities (cycling, cross-country skiing, snow-shoeing) carried out 4 times a week for one hour a session would also be significant to health (Bouchard, Shephard, & Stephens, 1994). For strength activity, alternate day training is recommended, while flexibility training can be, and should be, undertaken daily or twice daily to maintain ease of movement and relaxation.

The type of physical activity suitable for older people varies as widely as the individuals. But moderate aerobic activities such as walking, gardening, dancing, rowing, skating, hiking, slow cycling, doubles tennis, and stair climbing are highly recommended. More vigorous activities such as jogging, nonstop swimming, fast cycling, cross-country skiing, soccer, racket sports, basketball, aerobic dance, and running are excellent fitness activities, but only a few older adults appear to enjoy this intensity of activity. For older people, even milder activities such as badminton, croquet, lawn bowling, table tennis, and shuffleboard are considered to be worthwhile by the American Heart Association (Fletcher, Blair, & Blumenthal, 1994).

The heterogeneity of the elderly and their diverse activity needs and interests poses a challenge for the accurate and easy assessment of the activity component of their lifestyles. LaPorte and colleagues claimed that:

> More than 30 different methods have been used to assess physical activity. Calorimetry, mechanical and electrical monitors, and dietary measures, while precise, tend to be impractical on a population basis. No single instrument fulfils the criteria of being valid, reliable and practical although not affecting behavior. Surveys are the most practical approach in large-scale studies, although little is known about their reliability and validity (LaPorte, Montoye, & Casperson, 1985).

With this kind of measurement challenge, research has provided programmers little information about the *types* of activities chosen by seniors, and little about the frequency, duration, and chosen intensity level of their activities. Without this information, physicians, programmers, and exercise leaders will have difficulty motivating and addressing the interests of older adults. However, scientists have amply demonstrated that brief, low-cost physical activity estimates are well-served by simple questions about the number of sweat episodes experienced in the past week. While questions about physical activity are significantly related (correlation $r = .4$ to $.5$) with *direct* measures of oxygen uptake, they appear to be measuring a more narrow level of exercise. Moreover, the simple single-sentence questions do not solve some important questions about adult exercise.

To start off this chapter, the utility and limitations of a new instrument to assess the physical activity levels of older adults are presented. The "Older Adult–Exercise Status Inventory" is a seven-day self-report that can be completed by older in a matter of minutes (O'Brien Cousins, 1997a). For adults who have poor vision, or are frail in other respects, the OA-ESI can be administered by an interviewer.

The OA-ESI represents the weekly work and leisure time physical activities of older men and women in Canada and the United States. Having a list of activities enhances recall. The seven-day recall is considered to be suitable because it does not surpass the recall ability of most adults. The seven-day inventory provides a good deal of detailed information in that it assesses the duration, frequency, and level of intensity of types of activities popular among older adults. The design brings together the positive features of a number of instruments used in prominent epidemiological research (Blair, 1984; Canada Fitness Survey, 1983; Paffenbarger, Hyde, Wing, & Hsied, 1986; Taylor, Jacobs, Schucker, Kinedsen, Leon, & Debacker, 1978). In general, the OA-ESI compromises the brevity of the single question for the detailed information that we need about older adults.

The two-page inventory prompts subjects with categories organized in columns by the seven days of the week, and organized in rows with a list of 5 work categories and 37 optional or leisure time physical activities considered to be age-appropriate since they are based on the observed activities currently available for many older people in urban and rural communities across North America. Open categories called "other" capture novel activities that are not already on the list. These activity categories act as memory prompts; they are listed alphabetically from "aerobic fitness class" to "walking."

To reduce error in estimating intensity, aquatic exercise (aquacise) activity is subdivided into "vigorous" and "gentle," while cycling, gardening, jogging, and walking are subdivided into "sweat-inducing" and "no sweating." Precision is added by asking the respondent to report in minutes (rather than in hours) for each activity on each day.

The total amount of exercise in the past week, or current activity level (kcal) was calculated using metabolic charts giving MET units for physical activity with the MET being an *estimate* of the ratio of exercise metabolic rate to a resting metabolic rate (Cantu, 1980; Passmore & Durnin, 1955; Taylor, Jacobs, Schucker, Kinedsen, Leon, & Debacker, 1978; Wilson, Paffenbarger, Morris, & Havlik, 1986). Paffenbarger has recommended that a 60 kg body weight not be assumed, but rather the individual's actual body weight built into the calculation. Thus exercise status is the sum of weekly hours of each activity multiplied by the appropriate MET unit and multiplied by body weight in kilograms (kg). However, in my own research on 327 women over the age of 70, adjustments for individual body weight did not significantly alter the kilocalorie estimates for total exercise; the relationship between the two measures was $r = .97$.

How to Use the OA-ESI

A shortcut method is used whereby the MET unit is multiplied by the total weekly minutes reported for each row (activity). For example, to estimate the total weekly energy spent on walking or strolling slowly, we sum the number of minutes spent on this activity as accumulated over the seven days, and then multiply minutes times the MET unit for that activity.

	Slow Walking Calculation	
	Mon. Tues. Wed. Thur. Fri. Sat. Sun.	MET × minutes
Slow walking (min.)	_____ 15 5 _____ 40 15 ___	3 × 75 = 225 kcal

A weekly total can be summed for each row and then all the rows summed for the weekly kilocalorie total. The shortcut method assumes a standard weight of 60 kg.

For a sum of all the low-intensity activities (MILDCAL), add together all the scores for activities that are rated under 4 METs. For a sum of all the moderate (MODCAL) activities, add all the scores for activities between 4.0 and 5.9 METs. For a sum of the vigorous activities (VIGCAL), add activities rated at 6 or more METs together. The final weekly total is the sum of MILDCAL, MODCAL, and VIGCAL. The weekly total can range widely; in the leisure time category, women over age 70 ranged from 0 to 11,000 kcal in the Vancouver study. The mean energy expended on weekly leisure time exercise was about 1200 kcal.

Reliability of the OA-ESI

As a test of reliability (the ability of the respondents to reproduce the same scores after some time has gone by), the OA-ESI was administered twice in a four-week period to an active sample of 17 Edmonton women aged 58 to 80 (mean age of 68). Of the three activity categories assessed (mild, moderate, and vigorous), MILDCAL demonstrated poor reproducibility ($r = -.114$, not significant; there is little resemblance between the two scores. They appear to be unrelated and likely occurred by chance), MODCAL was reported more consistently at $r = .756$, $p < .001$ (significant relationship because 57 percent of the scores are alike and such an occurrence would be found by chance only one time in a thousand), while VIGCAL was .505, $p < .05$ (significant relationship; 26 percent of the scores are alike and this would be found by chance only 5 times in 100).

A second study involved a coed sample of 29 adults aged 65 to 90 (mean age of 71). The 22 women and 7 men reported on two different weeks of activity spaced by one week apart. In the second study, the two weekly exercise scores, unadjusted for body weight, were correlated $r = .771$, significant at the .001 probability level. In comparison, Paffenbarger's Physical Activity Index (PAI) produced a reliability coefficient of .73.

Ironically, the low coefficients for mild and vigorous exercise provide support for construct validity in the first study. The pilot study began in late summer followed by a second assessment four weeks later. In the interim, the seniors began their gymnastics season, resuming their vigorous involvement in U of Agers Gymnastics program at the University. In taking up this challenging exercise program, they apparently forfeited some of their less structured and milder summer activity. Although the reproducibility study of the OA-ESI was undermined, the seasonal shift in activity patterns lends support to the sensitivity and ultimately the construct validity of the instrument.

Validity of the OA-ESI

An assessment tool should have construct validity, predictive validity, and concurrent validity if it is to serve a variety of measurement purposes. Although the OA-ESI integrated the features of previously validated instruments (seven-day recall format, checklist, time in minutes) and therefore had some degree of assumed validity, other forms of validity were important to examine. Because alternative assessments for validating work activity in and around the home were not available, the validation study included only the leisure time aspect of the OA-ESI. The data here were derived from survey findings on 327 women with an average age of 77 (O'Brien Cousins, 1993, 1997a).

Predictive validity was demonstrated in the strength of the statistical relationships between *current activity level,* or *CAL,* and a number of psychological constructs with known or hypothesized relationships that were assessed at the same time. Weekly leisure time CAL, as assessed by the OA-ESI, was significantly and positively associated with beliefs about *Self-Efficacy* to participate in six fitness activities ($r = .324$, $p < .0001$), with perceptions about *Social Support* to exercise from family, friends, and physician ($r = .333$, $p < .01$), and negatively with beliefs about personal risks related to exercise ($r = -.185$, $p < .01$). These findings make theoretical sense: previous research acknowledges that exercise activity is lower in older individuals and in those with poorer health. In this study, CAL supported these hypothesized relationships with an $r = -.257$, $p < .0001$ with increasing age, and $r = .222$, $p < .0001$ with a favorable health rating. These statistical relationships with various psychological measures provide further support for the scientific capabilities of the OA-ESI.

Concurrent validity was demonstrated by examining the correlations of weekly exercise with other previously validated activity indicators in the same study. For example CAL was strongly associated ($r = .450$, $p < .01$) with a subjective question about lifelong activity involvement in physical activity similar to the question used by Godin and colleagues (1987). Their question was worded "How would you describe your physical fitness activity over your entire life course?" The five response choices ranged from "I have never been much involved" to "I have always been involved." Concurrent validity was also found with a separate assessment of the number of active days reported per week ($r = .491$, $p < .001$).

A question from Gaston Godin's (1982) unpublished survey instrument asked, "How often did you participate in vigorous physical activities *long enough to get sweaty* within the past 4 months?" With this single question, CAL showed a relationship of $.411$, $p < .0001$. In summary, the OA-ESI is significantly related to other more simple assessments already used in the field, but the substantial detail of the OA-ESI makes it unlikely that relationships above .45 to .50 will be found with crude measures of physical activity.

The participation patterns of the 327 Vancouver women are similar to that described in other studies, however, as volunteers, they were better educated and somewhat more active than expected. Still, only about one third of the women were exercising at an optimal level. CAL also had significant associations with the number of PARQ symptoms reported (people with poorer health did less activity). Concurrent validity was demonstrated by examining the correlations of estimated kilocalories spent on exercise (CAL) with other activity indicators on the same survey. For example, significant associations were found with life-long activity status (people reporting recent involvement, or lifelong involvement, were currently more active), and with number of sweat episodes in the past four months. People reporting more sweat episodes on one scale also reported more overall activity on the other scale. As expected, vigorous exercise in the OA-ESI held the strongest association with estimated sweat episodes.

The OA-ESI documents a number of descriptive details. For example, it is immediately clear the types of exercise that are most prevalent in each individual. In terms of mild exercise (<4 METS), walking is usually predominant. The most frequent response to moderate and vigorous activities is no response, suggesting that only a minority of older people are active at this intensity. Conclusion: The OA-ESI appears to be a sensitive, reliable, and valid instrument to assess broad activity patterns of large populations of older adults. The inventory provides a great deal of detail about the nature and scope of elderly physical activity. The assessment has limitations however. It provides indirect measurement of energy spent on exercise, and is merely an estimate. The individual reporting error of a seven-day recall is not specifically known for older adults. Further work with the instrument may indicate that there is utility in dropping the mild activities altogether in the calculations. More detailed information on the OA-ESI is published in the *Journal of Sport Behavior*.

Older Adult–Exercise Status Inventory (OA–ESI)
OA–ESI

Instructions: Did you do any of these physical activities in the past week? If so, HOW MUCH TIME IN MINUTES did you spend on each occasion? Add your own activities at the end if they are not listed here.

WORK ACTIVITIES in the past week
Time spent in MINUTES on each occasion

	Mon.	Tues.	Wed.	Thurs.	Fri.	Sat.	Sun.	(For office use only) MET × MINUTES
Work in the home (sweaty)	___	___	___	___	___	___	___	5.5 ___
Work in the home (light)	___	___	___	___	___	___	___	3.0 ___
Outdoor work (sweaty)	___	___	___	___	___	___	___	6.0 ___
Outdoor work (light)	___	___	___	___	___	___	___	3.0 ___
Other _____	___	___	___	___	___	___	___	___
LEISURE ACTIVITIES								
Aerobic fitness class	___	___	___	___	___	___	___	6.0 ___
Aquacize class	___	___	___	___	___	___	___	6.0 ___
Badminton	___	___	___	___	___	___	___	5.5 ___

LEISURE ACTIVITIES (*Cont.*)

Time spent in MINUTES on each occasion

	Mon.	Tues.	Wed.	Thurs.	Fri.	Sat.	Sun.	(For office use only) MET × MINUTES
Bicycling outdoors (sweaty)	___	___	___	___	___	___	___	6.0 ___
Bicycling outdoors (light)	___	___	___	___	___	___	___	5.5 ___
Bicycling indoors (sweaty)	___	___	___	___	___	___	___	6.0 ___
Bicycling indoors (light)	___	___	___	___	___	___	___	5.5 ___
Bowling (5 Pin)	___	___	___	___	___	___	___	3.0 ___
Bowling (Lawn)	___	___	___	___	___	___	___	3.0 ___
Bowling (Carpet)	___	___	___	___	___	___	___	3.0 ___
Calisthenics	___	___	___	___	___	___	___	4.5 ___
Canoeing or kayaking	___	___	___	___	___	___	___	3.0 ___
Curling	___	___	___	___	___	___	___	3.0 ___
Dancing (Square/Tap/Folk)	___	___	___	___	___	___	___	6.0 ___
Dancing (Ballroom/Ballet)	___	___	___	___	___	___	___	5.0 ___
Dancing (line, Hawaiian)	___	___	___	___	___	___	___	4.0 ___
Darts	___	___	___	___	___	___	___	2.5 ___
Golf	___	___	___	___	___	___	___	3.5 ___
Gymnastics, Rhythmics	___	___	___	___	___	___	___	6.0 ___
Hiking hilly terrain	___	___	___	___	___	___	___	8.0 ___
Horseshoes	___	___	___	___	___	___	___	3.0 ___
Jogging (warmth inducing)	___	___	___	___	___	___	___	10.0 ___
Jogging (sweat inducing)	___	___	___	___	___	___	___	12.0 ___
Rebounding (mini-tramp)	___	___	___	___	___	___	___	10.0 ___
Rope skipping	___	___	___	___	___	___	___	12.0 ___
Rowing (machine or boat)	___	___	___	___	___	___	___	8.0 ___
Skating (ice or roller)	___	___	___	___	___	___	___	6.0 ___
Stair climbing (continuous)	___	___	___	___	___	___	___	8.0 ___

LEISURE ACTIVITIES (*Cont.*)

Time spent in MINUTES on each occasion

	Mon.	Tues.	Wed.	Thurs.	Fri.	Sat.	Sun.	(For office use only) MET × MINUTES
Stretching	___	___	___	___	___	___	___	3.0 ___
Swimming (gentle)	___	___	___	___	___	___	___	7.0 ___
Swimming (nonstop)	___	___	___	___	___	___	___	10.0 ___
Table tennis (ping pong)	___	___	___	___	___	___	___	4.0 ___
Tai Chi	___	___	___	___	___	___	___	3.0 ___
Tennis	___	___	___	___	___	___	___	6.0 ___
Walking (slow strolling)	___	___	___	___	___	___	___	3.0 ___
Walking (warmth inducing)	___	___	___	___	___	___	___	4.0 ___
Walking (race or speed)	___	___	___	___	___	___	___	5.0 ___
Other	___	___	___	___	___	___	___	___
Other	___	___	___	___	___	___	___	___

THANK YOU VERY MUCH FOR COMPLETING THIS SURVEY. (FOR OFFICE USE ONLY)

Calculate weekly work and leisure totals separately.

Sum of MILDCAL (<4 MET activities)   = _____ kcal

Sum of MODCAL (4 to 5.9 MET activities)   = _____ kcal

Sum of VIGCAL (6+ MET activities)   = _____ kcal

TOTAL Current Activity Level (CAL)   = _____ kcal

STRATEGIES FOR ENJOYING A MORE ACTIVE LIFESTYLE

Active Living Is Innovative Living

Individuals who are older can incorporate physical activity into their daily routine if they utilize the concept of active living (Novak, 1994). By definition, active living encompasses leisure time physical activity, exercise, sports, occupational labor, gardening, and physical chores and hobbies such as house-cleaning and home construction. Active living acknowledges that any body movement that results in an increase in energy expenditure is relevant to health (Bouchard, Shephard, & Stephens, 1994). Everything from organized sport involvement to unplanned and spontaneous activities count. The goal is to stay nimble and strong for as long as is possible. As people get older, active living is ideally participated in every day.

According to Orban (1994), optimal active living ought to include vigorous physical challenges throughout the day. In this way, reserve energy capacity of the body adapts to the physical demands imposed on it. Building active living into one's routine takes some creative planning, but spontaneous ideas would work as well. For example, a stint of walking could be incorporated by picking up a bus at the stop further down the road, by parking your car a few blocks from your destination, by taking the stairs rather than an elevator, by adding a lap or two around the mall on a shopping trip, or pursuing a light errand on foot instead of by car.

People can look for ways to challenge their strength, endurance, mobility, and agility rather than avoiding such situations as they get older. This strategy for health promotion means that older women might choose not to defer the tasks requiring upper body strength to men. Carrying heavier objects and finding ways to open jars helps women to maintain strength and stimulates bones to absorb calcium. Similarly, men need to seek ways to maintain joint suppleness, balance, and dexterity. Perhaps supervised men could benefit by taking up activities (such as yoga) that make a point of enhancing flexibility. A variety of stretches done in the easy chair during T.V. commercials may be another solution. After-dinner walks for people of all ages are certainly appropriate. A single woman can take the neighbor's dog with her if she needs a companion.

Patrick and colleagues (1994) have provided a tool for physicians who are interested in encouraging activity for their patients called PACE (Physician-Based Assessment and Counseling for Exercise). In their instrument, they report 11 physical activity levels ranging from the precontemplator stage to the active stage.

PACE Activity Levels

Precontemplator Stage

1 I do not exercise or walk regularly now, and I do not intend to start in the near future.

Contemplator Stage

2 I do not exercise or walk regularly, but I have been thinking of starting.
3 I am trying to start exercise or walk.
4 I have exercised or walked infrequently for more than one month.

Active Stage

5 I am doing vigorous or moderate exercise less than 3 times a week.
6 I have been doing moderate exercise 3 or more times a week for the last 6 months.
7 I have been doing moderate exercise 3 or more times a week for 7 months or more.
8 I have been doing vigorous exercise 3 to 5 times a week for 1 to 6 months.
9 I have been doing vigorous exercise 3 to 5 times a week for 7 to 12 months.
10 I have been doing vigorous exercise 3 to 5 times a week for more than 12 months.
11 I do vigorous exercise 6 or more times a week.

In addition to the activity level list, Patrick and colleagues (1994) suggested that people need to select activities that they enjoy, that they know are available to them in their communities, than can fit time-wise in their day, can be increased in duration if necessary, and will be encouraged by someone who will support the activity or act as a companion.

WHO IS EXCUSED FROM BEING ACTIVE?

No one. Many people will excuse themselves from active living because they feel dizzy, need a cane, use a walker, or spend most of the time in a wheelchair. But none of these situations require a person to cease exercise. Getting old has its challenges, but some problems are only temporary and worse problems can be avoided for those who return to physical activity after a temporary setback. Rather than acting as excuses, the crutches, canes, walkers, and wheelchairs are actually *aids* to active living. Wheeling a wheelchair around is a health-promoting physical task, as is using a walker in which the arms assist the legs. Individuals who are physically limited are ironically in an excellent position to take advantage of this challenge. By thinking of canes and wheelchairs as aids to more active living, they become enablers of a more active lifestyle that ultimately can lead some people to independence from these aids (see Mrs. E. in Chapter 7).

Furthermore, many excellent exercises can be done while sitting in a chair and lying in a bed. If severe illness strikes, the days of inactivity can be severely weakening, and people must temporarily forego their habitual activities. The challenge is for individuals to gradually work back to their active living patterns. Without this persistence to be a moving, active individual, the downward spiral of illness becomes more difficult to reverse. Muscle weakness sets in, joints get stiffer and stiffer, balance declines, physical confidence is undermined, and it is a short road from there to increasing frailty, serious falls, and fractures.

The negative outcomes of prolonged bed rest are as serious as the outcomes of prolonged malnutrition. Deprivation of movement is another form of starvation whereby the body becomes severely weakened. Fasting one's body from food is a serious decision that invites public health intervention, but fasting the body of daily physical movement is also a health insult. However, inactivity as a type of body neglect is socially acceptable and occurs all the time with little concern by anyone. The time has come to rethink health behavior. If we are what we eat, then we also are what we do. As people get older, they need to keep moving in whatever way they can. This should be the main survival tactic in old age.

SUPERVISED EXERCISE: WHO NEEDS IT?

Referring to older adult recreation, a statement from the American Heart Association advocates a number of low-intensity physical activities that are informal and unsupervised activities.

Low intensity leisure activities like walking, golf, badminton, croquet, shuffleboard, lawn bowling, and ping pong are recommended for the elderly (Fletcher, Blair, & Blumenthal, 1994).

For the majority of older people, supervised exercise programs need not replace the informal recreational opportunities available to them in everyday life such as walking and gardening. But few adults get adequate variety of movement in informal settings and many older people like to join exercise classes for the camaraderie and fun associated with being with other seniors. Although there are many physical activities that older people can do alone in the privacy and convenience of their own homes (see "At Home Exercises" later in the chapter), a minority of individuals may need support when they are exercising. The individuals who most need guidance and encouragement in the exercise setting are:

- older people lacking knowledge about what to do
- cardiac patients who need to be monitored
- unmotivated people who have a medical condition
- frail elderly who are risk of falling
- cognitively impaired elderly

The American Heart Association stated that, "careful isometric training alone or with aerobic training is generally safe and effective in patients with cardiovascular disease who are medically stable and are in a supervised program" (Fletcher, Blair, & Blumenthal, 1994).

Supervised versus Unsupervised Exercise

One difficulty facing health promotion professionals is the determination of who is at risk of being physically active on their own. At first, it is tempting to consider the frail and very aged adults to be the highest risk group. But some might argue that the frail are at very little risk when they are doing simple stretches while seated and strengthening exercises within their capabilities. Frail adults are unlikely to take the initiative to push themselves to dangerously high intensities. Indeed it is a matter of course that some people in their 90s are already doing gentle exercises in their private lodgings every morning before rising out of bed (O'Brien & Vertinsky, 1995).

The more likely at-risk person is the previously athletic older adult who is familiar with rigorous training from years back. Physical educators sometimes encounter these highly capable, but out-of-condition athletes who can be at risk of overextending themselves because they know what to do and are impatient about progressing in a slower fashion (O'Brien Cousins & Burgess, 1992).

Several studies allude to a quite high-injury rate among older athletes, but there is also evidence that injury is not a concern in most older adult fitness programs. Certainly more information is needed, but for guidance at this point in time, a supervised exercise program is warranted if the older individual:

1 is motivated to exercise but does not like exercising alone;
2 has a concern about their health problems;
3 can do most of the activities of the group program being considered;
4 is likely to overexert or underexert themselves without proper guidance;
5 enjoys the social camaraderie of group exercise.

Supervised exercise can also occur under the care of a physical therapist depending on affordability of private assistance. In Canada, a basic but cost-limited therapy service is offered under health care. After 12 or so sessions, individuals must pay a fee (about $35.00) for each therapy session. Older people who can afford unfunded therapy may opt to hire a fitness professional to come to their home so that they can be supervised in the comfort and convenience of their own home. The downside to this latter strategy is that the social interaction of group exercise is lacking.

CONTRAINDICATED EXERCISE: WHERE IS THE RESEARCH?

A number of exercises, or at least certain body positions, are considered inadvisable or "contraindicated" (see examples in text box). What is confusing about this term is that some fitness professionals consider these positions to be highly dangerous. Obviously certain physical movements, under certain conditions or in certain settings, are judged to be risky for some individuals. What is frustrating about contraindicated movements is that we have no clear idea about what the injury rates actually are, and exactly who is at risk with these movements. Does one person get injured for every five people who do this movement one time? Or is the risk of injury 1 in 1,000 movements? One injury in 10,000 movements? Are high-fit adults at the same risk as low-fit adults? Are the risks the same for men and women? Are the risks the same for older adults? Are newcomers in the same risk bracket as people who have been doing this activity since childhood? Who is reporting injury rates and who is deciding what makes a movement contraindicated? If there are exercise risk studies, where are they being published?

Which exercises are contraindicated?

Exercises that put most of the body weight on the chest
Exercises with the chest lower than the torso
Straight-legged toe touch
Back lying with toes over the head to the floor
The hurdler's stretch (hard on the knee)
Tipping the head back to full extension
Jerky, percussive movements in general
Failing to stop or reduce activity at the point of breathlessness

---

The Dilemma Avoiding all contraindicated exercise can undermine an older adult's pursuit of some sport activities that are more health-enhancing than risk-taking. An example of the dilemma in adopting universal standards prohibiting contra-indicated movements is the gymnastics program at the University of Alberta. The U of Agers are a gymnastics club of 30 men and women who train two to five days per week in artistic and rhythmic gymnastics. The club has novice and advanced partici-pants, a few of whom have been training for many years. The difficulty of some of the skills suggests that these individuals may be at risk. But apparently they are not, for they have worked and played and laughed their way to fitness in the gymnastics center since 1986, and not a single major injury has occurred.

Even minor injuries, like bruises and scrapes are rare. For example, Stan Dyer, born in 1921, hops into a handstand whenever he feels like it. The physical and psychological benefits are highly apparent—but that is not to say that fitness exercise kept him risk-free of disease. Rather, the regular demands of training gave Stan Dyer an advantage in the early detection of heart disease. In 1988, while running his two-mile warm-up, Stan would notice a pain deep in his throat. This pain increased over the months until running was impossible and he had to consult a physician. The first consultation resulted in a prescription for antibiotics. The pain persisted. The second physician immediately diagnosed coronary heart disease and scheduled angioplasty. This preliminary procedure led to haemorrhage complications and open-heart surgery. The several physicians assigned to his case were amazed that he survived the four open-heart operations that he underwent in a week-long struggle for his life. The medical team attributed his survival of the ordeal to his initial physical stamina devel-oped for gymnastics. Incredibly, one year later, he had slowly worked himself back into condition again, claiming that he was "90 percent of where I was before the surgery" and now a few years later, he is back to running on the varsity track again with college kids 55 years younger.

Given that so little specific information is actually documented on what people are actually risking by participating in the more exciting and adventurous sports, it is impossible to know what to advise older adults and their leaders. The benefits of adrenalin-rushing activities are that they hold high rewards for those that love to do them. At best, the real risks are unknown. The fact that seniors of all sizes, shapes, and experience levels can do gymnastics year in and year out leads one to question the contraindicated exercise notion. On the other hand, the information surrounding contraindicated movements are so heavily endorsed among fitness professionals, sug-gests that readers will have to judge for themselves whether they will steer clear of the contraindicated movements.

One emphasis for health promotion and safety is on *regular* exercise activity. Exercise programs that are taken up erratically are considered less safe and effective because there will be little progress made if any, between one session and the next. A second emphasis for safety is on *progressive loading* of the body; the intensity or pace of the activity varies according to the fitness level of the participant. An intensity level that is optimal for a well-trained older person would be unenjoyable, overtaxing, and impossible for an untrained individual. This point highlights the complexity of exercise prescription for older people. The health and fitness spectrum varies from frail status to elite (high performance) status, and the worst thing professionals can do is to prescribe the same program to all older participants.

In certain settings, some simplification is warranted. For example, in regard to isometric forms of exercise, the American Heart Association does not advocate static contractions or isometric (same-position) exercise as an effective way to reduce cardiovascular risk (Fletcher, Blair, & Blumenthal, 1994). Rather, people with cardiovascular disease are usually asked to refrain from heavy lifting and forceful isometric exercises, although the use of light weights is highly recommended for developing muscle strength and joint flexibility. The question that remains is what is "light" weight and what is "heavy"? A simple guide is that heavy weights are ones that make the user strain enough to briefly hold his/her breath; light weights will fatigue the user's muscles after a few repetitions, but each lift is not enough strain to involve the facial muscles or alter breathing.

The training heart rate for people who can exercise their arms, but not their legs, is ten beats per minute lower than the heart rate calculated for leg training. The American Heart Association also recommends that the higher blood pressure that usually accompanies upper body exercise should be monitored.

FUNDAMENTAL MOVEMENT NEEDS OF THE AGING BODY

The aging body needs *more* than aerobic fitness. In 1992, the American Heart Association reported,

> Developing endurance, joint flexibility and muscle strength is important in a comprehensive exercise program, especially as people age (Fletcher, Blair, & Blumenthal, 1994).

For older people it could be argued that strength and flexibility may be even more important to independence and quality of life than having optimal aerobic fitness. An older jogger who has a fit heart but who is too stiff to clip their toenails will soon have foot problems serious enough to interfere with their ability to jog. An elderly woman, perhaps a participant in yoga, can still be too weak to get in and out of her bathtub safely. The independence of the older adult is only as good as the weakest physical trait. To obtain the full benefits of an active lifestyle then, one has to take part in a range of activities that may stimulate the body aerobically, but especially provide muscle strength and endurance, and furthermore, promote joint flexibility and balance. Although the main ingredients of an all-around program can be found in this chapter, some older people may find it more enjoyable to attend a high-variety exercise program in their community.

The First Steps to Fitness: Walking

The first steps to a more healthy lifestyle are one's own footsteps. Of all the fitness components, the foundation of aerobic fitness is considered to be the capability to sustain moderate forms of activity such as walking, cycling, jogging, or skating without getting breathless or unduly fatigued. This is called *aerobic fitness* because it represents a system dependent on oxygen. Aerobic fitness is one's capacity to absorb oxygen in the lungs, effectively transport the oxygen through the blood-stream to the working muscles, and to effectively transport the waste gas of carbon dioxide back to the lungs for disposal. The important organs to do that job are the heart, the blood vessels, the working muscles, and the lungs.

Brisk walking is a great aerobic activity because it uses more than half of the body's muscles (Health Canada, 1993). Over the short run, walking increases the body's need for oxygen and thereby trains the aerobic system to operate more efficiently over the long run. Walking strengthens bones since the weight-bearing forces stimulates leg bone to take up calcium. Moreover, walking is a low-intensity activity that is natural, virtually injury-free, refreshing, and enjoyable. These very features permit walking to be an easy social activity in which conversations are possible. The energy spent on a long walk leads to a relaxed feeling, and tends to be energizing and fatigue-reducing. Adequate amounts of regular walking lead to lower blood pressure, reduces LDLs (low density lipoproteins or blood fats), and has a number of important psychological benefits. In sum, there just is not any other activity that can quite compare.

Walking Technique   Older people are advised to start with a shorter stride length and maintain a rapid, but soft heel-to-toe action of each foot. As fitness improves, stride length can increase while maintaining the habitual rhythm. The arms are flexed at the elbows and oppose the leg action in a natural swing. The body is held tall with a straight back, shoulders relaxed, and head high. After a few minutes, walkers can take the "talk test," which is a guide to the intensity level of the chosen pace. The talk test involves reciting a poem, humming or singing, or speaking to a companion without interrupting the flow of the words. If breathlessness is evident, the walker is going at it too hard.

To get the most health benefit out of walking (or any other aerobic exercise), participants should exercise at a *target heart rate* (Figure 8.1). After taking a ten-second pulse reading at the radial artery (thumb-side of wrist) or carotid artery (neck), the participant locates their age on the bottom of the chart and then locates their pulse (number of beats per ten seconds) on the left side of the chart. The intersection of the two points should fall in the 70 percent training zone. If the participant is exercising below the training level zone, she may decide to work a little harder to get better health and fitness benefits. If the participant is exercising above the 70 percent training level, she may cut back on the intensity slightly and still derive aerobic benefits at a more comfortable exercise level.

Perceived Exertion Ratings   Target heart rates do not work for everyone. Many older people have difficulty finding their pulse. A miscount of even one beat can lead to an overestimate or underestimate when the brief 10-second count is multiplied by 6 to estimate beats per minute. Moreover, people who are on beta-blocker medication will not be able to use the target heart rate chart since their pulse rates are held constant. In all these cases, the perceived exertion scale is the most useful device to judge intensity. The Rating of Perceived Exertion (RPE) is a self-referent 15-point scale ranging from 6 to 20, with 6 representing "very, very light" exertion, and 20 representing "very, very hard" exertion (see Figure 8.2).

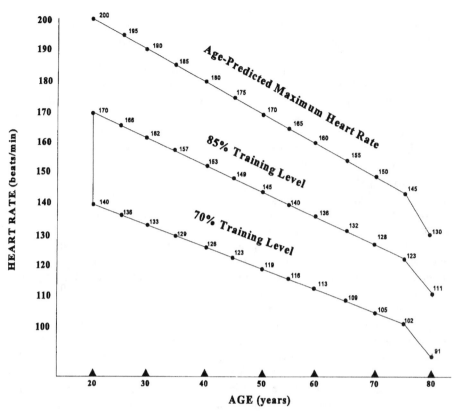

Figure 8.1 Target heart rate according to age.

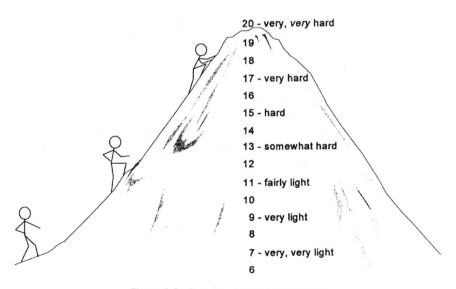

Figure 8.2 Ratings of perceived exertion.

Since the 1960s, exercise scientists have devoted considerable attention to a self-rated cue of effort called *perceived exertion* (Borg, 1970; Milhevic, 1991). Steinhardt and Carrier (1989) have reported that feelings of "effort" in physical activity were a significant barrier to adult participation. Indeed, "the major defining property of motivation is the level of effort mobilized and sustained in a pursuit" (Bandura & Cervone, 1986). High-intensity efforts are possibly lacking in older adults because 70 percent of adults aged 80+ are satisfied that they are already doing the right amount of physical activity for their age (Statistics Canada, 1992). Sallis (1994) reported that "one of the main influences on enjoyment is the amount of exertion required by the activity."

The exertion ratings, although highly subjective, are can be equated scientifically to objective physiological measures such as heart rate, metabolic rate, and blood lactate. For example, a self-rating of "6" represents a low exertion estimate (equivalent to the resting heart rate while seated). A rating of "13" would be reflective of moderate exercise intensity approximating 130 beats per minute. Several studies have shown that the RPE provides a simple and physiologically valid method of regulating exercise intensity. Subjective exertion during exercise have been shown to match monitored heart rates in young men about 65 percent to 80 percent of the time (Borg, Hassmen, & Lagerstrom, 1987; Dunbar et al., 1992; Monahan, 1988).

When people feel they are straining to keep up the pace, their psychological stress is apparently representative of their actual physiological state. The relationship is not as obscure as it might seem. A rapid and pounding heart rate, tightness in the chest or a feeling of breathlessness, elevated blood pressure, a feeling of overheating, and the sensation of sweating are some of the cues that act as indicators for personal exertion.

Preliminary work with anticipatory exertion found that sedentary women are more likely to have heightened beliefs about the effort required to engage in fitness activities such as walking, stretching, cycling, and strengthening activities (O'Brien Cousins, 1995b). Older women perceived exertion differently across the different fitness exercises. Curl-ups, push-ups, and a 50-minute aquatic class were viewed at the most exerting (scoring 14+). A sitting stretch to touch the toes, and walking briskly for 20 minutes were judged overall to be the least exerting (scoring 12 or less). In these measures of anticipated exertion for six fitness activities, elderly women were able to respond with 75 percent accuracy four weeks later ($r = .87$, $p < .0001$).

ParticipACTION provided the following chart, designed by Peggy Edwards, to guide walkers (Figure 8.3). The two levels of walking offer a suggested time and distance over a 20-week progressive walking program. The inexperienced walker (Level 1) can progress from 10 minutes, two walking sessions each week, to an advanced Level 2, walking briskly 45 minutes, four to five times each week. If walking at Level 2 was sustained, an adult weighing 80 kilograms will burn off 1500 calories in one week alone. That amounts to 75,000 calories of fat burned each year or about 20 pounds.

GENTLE EXERCISES FOR OLDER ADULTS IN THE HOME

Although close to 90 percent of older people are healthy enough to exercise, many of these same adults are unable to get out of their homes to join other seniors in commu-

Level 1 For people who are not used to exercise										
Week	1	2	3	4	5	6	7	8	9	10
Minutes walking Walks per week	10 2	10 3	15 3	18 3	20 3-4	20 4	25 4	30 4	32 4	35 4
Mileage	Start at Week 1 with about one-half mile or 1 kilometer and work up to about 2 miles or 3.5 km by Week 10.									

Level 2 For people who exercise regularly										
Week	1	2	3	4	5	6	7	8	9	10
Minutes walking Walks per week	20 3	22 3	25 3	30 3	30 4	35 4	35 4-5	40 4-5	42 4-5	45 4-5
Mileage	Start at Week 1 with about 1 mile or 1.5 km and work up to about 3 miles or 4.5 km by Week 10.									

Source: Reprinted with permission from Peggy Edwards, ParticipACTION.

Figure 8.3 Sample walking program.

nity exercise. Some older people are homebound because they are caregivers for grandchildren, an ill spouse or family member, or are afraid to go out in bad weather. Therefore, other active living alternatives must be found. Ironically, homebound adults who neglect their own health needs with regard to healthy exercise are likely to lose the ability to live at home themselves. Because of these commitments to others, personal health is vital to more than just the homebound adult.

Some older adults are already remarkably active in and around their home because they do most of their own home maintenance. Domestic chores such as housecleaning, gardening, snow removal, painting, mowing the lawn, and so on, do have some positive physical contributions in maintaining muscle strength and endurance, and do increase the energy spent in a day. At this point in time scientists do not know what contribution, if any, daily physical chores around the home have for health benefits. The fact is known that women are mainly responsible for housekeeping activities and this daily energy expenditure coincides with the fact that women also live seven years longer than men!

Even with a highly active living approach to life around the home, a balance of fitness activities may not be possible. For example, people tend to shovel, rake, sweep, clean, and scrub with the same arm and use the same side of the body. If the activities are pursued at a slow pace, the contribution to aerobic fitness may be negligible. Overall, joint flexibility may not be adequately addressed either. As was discussed earlier, any weak link in the fitness chain can eventually undermine older adult independence. What *are* the essential movements to maintain basic survival?

THE ESSENTIAL MOVEMENTS FOR INDEPENDENT LIVING

Mobility Requirements

- Hip flexion to reach the feet (to wash, clip nails, tie shoes)
- Shoulder extension to reach behind back (zippers, coats)
- Shoulder flexion ability to reach high objects overhead (hair grooming)
- Wrist flexibility to grip and twist (open doors, jars)
- Ability to be able to get down on the floor and get back up

Strength and Endurance Requirements

- Ankle strength to avoid trips
- Ability to carry moderately heavy objects (groceries, garbage)
- Ability to push or pull (furniture, doors, drapes, blinds)
- Arm and leg strength (to lift objects, get out of bathtub)
- Ability to walk up and down stairs without leaning on the handrail

Cardiorespiratory Requirements

- Ability to move around the home doing physical tasks without becoming breathless
- Ability to walk to and from a public transportation system
- Ability to enjoy sustained recreational activities such as walking

Balance Requirements

- Ability to move around the home with confidence and ease
- Ability to do simple tasks such as standing on a stool
- Ability to stand on one leg temporarily
- Ability to react quickly to uneven terrain

THE HOME EXERCISE PLAN

This program requires that various parts of the home are used as "activity stations." Once the warm-up is complete, the order of the movements are not particularly important; the idea is to "imprint" an activity on a certain region of the home. The program can be done like a circuit, with exercise stations that you visit in sequence. Or the movements can be done throughout the day, whenever you happen to enter that part of your apartment or residence.

Kitchen Warm-Up

DESCRIPTION	ILLUSTRATION

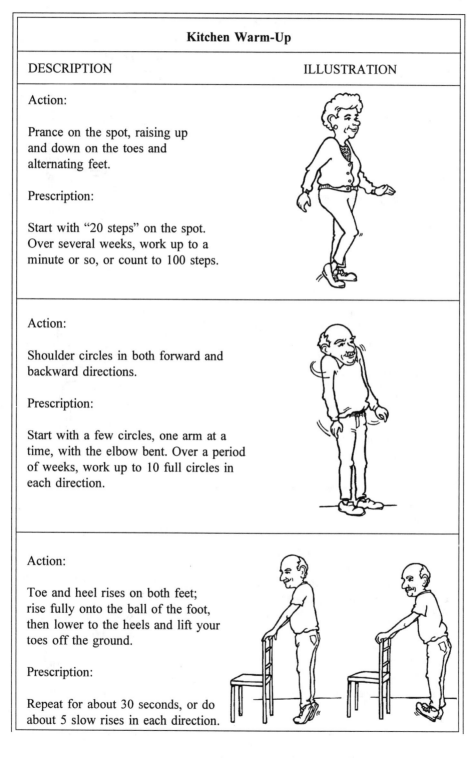

Action:

Prance on the spot, raising up and down on the toes and alternating feet.

Prescription:

Start with "20 steps" on the spot. Over several weeks, work up to a minute or so, or count to 100 steps.

Action:

Shoulder circles in both forward and backward directions.

Prescription:

Start with a few circles, one arm at a time, with the elbow bent. Over a period of weeks, work up to 10 full circles in each direction.

Action:

Toe and heel rises on both feet; rise fully onto the ball of the foot, then lower to the heels and lift your toes off the ground.

Prescription:

Repeat for about 30 seconds, or do about 5 slow rises in each direction.

Kitchen Warm-Up (*Cont.*)

DESCRIPTION	ILLUSTRATION

Action:

Shoulder stretch while seated
at a table.

Prescription:

Relax in this position for up
to 60 seconds.

Action:

This stretch works on the hamstring
muscles at the back of the leg. Sitting
in a sturdy chair, place one leg on a
stool or even on the table and relax
forward over the outstretched leg.

Prescription:

Hold a position of comfortable stretch
for up to one minute.

Action:

This stretch works the quadriceps
muscles at the front of the thigh. Hold
a kitchen counter for support and grasp
one leg at the ankle or pant-leg. Keep
the back straight and the knees close
together.

Prescription:

Hold 10 to 20 seconds on each leg.

Home Workout Ideas

The home workout can be carried out one time to start. As fitness improves, a the circuit can be repeated, and then eventually carried out for a total of 3 times, by moving from one station to the next, exercise becomes sustained and thus an aerobic effect is created. Some activities can be replaced if the exerciser has physical limitations.

DESCRIPTION	ILLUSTRATION

Action:

Repeated walking up and down stairs (with handrails) is an endurance exercise. Marching on the spot with high knees is a substitute.

Prescription:

Walk a steady pace up and down stairs, 1 to 5 flights. Use the handrails if needed. For the more fit, climb two stairs at a time going up and do more repetitions.

Action:

Marching is done on the spot 30 to 60 seconds or count your foot contacts (work up to 100).

Home Workout Ideas (*Cont.*)

DESCRIPTION	ILLUSTRATION

Action:

Wall push-ups. The exerciser stands near a wall at arm's distance, hands directly in front of the shoulders. The elbows flex and extend at a steady pace to a point of mild fatigue. Exhale on the push.

Prescription:

Start with 5 push-ups and work gradually up to 20 at a time.

Action:

Leg lifts: No breath-holding! One knee is lifted to the chest, the leg straightens, and lowers slowly to the floor.

Prescription:

Start with about 5 lifts on each leg and work up to a set of 10 on each leg.

Action:

Bicep curls for arm strength: Standing tall with knees slightly bent, and arms down, the yellow pages directory is held on the forearms (palms up). The book is lifted and lowered without holding the breath.

Prescription:

Start with 10 lifts and work your way up to 20. A substitute resistence could be a plastic bottle filled with sand or water, or a cast-iron frying pan.

Home Workout Ideas (*Cont.*)

DESCRIPTION	ILLUSTRATION

Action:

Wall sit. With back to a wall, the exerciser "sits" by leaning on the wall and bending the knees to nearly a 90 degree position. Maintain regular breathing while sitting.

Prescription:

Maintain the position until the thighs are feeling fatigue. A suggested starting range is 10 to 30 seconds.

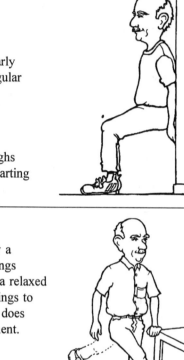

Action:

Leg swings. Standing sideways by a counter or table, the exerciser swings one leg forward and backward in a relaxed way, eventually increasing the swings to about hip height. The upper body does not twist or sway with the movement.

Prescription:

A series of about 10 relaxed swings is a starting point that can be increased to 20 swings on each leg.

Action:

Sofa curl-up. Use a firm sofa or bed, knees bent and feet flat. While exhaling, lift the head, shoulders and then the upper torso off the mattress. Reach for the knees. Lower back to lying by uncurling the body.

Prescription:

Start with 2 or 3 curl-ups, and work gradually up to 20.

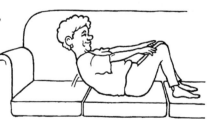

Home Workout Ideas (*Cont.*)

DESCRIPTION	ILLUSTRATION

Action:

Flutterkick: The exerciser takes a face-down position on a firm bed or couch resting the heads on the arms. Each leg is raised alternately from the hip.

Prescription:

Start with 20 flutter kicks and work up to 60 flutter kicks in 30 seconds.

Action:

Couch potato commercial breaks. While sitting in a large armchair, the exerciser lifts their hips off the seat using only the arm rests.
Then, while standing in front of the chair, the exerciser starts to sit down, but returns to stand without hips touching the chair.

Prescription:

Start with 5 arm lifts and 5 "sits"; work up to 20.

Cool-Down Activities

DESCRIPTION	ILLUSTRATION

Action:

Trunk stretches: Use a broom or
towel to keep the shoulders in position.
Gentle trunk twists can be done holding
the broom at waist height, or above the
head for a more advanced stretch. The
backscratcher is done with the broom
held behind the back with one arm
over the shoulder. The broom is raised
and lowered slightly to get a full stretch.

Prescription:

Do slow and relaxed movements. Do
not hold the arms over the head for long
periods of time. For the backscratcher, the
arm positions are reversed after 10 to 20 seconds.

Action:

Calf stretch: While a railing is held for
support, the feet are placed one in front
of the other, both toes facing directly
forward.

Prescription:

Hold the stretch for up to a minute with
relaxed breathing.

Action:

Shoulder stretch #1: The wrists are placed
palms down on a table while the exerciser
stands with the hips flexed at about
90 degrees, knees slightly bent, and the
back flat and horizontal to the floor.

Prescription:

Hold the position for up to 60 seconds
with relaxed breathing.

Cool-Down Activities (*Cont.*)

DESCRIPTION	ILLUSTRATION

Action:

Shoulder stretch #2: the exerciser stands
with feet apart, bends the knees and hip
area while clasping the hands behind the
back. The arms are raised gently backward
to the point of stretch.

Prescription:

Hold the position for up to 30 seconds.

Action:

Leg stretch: the exerciser slowly sits
and relaxes forward with the arms down
by the legs. Keep the head at chest height.
A foot stool can be used to get a more
challenging stretch.

Prescription:

Hold up to 60 seconds with relaxed breathing.

Action:

Shake out: Stand up slowly, and gently
shake out limbs, wrists, and ankles.

Prescription:

Shake out the body gently for
15 to 20 seconds.

Part Two

Toward a Theory of Older Adult Exercise Motivation

TWO MAIN THEORETICAL APPROACHES

A discussion of theory, rather than being a daunting task, has the intrigue of a detective story. As new information is presented in the scientific story, the plot thickens, and the observer tries to assemble the pieces of the puzzle. Making sense of why people do what they do is very much resembles a nonfiction mystery.

The complexity of predicting a health behavior such as physical activity has been aptly described as "a web of causation" (Sallis & Hovell, 1990; Thomas, 1984). Addressing this complexity are two major disciplines, representing two general research approaches: 1) social epidemiology, and 2) behavioral health psychology. Social epidemiology represents the extrinsic forces of society, history, and environment that affect population health while health psychology accounts for intrinsic factors such as one's interpretations and decision making. An understanding of these two approaches is essential to the study of exercise behavior and theory development because

> . . . the degree to which the true origin of the determinants [of exercise] resides in the person or the environment remains to be determined (Dishman, 1990).

Chapter 9 examines perspectives in health psychology that have been helpful in understanding health behavior. Some of the health behavior theories briefly presented and discussed in Chapter 9 are: the Health Belief Model (Rosenstock), Health Locus of Control Theory (Wallston & Wallston), the Theory of Reasoned Action (Fishbein & Ajzen), Protection-Motivation Theory (Weinstein), and Social Cognitive Theory (Bandura).

In Chapter 10, the personal attributes and life course situations that context-ualize individual beliefs and decision making (socialization and ecological models) are presented. The cognitive beliefs of older individuals (attitude–behavior variables) are presented in Chapter 11 along with a sampling of the research that has examined these beliefs in late life physical activity involvement. Chapter 12 presents an integrated view of the previous models, followed by a self-talk model of older adult exercise motivation in Chapter 13. Research challenges and unanswered questions are addressed in Chapter 14. The final chapter, Chapter 15, generally summarizes the findings and the implica-tions for health and social policy.

Chapter 9

Perspectives in Health Psychology

BEHAVIORAL HEALTH PSYCHOLOGY PERSPECTIVES

Behavioral research in health psychology is concerned with attitudes and behaviors of adults regarding their health and well-being. Some health professionals suggest that individual knowledge and beliefs about one's world are the main controlling determinants of one's behavior. Rosenstock's Health Belief Model is prominent in representing this stance in many contemporary health behavior change studies.

THE HEALTH BELIEF MODEL

The Health Belief Model (HBM) of Rosenstock, Strecher, and Becker (1988) defined health behavior as "any activity undertaken by a person who believes himself/herself to be healthy for the purpose of preventing disease." The HBM was first developed to understand why so few U.S. citizens were taking advantage of free tuberculosis screening in the 1960s. The HBM highlights the cognitive processes that act as barriers to taking preventive action through an emphasis of the role of subjective beliefs or expectations held by currently healthy individuals. Their most recent contribution to health behavior theory is seen in his modification of the HBM to include the component of self-efficacy. For example for an older man to take up exercise for health reasons, that individual must believe that the activity will generally benefit his state of health (outcome expectation) and also that he is capable of doing the activity (efficacy expectation).

PERSON ----------> BEHAVIOR -----------> OUTCOME
efficacy   outcome
expectations   expectations
"I can do it."   "It's worth doing."

This model, Rosenstock's 1988 model including efficacy, has a temporal orientation that implies that outcome expectations occur after the behavior is initiated. This is problematic: it is unlikely that outcome expectancies are part of the decision making processes right from the beginning and are instead part of the incentive process leading one to take action. Furthermore, the HBM does not account for the role of social forces and subjective norms—the notion that individuals interpret their world through role models and are socialized to act in the ways expected of them for their age, gender, race, and so on.

According to Rosenstock's (1974) and Becker's (1974) earlier conception of health beliefs, health-related action depends on perceptions about personal susceptibility to a specific disease in combination with the perceived severity of the disease, environmental modifying factors such as cues to act, and likelihood of taking preventive action based on the weighing of perceived barriers and perceived benefits (Figure 9.1).

The Health Belief Model has served as a conceptual core for general health behavior compliance studies and has been useful in predicting health, illness, and sick-role behavior. Health beliefs have been positively associated with exercise compliance and adherence in older adults when there is specific knowledge about the exercise regimen (Tirrell & Hart, 1980) and when individuals are adequately informed about their actual health situation (Rakowski, 1984).

Janz and Becker (1984) reported on a comprehensive review of 29 health-related investigations utilizing the Health Belief Model. Summary results provide substantial support for the HBM, with "perceived barriers" and "perceived benefits" proving to be the most powerful HBM dimensions in demonstrating associations with behavior. The Health Belief Model rests on the notion of beliefs *causing* behavior—a time order sequence that is not often addressed in other theoretical research.

Still, a number of conceptual difficulties and inconsistencies are associated with the Health Belief Model. First, health beliefs are understood to be a reflection of just how knowledgeable people are about the consequences of their own health actions. Blumenthal (1983) acknowledged that the sole basis of evaluating people's beliefs is to assess their biomedical knowledge. Thus health beliefs based on personal experience, or beliefs acquired through social, psychological, and cultural foundations may be good predictors of behavior but are rarely examined as such. In 1974, Kirscht was troubled by the fact that "supporting evidence for the utility of the Health Belief Model had come primarily, but not exclusively, from retrospective studies, and with exclusive reference to disease preventive behaviors" (Kirscht, 1974).

The Health Belief Model hinges on an individual's *perceived susceptibility* to a

The Health Belief Model

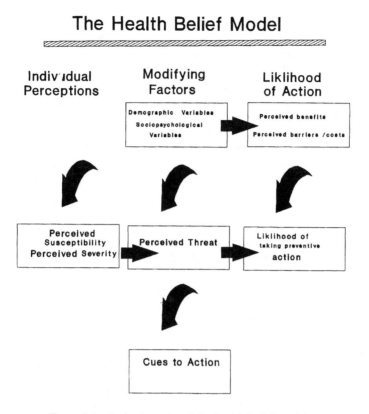

Indiv idual
Perceptions

Modifying
Factors

Liklihood
of Action

Demographic Variables
Sociopsychological
Variables

Perceived benefits

Perceived barriers /costs

Perceived
Susceptibility
Perceived Severity

Perceived Threat

Liklihood of
taking preventive
action

Cues to Action

Figure 9.1 Basic elements of the health belief model.

disease occurrence (Rosenstock, 1974). Yet some research has suggested that health beliefs are more predictive of health protective behavior in the well-elderly who perceive lower susceptibility to risk or health threats (Lindsay-Reid & Osborn, 1980; Segall & Chappell, 1989). Such findings do not support the notion of the HBM's *readiness or cue to act* because recognition of an illness threat (perceived susceptibility) in well adults is less meaningful.

Perceived severity of a health threat is another belief assessed by the Health Belief Model; the original HBM has a disease-avoidance orientation. Individuals who are emotionally aroused by the provision of knowledge about the severity of their present condition are predicted to initiate or adhere to preventive health practice. There are, however, potential shortcomings in using threat or knowledge of threat to promote health practice. Gintner, Rectanus, Achord, and Parker (1987) found that attendance at a blood pressure screening was cut in half when an illness-threat format was used to motivate participants. Participants were more likely to attend the preventive screening when a wellness appeal was presented.

The structure and reliability of health beliefs were examined by Jette and colleagues (1981). They identified six general health threats, perceived severity of five conditions, four perceived barriers to taking medications, four questions measuring general health concern, three items assessing trust in physicians, three items of perceived susceptibility, three items on perceived health status, and two questions about health locus of control. Factor analysis revealed that condition-specific measures of perception of susceptibility and severity and situation-specific measures of perceived barriers were empirically distinct from general measures of these beliefs. Their findings supported the original theoretical assumption that HBM dimensions were sufficiently distinct to be considered different beliefs, but warned against mixing specific and general questionnaire items within the same index.

After reviewing over 600 research articles in an effort to determine what was known about people's health habits and practices, Norman (1985) advocated a holistic approach to understanding health behavior:

> No one factor has been found to provide a sufficient basis for predicting health behavior. People's health habits and practices are often daily actions which have been influenced by a host of cultural, social, psychological and biological factors (Norman, 1985).

Norman claimed that even though personal knowledge and beliefs about the health consequences of behavior may have some impact on the way in which people behave, they do not on their own provide a strong basis for preventive health activities. This is because "it is an enormously complex task to present people with information in a way that will lead them to change their health beliefs." Norman suggested that health education initiatives may well be futile considering the discrepancy between people's health beliefs and their actual behavior. His scepticism about altering people's beliefs in the hopes of altering their behavior mirrored the findings of Haefner and Kirscht (1970) who found that merely changing the participants' beliefs about health was not enough to alter their behavior.

HEALTH LOCUS OF CONTROL THEORY

A second theory in behavioral health psychology that has the potential to predict late life exercise behavior is the Health Locus of Control Theory. Rotter (1954, 1966) proposed that a person learns or is conditioned operantly on the basis of his or her history of positive or negative reinforcement. Through these experiences, the person also develops a sense of internal or external locus of control. Those with an internal locus of control are more likely to self-initiate change, whereas those who are externally controlled are more likely to be influenced by others. Therefore, locus of control refers to an individual's perceived influence in regulating outcomes.

Wallston and Wallston (1978) proposed that an individual's sense of control varies by domains of experience and actions, such as health experiences. *Health Locus of Control* (HLC) is defined as perceived control over one's health. "Internal" locus of control refers to perceptions that a health outcome is due one's personal actions, but "external" locus of control refers to perceptions that a health outcome is due to chance, external factors or the actions of others (Kist-Kline & Lipnickey, 1989; Wallston & Wallston, 1978).

According to Health Locus of Control Theory, individuals exhibiting more control over their health ("internals") would be more likely to be participating in health-promoting behaviors such as physical activity. Indeed, many studies have found that participants who claim to be more physically active tend to be more internally controlled (Bonds, 1980; Carlson & Petti, 1989; Kleiber & Hemmer, 1981; Lumpkin, 1985; Moore, 1980; O'Connell & Price, 1982; Perri & Templer, 1984–1985; Sonstroem & Walker, 1973). Internality may be found in athletes, even in team sports where the actions of others are key events (Kleiber & Hemmer, 1981; Lynn, Phelan, & Kiker, 1969). However, so far, HLC has provided only modest associations with exercise behavior (Calnan, 1988; McCready & Long, 1985), specifically leisure time physical activity (Dishman & Steinhardt, 1990). One concern is that in some studies, health locus of control is not predictive at all of health behaviors (Calnan, 1988) or exercise behavior (Blair, et al., 1980; Dishman & Gettman, 1980; Kaplan, Atkins, & Reinsch, 1984; Laffrey & Isenberg, 1983).

People who believe in chance ("externals") tend to be older (Calnan, 1988); female (Calnan, 1988); less educated (Boyle & Sielski, 1981); and in manual occupations (Calnan, 1988). Recent research suggests that as soon as people learn that their health has deteriorated, they also exhibit more external perceptions of control (Waller & Bates, 1992). This loss of a sense of personal control is associated with depression (Mirowski & Ross, 1990).

THEORY OF REASONED ACTION/PLANNED BEHAVIOR

To date, little theoretical guidance has been given to the prediction of older adult exercise behavior, but two prominent theories have been explored (Dzewaltowski, 1989a, 1989b; Dzewaltowski, Noble, & Shaw, 1990). One prominent theory is Ajzen's and Fishbein's Theory of Reasoned Action (1980), revised and renamed as the Theory of Planned Behavior (TPB) (Ajzen, 1985; Ajzen & Madden, 1986). The formation of "intention" to act is central to this theory, and not the behavior itself. According to this model, an individual's intention to perform a given behavior is a function of attitude toward the behavior, and normative beliefs about what relevant others think one should do, weighted by personal motivation to comply with those relevant others. Behavioral intention is viewed as a type of expectancy and is indicated by the person's subjective probability that she or he will perform the behavior in question.

In regard to predicting exercise intentions, the TPB has been more useful in explaining exercise intentions in males (Godin & Shephard, 1987). TPB has been more effective in explaining exercise behavior compared to Kenyon's Attitudes Towards Physical Activity inventory (Godin & Shephard, 1986), but "has not identified a predominant cognitive profile of those who intend to exercise" (Godin, Shephard, & Colantino, 1986). Riddle (1980) obtained success with Fishbein's model obtaining a high correlation ($r = .82$) between habitual jogging behavior and further intention to exercise. However, Riddle noted that her most important finding was that "joggers had stronger positive evaluations of the beneficial consequences of regular jogging" but nonexercisers "were not as convinced." The importance of these perceptions about the "consequences of exercise" is that "consequences" is not a theoretical element in the Theory of Reasoned Action, but rather matches a component called outcome expectations in Social Cognitive Theory.

Recent attempts have been made, with some success, to improve the Fishbein-Ajzen model by adding a self-efficacy component from Bandura's Social Cognitive Theory (Wurtele & Maddux, 1987).

SOCIAL COGNITIVE THEORY

Social Learning Theory

Although Social Cognitive Theory arose from a behavioral psychology perspective, the theory incorporates important features related to socialization and social learning. Perry, Baranowski and Parcel (1990) traced the 50-year history of social learning theory noting that it was originally introduced to explain imitation or modelling behavior among animals and humans. Rotter first applied early social learning principles to clinical psychology (1954), which in turn led to his development of the idea of "generalized expectancies of reinforcement" (1966).

Building on Rotter's social learning perspectives, Bandura is credited for the contemporary development of Social Cognitive Theory (1986, 1989, 1995). Social Cognitive Theory (SCT) continues to evolve as a broad conceptual domain that incorporates many theoretical ideas and is employed by many areas of practice. Thus, with such breadth of application, abuse or misuse is possible. Perry and colleagues (1990) pointed out one theoretical pitfall of research using SCT; the pitfall is that "one concept was often explored but the others were excluded completely." For example, the concept of internal and external locus of control dominated social learning research at one time. Then Bandura's identification of self-efficacy as the single most important factor in promoting behavioral change led to a narrow examination of this construct. The emphasis on a single variable oversimplifies reality but is "a reflection of the structure of experimental research, which usually permits analysis of only a few variables at a time" (Perry et al., 1990). Clearly, research that examines all of the main constructs of Social Cognitive Theory should be encouraged.

The Constructs of Social Cognitive Theory

Originally, social learning theory emphasized the role of self-referent beliefs or subjective expectancies held by the subject. Beliefs or subjective expectancies about the possibilities and consequences of personal action were considered to be the key mediating forces between a person and a specific behavior (Figure 9.2).

Recent years have witnessed a resurgence of interest in the study of self-referent phenomena. Bandura (1989) pointed to several reasons why self-processes have come to pervade many domains of psychology.

> Self-generated activities lie at the very heart of causal processes. They not only contribute to the meaning and valence of most external influences, but they also function as important determinants of motivation and action (Bandura, 1989).

Figure 9.2   Basic elements of social learning theory.

According to SCT, individuals' beliefs of self-efficacy are central to their decision to participate in physical activity. Efficacy expectations are defined as a person's
judgments of their capability to organize and execute their skills and resources and
that of the environment to perform an action that will lead to a designated outcome
(Bandura, 1977a, 1977b, 1986). Specifically Bandura's theory claims that human action is guided by a core set of four beliefs: motivation to obtain a goal (*Incentive to
Act*), beliefs that a certain behavior will be beneficial in reaching a goal (*Outcome
Expectations*), a belief in one's ability to perform the action (*Self-Efficacy*), and finally, a perception that the action will be endorsed or "positively reinforced" (*Social-
Environmental Support*). Thus the four expectancies encompass internal and external
factors that may affect individual behavior. In contrast, perceived behavioral control
(in the Fishbein-Ajzen model) and perceived barriers (in the Health Belief Model) are
assumed to reflect external factors (availability of time, facilities etc).

Exercise behavior, using a social cognitive perspective, is predicted to occur when
an individual:

1   Highly values (wants) the outcomes of physical activity, (Incentive or Mo-
    tive);
2   Perceives that specific forms of physical activity will lead to health benefits
    and that harmful outcomes are not likely, (Positive Outcome Expectancies);
3   Believes that they are physically able to do the specific activity, (Efficacy);
    and
4   Perceives that they will be socially reinforced for participating (Social sup-
    port).

To the extent that individuals "learn" what to value, what is risky for them, how
competent they really are, and how much endorsement society will offer for their
activity, SCT beliefs indirectly reflect the socio-environmental milieu, cultural learning, and past experiences of the individual. But individuals are not considered to be
passive recipients of environmental influence. Inherent in SCT is the idea that people
self-regulate their social and physical environment as well as their actions.

Bandura described the nature and function of human agency as a "conceptual
model of triadic reciprocal causation" (1986), also known as reciprocal determinism.
Self-functioning is viewed as a continuous interaction between environmental factors,
beliefs and behaviors (Bandura, 1986) (Figure 9.3). The interaction is such that a
change in one has implications for the others. According to SCT, the environment

Reciprocal Determinism Model

Physical Activity

Type
Intensity
Frequency
Duration

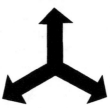

Cognitive Beliefs

Motive
Outcome Expectations
Exercise efficacy
Social Reinforcement

Situational Environment

Age
Health Status
Education
Work Role
Marital Status
Family size
Financial Status
Cultural Background
Past Mastery
Past encouragement

Figure 9.3   Concept of reciprocal determinism.

provides the social and physical situation within which the person must function and thus also provides the incentives and disincentives (expectancies) for the performance of behavior.

SUMMARY

Individual knowledge and beliefs about one's world are thought to be the determinants of one's behavior. In this chapter, the Health Belief Model, Health Locus of Control Theory, Theory of Reasoned Action/Planned Behavior, and Social Cognitive Theory were introduced as the main models used to understand exercise cognition. In the next section, the life situation and circumstances of an individual provide the opportunities and constraints to their participation in active living. Contextual factors are shown to play a critical role.

Chapter 10

Contextual Explanations

When viewed in terms of the size of population affected, and the serious outcomes for health, *physical inactivity* could be considered to be an epidemic. In typical epidemics, medical researchers attempt to quickly identify the source of the social problem, and the population characteristics that increase public susceptibility. In a similar way, certain social groups can be identified for their vulnerability to sedentary living. The material in this chapter introduces social epidemiology as a theoretical perspective that attends to the broad characteristics and contextual situations of sedentary adults. These characteristics and circumstances of people provide social constructions (opportunities and barriers) by which their lives and activities are guided. In this chapter, ten characteristics are reviewed for their known relationship to physical activity: age, health, gender, culture, education, financial status, employment history, marital status, family size, and previous experience in physical activity.

SOCIAL EPIDEMIOLOGY

The social epidemiological perspective focuses upon personal characteristics and the environmental situation of the individual. The personal qualities and social circumstances of individuals have important associations with health and activity behavior and thus are considered to useful predictors (Belloc & Breslow, 1972; Berkman & Breslow, 1983; Dishman, 1990).

Such predictors imply that people are not the creators of their behaviors, but rather are victims of circumstance. Bandura called this "environmental determinism" or the study of human behavior in terms of "mechanical agency" (Bandura, 1989). In this view, internal events are mainly products of external ones devoid of any causal efficacy on the part of individuals. For example, environmental determinism seems to explain the findings of Sidney, Niinimaa and Shephard (1983) who found that both active and inactive senior citizens had equally positive attitudes toward physical activity. They then wondered why there were discrepancies between the activity behavior of the two groups, and concluded that "there must be other factors, perhaps more important than attitudes, which influence behavior." As another example, one's life occupation can alter possibilities for active behavior later on. Svanborg (1988) reported on a longitudinal study that found previously sedentary workers were more limited in activities of daily living than those whose work had been strenuous.

At the level of the individual, personal attributes and life situations are not easily altered, and therefore are not very suitable for social intervention and health promotion. Even so, epidemiological approaches are useful because they identify specific social groups that can be targeted for particular assistance. Theoretically, however, demographic variables, on their own, are deficient because they only provide association, not explanation. Once descriptive associations are found, however, hypotheses can be developed to explain the findings that then can be tested in further research. For example, if never-married women are found to be significantly more active in late life, hypotheses would then be generated and tested as explanations for this finding (See Parenthood and Family Size later in the chapter).

McPherson (1986) emphasized that demographic characteristics can interact or confound one another. For example, intracohort (age) differences, which could explain activity involvement, can vary dramatically by education, marital status, health status, economic status, degree of mobility, employment status, and social network. Nixon II, (1986) claimed that sport socialization research "needs to address these issues of 'contextualization.'" In Sweden, understanding contextualization was essential to the development of a comprehensive health promotion intervention of 1200 adults over age 70 (Eriksson, Mellstrom, & Svanborg, 1987). For the Swedish study, a "lifestyle" hypothesis was proposed: that the kind of everyday life led by the individual had consequences not only for social performance but also for functional well-being.

> We are only beginning to understand why some people are physically active and others are not. The behavior is determined, at least in part, by characteristics of the person, the environment, and the activity itself (Powell & Paffenbarger, 1985).

Ten contextual or situational variables appear to have significance as potential determinants for late-life exercise: age, health, education, socioeconomic status, marital status, family size, employment history, culture, gender, and childhood socialization (Figure 10.1).

Life situational factors

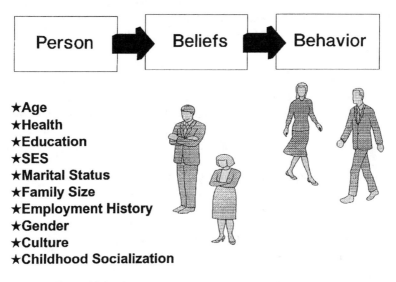

| Person | ➡ | Beliefs | ➡ | Behavior |

★Age
★Health
★Education
★SES
★Marital Status
★Family Size
★Employment History
★Gender
★Culture
★Childhood Socialization

Figure 10.1 Contextual explanations for late-life exercise.

AGE AND EXERCISE

Among the most significant social roles affecting activity patterns, and notably, physical activity behavior, is "old age." For example, being old in the 1990s is the present identity of a particular social group who have experienced a certain social isolation to old age and look upon retirement as "a well-earned rest."

> Age is not just a chronological variable but also a social construct that defines social behavior at specific points in the life cycle. Age is an important form of social differentiation that can result in social inequality because of ageism (McPherson, 1984).

Ageist practice is recognized as a social construction whereby adults are reinforced for more mature roles and age-expected behaviors (Teague, 1987), for learning helplessness and carrying out a self-fulfilling prophecy of age decline, frailty and illness. Chronological age can therefore be hypothesized to play a role in physical activity and sport behavior.

There is a well-documented and universal pattern of declining physical activity and sport participation by age, especially in the early twenties and again after retirement. These sharp decreases in participation have been tied to two major life events—leaving high school and/or entering the work force, and leaving the work force (McPherson, 1984).

The pattern of declining involvement with age appears to be more pronounced among the less educated, those with lower incomes, those in rural and smaller communities, among females and blue collar workers, and among those who live in countries where sport participation is not highly valued or promoted (Shephard, 1997; Stephens & Craig, 1990). McPherson (1978) made the point that, after peak performance age in many sports, incentives are lacking for adult participation. Community programs, facilities and coaching time tend to be allocated to high performance children. With only younger role models present in a sport, older adults readily assume that sports events are for the young.

Canadian data states that 42 percent of men over 65 and 23 percent of women over age 65 are active (spending 3+ kilocalories per kg per day on exercise), a level that exceeds the activity of middle-age groups (Stephens & Craig, 1990). In the age group of 45 to 64, only 30 percent of men and 20 percent of women are classified as active, suggesting that adults are at their most sedentary in the years just approaching retirement (Stephens & Craig, 1990).

Little is known how physical abilities and skilled motor patterns actually deteriorate over the years, although disuse, muscle wasting, muscle deactivation and neural decline are thought to be interrelated. There is evidence that simple daily motor patterns of adults over the life course are developmentally altered in adaptation to other age-related declines. More likely, however, individual lifestyle changes, such as reducing the more vigorous activities with age, are just as responsible for developmental changes as are actual maturational processes.

EDUCATION AND EXERCISE

The phenomenon of older Canadians being less physically active may be determined, in part, by lower levels of education (Rudman, 1986b). Education has strong associations with physical activity level in both free-living and supervised exercise settings (Dishman, 1990). Many older individuals had only a few years of schooling and thus may lack knowledge, skills, or habits related to physical activity in public settings. For example, in 1911, only 80 percent of those ages 10 to 14 were attending Canadian schools. Boys and girls attended about equally, although young people often withdrew in their teens to work (Harrigan, 1990).

Today, about 60 percent of Canadians over the age of 65 claim to have a Grade 9 or better education. The Canada Fitness Survey (Stephens & Craig, 1990) reports that 52 percent of adults with incomplete high school education are inactive compared to only 33 percent of those with a university degree. Among active Canadians, 89 percent of university educated adults, 65 years and older, spend over 3 hours per week on physical activity in their leisure time compared to 71 percent of those who did not complete high school.

> The interest in advanced education and participation in sports activities also increase with economic status and level of education. This makes the following very clear: *The course for successful aging is set predominantly in childhood and youth* (Meusel, 1991).

If this is true, then the challenges of activating individuals in adulthood will continue for some time. Recent studies reveal that contemporary lifestyles of children are predominantly sedentary and yet hyperactive behavior in school settings is believed to be the most common problem referred to child-guidance clinics in the United States.

Other studies also support the link between education and physical activity. Baecke, Burema, and Frijters (1982) reported highly significant relationships between level of education and leisure time physical activity in males ($r = .38$, $p < .001$). Godin and Shephard (1986) examined psychosocial factors influencing intentions to exercise in a group of individuals ranging from 45 to 74 years of age. Education influenced intention to exercise by interacting with "subjective norm," a construct representing a subject's perceptions about social expectations. Less educated subjects were influenced by social norms, and more educated people tended to exercise independently of external influences.

HEALTH AND EXERCISE

Subjective Health and Exercise

Self-assessed health is perhaps the most important individual attribute affecting a person's late-life involvement in physical activity (O'Brien Cousins, 1997c). Individuals may simply not feel well enough to exercise. Yet the process by which a person comes to understand and evaluate personal health is, in itself, poorly understood.

Self-rating of health is thought to be a multidimensional construct that encompasses a global sense of well-being. There is surprising statistical support for such a simple and subjective scale. Maddox and Douglas (1973) found "self- and physician-ratings of health are predominantly congruous." Indeed, several studies have found subjective ratings of health to be superior to objective measures of health in terms of predicting well-being, happiness, morale, and life satisfaction.

Mortality rates are even predictable by self-rated health. Mossey and Shapiro (1982) followed over 3500 randomly selected Manitoban residents ages 65 and over and found a risk of early mortality almost three times greater for individuals who had rated their health as "poor" only two years earlier.

Idler and Kasl (1991) studied mortality in over 2800 older adults with the mean age for females being 74.9 years. About 12 percent of the women rated their health as "excellent," 46.5 percent as "good," 33.7 percent fair, and 8.4 percent as "bad" or "poor." At the four-year follow-up, Idler and Kasl found that "the odds of death increased at every lower level of self-evaluation of health." What this means is that people who ranked their health as "bad" or "poor" were over three times more likely to die within the four-year period as were people who had rated their health as "excellent." Idler and Kasl concluded,

> The knowledge that expressions of subjective health status are sensitive indicators of survival length should engender new respect among health professionals for what people, especially the elderly people they treat, are saying about their health.

Larson (1978) suggested that although physician ratings should provide the most objective evidence of the severity of illness in absolute terms, they may not accurately reflect the extent to which an individual's physical condition is actually debilitating. Although physician's ratings may be age-biased in favor of younger adults, the "old-old" category (75+) of adults tend to rate their health more positively than "young-old" groups. Gender bias and age bias may be operating because older groups are predominantly women, and older adults may have reduced expectations for optimal health. Thus deteriorating health may not necessarily be reflected in the subjective self-rating of the old-old.

A self-perception of good health can act as a barrier to exercise. The majority of inactive older adults perceive themselves to already have good to excellent health and therefore do not believe that they need more exercise. These beliefs persist in spite of the fact that the prevalence of illness and disability increases with age and is significantly greater for women than for men.

Charette (1988) stated that only 25 percent of inactive Canadians actually have an activity limitation, and of these, more than half think that exercise will improve their health either moderately or a great deal, regardless of their activity limitation status. What can explain why older adults, who are physically inactive, and who state that exercise could improve their health, are still inactive anyway?

In most of the literature relating late-life exercise behaviors to health outcomes, positive relationships are found (O'Brien Cousins & Horne, in press). Exercise participation is related to better health, and better health is associated with increased levels of physical activity. The difficulty in the interpretation is which comes first? Do people exercise more because they have better health to start with, or do people who exercise actually create and/or perceive, better health? The problem of causality is partially answered in large population demographic studies such as that of Belloc and Breslow (1972) and the longitudinal study on college males by Paffenbarger, Hyde, Wing, and Hsied (1986). These studies have linked habitual exercise in the lifestyles of large populations to favourable mortality outcomes. More answers and confirming evidence need to be sought, especially for women who, with a life-span advantage over males of 7 to 8 years, are possibly more concerned about health outcomes and quality of life than extending their life span.

Worries about one's health may be the germinating force leading to specific kinds of self-protecting behaviors. Possibly the prospects of chronic illness provoke certain women to action, while convincing others that it is time to slow down. Both strategies can be considered health protective even though the behaviors are oppositional lifestyle choices. Such a dichotomy needs further exploration because women, in general, exceed males in all other personal health care behaviors *except* exercise (Verbrugge & Wingard, 1987).

A plausible explanation for the reluctance of females to be diligent about promoting their health through exercise is that the way girls and women have been socialized over the life course has lessened their belief in exercise and sport as valued behaviors (Csizma, Wittig, & Schurr, 1988). By late life, vigorous physical pursuits are not only seen as socially inappropriate, but also viewed as high-exertion (Winborn, Meyers, & Mulling, 1988), and therefore potentially life and health-threatening.

Evidence is accumulating that adults who perceive their health as poor are more reluctant to adopt exercise than those who perceive good personal health. In a randomized walking exercise intervention on older women, those who adhered to the two-year exercise program were, at base-line, of lighter weight, already more active, and non-smokers (Kriska, Bayles, Cauley, LaPorte, Sandler, & Pambianco, 1986). However, the variable that best differentiated between compliers and noncompliers was the frequency of reported illness over the two-year period. Women who adhered to the exercise program reported significantly less illness "emphasizing the fact that the limiting factors to physical activity in this population may be quite different from factors limiting physical activity in the young" (Kriska et al., 1986).

Morgan and colleagues (1984) studied an unspecified age group of General Foods employees and found that although male participants who enrolled in the fitness program perceived good health and positive beliefs about exercise, women who were signing up to exercise associated exercise with *poorer* health. Furthermore, female exercise adopters did not improve their perceptions of personal health at retest, although male adopters did. In short, Morgan's team found that the exercise and health relationship differed for men and women.

Objective Health

Although women are outliving their male counterparts by seven or eight years, aged women are vulnerable to one or multiple chronic conditions through much of the period of this extended life. A survey of Canadians in the mid-1980s found 55 percent of adults over 65 reporting arthritis/rheumatism, 39 percent reporting hypertension, 26 percent reporting heart trouble and 24 percent with respiratory problems (General Social Survey, 1987). "Normal aging" for elderly women typically follows this profile: almost half are physically limited in daily activity; 60 percent of women over 65 were screened out of random public physical fitness testing for reasons of health risk (Canada Fitness Survey, 1983); and 46 percent are institutionalized by age 85. Many are truly unfit and cannot complete even modified fitness tests of basic strength (O'Brien & Conger, 1988). This lack of basic strength is blamed for the majority of the falls experienced by one third of all adults over age 65. One third of women ages 65 years and up will have one or more vertebral fractures. As women survive into their eighties, one third are expected to experience a hip fracture (Nelson, Fisher, Dilmanian, Dallal, & Evans, 1991).

With widowhood, poverty and declining health as the norm for about half of all older women, women over the age of 65 are more likely to report stress than men. Contributing to this stress are psychosocial and physiological effects of motor-sensory deprivation due to physical inactivity.

In contrast to women, older men face more mortal concerns. Of primary concern is the gender difference in the age of onset and the overall incidence of heart disease.

Although more women actually die each year of coronary heart disease, men contract the disease about 15 years sooner than women. Incidence of male heart problems can begin at age 35, although heart disease becomes more of a concern for postmenopausal women.

Another gender difference is evident in survival rates after first heart attack. Perhaps because of earlier appearance of the disease in males, men seem to be better able to survive first heart attack better than women, and consequently, middle-age to elderly men are in the majority in cardiac rehabilitation programs. Some research has suggested that the health promotion potential of physical activity may be stronger for men, especially if pursued during the middle years of life (Hein, Suadicani, Sorensen, & Gyntelberg, 1994). This finding makes sense if one considers the risk-reducing qualities might have the greatest effect on men by delaying the onset of the disease until old age. However, Hein and colleagues warm that prior athleticism may not guard against coronary heart disease unless physical activity patterns are maintained over the life-span.

The inverse gradient in the fitness–mortality relationship is strong and steep for men, possibly because there have been far more mortality and physical activity studies done on men. For example, Paffenbarger and his colleagues from Stanford University have done a series of longevity and all-cause mortality studies on large convenience samples of men— longshoremen and 17,000 college alumni (Paffenbarger, Hyde, Wing, & Hsied, 1986).

For women, the gradient is less steep; Bokovoy and Blair (1994) found that both moderately and highly fit older women had a lower all-cause mortality risk than unfit women, but did not differ from each other. This means that the mortality protection for women is potent even for moderate exercise, but overall, women gain less longevity advantage than men in pursuing moderate to vigorous exercise. The wider range of fitness levels among men may be part of the explanation for the strong male gradient. Another explanation may be that unfit women may be less fit than unfit men, so females may reap greater benefits at even moderate levels of physical activity (CFLRI, 1995). Also the longevity of women is greater than men, and therefore the potential to increase women's longevity even more may be limited.

MARITAL STATUS AND EXERCISE

An active life partner has been hypothesized to have a strong influence on the activity patterns of their mate. In 1976, Spreitzer and Snyder advocated a social learning perspective and suggested that involvement in sport resulted from exposure to role models and reinforcement from significant others. Using self-administered questionnaires with a systematic probability sample on 264 adults under the age of 61, these researchers found that female involvement appeared to be determined more by their spouses' degree of involvement than the extent to which women participated in their youth.

Having a spouse who is indirectly involved in sports tends to reinforce earlier encouragement from one's parents and to interact with perceived ability partly to explain the degree to which one is involved in sport as an adult (Spreitzer & Snyder, 1976).

Tait and Dobash (1986) claimed that women consciously or unconsciously marry a male whose orientations in lifestyle are similar to their own. They suggest that "women who take part in sport perceive a very high degree of support from their nominated or significant male" (Tait & Dobash, 1986).

The relationship between marital status and cardiovascular risk behaviors was the focus of a study on 7,849 midwestern men and women. Separated or divorced persons reported higher levels of relaxation-enhancing behaviors such as smoking and drinking and higher levels of physical activity. Married men showed lower mortality rates over single men, but married women were not advantaged in this way over single women. For women, "never having been married" was the most favorable status with respect to educational attainment and reported history of heart attack and stroke. Being married, or over the age of 40, were situations that were accompanied by less physical activity (Rudman, 1986b).

Ishii-Kuntz (1990) studied the formal activities of elderly women and the determinants of their participation in senior's centers. Using a nationwide probability sample of 1,051 women over the age of 65 (data collected in 1981), this research categorized variables as: "predisposing" (age, race, education, and marital status), "enabling" (income, employment status, health status, and transportation) and "need" (loneliness and living arrangement). The average age of the women was 73.2 years and 62 percent were widowed. Elderly widows were more likely to participate in voluntary organizations than married women and loneliness had a positive impact on their senior center participation.

PARENTHOOD AND FAMILY SIZE

Exploring the parenting role and the impact of family on physical activity and health outcomes has received little attention. Parenthood and grandparenthood are important social roles that last a lifetime. These roles are significant to the status of men but have particular salience for women. Motherhood and grandmotherhood are the most enduring social roles with which women identify. Yet little research has examined the role of motherhood on women's exercise patterns in middle age and beyond. The number of children born, number of children raised in the household, the spacing of children, and the health of children cared for are plausible factors affecting women's leisure and physical activity patterns over much of the adult life course (Henderson, Bialeschki, Shaw, & Freysinger, 1990). The impact of family size on women's exercise patterns is likely to be a reflection of available leisure time, availability of financial resources, and a mother's interest in being physically active in the play patterns of her family.

> Leisure for women has been, and largely still is, home-based. Because home is also a place, if not the place, of work for women, it is not surprising that work and leisure activities are often intertwined and indistinguishable (Henderson, et al., 1990).

A Canadian time budget study by Shaw (1985) examined the distribution of leisure of 60 married women for a 48-hour period. Although over 70 percent of gardening and animal-care chores were considered by the women to be leisure, only 4 percent or less of home chores and laundry were defined as leisure. Henderson and colleagues (1990) argued that women have typically been oppressed in most aspects of their lives, including leisure. Allen and Chin-Sang (1990) studied the meaning of leisure and work for 30 aging black women. When asked how their definition and experience of leisure had changed over the years, most women said they "had no leisure in the past." Housework was clearly the predominant feature of their lives, but gardening was classified by many women to be a leisure activity. Even though housework may be the predominant physical activity for many women, Verbrugge (1990a) reported that homemakers are not particularly enthusiastic about their work compared to employed men and women. Furthermore, employed women usually liked unpaid housework less than their paid jobs.

An important example of family leisure is the holiday, yet the family holiday is "often a breeding ground for arguments and family conflicts and where the domestic labour for women may actually increase. . ." (Deem, 1982). Leisure outside the home has often been viewed as something that mothers should willingly sacrifice.

As with today's contemporary women, even if pioneer women had been physically inclined, traditional roles of child rearing, housekeeping, and domestic skills such as cooking and sewing, would have consumed much of their time and energy during their maternal years. Housewives with young children were likely to perceive little freedom in their lives because of constantly being "on call."

> Children constrain women's leisure not just because of the considerable physical care required by babies and young children, but also because of their social and emotional needs. The responsibility of child care, which falls disproportionately to women in society, reduces women's leisure options and inhibits a considerable number of leisure activities. . . (Henderson et al., 1990)

Many pioneer women worked farmland or ranches or provided support systems for their husband's occupational pursuits. Home industry and responsibilities were often were initiated in the adolescent years, no doubt heightened during the depression and war years, so that leisure time physical activity may have been limited. Certainly the time required for skilled athletic development would not have been highly valued by society as the preferred way for average women to spend their time.

> Some work has suggested that women's private leisure time is of less value than men's. Women's time (each day and across their life span) was (and still is) perceived as time that could be interrupted for whatever needs or crises arose, particularly those needs related to the family, although the time of men was respected as private. (Henderson et al., 1990).

Deem (1982) contended that leisure spaces are particularly difficult for women to find in their own home. When older, most females have established lifestyles without sport skills or habitual fitness activities, and the normal course of action is to taper activity in the later years, not increase it.

An interaction effect between income and number of children demonstrates the complexity of developing a simple understanding of exercise behavior and one's family situation. This interaction effect indicates that as number of children increases for lower income persons, participation in individual physical activities decreases. For high income persons, participation increases with more children. Women who have adequate financial resources may be better able to afford the time and cost of engaging in activities alongside their children. Children of middle-class families may experience more instruction in lifelong activities such as tennis, swimming, skiing, skating, and golf. They, therefore, are in a better situation to participate in sports in which whole families can enjoy.

Beliefs about personal risk are known to be important to people's decisions about participation. Relevant to this topic are findings that mothers, ages 52 to 73, perceived significantly less risk in fitness activities than same-aged women who were never mothers (Branigan & O'Brien Cousins, 1995). Moreover, the more children raised by the mothers, the less risk they felt for challenging fitness activity. Because health, age, and education were all statistically controlled for in this study, other explanations had to be sought. Beliefs about low risk in exercise settings by aging mothers may be attributed to an attenuation to exerting activities after a lifetime of raising children. Perhaps mothers become more risk-accepting by taking on the risks of bearing and raising larger families. Through their children, perhaps mothers learn a good deal about the benefits of play and vigorous exercise, and consider the risks to be small in comparison.

WORK ROLE, EMPLOYMENT, AND EXERCISE

Changing patterns of activity involvement are thought to be the result of altered role transitions and altered opportunities across the life cycle (McPherson, 1984). Particularly relevant to leisure time activity are the demands of an individual's employment and non-paid work. McPherson suggested that,

> the decisions concerning how to minimize costs and maximize rewards with respect to physical activity involvement are related to commitment, adherence, and the relationship between work and leisure and between work and family responsibilities (1984).

Neither women's employment, nor domestic work role, have been studied extensively for their role in determining physical activity patterns. Life work is thought to be closely tied to level of education, marital status, number of children raised, health status, social class and so either types of work, as activity-promoting forces for women, are difficult to study in isolation. Morgan (1986) pointed out that it is physical activity of any kind, not athleticism, that is associated with quality and quantity of life. To date, little or no research on the fitness and health outcomes of women's domestic work activities have been reported. However, employed women of higher means are apparently more physically active. Almost 60 percent of Canadian women in manager/ professional occupations report they are active compared to only 44 percent of women in blue collar work (Government of Canada, 1984).

Recently, there has been information to suggest that employed women carry most of the domestic work load at home in addition to full-time engagement in employed labor. This means that leisure time opportunities for employed women may be even more severely limited than full-time homemakers, and that opportunities for exercise may be lacking for employed women unless they undertake fitness activity during their normal work day.

Fishwick and Hayes (1989) surveyed 401 adults ages 18 to 83 years of age to determine differences in recreational activity by age, race, gender, and social class. In contrast to much of the literature, they found that women were not underrepresented as leisure time sports participants but were vastly underrepresented as team sport participants. Possibly time constraints made it difficult to schedule practices and games with other adults. In addition, Fishwick and Hayes emphasize that normative expectations channel women into "gender-appropriate" activities such as aerobics.

Steinhardt and Carrier (1989) examined early and continued participation in a corporate work-site health and fitness program (Conoco Inc.). Using a broad array of variables representing socio-environmental factors, physical-behavioral factors and psychological factors, they obtained physiological and questionnaire data on 143 women ages 19 to 60 years old. They found younger employees were more likely to be "starters" in the program. Those who were adherers claimed more "attitudinal commitment" and perceived the health and fitness program to be more convenient.

McPherson and Kozlik (1987) reviewed studies on Canadian leisure activities by age, and noted that participation rates dropped severely after age 19 and again at age 64—two points regarded as endpoints of labour force activity. At these transition points, men participated in sport activity to a greater degree than women, and rates of participation increased in a linear pattern with income and level of education. More study is needed to understand how paid work facilitates or undermines active leisure patterns, and how retirement from employment encourages or discourages future participation.

SOCIOECONOMIC STATUS AND EXERCISE

Findings from Canada's Health Promotion Survey (1990) suggested that:

- Canadians who rate their health as excellent are three times more likely to be in the highest income bracket than those who consider their health to be poor.
- Canadians in the lowest income bracket are four times as likely to rate their health as only fair or poor as those in the highest income bracket.

However, direct information on the role of financial situation and older adult exercise is lacking. McDaniel (1989) pointed out that economic inequities tend to accumulate in old age and are exacerbated by a pension system that is not workable for many women. More research will be needed to tease out the interwoven elements of socio-economic status, gender, educational level, occupational level, and race, which, in various ways, are likely to limit lifestyle choices, activity patterns, and outcomes of good health.

GENDER, CULTURE, AND CHILDHOOD SOCIALIZATION

"Social system theories" reflect the cultural interaction between society and individuals (McPherson, 1990). General sociological theory advocates the importance of social structure, social processes, social roles, and the effect of the cultural environment on human behavior (George, 1985).

> Socialization is a lifelong process that enables an individual to participate in a society. . . . Socialization is both a process and a product. As a process, socialization involves learning skills, traits, knowledge, attitudes, language, beliefs, norms, values and shared behavioral expectations associated with present or future roles. The process may vary because of such factors such as gender, socioeconomic status, community or ethnic differences, cultural differences, and individual differences in the lifestyle and values of socializing agents. (McPherson, 1990)

In this section, a life course perspective is utilized. Particular attention is given to the elements of childhood at the turn-of-the-century that would promote or deter one's physical activities throughout the remainder of the life-span. In particular, a focus is given to social systems, such as gender and age, that expose certain social segments to experiences which could lead to positive feelings of physical skill, control, and mastery.

One of the most significant social roles affecting human behavior is that created by gender. A wealth of evidence exists to suggest that males and females are socialized very differently from an early age, particularly with respect to aggressive play and choice of toys. Traditionally, females have had little encouragement to engage in certain vigorous and challenging forms of physical activity and sport (Vertinsky, 1991). Females are socialized to be more passive physically, and in particular, are lured away from combative and other aggressive forms of sport. Wakat and Odom (1982) noted that "although infant males and females start out with roughly the same physical capabilities, they soon begin to experience different courses of development, as set down by society according to what is appropriate for little boys and what is appropriate for little girls." Media interest and the public popularity of contemporary male professional sport heroes attest to important differences in gender support for physical activity that still persist today. Hall (1976) reported that women's attitudes toward activity are generally favorable, and concludes that socialization and opportunity are therefore most responsible for the inadequate participation of females.

Apparently, contemporary females still experience considerable role conflict in certain athletic settings and the female in sport is still considered to be in man's territory (Csizma, Wittig, & Schurr, 1988). Since the 1970s, sport sociologists recognize that physical activity and sport are used as an important medium in which males are "masculinized." Conversely, the same cultural values, if applied to females, would be construed as "defemininizing."

Hauge (1973) wrote an early review paper of the influence of the nuclear family on female sport participation. She raised the possibility that a propensity toward tomboyish behavior might be affected by sibling order, family size, parental model-ling, and childhood opportunity. As important as the family in socializing young people, is probably their school experience. Vertinsky (1992) presented a thorough summary and discussion of the challenges and opportunities physical educators face in providing gender equity in contemporary school settings. With strong social forces operating at school and in the home, the socializing determinants for physical activity participation are likely to be quite different for men and women.

One's early circumstances and socializing experiences are apt to play some role in determining how active one would want to be over the life course (Rudman, 1986b). Sport socialization theory more specifically recognizes that individuals are socialized differently in physical activity settings often starting at a very early age. A number of studies support the hypothesis that early experiences in childhood physical activity create advantages for adult participation later on (Dishman & Dunn, 1988; Spreitzer & Snyder, 1976). Even exposure to activity opportunities in early adulthood may be effective in lifelong involvement. Adams and Brynteson (1992) reported that middle-age adults exercised more frequently, and held higher health value for exer-cise, if they simply had more hourly exposure to physical activity training as col-lege students. Howell and McKenzie (1987) also found varsity and non-varsity sports participation in high school increased adult sports involvement for both men and women.

At least two studies do not support the early socialization hypothesis (Adams & Brynteson, 1992; Steinhardt & Carrier, 1989). Dishman and Dunn (1988) warned that the "available evidence on the relationship between childhood and adulthood exercise patterns is not compelling" because the associations come exclusively from cross-sectional and retrospective surveys with adults and is limited to sport and physical education experiences.

Past Experience and Socialization
for Childhood Physical Activity

A collection of studies identified relationships among childhood activity opportuni-ties, perceived physical ability, and social support by one's parents, peers, male sib-lings, teachers (Greendorfer, 1983; Griffin, 1982). Research indicates that physical play and recreation during childhood contributes to an awareness of one's physical world and enhances the ability to manipulate and control one's surroundings (Lewin & Olsen, 1985).

Moore and colleagues (1991) researched the relationship between activity levels of parents and those of their young children ages four to seven. Caltrac accelerom-eters monitored children, mothers, and fathers for more than ten hours a day for eight days. Children of active mothers were twice as likely to be physically active as the children of inactive mothers. The relative odds of being active for the children of active fathers was even higher at 3.5. When both parents were active, the children were 5.8 times as likely to be active.

Possible mechanisms for the relationship between parents' and child's activity levels include the parents serving as role models, sharing of activities by family members, enhancement and support by active parents of their child's participation in physical activity, and genetically transmitted factors that predispose the child to increased levels of physical activity (Moore et al., 1991).

A number of studies support the important role of early childhood physical activity in the development of role play, sense of group membership, fitness and motor skill, bodily awareness and improved self-concept. Sex differences in motives for participation have been identified, with boys placing more emphasis on achievement, rewards, and status. Powell and Dysinger (1987) reviewed the available literature on the association between childhood and adult phy-sical activity patterns. In summarizing the available studies, they felt that the Harvard alumni study, which connected college sport to current activity patterns and absence of coronary disease (Paffenbarger, Hyde, Wing & Hsied, 1986), provided the strongest evidence supporting an association between youth and adult activity in males.

Butcher (1983) examined three categories of variables that influenced the physical activities of 661 adolescent girls: personal attributes, socializing agents, and socialization situations. For competitive interschool teams and intramural activities, four personal attributes: movement satisfaction, self-confidence, independence, and assertive (self-description) were most important. For community-organized activities, socializing agents (parental influence) and socialization situations (socioeconomic status) were most influential, although for the total activities participated in, the amount of sports equipment was the crucial factor. Butcher noted that by Grade 10 there was a noticeable drop in girls' school physical activity participation, but not in physical activity in the community setting. Three types of social influence were family (parents and siblings), peers, and teachers or coaches. Representing a European perspective, Meusel (1991) claimed that,

> The physical education teacher is better qualified than most to open the path towards successful ageing to individuals and society with their work. Should not the physical education teacher also learn and teach how sport activity is to be adapted not only to the immediate but also to the long-term interests of the individual! (Meusel, 1991)

Spreitzer and Snyder (1976) developed a path analysis model of early sport socialization using self-administered questionnaires with a middle-age population of 110 women and 154 men (mean age = 42 years), and an average education level of 13 years. From seven predictor variables, 46 percent of the variance in sport involvement in men and 40 percent of the variance among women was explained. From the results they formed a causal framework stated as follows:

> Parents (especially the father) who are interested in sports tend to encourage their offspring to participate in sports, which markedly increases the likelihood of a youth's participation in sports. One's participation as a youth markedly affects how one perceives his/her athletic ability. This perception, in turn, has a strong impact on the degree of adult participation in sport. (Spreitzer & Snyder, 1976)

Howell and McKenzie (1987) found that participation in high school athletic programs was related to team sport activity later in adulthood with some gender differences. The effects of high school varsity sport experience on later life sport involvement was greater for men than for women. This finding similar to that of Spreitzer and Snyder (1976) who obtained a correlation of .25 between youth and adult sport involvement for males, but no relationship at all for females. These findings suggest that even when sport organizations are available to young females, other barriers exist to their involvement later in life.

Steinhardt and Carrier (1989) set up an interesting study of men and women attending a health and fitness program in a large corporation. Their findings contradict research that indicates youth participation has positive effects on adult participation. Instead they found that the individuals who were among the first to participate in the corporate fitness program appeared to have been sedentary as youth. They suggest "that those individuals who were active as youth may be less attracted to an organized program or perhaps less dependent on an organized program to exercise" (Steinhardt & Carrier, 1989).

Childhood Situation: Opportunity, Mastery, Movement Competence

Growing evidence suggests that physical mastery, or an individual's self-concept of physical ability, may be the most important determinant of both affect and expectancy, and therefore, an important mediator of human motivation and movement behavior. Evidence is lacking, however, at what stage in human development the self-concept of movement ability must be realized to be incorporated into one's identity.

Positive and early experiences with physical activity and sport seem to have lasting effects in other ways. Raivio (1986) reported that interviews with Finnish female sport administrators, ages 29 to 60, indicate a similar childhood background; all ten women had participated in outdoor activities as young girls, and all but one recalled a parent or close relative encouraging their participation in physical activities. Morgan (1986) found that former male high school athletes reported significantly more positive attitudes towards activity and their estimation of personal physical ability in young adulthood, yet were not necessarily more active in adulthood than former non-athletes. He concluded that former athletes appeared to base their subjective judgments of physical ability on an earlier reference point. Furthermore Morgan noted that former athletes, who were no longer active, still regarded themselves as athletes.

Dishman (1990) claimed that organized sport experience in one's youth might contribute "knowledge, skills, and predispositions useful for activity in later years and is amenable to large-scale public intervention." Thus, a causal relationship between skilled participation in childhood and adult activity would have strong implications for public health (Dishman, 1990). Yet no prospective study has been conducted to specifically show this relationship; long-term studies of childhood sport or physical education as a determinant of contemporary adult activity have not been reported. For now, the numerous cross-sectional and retrospective studies that link youth sport with adult physical activity must be viewed with caution. Thus, the question of whether physical activity determinants for the individual who begins habitual activity at middle age are the same as those of a person who was active because childhood remains unclear.

Research is consistently finding that perceived competence in physical skills is an important influence on the participation and motivation of children in sport contexts. Young participants in organized sports are found to have higher perceived competence, more persistence and higher expectations for future success than non-participant children. Self-efficacy ratings and experience level in gymnastics were significant predictors of the actual success of boys ages 7 to 18 in competitive gymnastics settings. There is preliminary evidence that mastery of high-risk sport skill may even generate increased self-efficacy for other physical and social tasks (Brody, Hatfield, & Spalding, 1988).

Social comparison to peers is one way that individuals may judge their capability for activity. What children say and do in physical education classes may be highly sex-differentiated; subtle socialization is part of a "hidden curriculum" whereby children learn that female activities are less valued (Griffin, 1982). Boys may limit girls' opportunities to master physical skill by excluding female players on passes, "hogging" the ball, and by dominating coed games in general. In a variety of ways, boys unintentionally or intentionally undermine the confidence of female players.

Similarly, family members are thought to be powerful determinants of the activity behaviors of children. Parents, in particular, are key role models and may at first support the athletic achievements of a daughter. But "when parents decide that sport achievement is a threat to her social life and eventual marriage, they push the feminine role" (Hauge, 1973). There is a tendency for a same-sexed parent to have more influence on a child's involvement than does the opposite-sexed parent (Snyder & Spreitzer, 1973).

Petruzzello & Corbin (1988) also advocated that experience and gender are important determinants of performer confidence. They conducted two studies on college-age males and females that indicated that even on gender-neutral motor tasks, females rate themselves with significantly lower levels of confidence. They concluded that the greater experiences and social rewards for males in physical activity raises their expectancies for success on new tasks.

> It becomes increasingly clear that experience affects self-confidence. Successful experiences/mastery attempts can serve to enhance self-confidence. As such, the more experience one has at a variety of tasks in a variety of physical situations, the greater the possibilities are that self-confidence can be generalized to more situations (Petruzzello & Corbin, 1988).

A construct called *movement confidence* was employed for predicting children's physical performance and play decisions. Griffin and Keogh (1982) developed a working model that describes "movement confidence as both a consequence and a mediator in an involvement cycle." Movement confidence was defined as a feeling of adequacy in a movement situation.

The confidence or assurance with which an individual approaches a movement situation should be an important determinant of what an individual will choose to do and how adequate the movement performance will be (Griffin & Keogh, 1982).

The Griffin and Keogh Model of Movement Confidence assumes that a cognitive evaluation of self in relation to the perceived demands of a task is an antecedent to confidence. Utilizing a Movement Confidence Inventory (MCI), Griffin, Keogh, and Maybee (1984) studied perceptions of movement confidence of 450 college-age students for performing 12 different movement and sport-related tasks. In that study it became clear that movement competence was not a lone predictor of performance confidence; rather, it was accompanied by perceptions of potential pleasant and unpleasant movement experiences. A playground movement confidence inventory (PMCI) and a stunt movement confidence inventory (SMCI) were developed to identify children who may be in need of special assistance in learning sport and physical activity. Griffin and Crawford (1989) noted that level of confidence varied according to the nature of the specific task and context. The Stunt Movement Confidence Inventory was able to reliably discriminate between high- and low-confidence children ages 9 to 11 on six "stunting" tasks.

SUMMARY

This chapter has explored ten contextual elements that can affect one's propensity or aversion for late life physical activity. In the next chapter, a different perspective is presented—that is, a conceptual stance that the individual is the significant controlling force over their actions.

Chapter 11

Cognitive Explanations

THE COGNITIVE DETERMINANTS OF EXERCISE

Developing an understanding about the mechanisms underlying regular physical activity participation poses a challenge. Many studies on motivation and exercise have concentrated on adherence, or the problem of keeping participants exercising once they have started. Less has been studied on the reasons why people start exercising in the first place, and little information is available on the motives behind the late-life initiation or resumption of exercise regimens of older adults.

> Despite a remarkable growth in applied interest about exercise adherence, the development of conceptual models leading toward a motivational theory of habitual physical activity has lagged far behind (Sonstroem, 1988).

Sonstroem (1978) advanced one of the first models for prediction of exercise involvement. Key to his theoretical model was the notion of "self-esteem." In predicting exercise participation, Sonstroem's model posited that self-perceptions of physical ability (Estimation) influence an individual's interest in physical activity (Attraction) and that Attraction provides the greater influence on exercise participation. Although Sonstroem's model has enjoyed only limited success in explaining the activity patterns of high school boys, it provides some important information: that is, people who are motivated to be physically active will turn first to those activities to which they are most attracted, in which they feel competent and confident and through which their self-esteem is likely to be maintained.

Psychologists hold the perspective that the individual is the controlling aspect of behavior. Although every individual confronts social forces that may shape their values and beliefs, ultimately the individual's motivation, and the way they interpret their world, leads to predictable patterns of behavior. Social Cognitive Theory is the main focus of this chapter because this broadly applied behavioral theory has already met with good success in the explanation of older adult physical activity.

Self-referent perspectives are important to understand because attitudes, opinions, and beliefs are formative and modifiable (Dishman, 1990), creating the potential for health promotion initiatives and program experiences to profoundly and quickly transform individual perspectives and behavior. When health promotion programs are aimed at older adults, they can have a significant impact on mortality outcomes even after age 70 (Kaplan, Seeman, Cohen, Knudsen, & Guralnik, 1987). Creating behavior change is not easy, but understanding how perspectives are formed, and also how they are changed, are important steps in being able to convince more adults to age better by making lifestyle changes.

Conceptual models to understand and explain the diverse determinants for participation in physical activity among elderly adults are relatively undeveloped. In newer studies, motivational factors that have had some success are now being combined for further strength in prediction (Sharpe & O'Connell, 1992). Incentives, attitudes, beliefs, expectancies, perceived barriers, cues to act, and self-perceptions are among the most common constructs used in contemporary theoretical models. In this chapter, key studies pertaining to the cognitive determinants of late-life exercise are presented. The literature is organized according to four main cognitive components: 1) motive or incentive; 2) outcome expectations; 3) social reinforcement; and 4) self-efficacy. Other health behavior constructs, such as health locus of control, will be discussed in relation to their conceptual overlaps with Social Cognitive Theory.

SOCIAL COGNITIVE THEORY

An important theoretical stance in behavioral psychology is that individual beliefs about one's world are the controlling determinants of one's behavior. Social Cognitive Theory (SCT) successfully represents this stance in many contemporary studies (Bandura, 1986, 1989, 1997; Bandura, & Cervone, 1986;). Dzewaltowski (1989) has twice shown that SCT is a superior theoretical model for the prediction of exercise in adults.

Bandura's SCT accords a central role to self-reflective, cognitive processes and predicts human behavior by examining individual beliefs or subjective expectancies about the personal outcomes of their actions. Specifically, Bandura's theory claims that human activity is guided by a set of four main beliefs: motivation to obtain a goal (*incentive to act*), beliefs that a certain behavior will be beneficial in reaching a goal (*outcome expectations*), a belief in one's ability to perform the behavior or *action (self-efficacy)*, and finally, a perception that the action will be rewarded (*social-environmental reinforcement*) (Figure 11.1). Exercise behavior, in this perspective, is predicted to occur when an individual: 1) wants to maintain or improve their health (MOTIVE, GOAL, INCENTIVE); 2) perceives that exercise participation will lead to health benefits and that harmful outcomes are unlikely (BENEFITS, RISKS); 3) believes they are capable of performing the activity successfully (EFFICACY); and 4) perceives that those around them will support their participation (SUPPORT). To the extent that individuals "learn" which actions contribute to health, which activities are risky, which are beneficial, how competent they really are, and how much endorsement society will offer for their behavior, self-referent beliefs reflect the cultural-environmental milieu and social learning of the individual (See Reciprocal Determinism, Chapter 9).

INCENTIVES OR MOTIVES TO EXERCISE

Bandura's "incentive to act," behavioral goal or motive, could be represented as the incentive to live a long and healthy life. Setting goals for maintaining or improving health is considered to be a key determinant explaining why adults might take up health-promoting exercise in late life (Duda & Tappe, 1989). We do know that many people hold the expectancy of gaining or maintaining health from participation in physical activity; we also know that people who place a high value on health may exercise more than persons who place a low value on health.

   In contemplating more active living, people need a good reason to even think about starting. Bandura claims that people have to have a goal that they seek to

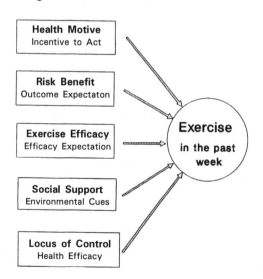

Figure 11.1 Cognitive model of late-life exercise.

achieve, and their action must be highly valued if they are going to develop the motivation to achieve it. There are many participatory motives for older adults. Older adults say they seek physical activity as a way to relieve boredom or stress and get out of the house, to socialize, to have fun, to maintain or learn physical skills, to follow doctor's orders, to demonstrate self-discipline, to experience competition or self-measurement, to promote beauty and/or to obtain health and fitness benefits. Some research suggests that motives may differ by gender and life stage.

Finkenberg (1991) used Kenyon's Attitudes Toward Physical Activity Scale and found, in college students, that males were significantly more motivated to exercise for competition, but females were more motivated to exercise for health and fitness. Among older people, O'Brien and Conger (1991) found that men and women participating in Seniors Games were motivated by different expected outcomes. Male participants reported they enjoyed maintaining a degree of public acclaim for sustaining their physical prowess into old age. In contrast, older women said that sport participation promoted their functional health and personal independence so that they could sustain more active caregiver roles within their families.

Godin, Shephard, and Colantino (1986) focused their study on middle-age employees who expressed a willingness to exercise but actually did not exercise. The overall findings identified surprisingly little difference between cognitive profiles of inactive and active adults. Individuals who had intended to exercise, but didn't exercise during the two-month period of the study, differed from fellow exercisers in perceiving a problem with "lack of time," and believing that exercise required more effort and provided less health value. The researchers suggested that motivation might not be the limiting factor for many inactive people; sedentary intenders might simply be confronted with more social and environmental constraints than those who are active. However, lack of leisure time as a barrier to exercise, is a perplexing factor considering the situation of elderly adults, most of whom are retired.

Health as Incentive to Act

Of interest to the motivation issue is the expectancy of gaining health from participation in physical activity. Expectancy value is an important construct in Social Cognitive Theory and is seen as central to one's motivation. Simply, people must value what they do, or why would they bother? For example, physical activity must be highly valued for its role in "producing" health in order to be considered to be a potential incentive. That is, those individuals who place a high value on maintaining their health, and who understand the role of regular moderate exercise in maintaining health, would be hypothesized to be more likely to be physically active. There is scant evidence to support this hypothesis. The Campbell's Survey (Stephens & Craig, 1990) reported that, by age 65, less than half of Canadian adults judged physical activity as very important to their health. Furthermore,

> females attach more importance than males to all factors, especially body weight, a good diet, and rest and sleep, with *only one exception*: regular physical activity (Stephens & Craig, 1990).

Other evidence suggests that older people are not particularly concerned with promoting their health. For example, Karen Altergott, editor of *Daily Life in Later Life* (1988), included a chapter titled "Life course and the daily lives of older adults in Canada" written by Zuzanek and Box. They claim that, as a result of retirement, older Canadians gain approximately 38 extra hours of disposable time per week.

> Paradoxically, although older adults possess greater amounts of free time, their rates of participation in leisure activities, and the number of leisure activities they engage in, decline after retirement (Zuzanek & Box, 1988).

Substantial participation declines are noted to occur in the post-retirement period in sports, sport spectatorship, and outdoor recreation (especially for women), although activities affected little, or even slightly expanded, are visiting, reading, radio listening, watching television, playing cards, hobbies, pleasure driving, and physically less demanding forms of outdoor activities such as walking. These, then, are the activities that appear to most interest older adults. Closer scrutiny of the main activities chosen by seniors illustrates that few of them appear to have been chosen for their physical "health value."

Rather, the recreational activities of the older Canadians often seem to have been selected instead for their social and entertainment value. Thus one might question the assumption that health value acts as an "incentive" in explaining older adult involvement in physical activity. Many older adults may not be aware of the health-promoting effects of exercise participation. Other older adults may see less relevance to sustaining or taking up health-promoting activities as age advances, particularly if they believe that such efforts are only likely to contribute to short-term gains. Seniors may indeed feel that their "life time" is running out and they are too late to realize any significant gains from serious participation in physical activities (O'Brien & Conger, 1991). They may feel that the finite lifespan may cut short the gains from an exercise program giving little "health value" to regular exercise participation. Perhaps there comes a point in the life course when people stop doing "the right thing" for their health because they perceive that life will soon end anyway. In these circumstances, older adults may be motivated to undertake activities primarily for pleasure and entertainment.

Outcome Expectations

Outcome expectations are beliefs about the probable consequences of personal actions. Because participation in fitness exercise is a high-effort and often skilled undertaking, individuals take action when they believe that the beneficial outcomes of participation are high and will outweigh the costs (Rosenstock, Strecher, & Becker, 1988). Previous research has advised that about 20 percent of older adults perceive that regular exercise does them more harm than good. Thus many older adults seem to believe that exercise participation is more a risk-taking action than a risk-reducing action. In reality, sport injuries affect less than five percent of the over 65 age group of Canadians (Stephens & Craig, 1990), yet preliminary evidence suggests that *perceived risks* associated with vigorous activities may be a particularly significant barrier to participation (Koplan, Siscovick, & Goldbaum, 1985).

Heightened risk perceptions may be a particular feature of being older. Women, especially, may feel at risk because their minimal involvement in vigorous activity reveals major constraints (Calnan & Johnson, 1985; O'Brien & Vertinsky, 1991). In experimental settings, older adults perceive that they are exerting themselves more than younger adults at age-equated training loads and thus they may fear the consequences of engaging in more exerting activity. Exacerbating these fears, media campaigns may have misled the public to believe that exercise must be highly strenuous to be health-promoting (Blair, Kohl, Gordon, & Paffenbarger, 1992). With an all-or-none view about the intensity of exercise necessary for health benefits, older adults may perceive there is little point in engaging in brief and lower intensity activities, and they simply may not feel capable of, and safe with, longer or more intense exercise.

Expectations about positive or negative consequences (benefits or risks) are important to the actions taken by individuals according to both Social Cognitive Theory and the Health Belief Model. The ability to envision the likely outcomes of prospective actions is one way in which anticipatory mechanisms regulate human motivation and action. "People strive to gain anticipated beneficial outcomes and to forestall aversive ones" (Bandura, 1989). In addition, the effects of outcome expectancies on performance motivation are partly governed by self-beliefs of efficacy. In activities in which the level of competence dictates the outcomes, the types of outcomes people anticipate depend largely on their beliefs of how well they will be able to perform in given situations. The strong statistical relationship between outcome expectations and efficacy are such that "when variations in perceived self-efficacy are partialed out, the outcomes expected for given performances do not have much of an independent effect on behavior" (Bandura, 1989).

Positive outcome expectations for physical activity would require that the individual believes that the outcomes of participation would be personally beneficial and the risks of participation would be reasonably low. According to Bandura's interpretation, perceptions of risk would then be predicted to be higher for individuals who have low self-efficacy for physical activity. Conversely, perceptions of positive outcomes would be predicted to be higher for those who exhibit high self-efficacy for physical efficacy.

Self-Efficacy and Movement Confidence

Self-efficacy is the most studied component of social cognitive theory. Perceived self-efficacy appears to play an influential role in ways that affect motivation and "intention" for involvement in physical activity and sport. Because physical activity is often conducted in public settings, and performance is visible to any observer, confidence to perform may be particularly important in the skilled forms of exercise and sport.

Bandura (1977a) defined self-efficacy as the strength of an individual's perceived self-confidence or belief that he or she can successfully complete a task through the expression of ability. Although those who view themselves as having high ability for a task are also apt to feel efficacious for performing it, simply possessing the ability to perform a task does not guarantee a high degree of self-efficacy. In addition to efficacy perceptions, Schunk and Carbonari (1984) claimed that "ability" involves effort, luck, and task difficulty—three additional elements that can explain the success or failure of personal actions. Furthermore, competent behavior is unlikely to occur if social, psychological or structural barriers exist, or if there are inadequate incentives. Self-referent perceptions of efficacy are at least partly responsible for the kinds of challenges that people choose to undertake, how much effort they will spend on an activity, and how long they will persevere in the face of difficulties (Bandura, 1986).

Falling just short of one's goals can be motivating to a point. Social Cognitive Theory claims that discrepancies between performance feedback and personal standards lead to a self-dissatisfaction that then serves as a powerful motivational inducement for enhanced effort. Those who distrust their capabilities are easily discouraged by failure, whereas those who feel assured of their competence to achieve a goal will intensify their efforts when their performances fall short, and persevere until they succeed (Bandura & Cervone, 1986). Dzewaltowski (1989b) therefore suggests that a measure of efficacy in the exercise setting should "examine individuals' efficacy toward coping with difficult situations and still adhere to an exercise program." Recent research suggests that task-specific efficacy measures are superior predictors of behavior over general efficacy measures (Bandura & Cervone, 1986). Thus self-efficacy in exercise research has been defined in many ways such as self-rated confidence to perform specific movements, to adhere to an exercise program, or to sustain exercise for 60 minutes.

The need to be specific in the assessment of physical efficacy has prompted researchers to develop their own measures to deal with their particular research questions. Consequently, the available research on efficacy and exercise at times appears to be haphazard. Some studies merely verify what Bandura's theory has already demonstrated. Others add some interesting information but theoretical direction is lacking. Even with these problems, expectations about personal *efficacy* to do an exercise task is a powerful predictor of exercise behavior (Dzewaltowski, 1989b; Ewart, Taylor, Reese, & DeBusk, 1983; Ewart et al., 1986a, 1986b; Marcus, Selby, Niaura, & Rossi, 1992), particularly in high-skilled settings (Barling & Abel, 1983; Brody, Hatfield, & Spalding, 1988).

BARRIERS TO PERCEIVED EFFICACY TO EXERCISE

The Campbell's Survey (Stephens & Craig, 1990) indicated that barriers and lack of perceived control interfere with the desire of 70 percent of 65+ Canadian women to exercise more. In general, males *at all ages* felt they had more control over their life situations than did females. The major gender differences in perceived barriers were a greater emphasis by females on family time pressures, lack of energy, and lack of ability. Lack of a partner and lack of ability were important explanations among those who resisted or lapsed in their activity programs.

Health, too, can undermine self-efficacy. Davis-Berman (1989) provided evidence that physical self-efficacy in aging women may be minimized by the effects of depression. Thirty percent of the variance in depression scores were explained by a physical self-efficacy score. Kelly (1987) suggests that the low rates of participation in exercise, sport, and outdoor recreation for those age 55 and above reflect the likelihood that real health and physical ability limitations are operative. Exercise and sport settings are high-investment activities that call for special facilities, expert supervision and guidance, eager companions, specialized equipment, and often high levels of effort, skill-requirements and resources that may be harder to fulfill as people reach advanced age. Therefore, social contexts for physical activity tend to become more unstructured, limited to family and friends although the locales of activity may become limited to one's private residence.

Along the same lines, Godin, Shephard, and Colantino (1986) found that sedentary adults (average age 39) who had positive intentions to exercise perceived regular exercise to be "tiring," "time-consuming," and placed less value on "being healthy." The major perceived obstacles of intenders to exercise participation was "lack of time" and "perceived exertion." Both of these factors can be linked to one's perceived ability to carry out a program of exercise.

Waller and Bates (1992) studied self-efficacy beliefs, multidimensional health locus of control, and lifestyle behaviors in 57 healthy elderly subjects (mean age 74.7) with a view to determine who could benefit most from health promotion programs. Most of the subjects were characterized by an internal locus of control belief (91.2 percent), high generalized self-efficacy (57.9%), and good health behaviors. Waller and Bates (1992) suggested that individuals with an internal locus of control and high generalized self-efficacy are most likely to benefit from a health education program compared to those with an external locus of control and low self-efficacy.

Woodward and Wallston (1987) examined age, desire for control, information, and general self-efficacy in 116 adults ages 20 to 99. They found that individuals over 60 years of age desired less health-related control than did younger adults, and preferred that health professionals make decisions for them. Perceived self-efficacy was lower for individuals over 60 years of age. The findings suggest that "those individuals most at risk for chronic illnesses and hospitalization are also those who are most likely to fail to take an active role in their health care."

The Role of Habit and Previous Physical Activity

The important role of "habit" was highlighted in a University of Toronto study. Using a random sample of 136 University of Toronto employees, Godin, Valois, Shephard, and Desharnais (1987) examined the influence of past physical activity on subsequent activity. Three measures of "habit" were used: Immediate Past Behavior (weekly score using MET units to quantify activity level), Past 4 Months Behavior, and Adulthood Behavior (frequency of getting sweaty during leisure time as an adult). They found that "distal" exercise behavior (three weeks and two months later) was predicted by both intention to exercise and Immediate Past Behavior.

Godin and colleagues concluded that if a person has never engaged in a particular behavior, it remains uniquely under the control of behavioral intentions. However as the behavior is repeated, the importance of the habit increases, with a corresponding diminution in the importance of behavioral intention.

> . . . the decision to adopt an active life-style, over the previous habit of being sedentary, requires more "girding up of loins" than the decision to continue to exercise for an individual who has a well-established habit of exercising. Consequently, a process of change has to take place, this requiring "will" in order to compete and resist the forces of the old habit in establishing a new habit (Godin, Valois, Shephard, & Desharnais, 1987) .

Although the role of "habit" has received only preliminary attention in predicting late-life exercise behavior, habitual activity may have some bearing on advancing intention into actual action. In a study by Griffin and Crawford (1989), the notion of "habit" was accommodated in the variable "movement confidence" which combined self-efficacy ("I am sure I can do this") with habitual experience ("I have done this a lot").

The Role of Efficacy on Exercise Behavior

A number of contemporary studies are linking physical self-efficacy, perceived movement competence, or self-rated physical ability to predictions of exercise behavior, physical fitness, and adherence to fitness programs. For example, self-efficacy has been found to be the most powerful and statistically significant correlate of both walking and vigorous exercise among ill and healthy groups alike (Hofstetter et al., 1991).

Ryckman and colleagues (1982) developed a general Physical Self-Efficacy Scale (PSE) in order to identify an individual's perceived physical self-confidence. Although this instrument demonstrated adequate reliability and validity in predicting *general* self-efficacy in sport settings, McAuley and Gill (1983) did not find this to be a useful instrument in evaluating efficacy for college gymnastics. Rather, the Perceived Physical Ability scale (PPA), a sub-scale of the PSE, was more situation-specific and offered better prediction of performance outcomes.

Using the same PPA sub-scale, Duda and Tappe (1989) studied 145 adults ages 25 to 81 years of age with the purpose of examining motivational differences to exercise by gender and age. They found that older and younger physically active adults did not differ in physical self-efficacy and health status. However, middle-age and elderly adults tended to engage in exercise more for the positive consequences on health status than young adults. Males engaged in exercise more for competition than females although females exercised more for fitness reasons. There was also a trend for females to exercise more for affiliative reasons than males. Women tended to view themselves to be less physically able, perceive greater need for support for their involvement in exercise, and believed that one's fitness status is primarily due to fate or chance occurrences (externality). Duda and Tappe concluded that exercise has different meanings to young, middle-age, and elderly men and women noting that perceptions of efficacy and social support for exercise were the major differences between men and women.

According to Bandura, efficacy beliefs are thought to be specific to particular behaviors and not necessarily generalizable to other behaviors. However, evidence exists in one study that efficacy for exercise may be generalizable to related kinds of tasks. Kaplan, Atkins, and Reinsch (1984) examined specific versus generalized efficacy expectations for exercise in older patients with chronic obstructive pulmonary disease (COPD). All subjects (mean age was 65 years) were given a prescription to undertake two daily walks. The experimental group of the randomized design received three months of supervised training and advice although the control group received only advice. After three months, only the experimental group had significantly increased their activity level, their perceived efficacy for walking and also their efficacy expectations for *other similar physical behaviors* in comparison to the control group. These results suggest a "bidirectional" type of causation or a "reciprocal-causal" model meaning that "efficacy and performance attainments may affect each other in reciprocal fashion" (Kaplan, Atkins, & Reinsch, 1984).

Such a finding supports SCT as does Dzewaltowski's study (1989b) conducted on 328 students comparing Bandura's Social Cognitive Theory to Fishbein and Azjen's Theory of Reasoned Action. The theories' constructs were assessed prior to collecting data on the total days exercised over an 8 week period. With all the variables entered in a regression equation, the Theory of Reasoned Action could only account for 6 percent of the variance in exercise behavior. When Social Cognitive Theory variables were entered into the equation, they accounted for more (14%) of the exercise variation. Dzewaltowski (1989a) concluded "it may be that those who exercise are confident that they can exercise despite uncontrollable factors."

Self-efficacy assessment led to a useful application for conducting safe exercise rehabilitation among older men. In Ewart's study (1986b), 40 men were recovering coronary artery disease patients with an average age of 55 years. Their confidence in their ability to jog various distances was measured with a jog self-efficacy (SE) scale before an eight-week group exercise program was begun. Heart rate monitoring during ambulation disclosed that there was significant noncompliance with the prescribed treadmill exercise; 33 percent of patients *exceeded* their prescribed range (70 to 85% of maximum heart rate) for at least half of the 20-minute exercise bout. Another 25 percent spent at least half of their training time exercising below the prescribed range. "Overachievers" were described as patients who overestimated their ability to jog, and "underachievers" were those who overestimated their exercise heart rate. Jogging SE proved superior to treadmill performance, depression measures, and Type A personality measures in predicting patient adherence to exercise prescription.

The Role of Exercise on the Development of Efficacy

The literature generally supports Bandura's theory that efficacy and actual performance strengthen each other in a two-way relationship (reciprocal causation) (Kaplan, Atkins, & Reinsch, 1984). This means that previous successful performance leads to stronger efficacy expectations, and in turn, stronger efficacy perceptions increase the likelihood of further successful performance. Marcus and colleagues (1992) found a linear relationship whereby higher levels of self-efficacy for exercise accompanied higher levels of exercise activity in blue collar employees. In contrast to those who exercise regularly, employees who had not yet begun to exercise had little confidence in their ability to exercise.

Specificity versus Generalizability?   Self-efficacy is understood to be a specific judgement about one's capability and not understood to be generalized to other abilities. However, Stewart and King (1991) suggested that exercise may enhance a sense of more generalized mastery or control through the operation of two mechanisms.

> Regular exercise may provide people with an enhanced sense of their ability to handle problems. Regular exercise may also provide a model of control (e.g. "I obtain improved health by exercising") that may generalize to other life domains. (Stewart & King, 1991)

However, no differences in a general sense of control were found in at least one randomized study of a 12-week aerobic exercise and strengthening program for 15 men and women ages 61 to 86 compared to a social activity control group (N = 15) or a waiting list control group (N = 18) (Emery & Gatz, 1990).

Another finding supports Bandura's specificity of SE and suggests that physical efficacy perceptions can be quickly improved by successful performance on a related activity. The effects of running the treadmill only three weeks following myocardial infarction (MI) on subsequent physical activity were evaluated in 40 men with a mean age of 52 years (Ewart, Taylor, Reese, & DeBusk, 1983). The men were examined for self-perceived ability to walk/run various distances (from one block to five miles), climb stairs (from several steps to four flights), engage in sexual intercourse (from one to 20 or more minutes), and lift and carry objects (from 10 to 75 pounds). Patients' confidence in their ability to perform these activities were assessed before and after a symptom-limited treadmill test of aerobic fitness. Significant increases in self-efficacy occurred after the treadmill test for activities most similar to the test: walking, stair climbing, and running.

In contrast, Hogan and Santomier (1984) examined the effects of participation in a learn-to-swim program on the self-efficacy of older adults. The subjects were 38 volunteers 60 years of age or older. This study was quasi-experimental in that it utilized a non-randomized control group. As such, the study is vulnerable to the confounding effects of self-selection. As expected, significant changes in swimming efficacy were found, but more importantly, this efficacy generalized to other performance-related situations. Open-ended questioning indicated that other aspects of their lives had been affected such as "now able to handle a trip to China," "my walking has improved," and "chores are more easy." Although such generalized efficacy outcomes are not in agreement with Bandura's theory that efficacy expectations are specific, it should be noted that walking, doing chores, and travelling have a strong physical activity component.

Exercise programs can contribute to efficacy better if the participant is regularly involved. A ten week exercise program containing 69 percent women ages 55 to 80 was conducted by Howze, DiGilio, Bennett, and Smith (1983). "High-attenders" were those who attended 15 or more sessions out of the 20 two-hour sessions. "Low-attenders" were less confident of their physical abilities and were more worried about injury. Ninety-two percent of the participants said that they "felt better in general" and felt more physically fit after the program. Howze and colleagues suggested building self-confidence by progressive exercise, which provided successful participation all along the way.

Also, Ewart and colleagues (1986b) examined 43 men with coronary artery disease proposing that highly specific estimates of personal capabilities mediate adoption of new or difficult exercise settings. Correlational analyses of self-efficacy in relation to strength and endurance tests strongly supported the contention that the adoption of novel activities is governed by highly specific self-perceptions. The pattern of findings suggest that favorable appraisal of one's athletic ability increases motivation to pursue sport, leading to greater participation, increased skill, more positive self-appraisal, and consequently, higher motivation.

The Role of Experience and Past Mastery on Current Efficacy Previous performance has an important role in predicting efficacy perceptions. Feltz (1988) examined gender differences in the causal elements of self-efficacy on a "high-avoidance" motor task (the back dive) in college age students. Feltz proposed a respecified model of Social Cognitive Theory that included both self-efficacy and previous performance (experience) as direct predictors of approach/avoidance behavior on the dive. The diving efficacy scale asked the subject to rate the degree of confidence he or she felt about accomplishing the back dive successfully for each of four board heights. Each rating was made on a 10-point scale from 0 (great uncertainty) to 10 (great certainty). Actual performance was measured by two trained observers using an objectively designed performance evaluation. No sex differences were found in self-efficacy scores, and both males and females significantly increased self-efficacy perceptions from Trial 1 to Trial 2. Previous performance and self-efficacy measures were both strong predictors of subsequent performance for males and females.

One of the best studies demonstrating the dose-response nature of self-efficacy and exercise was recently reported by McAuley, Courneya, and Lettunich (1991). Fifty females and 50 males (average age of 54) were examined for the effect of acute and long-term exercise on self-efficacy responses in sedentary adults. Three measures of self-efficacy were employed to determine subject's beliefs in their physical capacities as related to exercise and fitness. Specifically, the efficacy scales represented subject confidence to be able to succeed with 1) increasing numbers of sit-up repetitions in one minute, 2) cycling longer at increasing work loads, and 3) walk-jog successive quarter-mile distances within 4-minute intervals. Subjects participated in a 5-month aerobic exercise program, three times per week in one-hour sessions. Both males and females demonstrated significant increases in efficacy following acute exercise. Females, who had demonstrated initially lower self-perceptions than males, made dramatic increases in efficacy during the exercise program, equalling or surpassing those of males. Increased self-efficacy closely accompanied the actual measured physiological gains in performance as expected. McAuley and associates concluded that their results are encouraging because sedentary individuals in their middle years were able to make significant health-related gains through a relatively low-impact activity such as walking.

The reciprocal nature of efficacy and p
study. Barling and Abel (1983) studied self-effic
40 active males (26.6 years). Three 10-item scale
can play most of my strokes correctly"). Two judg
mance (inter-rater $r = .91$, $p < .001$ in all 12 rated ι
higher self-efficacy for tennis were rated as the most sk
relationship between efficacy and performance holds even wι
by others.

In summary, self-efficacy estimates are powerful predictι
though SE is theoretically conceived as a highly specific belie
evidence suggests that physical forms of efficacy are potent enoι
general forms of self-confidence. More work will be needed to finα
nation for this is biological or psychological.

SOCIAL SUPPORT

The objective of this section is to review the known interrelationships of p
activity, aging, and the social environment. Understanding the impact of variou
cial reinforcements on individual and group behavior holds promise for cost-effectι
community-level intervention.

Ageist Practice in Communities

Ageism, or the explanation of behavior using age considerations alone, is thought to be
a powerful social element governing the present active living choices for adults as they
age. One major theory of aging rests on this assumption: disengagement theory en-
dorses the withdrawal from social participation as a natural and healthy course of aging
(Cumming & Henry, 1961). Others would argue that disengagement is not at all a
choice, but rather is aggressively driven by publicly held stereotypes and the political
economy of age stratification. Certain privileges are denied and access to social participation limited based simply on the age or life stage of individuals. Examples of age
discrimination in physical activity are: an emphasis on youth participation by sport
agencies; limited programs for the elderly to public sport facilities; few opportunities
to receive expert coaching and instruction; disinterest by the media and general public
in master's events; and a lack of publicly organized events and community programs
representing the broad interests of older adults (Curtis & White, 1984).

Ageist practice socializes older adults into a narrow range of "appropriate" activities, even though those activities may not represent those in which older adults have
developed lifelong skill or interest. Views that older adults should exert themselves
less as they age, and should become less competitive at the activities they do, are
consistent with the social stereotypes that are present in much of contemporary society. When these social forces are evident, it becomes clear to older adults that social
acceptance is lacking for them to publicly demonstrate athletic excellence. Ageism is
probably the most obstructive form of adult socialization preventing older adult participation in some of our most valued forms of physical activity.

port Research

to our current understanding of exercise and social reinforcement are two
udies: 1) those that identify the types of people who lack interest and desire
e; and, 2) those that identify the kinds of physical and cultural environments
g more physical activity. Among the prominent relationships between the
nvironment and optimal health is a powerful construct called "social support."
any gerontology studies have already demonstrated with clarity that social sup-
s important to the maintenance of good health (Pilisuk & Minkler, 1985), includ-
educed psychological distress (Holohan & Moos, 1981), and reduced mortality
lderly populations (Blazer, 1982). Exercise scientists are similarly beginning to
reciate the significance of social support in physical activity settings. Indeed, al-
ough physical activity settings may be among the most important *sources* of social
ontact and support in the lives of older adults, other forms of social support may be
needed. For older adults to live actively, some degree of social endorsement or incentive may be *an essential prerequisite.*

Expectancies about social support for exercise represents an important environmental reinforcement. Verbal cues from friends, family, and significant others such as
physicians can provide encouragement or discouragement, and in this regard, social
support can be thought of as a social efficacy to exercise. For women, such affiliative
factors have been emphasized as important personal incentives to be physically active
(Duda & Tappe, 1989; O'Brien Cousins, 1995a).

Perceived social support to exercise in late life is considered to be an important
motivating force because some older women report that they have experienced: 1)
disapproval from their spouse (Andrew et al., 1981; Perusse, LeBlanc, & Bouchard,
1988; Tait & Dobash, 1986); 2) lack of peer interest and companionship (Hauge,
1973); 3) discouragement by the immediate family (McPherson, 1982; Spreitzer &
Snyder, 1976, 1983); and 4) inadequate encouragement from physicians (Dishman,
1986; Gray, 1987; Wechsler, Levine, Idelson, Rohman, & Taylor, 1983).

Defining and Measuring Social Support   The scientific measurement of social
support is a recent phenomenon requiring clear operational definitions. Social support
has seen a rapid evolution of conceptual meaning ranging from individualized emotional and affective dimensions to large, contextual features of a particular society
(Esdaile & Wilkins, 1987). Most measurement to date has addressed social support at
the "micro" level. For example, an early definition of social support was given by
Cassel (1976) as the gratification of a person's basic social needs (approval, esteem,
succorance). Cobb (1976) conceived social support to be information leading a person
to believe that they were cared for, esteemed, and belonging to a network.

The measurement of a multidimensional construct such as social support is difficult, if only because there are now a legion of available instruments that tap into
emotional support, tangible support, informational support, and support provided to
others at both perceptual and enacted levels. Social support, as a *quantity*, can be
measured objectively as the number of confidants one has, or the number of phone
contacts or visits from friends in the past week. The *quality* of social support can be

subjectively assessed with perceptual rating scales about the adequacy of one's support network.

Physical Activity as Social Networking

Recreation centers, seniors' groups, sport clubs, and even shopping malls provide positive settings in which to engage in socializing and physical activity (Graham, Graham, & MacLean, 1991). Within these social settings, both formal and informal structures can provide instrumental aid, information, and advice. In addition, such settings supply one of the biggest benefits of leisure activity—companionship (Ishii-Kuntz, 1990; Tinsley, Teaff, Colbs, & Kaufman, 1985). Institutionalized elderly are known to place high priority on the social context of physical activity, although they also hope that exercise will also enhance their health and fitness (Mobily, Lemke, Drube, Wallace, Leslie, & Weissinger, 1987).

Some older people are apparently reluctant to take advantage of existing community networks for participation in physical activity and sport. Older men may dislike being a follower of an exercise leader, or feel that they do not need exercise supervision. Women, on the other hand, are not always in a position to leave their home to take advantage of existing community networks for participation in physical activity and sport. Thus, finding companionship for physical activity outside the home is easier for males than females (Curtis & White, 1984); women often have no choice but to exercise at home alone. From young adulthood on, females are found more often in caregiving and domestic situations that may limit their ability to formalize social networks outside the home environment.

According to a national survey on women with disabilities, social barriers rather than physical limitations and medical concerns, are considered to be their primary limitations to activity participation.

> The primary changes that would encourage greater participation in physical activities were accessible facilities that are closer to home, knowledgeable instructors, people with whom to participate, and more available information on programs (Fitness Canada Women's Program, 1990).

Social encouragement from other adults may be particularly lacking for older women with limitations. Almost half of the physically limited women surveyed said they alone were responsible for getting involved in activity although family and friends were influential in activating only 13 percent of respondents.

For older adults, ease of transportation to physical activity settings and costs of participation may be practical barriers to obtaining the support they need to be more active. Some elderly women never learned to drive the family car, or can no longer afford to maintain a car, and therefore limit their activities to whatever is available in their neighborhood.

Role of Group Cohesion   Social support and group cohesiveness have been studied with a view to understanding why people begin physical activity, why some maintain their involvement, and why others stop participating altogether. Dishman (1986) noted that after six months, over half of those who begin an exercise program have already dropped out. As might be expected, people who do not adhere to a specific fitness or sport setting are less attracted to the group's task and to the group as a social unit (Carron, Widmeyer, & Brawley, 1988). The literature underscores the need for an awareness of how the social and physical environment can affect the elderly individual's sustained involvement in group activity. We need better understanding of how activity engagement may relate to the individual's evaluation of the environment and of the self (Barris, 1987). A series of six studies examined the behavioral and cognitive procedures that would enhance adherence to a 3-day-per-week walking/jogging program in sedentary adults (Martin et al., 1984). Overall, the results of these studies confirm the importance of social reinforcement, including instructor feedback and praise during exercise.

Role of Companionship   Lack of social support for older women in the form of sport opportunities and companionship is one of the key findings of a study by Curtis and White (1984). Using a sample of 33,762 native-born Canadians who filled out a nine-page survey questionnaire, they found that older females participated in fewer types of sport activities than younger women, but participated more frequently in those activities in the past year. Still, only 10 percent of women over age 60 had at least one physical recreation that they had pursued one or more times on an annual basis.

Problems in finding others with whom to participate was a problem for over 20 percent of the elderly women, and they were the one age group who had the most problems with finding companionship. Older women had twice as much difficulty as same-age men with finding companionship, yet at the same time, reported that time conflicts in activities were only half the problem that men had experienced. This finding is congruent with other work that has found women's workloads to be flexible, but time-consuming (Edwards & Hill, 1982). Ishii-Kuntz (1990) reports that widowed women, in particular, are likely to be seeking companionship and social opportunities in seniors' centers.

The Role of Spousal Support   One hypothesis linking social support to physical activity is that people who have active life companions, active partners, or active spouses are more likely to be physically active themselves (Snyder & Spreitzer, 1973). Having a spouse who is indirectly involved in sports is thought to reinforce earlier encouragement from one's parents and to increase one's perceived ability to be involved as an adult (Spreitzer & Snyder, 1976).

In analyzing family influence on sports involvement, social scientists have claimed that there is considerable similarity of activity patterns between a couple.

> Evidently, they mutually reinforce one another's interest in this sphere of leisure behavior. Explanations of this finding might lie in the mate selection process where a common interest in sports might serve as an additional inducement for the match; also, the findings might suggest that a strong interest in sports on the part of one spouse is gradually transmitted to the partner (Snyder & Spreitzer, 1973).

Other research suggests that "women who take part in sport perceive a very high degree of support from their nominated or significant male" (Tait & Dobash, 1986). This evidence notwithstanding, compared with men, women ages 45 and older reported *less support* from their spouse and experience less encouragement to be active with advancing years (Stephens & Craig, 1990). Furthermore, Hauge (1973) suggested that "middle class men look outside the home for sport companions almost twice as frequently as the women do." Therefore men seem to be active even if their spouse is not.

One of the few available studies on the role of spousal support to exercise adherence is unfortunately available only in relation to men. Myocardial patients were studied for drop-out rate from an exercise program over a seven year period (Andrew et al., 1981). Of all the determinants being considered, spouse approval was the most significant finding. The drop-out rate of those with little or no support from their wives was three times greater than in those men with positive spousal encouragement.

Ishii-Kuntz (1990) examined how predisposing, enabling, and need factors influenced elderly women's participation in voluntary organizations and senior centers. A nationwide probability sample provided data that indicated that age, race, and health status influenced participation. Elderly widows were more likely to be involved in voluntary organizations than married women, with loneliness being a major factor leading to seniors center participation.

The Role of the Physician The cautionary warnings that one must always consult a physician before taking up any interest in physical activity may be doing more harm than good.

Certainly anyone who is doubtful about one's personal state of health should consult a physician. In principle, however, there is less risk in activity than in continuous inactivity. In a nutshell, our opinion is that it is more advisable to pass a careful medical examination if one intends to be sedentary in order to establish whether one's state of health is good enough to withstand the inactivity (Astrand, 1986).

Evidence suggests that ordinary people will not get extraordinary advice from a physician about how to start an exercise program. Moreover the "see your physician" prescription may prevent many adults from ever getting started because a chain of dependency is then formed (O'Brien Cousins & Burgess, 1992). Becoming more physically active depends on seeing the doctor, and it also depends on what the doctor has to say. Because of time constraints and a billing system that is funded by the number of patients seen, physicians often do not discuss their attitudes and knowledge about exercise with their clients. The dependency continues as one then seeks out an activity program in which exercise needs are met. If the program is really enjoyable, the participant may become dependent on the motivational skills of its leader in order to meet their exercise needs.

Regular pulse rate checking serves to remind individuals that they may be at risk of something going wrong with their heart, and consequently individuals may become too anxious to exercise on their own. This scenario is an example of how some forms of social support can backfire and become barriers to individualized and independent involvement in physical activity.

Health promoters have begun to examine the interest and competency of physicians to provide encouragement for their patients' activity patterns. It has been noted that physicians who have graduated since the late 1960s are more likely to believe in the importance of regular aerobic exercise, but overall, only about one quarter of physicians think engagement in aerobic activity three times a week is very important to health (Wechsler, Levine, Idelson, Rohman, & Taylor, 1983). Internists are more likely to ask about exercise behaviors than general practitioners (53% to 31%) and all physicians are more likely to ask about smoking, alcohol, and other drugs, than they are likely to ask about diet, exercise, and stress. Only three percent to eight percent of physicians thought they were "very successful" in helping patients achieve changes in various health behaviors, but 21 percent were optimistic about their ability to help patients increase exercise.

Surveys of physicians in Massachusetts and Maryland indicated that just less than 50 percent of primary care physicians routinely inquire about their patients' exercise practices (Wechsler et al., 1983). In an exercise intervention study on women ages 55 to 80, only 5 percent of the participants noted that regular exercise had been recommended to them by a physician (Howze, DiGilio, Bennett, & Smith, 1983). In another study, only 27 percent of the physicians felt that exercise was "very important" for the average person. Thus "a large proportion of physicians are not fully convinced of the value of exercise for health" (Powell, Spain, Christenson, & Mollenkamp, 1986). Whether physician inquiries include in-depth questions about intensity duration or frequency of exercise is not known, nor do we know how physicians alter their questioning strategies with younger and older individuals.

Current views on the athletic potential of older adults, and older women in particular, are considered to be overly conservative even by health promotion experts and exercise physiologists. Most professionals may be concerned more about the risks of participation for frail elders and the potential for harm and litigation outcomes than they are for raising activity levels of the entire community (DeLorey, 1989).

Recent work examining the physician's role in exercise promotion among older adults suggests that the health care setting may not be the appropriate place to conduct exercise counselling (Branigan, 1995). A random sample of 64 Edmonton-area physicians along with a volunteer sample of 121 advanced education adults over age 55 provided survey information on their views of physician involvement in exercise counseling. Branigan's study found little congruence between physicians and older adults regarding their beliefs about physician support for exercise as an important health promotion behavior. The study further found that beliefs about physician support had no bearing whatsoever on the activity patterns of older adults, leading her to conclude that,

> a large number of adults in this group tend to take responsibility for their own health and well-being. As much as 90 percent stated that their biggest motivation to exercise was their own incentive.

Older adults reported the minimal time per visit was the most restricting factor to physician counselling for exercise, although physicians reported that their biggest barrier to exercise promotion was poor patient compliance. Physicians felt they were wasting their time asking for patients to increase activity levels.

Added to professional conservatism has been a persistent belief among older adults endorsing the scientific concept of "conservation of energy." Retirement, for many, means that it is time to take a long-deserved rest from lifelong physical work demands. The social norm for retired individuals has been rather passive leisure pursuits, and it is difficult to change expectations about activity choices if the participant is perceived to be already more ambitious than others of the same age. Particularly if an adult has been physically inactive in recent years, physicians and friends are unlikely to try to convince him or her that now is the time to start exercising.

The Role of Friends and Family   The number of close friends that a person has, appears to be significantly associated with the pursuit of general preventive health behaviors such as non-smoking behavior and exercise (Calnan, 1985). Although companionship for physical activity is considered to be a reinforcing factor, in recent decades, time pressures for couples are evident, at least in middle-age families. Inflationary pressures and changing attitudes towards the social roles of men and women have seen the rapid rise of two-career families and what some call the "death of leisure" (Posner, 1991).

Over half of the adult female population is in the labor force full-time; this means that there has been a significant change in the workload patterns of women. About one quarter of Americans at work are spending 49 hours or more each week on the job (Kilborn, 1990). It has been estimated that women average 66 to 75 hours per week at combined job and family responsibilities as compared with 42 to 49 hours per week 50 years ago (Edwards & Hill, 1982). The implications of this for women's physical activity patterns is that employed women may have too little leisure time in which to be physically active, and friendships and social networks may also become more difficult to sustain under these kinds of time pressures.

SUMMARY

Conceptual models that understand and explain late-life exercise behavior are under development. Beliefs about physical activity are important to identify since, compared to situational variables, attitudes, opinions, and beliefs are modifiable. Understanding how perspectives are formed and how they are changed is an important step in being able to convince more adults to adopt more active lifestyles.

Chapter 12 identifies a composite theoretical framework and the utility of this model for the prediction of late-life exercise among women. The results of survey data on 327 women over age 70 are presented. Chapter 13 examines the work of Weinstein and the Precaution-Adoption Process as it might be applied to the older adult exercise setting. A self-talk model of older adult exercise motivation is proposed.

Chapter 12

The Synthesis of Theory: A Composite Model

Conceptual models to understand and explain the diverse determinants for participation in physical activity and exercise in the elderly are relatively undeveloped. Motivational theories that have had some success are now being reconceptualized and, in some cases, combined for further strength in prediction. Incentives, attitudes, beliefs, expectancies, perceived barriers, cues to act, and self-perceptions are among the most common constructs used in contemporary theoretical models. In this chapter, a composite model is tested for its utility to predict late-life exercise among women.

THE INTEGRATION OF THEORY

Justification for a Composite Model

The benefits of using multiple theoretical perspectives were advanced by Rodgers and Brawley (1993). With single construct theory, only a modest amount of explanation for exercise behavior has been possible (Dishman, 1990; Dzewaltowksi, 1989a; Dzewaltowski, Noble & Shaw, 1990). Brawley (1993) and Maddux (1993) suggested that it is timely to integrate cognitive models of health and exercise behavior. Maddux recommends that instead of pitting one theory against the predictive power of another,

... theorists and researchers [should] focus their efforts on integration of the major social cognitive models and on determining the relative predictive utility of the various social cognitive factors with various health behaviors and in various contexts (Maddux, 1993).

Using the single construct of self-efficacy, most exercise studies have not advanced our theoretical understanding. Findings simply confirm what we already know from Social Cognitive Theory (Bandura, 1989), that is that, 1) personal efficacy for a behavior is a good predictor of the future occurrence of that behavior; and 2) exercise interventions elevate perceptions of personal efficacy for related physical activity (Ewart et al., 1986a, 1983; Hofstetter et al., 1991; Hogan & Santomier, 1984; Kaplan, Atkins, & Reinsch, 1984; McAuley, Courneya, & Lettunich, 1991). The composite model uses four elements of SCT, interprets outcome expectations according to the HBM, and adds the construct health locus of control and thereby may provide for a more comprehensive explanation for less physical activity in late life.

A composite model of late-life exercise is illustrated (Figure 12.1) with 16 variables represented. Under "Situational Environment" are ten life situational factors that can act as incentives or barriers to physical activity. Under "Cognitive Beliefs" are the cognitive factors that are considered to be the important mediators of physical activity. On the right is the dependent behavior, weekly exercise. The Composite Model is a triadic depiction of late-life exercise behavior; older adult physical activity is potentially explained by both contextual and cognitive elements.

The model has conceptual merit in that it embraces the main theoretical elements of SCT, locus of control theory, and the HBM. Combining HLOC Theory with Social Cognitive Theory has been advocated as an important theoretical step (Long & Haney,

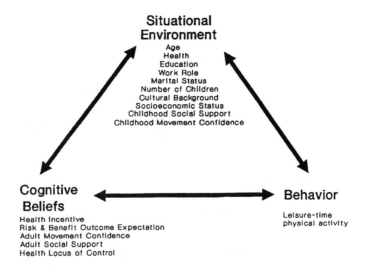

Composite Model of Adult Physical Activity

Figure 12.1 Integrated model of late-life exercise.

1986; McCready & Long, 1985) for this reason: an older individual may be highly motivated to live a long and healthy life, but if an individual perceives they have little control over their health, they are unlikely to take on a high-effort, health-promoting behavior such as exercise.

Interpretation for Bandura's outcome expectations comes from the cost/benefit decision-making process of the Health Belief Model (Rosenstock, 1974). The Health Belief Model assumes that people weigh the expected benefits of a precaution against its costs and adopt the precaution if the balance appears favorable. Because there are indications that late-life exercise may be viewed as a high risk behavior, outcome expectations are assessed in this study as perceived health benefits and perceived health risks.

RESULTS OF A STUDY USING THE COMPOSITE MODEL

The composite model was used with good success to predict the weekly exercise patterns of elderly Vancouver women. Details of the geographic sampling procedure used, the specific assessment instruments, and the statistical analyses are explained elsewhere (O'Brien Cousins, 1993, 1996). The purpose of the study was first, to describe the variability among elderly exercise behavior in women, and second, to examine the utility of the Composite Model in explaining this variability. A third purpose was to explore the childhood roots of movement confidence and social support as possible historical determinants to older adult physical activity participation. The measurement and etiology of elderly women's physical activities have received little previous study and thus this research was considered to be exploratory in nature. This study was, however, able to confirm the heterogeneity of older women's activity patterns and provide preliminary support for a Composite Theory of exercise behavior.

Descriptive Findings

A geographically representative community sample of 280, and a strategic sample of 47 Vancouver women, ages 70 to 98, filled out survey questionnaires. Current exercise level was assessed using a seven-day inventory of the type, intensity, and duration of 38 leisure time activities. Metabolic estimates were applied to each reported activity thereby providing a weekly energy expenditure in kilocalories for each woman.

This study was among the first to collect field data on the specific nature and scope of older women's leisure time physical activities in Canada. Over one half of the elderly women consulted reported no current participation in *vigorous* activities (6+ METS) and over one third reported no current participation in *moderate* activities (4–5.9 METS). Walking was the predominant *mild* (<4 METS) exercise with 60 percent of the women reported having walked in the past week. Out of six different fitness activities, walking briskly for 20 minutes was rated the lowest in perceived risk to health, the highest in perceived benefit to health, and the one activity about which women over age 70 reported the most confidence.

Energy Expended in the Past Week   The 327 women in this study, although all over the age of 70, displayed substantial heterogeneity in their exercise patterns, ranging from 0 to 11,000 kilocalories of weekly energy spent on exercise during a seven-day period. Over half of the women said they had "never exercised long enough or intense enough to actually get sweaty" in the past four months. But, overall, the participants in this study were substantially more active than older adults studied elsewhere (Stephens, Craig, & Ferris, 1986; Teague & Hunnicutt, 1989). This outcome supported Brook's (1988) finding that individuals living in western regions of the continent tended to be more active than those living in other regions. As a group, the elderly women in this study met the "adequately active" criterion of 3+ kcal/kg/day in physical activity (Paffenbarger, Hyde, Wing, & Hsied, 1986). Although 35 percent of the women in this study were substantially above the criteria however, the majority of women in this study (65 percent) were inadequately active to receive full health benefits.

The majority of the 327 women in this study reported activity levels below the prescribed ideal of 2000 kcal per week for middle-age men (Paffenbarger, Hyde, Wing, & Hsied, 1986). The average energy expenditure spent on exercise in the past week was about 1500 kcal but the median was well below that at 1079 kcal. As anticipated, the activity level of women in this study was highly variable with a large positive skew toward extremely high activity levels of several dozen women.

About 25 percent of the women reported activity levels that placed them in an "ideal" category of 1500 to 3000 kilocalories per week. This is equivalent to a 60 kg person walking briskly for an hour, seven days a week—an activity level that exercise physiologists might consider optimal for aerobic fitness and health promotion, at even younger ages. Most women in the study were far less active than that, with 38 percent exercising at a level of 500 to 1500 kcal/week, an amount that is comparable to walking briskly a total of two hours per week—and an amount that, while deficient according to current recommendations, may contribute some important benefits to the maintenance of overall health and physical ability. About one quarter of the women reported physical activity below 500 kcal/week ("low"), and half of those women reported less than 250 kcal/week in terms of total activity level ("very low"). In contrast, as many as 10 percent of the women in this study were exercising at levels above 3000 kcal per week, and a few women appeared to be highly active (5000+ kcal).

The six cognitive variables (health motive, movement confidence, social support, perceived risks, perceived benefits, and health locus of control) are described in detail in O'Brien Cousins's (1996) *Exercise Cognition Among Elderly Women*.

Descriptive Results of the Cognitive Variables   Table 12.1 shows the range of scores, means, and standard deviations for each cognitive variable.

Health Motive   Motivation to live a long and healthy life was high for almost every participant in the study. The median score was 3.5 out of a possible score of 4.0.

Adult Social Support to Exercise   Table 12.2 shows that perceptions about social support to exercise varied. About half of the sample felt they had received

Table 12.1 Ranges, Means, and Standard Deviations for the Cognitive Variables

Cognitive variables	Range	Mean	Standard deviation
Health Motive	2–4	3.48	.51
Movement Confidence	6–24	14.38	4.24
Social Support	4–20	12.20	3.84
Perceived Risks	6–30	14.17	5.60
Perceived Benefits	6–30	17.86	5.95
Health Locus of Control	15–58	36.45	6.67

at least some encouragement from at least one person to maintain their physical ability since middle age. Similarly, about half of the women reported that they currently had friends active in physical fitness activities, and half of the women had athletic families who were athletically inclined. Almost 70 percent did not have their physicians' support for vigorous physical activity. Almost 40 percent were not sure what their doctor thought about their personal participation in vigorous activities, and another 30 percent said their physician would not approve of vigorous forms of exercise. The older women in the study reported the lowest levels of encouragement for physical activity (Figure 12.2).

Adult Movement Confidence (Exercise Efficacy)   Women felt most confident about their ability to walk (Figure 12.3). Over 54 percent of the women were "very sure" and 21 percent were "pretty sure" that they could walk briskly for 20 minutes. But over 13 percent claimed they could not do brisk walking for that duration. The activity rated by the women with the least overall confidence was the aquafit class of 50 minutes. Almost 65 percent of the women claimed they were unsure or knew they could not do this activity. Efficacy was lowest for the modified push-up with about half of all women reporting that they knew they could not do five push-ups. Efficacy showed a strong linear relationship to weekly activity level (Figure 12.4).

Table 12.2 Proportion of Women Aged 70 + Who Perceived Social Support to Exercise (%)

	Living in an active family	Encouraged by someone	Physician approves of vig. exercise	Friends are active in fitness
Strongly agree	30.8	19.7	12.3	20.3
Agree	18.6	31.1	19.0	25.9
Unsure	12.2	11.4	38.3	7.3
Disagree	21.8	10.8	6.6	24.1
Strongly disagree	16.7	27.0	23.7	21.8

Age differences
in Support to Exercise

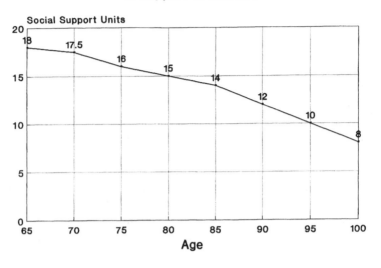

Figure 12.2   Age differences in support to exercise.

Perceived Efficacy
for Six Adult Fitness Activities

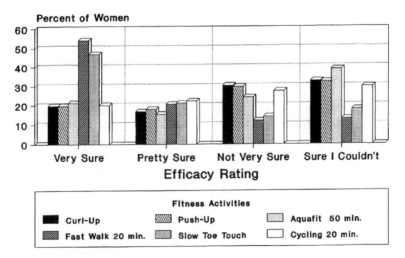

Figure 12.3   Movement confidence (efficacy) for six adult fitness activities.

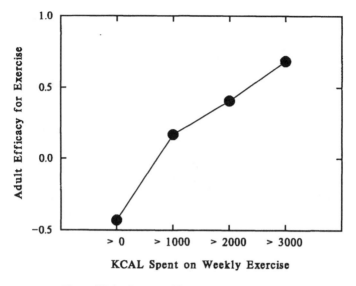

Figure 12.4 Current efficacy and exercise level.

Outcome Expectations   Ten repetitions of the curl-up was rated as the riskiest activity of the six fitness exercises presented, with many women reporting that they believed they might hurt their back or neck (Figure 12.5). Both walking and stretching were considered to be of low risk with only 14 percent finding these activities to be of any risk. As for perceived benefits of the six fitness exercises, brisk walking for

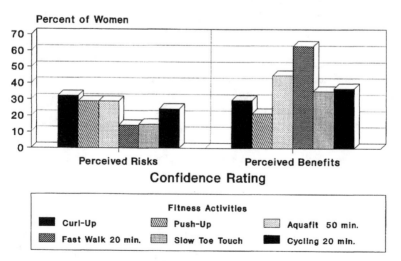

Figure 12.5 Perceived risks and benefits of six activities.

20 minutes was ranked first because 63 percent of the sample rated brisk walking to be moderately to highly beneficial. Aquatic fitness exercise was ranked second and was thought to be beneficial by 45 percent of the women. Doing the five push-ups was perceived to be of the least benefit. For the curl-up and the push-up, the risks were rated higher than the benefits; for the aerobic activities and the toe touch, the benefits were rated higher than the risks.

Health Locus of Control   Scores for Health Locus of Control ranged from 15 to 58 (possible range was 11–66) with a mean of 36.45 (*s.d.* = 6.67). Lower scores indicate feelings of personal control over one's health (internality), while higher scores indicate stronger beliefs that one's health is under the control of external forces (externality). Compared to college students and an older sample of hypertensive outpatients with HLOC scores of 40 (*s.d.* = 6.2), women in this study demonstrated more internality.

THEORETICAL FINDINGS

One purpose of this study was to test the utility of a Composite Theoretical Model by combining constructs from psycho-behavioral theory (Social Cognitive Theory and Health Locus of Control Theory) with constructs found in social epidemiology (life situation and personal characteristics). Thus the theoretical explanation for the variability in older women's activity levels in this study was based on 1) 10 life situational and personal attributes of individuals (Age; Health Status; Marital Status; Education; Socioeconomic Status; Cultural Background; Family Size; Work Role in mid-life; Childhood Social Support for physical activity; and Childhood Movement Confidence for physical skill), and 2) six self-referent beliefs about late-life physical activity (Health Motive; Self-Efficacy to do fitness exercise; Environmental Cues/reinforcement in the form of perceived social support; Expected Outcomes in the form of perceived risks and benefits; and Health Locus of Control). Using the triadic reciprocal determinism model of Bandura, Figure 12.6 shows the main statistical relationships between the elements of the Composite Model.

A series of three multiple regression analyses (O'Brien Cousins, 1993) were used to examine which theoretical elements provided unique explanation to late-life exercise behavior. In the first regression, the ten situational variables were reduced to four significant predictors of energy spent on exercise in the past week: Health Status; Childhood Movement Confidence; Age; and Cultural Background according to school location. Together these four variables explained 18 percent of the variance seen in late-life exercise level. In the second analysis, only two cognitive variables, Adult Movement Confidence and Adult Social Support, emerged as significant variables *(R² = .22)*.

A full regression model was tested by including the four significant contextual variables and the two cognitive variables that had probability levels below .05 in the preliminary analyses. The third regression included all six significant predictors; Childhood Movement Confidence and Age were dropped from the regression equation. Adult Movement Confidence, Adult Social Support, Composite Health, and Cultural

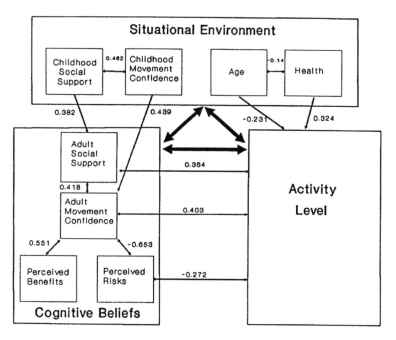

Figure 12.6 Proposed model of explanation of older women's physical activity.

Background (School Location) remained to explain 26 percent of the variance seen in exercise participation (O'Brien Cousins, 1995).

The factors from the model that best explained why older women were physically active were: 1) they perceived high levels of social support to exercise; 2) they felt personally efficacious for fitness-types of activities; 3) they had satisfactory health; and 4) they were educated in northern European countries.

Interpretation of the Regression Analysis

> Weekly exercise level = .03 + .248 Adult Social Support + .195 Efficacy + .174 Health − .126 School Location + residual error

The regression coefficients are estimates of the effects on Y of a one-unit change in X given the other variables in the model. For example, the estimated effect of age was −.014, which suggests that for each year of age, exercise level drops by .014 amounts per week, or .014 of the standard deviation of the exercise level mean (1800 kcal) or 25 kcal. This means that, on average, with each year of age examined, exercise level dropped 5 kcal per week, or about 1400 kcal *less* each year. This seems to be a small effect that would translate into a difference of one flight of stairs per day (Paffenbarger, Wing, & Hyde, 1978) or about 20 miles of walking in a year. However, over a ten year period, if eating patterns did not compensate, an individual could expect to gain up five pounds of extra body fat.

The best explanatory variable was Adult Social Support, or current encouragement from family, friends, spouse, and physician. In the final model, exercise level was predicted by .25 of a standard unit of Adult Social Support. Adult Social Support had a mean of 12.2 out of a possible score of 20. The standard deviation was almost 4 points. This means that for every four unit score on the social support scale, women increased their exercise level .25 of the standard deviation unit of exercise level, or 450 kcal. This is a very large effect, because it indicates that for each social support unit, women would change their exercise by over 100 kcal, or over a mile of walking per week. Providing an older woman with encouragement for exercise is thus very important. If she is unsure about the opinion of her physician in regard to her exercise behavior, and then finds out that her doctor is fully in support, she would experience an increase in social support that could elevate her motivation to the equivalent of brisk walking two or three miles a week. On the other hand, if a woman suddenly loses a committed walking companion, and this companion cannot be replaced, social support could drop by 4 points—the equivalent of omitting a customary 4 to 5 miles of walking per week.

Adult Movement Confidence had a significant and important effect on exercise level too ($b = .20$). This efficacy measure had a mean of 14.4 units out of a maximum score of 24 and a standard deviation of 2.4. Raising a woman's confidence to be able to try walking by only one unit, say from "not very sure" to "pretty sure" would mean an increase of activity expending as much as 150 kcal per week. This would be the equivalent of walking about two miles each week or over one hundred miles in a year.

Where women went to school as children was a significant predictor of their current exercise level. For example, the estimated effect of being educated in Canada, Britain, or the United States was $-.125$. The dummy code for these women was 1, and the standard deviation of exercise level was 1800 kcal, therefore women who were educated in Canadian, British, or American settings could be predicted to exercise 223 kcal *less* per week than other respondents in the study. This is a large difference. For example, a woman older than age 70, educated in the United States or Canada, is predicted to be exercising significantly *less* than immigrant women of her age *every* week, and the exercise she is missing is equivalent to about three miles of walking, or over 50 flights of stairs. In a year, this would equate to over 150 miles of walking which would burn about 12,000 kilocalories.

DISCUSSION OF THE FINDINGS

Explaining Late-Life Exercise

Although the R^2 coefficient of .26 is quite low (74% of the variability in exercise level went unexplained), it is important to note that R^2s of this magnitude are typical in the social sciences. The explanation of exercise level in this study substantially exceeds that provided by other studies of this type. The unexplained portion includes variance attributable to: 1) measurement error in estimating the intensity of exercise reported, 2) subject error in the recall of physical activity, 3) weekly fluctuations in individual activity levels, and 4) seasonal and uncharacteristic weather patterns that interfered with normal outdoor activities such as walking and gardening. Because any of these portions of variance may be quite large, it may not be possible to achieve a substantially higher R^2 by including more variables in the model, unless there are major deficiencies in the model such as the omission of constructs that represent important explanation.

One suggestion would be to use repeated measures of weekly exercise so that human and seasonal fluctuations of actual activity level are considered. A second strategy would be to seek ways to increase the diversity of the volunteer sample in order to strengthen the power to explain differences in exercise level. If a sample is composed of people who are all fairly alike, except for variation in the dependent variable, the reason for this variability is unexplainable. Thus R^2 in this study was limited to some extent by the homogeneity of the sample. The people in this study were alike in these respects: all the subjects were women; all were over age 70; the majority were of adequate health to be mobile in their community; and the 327 women had sufficient will and competence to complete the 30- to 60-minute survey questionnaire. In addition, two independent variables showed little variability; most of the women in this study wanted to live a long and healthy life (motive), and most of them were "internals" in terms of health locus of control.

Still, the Composite Model substantially exceeded the explanation of exercise in other studies. For example, Dzewaltowski (1989b) compared the ability of two different theoretical models to predict exercise prediction. The Theory of Reasoned Action (Fishbein & Ajzen, 1975) assessed intention to exercise, attitude toward the activity, and the social environment (subjective norm), but only 5 percent of the exercise behavior variance was explained in 328 undergraduate students. In the same study, two social cognitive constructs (self-efficacy and self-evaluated dissatisfaction) predicted 16 percent of the exercise variance. In a similar study comparing the two theories, Dzewaltowski, Noble, and Shaw (1990), found 10 percent of the variance in under-graduate students exercise behavior was explained with measures from the Theory of Reasoned Action. When self-efficacy measures were added to the regression analysis, another 7 percent of the variance in exercise behavior was explained.

Brooks (1988) reported on causal modeling analysis using sociodemographic information to predict five levels of physical activity behavior in 19,110 Americans over age 18. The sociodemographic measures were age, sex, marital status, education, household income, region of the country, and county size. Only age, education, and income were able to predict physical activity levels, and the variance explained was only 8 percent. Brooks concluded that her results indicate that education and income "in fact contribute very little to our understanding as to why some adults choose to lead physically active lifestyles while others do not" (Brooks, 1988).

Another study of 98 adults found self-efficacy for exercise program adherence and outcome expectations from the program, in a linear combination, predicted 12.5 percent of the variance between adherers and dropouts (Desharnais, Bouillon, & Godin, 1986). A path analysis model of achievement behavior designed to predict physical activity performance was able to explain 16 percent of the variance.

Relative to all of the above studies, the Composite Model used in this study performed well, because, in the present study, 26 percent of the variance in exercise behavior was explained. To improve on this prediction, one may choose to employ more costly and time-consuming means of measuring exercise levels, such as oral interviews or daily diaries, in order to reduce error. Providing monetary incentives or using quota sampling are ways to obtain more diversity in samples.

Life Contextual Variables

Of the contextual variables only health, school location, age, and childhood movement confidence were prominent in explaining late-life exercise. As has been found in other studies on older women in exercise settings, women who were more active reported better health (Kriska et al., 1986), tended to be educated in north European countries (Brooks, 1988), were younger (Brooks, 1988), and recalled being efficacious and experienced with challenging physical skills in childhood. The impact of childhood physical education in lifelong involvement deserves further exploration because the implications for lifelong life quality and public health are enormous.

One might wonder why other measures such as Education, Marital Status, Number of Children, Work Role, and the Composite SES Index did not add more explanation to the criterion variable. Many of these indicators, although they are potent predictors of behavior in younger people, are probably "leveled" by the later years. For example, the financial status of middle-class older women is reduced by old age, everyone is receiving Old Age or Social Security, and those who have marginal means are "boosted" with the Guaranteed Income Supplement. Thus SES differences, which are difficult to measure in the elderly anyway, are further masked by federal assistance programs. Education, employment, marital status, and raising children are often interrelated and therefore may confound or weaken each other in statistical effect.

Cognitive Variables

Adult social support and adult exercise efficacy were the two outstanding variables of the cognitive variables explaining late-life exercise, suggesting that feeling capable to do fitness activity, and feeling encouraged to participate were two important beliefs that lead older women to pursue more active lifestyles. This study confirms the findings of other studies that positive relationships exist between social support and involvement in physical activity (Andrew et al., 1981; Gottlieb & Baker, 1986; Heinzelman & Bagley, 1970; Langlie, 1977; Wankel, 1984). Other researchers are also recognizing the importance of social support in a variety of activity settings. Shivers (1991) suggested that intense socialization is fundamental to the older adult recreational experience. In studying the meaning of physical activity in old age, Takala (1991) noted that partway through his research more emphasis was given to the social meaning of physical activities. In a study on exercise adherence, Danielson and Wanzel (1977) found that women were more likely to be attending fitness classes if they were accompanied by a companion. Wankel (1984) succeeded in improving adherence to an exercise program by creating "a buddy system."

Exercise scientists are only beginning to appreciate the significance of social support in physical activity settings. The socializing characteristics of physical activity, exercise, and sport appear to be among the key reasons older adults participate (O'Brien Cousins, 1995a; Rudman, 1986a, 1986b). An irony that is becoming evident is that although physical activity settings may be the best source of female encouragement and companionship, other forms of social support may have to exist for women in order for the potential of these activity settings to be tapped. Further research is needed to clarify how fragile or resilient women's confidence and support systems are. For example, women may suddenly become more, or less, active upon the death of their spouse.

The findings suggest that self-perceptions about early skill mastery accompanied by childhood encouragement and opportunity in physical activity may give many females an advantage in fostering adult support networks and an efficacious view about lifelong exercise involvement. This finding speaks to the lifelong, lifestyle consequences of present-day girlhood experiences in challenging sport and play—stemming from processes of opportunity, encouragement, and acquired skills in physical settings such as school physical education and community sport programs. Contemporary families, schools, and communities must be effectively providing these opportunities, supports, and skills for young females, and society must help to sustain active women with incentives throughout the adult years if females are to age with optimal activity levels, and thereby sustain health, independence, and a fuller quality of life. Life circumstances and inadequate encouragement apparently limit opportunities, from childhood on, to develop the kind of confidence in one's physical abilities that would promote an active lifestyle through to women's oldest life stage.

Health Locus of Control did not play a significant role in this study, but the effect was in the expected direction with internals exhibiting more physical activity. At the over-70 age level, day-to-day health may be variable enough that the elderly may begin to question their personal control of it. Also among those women who reported their health as only "poor" to "fair," a good number were exercising extensively. In this study, women at both ends of the health spectrum were among the heaviest exercisers. Also, those who felt the *least* control and *most* control over their health exhibited greater involvement in physical activity. Those in the low end of the health rating were likely following medical advice to rehabilitate themselves with increased exercise, or perhaps they viewed their increasing illness as a "cue to act" before it was too late to do something to improve their health. Many of the most healthy women were highly active and felt they had some control over their health. Perhaps they had gained earlier knowledge about the personal benefits of physical activity and were now reaping the beneftis of their involvement.

Health Motive also failed to significantly explain late-life exercise because virtually everyone wanted to live a long and healthy life. Living a long and healthy life may have been too distant from the behavior of exercise to be conceptually linked. Incentive might have been more useful as a motive variable if it had been replaced by the health value of exercise. Behavioral value could have assessed using a semantic differential scale (loving or hating exercise) or more closely tied to exercise such as "I would walk everyday if I knew it would give me 500 more days of quality life" or "I would do 15 curl-ups a day if I knew it would keep my stomach flat."

The reasons for engaging in late-life physical activity appears to be motivated by other factors unrelated to health maintenance and disease prevention. Other motives should be explored such as personal enjoyment, improved appearance, and in the case of women, an incentive possibly related to "beauty." Many women of the over 70 generation were involved with the Women's League of Health and Beauty, which originated in Britain and spread to the Commonwealth Countries. Older women often lament over negative changes in their physical appearance as they get older. Therefore, physical attractiveness may be more important than health to many women, particularly if they perceive their health to be good and their appearance to be a problem.

Outcome expectations, assessed as perceived risk and perceived benefits, were quite highly related to efficacy and therefore lost their predictive power in the overall model. When perceived risk was entered into the regression equation on its own to explain exercise level, it explained about 7 percent of the exercise criterion; when benefits was entered on its own, it explained about 3 percent.

DISCUSSION OF THE MODEL: THEORETICAL SIGNIFICANCE

The Composite Model was supported as being more effective than other theories advanced so far that have focussed exclusively on either situational barriers, or cognitive determinants. In this study, *both* contextual variables and cognitive variables played important and independent roles in explaining 26 percent of the variance in late-life exercise. Thus the findings support Bandura's triangular model that the cognitive profile of people along with their life situation are both influential determinants of their actions. This study confirms Bandura's principle of reciprocal determinism, that is, situational and cognitive determinants both have important relationships with exercise behavior and with each other. The associations may be bi-directional in causation or reciprocal in effect (Kaplan, Atkins, & Reinsch, 1984).

The Composite Model performed well in this study because explanation of the exercise patterns of a large elderly sample was superior to that of other research using other theories and combinations (Dzewaltowski, 1989a; Dzewaltowski et al., 1990). The recent addition of SCT's construct of self-efficacy to other theoretical models also suggests that the time may have come to rework present theoretical models according to the specific human behavior under study. Some consistently successful predictors of human health behavior appear to have been identified across various models, but few researchers have been willing to address more than one contruct or theory at a time. Indeed, the application of current theory has usually occurred with only one or two of the theoretical constructs put to test. Self-efficacy has received the most emphasis and has often stood on its own as the only construct used.

The present study extended previous research by examining a more complete Social Cognitive Model, which included: 1) a health and longevity motive to exercise; 2) perceived personal risks and benefits of fitness activities; 3) social support to exercise; 4) self-efficacy to participate in fitness types of exercise, and 5) Health Locus of Control. Because Bandura's work suggests that cognitive beliefs are already a reflection of the personal and socio-environmental context of an individual, previous researchers using SCT have not examined individual attributes and social situations for competing explanation. Because one's life situation is considered to be less alterable than beliefs, less attention has been paid to the interrelationship of life situation to beliefs and behavior.

Cognitive theorists have studied behavior as an outcome of cognitive processes only, because they have assumed that the influence of one's life situation and personal attributes are imbedded in these cognitive processes. Of importance to future research, this study found that cognitive beliefs do not account for all of the explanation of late-life exercise. In other words, life situation and personal attributes can add significant influence to the explanation of physical activity over and above the assessed cognitive beliefs about physical activity. Because late-life exercise is independently explained in this study, in part, by health, age, and cultural upbringing (school location as a child), future researchers are encouraged to assess more than just the cognitive beliefs of individuals.

Overall, the findings do not support the inclusion of all ten situational variables and all six cognitive beliefs in the Composite Model of late-life exercise. Still, this study provides strong, confirmatory support for two key constructs of Bandura's Social Cognitive Theory; Self-Efficacy to participate in fitness exercise and Social Support to be physical active offer significant explanation of physical activity behavior in elderly women. Risk and benefit outcome expectations are beliefs that have more important relationships to one's judgements about ability than to late-life exercise itself.

Social Cognitive Theory was not significantly aided by adding the Health Locus of Control belief. Similarly, health and longevity did not appear to act as important motive or incentive to participate in late-life physical activity. Health Locus of Control and Incentive to Act operate in a context of health, which, in this study, might not have been conceptually related to physical activity patterns in the minds of older women. Together, their lack of explanation points to the possibility that many women are motivated to exercise for reasons other than health. This possibility raises the question, what IS the main motive for the high activity levels of women after the age of 70?

SUMMARY

Although the next stage of theoretical work might attend to eliminating ineffective variables and examining new combinations of the strongest constructs across the theories, the evidence is not convincing that any elements of the Composite Model should be abandoned yet. For one thing, the main determinants of exercise behavior have not been fully identified. If this study was to be replicated, perceived outcome expectations would be assessed more specifically. Ongoing work suggests that providing a list of common beliefs may help people comprehensively identify the beliefs most relevant to them. Using the measures in this study, beliefs about benefits and risks could be summed to see if an individual's overall attitude regarding physical activity would be a positive or negative.

In addition, a better understanding of "motives" or "incentives" are needed if we are ever going to understand the "triggers" that lead to more active living. Interviews and focus groups with recently active older people are appropriate ways to document the stories of what motivated them to get started. Future refinements of this research will not be a trivial undertaking. The identification of the specific fears of older adults about exercise, as well as their beliefs about specific benefits, will demand a major research project with strong funding support for both qualitative and quantitative assessment. The study of motives for late-life exercise will involve similar resources. The list of ten life situational variables might be reduced, but if the Composite Theory is to have wide applicability to different populations and health behaviors, inclusion of a full contextual list of variable might be advisable. In this way, the unique explanation of various "life situations" can be accounted for in distinctive populations.

Chapter 13

A Self-Talk Model of Exercise Motivation

THE DIALOGUE OF THINKING, DECISION MAKING, PLANNING, AND TAKING ACTION

In an article in *Health Psychology* titled, "The Precaution Adoption Process," Weinstein (1988) presented a critique of current models of preventive behavior and discussed a variety of factors that are generally overlooked—including the role of cues to action, and the problems of competing life demands. He also expanded on the ways that actual decision-making differs from the "rational ideal." Weinstein's alternative model portrays the precaution adoption process as an orderly sequence of five qualitatively different cognitive stages. The stages are accompanied by proposed self-talk that an individual may be using at the time of deciding whether to take action about one's health. His model has contemporary appeal because it brings the contemplative processes of exercise behavior to a level of internal dialogue and decision-making.

Weinstein's ideas concerned the initiation of new and relatively complex behaviors. These behaviors assumed a knowledge of a health risk or "personal susceptibility" to that risk. He stated that "new preventive actions usually involve high-level cognitive functioning and advance planning."

> If avoiding future harm is the major goal of an action, then beliefs about the need for protection and beliefs about the ability of a given action to provide protection are certainly central issues (Weinstein, 1988).

Stage 1:

Recognizes a health hazard

Stage 2:
Believes in significance of the hazard for others/
Believes that a precaution exists that is effective

Stage 3:
Acknowledges personal susceptibility to hazard/
Acknowledges that precaution is personally effective

Stage 4:
Decides to take the precaution

Stage 5:
Takes precaution

The theoretical framework that Weinstein sketched is viewed as more complex than the cost-benefit model originally found in the Health Belief Model. In that model, beliefs about positive and negative outcomes are treated as continuous dimensions in which quantitative assessments are made. Cost-benefit models assume that progress from first thoughts to action are adequately explained by quantitative differences in the value of the decision equation. In contrast, Weinstein presents the precaution adoption process as "a series of distinct stages." This view changes conceptual understanding about how people think, plan and act. A stage theory of preventive behavior places people at discrete points in cognitive processing.

Although the stages are considered discrete variables, each belief can have varying strength. A stage model implies that a qualitative change occurs in both behavior and thought when each of these beliefs passes a threshold. Therefore, a person has either reached a stage or has not. Weinstein claimed that the kinds of interventions and information needed to move people closer to action will vary from stage to stage. He suggested that the transitions between stages can be viewed as barriers that must be overcome before action is taken.

In this chapter, a composite stage model unique to adopting physical activity is presented (Figure 13.1). This model is called the Self-Talk Model of Exercise Motivation because each stage has the potential of exhibiting positive or negative self-talk. Each stage can move closer toward, or stop, mobilization for physical activity.

The Self-Talk Model starts with a *triggering event*, instead of Weinstein's Stage 1 (recognizing a hazard). Eight other phases of thinking are presented, some of which are compatible with the Precaution Adoption Process. For example, Stage 4 (decides to take the precaution) fits somewhat with *Setting Goals* and *Mobilization* phases. To confirm the coherence behind the Self-Talk Model used in this chapter, self-referent

Self-Talk Model
of Older Adult Exercise Motivation

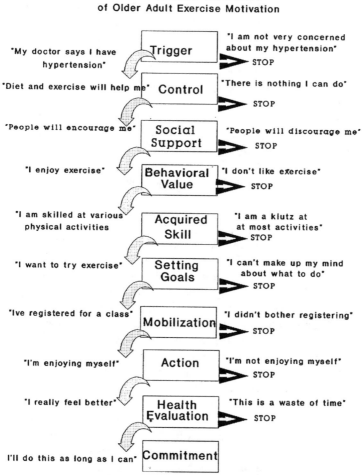

"My doctor says I have hypertension" — **Trigger** — "I am not very concerned about my hypertension" STOP

"Diet and exercise will help me" — **Control** — "There is nothing I can do" STOP

"People will encourage me" — **Social Support** — "People will discourage me" STOP

"I enjoy exercise" — **Behavioral Value** — "I don't like exercise" STOP

"I am skilled at various physical activities" — **Acquired Skill** — "I am a klutz at at most activities" STOP

"I want to try exercise" — **Setting Goals** — "I can't make up my mind about what to do" STOP

"Ive registered for a class" — **Mobilization** — "I didn't bother registering" STOP

"I'm enjoying myself" — **Action** — "I'm not enjoying myself" STOP

"I really feel better" — **Health Evaluation** — "This is a waste of time" STOP

"I'll do this as long as I can" — **Commitment**

Figure 13.1 Self-Talk Model of exercise motivation.

statements are offered alongside nine theoretical constructs amalgamated from behavioral theory. The model, even though it is inclusive and integrated, depicts cognitive processes occurring in a hierarchial format. This format may be overly simplistic, and presumes (with no supportive evidence) that human brain uses a path of orderly thinking. Such comprehensive and orderly thinking is probably not realistic, but the model does capture key constructs from major health behavior models, and does approximate the stages of behavior change of Prochaska and DiClemente (1983). However, the Self-Talk Model is in early conceptual development and thus is not fully prescribed. Weinstein's "messy desk" analogy would lead us to think that such orderly processing is unrealistic, yet Weinstein himself has proposed a five-stage model of behavioral decision-making.

The proposed Self-Talk Model represents a series of thoughts and physical actions related to exercise adoption. Some or all of these thoughts have been processed by older people in discussing exercise in various interviews and groups. The theoretical concepts supporting the vocalized thoughts are found in the center column of boxes. People who hold positive thoughts for activity will be more likely to work through the left-hand side of the model and move downward through the various cognitive phases and successfully reach a point of action and possibly commitment to regular physical activity. But at each cognitive level, negative dialogue is possible, and thus exiting the thought process is easy. Positive self-talk is needed throughout all the contemplative thoughts in order to succeed in reaching a level of preparation for activity. Those who hold any of the beliefs on the right side, are ready to quit their initial contemplation of exercise. The model begins with a triggering event or "cue to act," which acts as a call to attention for the individual.

Trigger

The "trigger" represents the *motive or incentive to act* in SCT, the belief about personal *susceptibility* in the Health Belief Model, or the *hazard* in the Precaution-Adoption Process, and the shift from *precontemplation* to contemplation in Prochaska's Stages of Behavior Change. The triggering act for sedentary people is often a rude awakening about the actual state of one's health or performance abilities. Previously sedentary individuals say they can recall this turning point very clearly, and that it was this single event that changed their activity behavior forever.

Triggering events can be positive or negative in affect. Some examples of negative triggering events are: not being able to get up after sitting on the floor without the use of furniture or assistance; noticing that certain favorite clothes no longer fit; or having a younger relative die of heart disease. Examples of positive triggering events are experiencing firsthand that an activity that really is fun; and encountering an appealing role model (an active person who is far older but far more mobile.

In the Self-Talk Model, being informed of a personal health hazard (hypertension) is used as an example of a triggering event. For the less concerned individual, the health issue is either ignored or conceived to be a trigger to *reduce* activity. This trigger, if interpreted negatively, acts as a barrier to further thoughts about becoming more active. For the skilled individual who holds positive values for exercise, the recognition of personal hypertension becomes a trigger to increase motivation for taking action. Thus, health problems can act as either strong motivators for active living, or can act as powerful deterrents depending on the individual's interpretation. If the trigger is salient to the individual, the individual then may pursue strategies toward controlling the problem.

Control

A person's sense of control is built on a number of current attributes as well as past and present circumstances and experiences. A sense of health control has been described earlier as health *locus of control*, but in the Self-Talk Model, control would be specifically tied to the specific problem that was the trigger event or events. For example, if someone was recently widowed, just helped their daughter out of the hospital from a serious car accident, and then encountered some financial difficulties, their sense of life control would be threatened. Their ability to handle all the immediate difficulties would be compromised, their personal confidence would slide, and they would sense a certain level of helplessness and depression. In this state of mind, it would be easier to give up on optional high-effort tasks like a regular exercise program. Even though maintaining their physical activity could act as an effective coping strategy and buffer for stress, assembling the limited resources needed to mobilize oneself for exercise would be unlikely.

For older people, simply approaching the end of a finite life provides a serious control problem. Although a 79-year-old individual might live another 20 years, mortality statistics suggest the end of life may be approaching. Such an uncertain future may be one reason that so many older people will say "why bother?" or "what's the point?" Individuals of this age group feel enough uncertainty about the future that very few make long-term plans or feel motivated to invest energy in activities that have long-term benefits.

In contrast, an adult who has more financial resources, who is younger, who has a living spouse who is healthy, supportive, and keenly active, who feels that life is stable and of good quality, who has been taking positive steps to age more successfully and notices progress, who is still learning, growing, and developing, may feel a stronger sense of control. The *Control* construct has much to do with recognizing available resources and applying these resources to a better aging experience.

Social Support

When an individual contemplates his or her prospects for physical activity, they are likely to consider the social ramifications of their potential involvement relative to significant people in their lives. If they visualize a discouraging response from one or more of the people close to them, they may reconsider the course of action. But if they perceive that a number of positive social outcomes are likely, the idea of becoming more active will be more appealing to them, and they can use these people to garner more motivation for their eventual participation.

Behavioral Value

Behavioral value is the individual's basic attitude or value held for the behavior in question (physical activity). If an individual holds little value, or negative value for physical activity ("I don't like exercise"), the cognitive process has already reached a dead end as far as motivation is concerned. However, if behavioral value is positive, then the individual views the action as potentially meaningful behavior; eventually they might contemplate their personal potential to engage in one or more types of physical activity. Therefore people who hold high regard for physical activity, exercise, and sport are more likely to contemplate their future involvement in it.

Acquired Skill

Individuals who have a good deal of past experience and mastery in skilled activities such as sport activities are likely to have more self-confidence about their future ability to participate. Past opportunities are often linked to family sport involvement, school opportunities, geographically situated cultural events, and social reinforcement at earlier life stages. People who judge themselves to be athletically inclined should be advantaged for future participation because they have held strong self-efficacy beliefs at one time, and maintain higher performance expectations. On the other hand, people who have acquired few skills in physical activity, or have experienced some kind of failure (the self-proclaimed klutzes) are probably far less confident about their ability to participate; they may be afraid of embarrassing themselves. So even when people agree that exercise has health benefits, they may avidly resist doing the activities that they feel are going to undermine their self-esteem.

Setting Goals

The individual who feels that increasing physical activity is one thing they can do for their hypertension will likely contemplate increasing their level of involvement. No doubt, the physician who first identified the problem will at least mention "exercise" in counselling their patient about how to deal with the problem. So the next step for the inactive but motivated adult is to consider the options and select one or more health behavior activities. If there is a serious interest in becoming more active, some future goal for activity is identified ("I should try an exercise program"). More specific goals have to be framed for future action to be taken ("I will register for an exercise class this week").

A health or fitness professional may be asked to assist in the formation of an exercise plan. Or the individual may prefer to seek out an active friend for their recommendation of an exercise program. The individual who perceives that the recommended activity is not exactly suited to their needs may procrastinate in their goal setting ("I can't make up my mind about what to do"), and will exit the contemplation process regarding exercise. To justify this decision, they may say they have "no time for exercise," but they really mean that they have other priorities for their discretionary time (different layers of priorities on the messy desk).

Mobilization

Setting goals for regular exercise takes the individual a long way into the motivation process, but easy exits are still possible. To this point all the energy spent contemplating activity has been cognitive. With some goals in place to become more active, the next step for the motivated older adult requires more effort. In the self-talk model, getting ready for engagement in physical activity is called mobilization. The older adult has to mobilize resources and develop a plan to meet his or her needs. Phone calls to recruit a companion, enquiries to recreation centres, selecting a program, filling out forms, paying fees, purchasing needed footwear, and preparing a kit-bag to take to the locker room could be just some of the mobilizing activities that have to occur before the individual actually becomes physically active.

Some people who are motivated to become more active will capitulate to sedentary living at this stage because of the extra physical drive needed at this stage to follow-through. Many people just don't get around to making the necessary phone call to get program information, or back out when they see how expensive a swimsuit is going to cost, or somehow just fail to be bothered enough to make active living happen. They have formed some intention to act in the goal-setting phase, but they exit the mobilization process simply because they "didn't get around to it." The messy desk is once again presenting them with other more appealing life priorities; or somehow the steps of mobilization get lost under higher priorities.

Action

The sedentary adults who make it to this stage are to be commended. They have experienced a triggering event or somehow developed an awareness and explored their personal resources and their sense of control; they have examined their values for increasing physical activity; they have had to explore their efficacy beliefs to choose an appealing physical activity; they have set themselves a goal for which to aim; and have probably gone to some trouble and expense to get ready for that activity. In the Action phase, they have carried through with their plan, but there is still a possibility to get out of the engagement process. If they decide that the activity undertaken is not up to expectations (not enjoyable for them, they don't fit in, it's harder than they thought, or not suited to their needs), their first encounters with the activity will fail to maintain their interest. Even if they do stick with the activity for enough weeks or months to experience the benefits, they still may drop out when re-registration is required. However, people who find an activity they enjoy, who find new friends in that activity, who get bolstered by the encouragement of the activity environment, and who learn enjoyable skills, will tend to develop high value for their behavior and be rewarded with positive views about the outcomes they are receiving.

Health Outcome

If individuals stay with an activity program long enough, and participate frequently enough, the benefits of their actions should become evident in terms of observable health outcomes. Over weeks and months, people will notice that they can move with less effort, can lift heavy objects with ease, can walk faster, and so on. Over the short-term, the benefits of exercise are so potent that even same-day improvements can be noticed in flexibility, improved circulation, the contented feeling of relaxation, and uplifted spirits as a result of doing something good for the body. Unfortunately, not all the early outcomes will be beneficial. Muscle soreness may occur for a day or two. It may take time to get in tune with the program. But the people who "feel better" after the program are reinforced for their efforts and tend to become "converts." They will want to return as much as they can to experience that good feeling over and over.

On the other hand, the participant who is trying to get involved may fail to succeed in maintaining a regular program of activity if they perceive few real health benefits, fail to fit in the available social network, or encounter competing priorities for their time. Some adults will lose their momentum and quit because of a temporary illness. For these near-adherers, the motivation to get this far is noteworthy. Even if health benefits seem to be marginal at the time, the fact that they have found certain activities to be enjoyable, and have succeeded at mobilizing themselves for exercise participation, bodes well for future involvements in physical activity.

COMMITMENT

People who develop strong habitual activity patterns may move into a long-term commitment phase. Commitment to an active lifestyle means that the individual is prepared to continually bring physical activity involvement to the top of their priorities on life's messy desk. Even then, a specific commitment is not a permanent commitment. A person's commitment to a specific physical activity program may wane if the activity becomes boring to them. In that case, motivation for that activity may drop, and often the habitually active person replaces it with another. They may appear to be a "drop-out" but they are really just changing activities. The older adult is still highly motivated to participate in something because they have already passed through at least nine phases of motivation.

SUMMARY

Although the Self-Talk Model may be a humble beginning to attempt to understand the complexity of exercise motivation, it does provide a starting framework that accommodates the insights of most current theories. The hierarchial nature of the model speaks to the future need to explore this type of model with path analysis.

Chapter 14

Research Challenges: The Limits of Current Knowledge

THE CHALLENGE OF RESEARCHING OLDER ADULTS

Self-Selection Bias and Survivorship

Older adults participating in research focused on physical activity are often not perfect representatives of the general population in their age group. Self-selected volunteers are usually more active, better educated, less overweight, and in better health than seniors who do not choose to be part of a research study. Recruiting representative samples of elderly participants for research is a challenge that has been reported before (Carter, Elward, Malmgren, Martin, & Larson, 1991).

Subjects willing to participate in gerontology studies are mainly found in community programs or seniors' lodges and therefore represent study populations who are independently mobile, who are currently involved in leisure activities in their communities, and who enjoy a reasonable level of health. Seniors assessed on the west coast of North America live in temperate cities and this may bias the sample toward more wealthy, healthy, and activity-conscious individuals. National studies suggest that the adults living "in the west" surpass national averages for activity level, freedom from physical limitations, not being overweight, and overall health status (General Social Survey, 1987).

One should also remember that adults living to their seventh, eighth and ninth decade of life already represent a biased population of survivors—individuals who may have certain social, psychological, and biological advantages not available to every female born in 1921 or earlier. Age group mortality statistics indicate that 62 percent of the women who were born in 1919 survived to age 60 (Golini & Lori, 1990). Women in the Vancouver study averaged a mean birth year of 1913 and had lived at least to age 70. They therefore represented about 30 percent to 50 percent of their particular birth cohort.

Mortality statistics also suggest that five percent to six percent of North American women over age 70 in 1990 would not be alive just one year later—an attrition rate of about 50 to 60 per 1,000. Researchers can potentially lose 16 to 20 subjects out of every 300 volunteers to annual mortality (U.S. Department of Health & Human Services, 1991). The uncomfortable reality of gerontological research is that some of the subjects are not alive just one year later to learn about the findings!

Finding representative samples of large populations will continue to pose difficulties in the future. One solution is that future research could focus on targeted social groups, such as those in poverty, long-term care, aboriginal elders, widowed adults, rural people and so on, in order to provide understanding of the activity patterns and unique determinants of physical activity in more specific contexts. As data collects on the situational barriers to older adults in various sport and exercise settings, commonalities and unique features will emerge.

Variables with Poor Response Rate

Further bias and error is added to a study when subjects choose not to answer certain kinds of questions. Post hoc analysis on the Vancouver women with missing data indicated they were significantly less active, had fewer children, were older, had less childhood confidence for skilled movement, had less adult social support for exercise and perceived more risks with the six fitness exercises. Ethical protocol at many universities require that all subjects are informed that they are not required to complete the study and can drop out at any time. Thus, other than paying subjects (which adds another type of bias), there is little gerontologists can do to eliminate bias.

Older women are particularly reticent to answer questions about income, age, and marital status. Also questions requiring open-ended answers are often left blank. Beliefs about risks and benefits of exercise can have a poor response rate compared to other cognitive variables. In previous work, complete data on only 47 percent of the participants were available on the perceived benefits and on just 55 percent for the perceived risks. Open-ended questions of, "The major benefit for me would be . . ." and "The major risk to me would be . . ." were rarely filled in, and when they were, quite often the specific benefit or risk identified was clearly a guess. A written evaluation by one of the researchers involved in administering the questionnaire to a 77-year-old woman stated:

> You will notice that some questions are partially completed or not completed at all. The
> subject felt they were inappropriate, for example, "rate the possible risk to your health"

because she had no way of knowing for certain. Those questions she felt sure about she answered quickly (Oral survey given by A.E.L., February 12, 1991).

Thus the data on risks and benefits, although conceptually promising, were weakened by many non-responses. A more appropriate format might be to use the perceived risks and benefits scales in a forced-choice Likert format such as "This exercise 1) has no risk for me; 2) has some risk for me; 3) is very risky for me." Possibly oral interviews would facilitate the response rate and a checklist of possible risks and benefits might also help respondents select their responses with more ease.

Explanations for missing data are lacking. If missing data is found in the middle portion of the questionnaire, it is unlikely that the subjects are fatigued. Missing data can be prevalent for efficacy and experience estimates of physical activity. Such questions require the subject to identify their experiential or acquired knowledge and this could feel threatening to many participants, especially if subjects feel inexperienced at specific activities and are not sure how able they are to perform them. One woman commented that she had never done *any* of the activities, and was sure that she could not do them, so for her, it was demoralizing to keep reporting the same negative response for each of the six skills. One can imagine that women without firsthand experience with adult exercise would find it extremely difficult to perceive *any* specific risks or benefits. On other sections of the survey, there was a remarkably high completion rate of about 92 percent with over 300 people providing data on almost every question. This shows high cooperation. Although little is known about response rates in the elderly, the quality of response in the Vancouver study appears to be good. A few studies have reported response/participation rates. In a recent random telephone survey to older adults, Graham, Graham, and MacLean (1991) reported that a 50 percent participation rate seriously jeopardized the representativeness of their sample. A Polish study on excessive weight and hypertension in adults ages 65 to 84 reported a participation rate of 28 percent in the 65 to 74 age group and only 9 percent in the 75 to 84 age group. They therefore warn the reader that,

. . . the conclusions should be drawn cautiously as the results of the study presumably are affected by the differential survival between sexes as well as by selection bias. It was disclosed that those in the older age group (75 to 84 years) were under-represented compared to younger subjects (Jedrychowski, Mroz, Bojanczyk, & Jedrychowska, 1991).

THE CHALLENGES OF ASSESSING THE ELDERLY

The challenge of collecting data on several hundred older adults brings attention to the methodological problems of written surveys. Colsher and Wallace (1989) claimed that previous research indicates that data quality tends to decline with respondent age. For example, elderly adults are more likely than younger individuals to refuse to participate in surveys (Carter, Elward, Malmgren, Martin, & Larson, 1991) and to refuse to answer specific questions. Elderly nonrespondents have indicated that they dislike investigations (Eriksson, Mellstrom, & Svanborg, 1987).

Although it might be expected that these problems would be similar to those experienced with younger persons, the prevalence of impaired physical health, declining sensory function, cognitive impairment, and abnormal affect among the elderly population may complicate surveys by reducing both data quality and sample representativeness (Colsher & Wallace, 1989).

Older persons are thought to be more prone to response biases such as choosing socially desirable responses; they may tend to be more cautious in making choices (Okun, 1976) and may require more information before making decisions (Denney & Denney, 1973; Kesler, Denney, & Whitely, 1976). However, some investigators have found increased accuracy among older respondents (Traugott & Katosh, 1979). But income, in particular, is one item that receives many omissions, especially among women who may feel vulnerable by revealing such information to strangers (Colsher & Wallace, 1989).

A problem that needs to be addressed in future work is that of improving public understanding about research. Many older people, and women in particular, do not feel "worthy" of scientific research; one woman suggested that her husband would be "much more interesting to study." In contrast, an older man who wanted to be in the study asked "Why are you studying older women? Their lives are so uneventful." Even after explanations of the importance and value of the research, some individuals did not see the relevance of the study to their present or future lifestyles, or could not appreciate the relevance of the study to benefit others. In addition, older people generally lacked understanding about a need for following scientific protocol, such as limiting the study to women of a specific chronological age.

Overall, the most prevalent concern of older women was that of a personal vulnerability to criminal behavior. Some women thought they were being "tricked" or screened for committal to an institution. Many women thought that reporting their age, medications, health, marital status, education, and income characteristics was "too personal" and risky. They worried they would be taken advantage of in some way.

Future researchers can improve on their data quality with older adults by: having a trusted member of the group ("ringleader") explain the importance of their time and the value of the study outcomes; conducting the survey in smaller units over a period of sessions; scheduling special survey times for the questionnaire; using at least 12-point font size lettering on the survey instrument; spacing the questions out well and using pictures for visual interest; starting off with objective questioning and concluding with more subjective items; and having seniors read through the questionnaire in advance for clarity and understanding.

DIRECTIONS FOR FUTURE RESEARCH

Identifying Motives for Physical Activity

One motivating belief that has not received the attention that it deserves is described by Bandura as "self-dissatisfaction" with performance. In Bandura's work, people who perform under their expected standard tend to strengthen their resolve to perform better in the future. When cyclists were given bogus feedback that they were going slower than they actually were, they immediately altered their performance to achieve a better standard. Cyclists who were given bogus feedback that they were high above the standard tended to slacken their efforts.

For older people, indicators that health or performance is declining may act as a "trigger" or cue that one is entering the downward spiral. This moment of reckoning or turning point can be interpreted as the time to take life easier, or the time to take action. For example, one woman identified her critical moment of behavior change was not having the strength or flexibility to be able to get up after losing her balance while skiing. Yet, for others, having two or three medical symptoms can mean lower exercise involvement. However, data on activity level according to the number of medical symptoms has shown that women reporting four or more symptoms were, as a group, almost as active (1800 kcal per week) as women taking no medications (1900 kcal per week). Future studies will need to attend to the possibility that people may be motivated, or demotivated, to take up physical activity when they develop a concern for, or dissatisfaction with increasing health problems. A realization about personal vulnerability may provide an important incentive to take action; such a realization is fundamental to Rosenstock's perceived susceptibility construct in the Health Belief Model.

Identifying the Perceived Risks of Exercise

Apparently many older people feel that exercise is risky for them. The fact that older women are unable, or unwilling, to comment freely upon what they considered to be the personal risks of participating in six fitness activities, suggests that more detailed and positive public education strategies are needed. Reminding people to consult their physician before increasing activity levels can be a deterrent. There is evidence that most seniors feel that there are general benefits to their health and well-being, but are not able to divulge what these benefits could be. Here is the challenge for health educators. Without information about the older people's attitudes and knowledge regarding risk and exercise, advocates will find it difficult to favorably direct health promoting messages to the older public. New instruments and more strategic research will need to be aimed at the exercise risk perceptions of various social segments of the population.

The Significance of Domestic Activity

One missing link in past work is the lack of attention paid to older people's lifelong energy expenditure in mild, moderate, and vigorous forms of work. The lifelong domestic work activity of women, carried on usually seven days a week, has been virtually overlooked. Women often point out that they have little leisure time to exercise, but do put a great deal of physical energy into their chores around the home. Recent research suggests that women's energy spent on domestic activity has been greatly underestimated (Mattiason-Nilo, Sonn, Johannesson, Gosman-Hedstrom, Persson, & Grimby, 1990).

Discussion with older people indicates that one of the supportive situations that fosters regular indoor and outdoor exercise is that of living in a residential dwelling with house and yard. Women in their seventies and older have indicated that their previously active lifestyles took unplanned turns for the worse when they gave up their residential homes and relocated into small apartments or seniors' lodges. The activity patterns of moving from one's residence is not at first evident—but selling a home with yard means that housework and domestic cleaning are reduced to a minimum, there is no more raking, hoeing, and digging in the garden, there is less garbage to dispose of, and less distance to carry it. The devastating physical implications of such a move is best described by an 86-year-old woman:

> I have been in this 'home' for only one year. I have been shocked by the number of women who just 'sit.' There are arrangements for drives and rides, but never for walks. The exercises are mostly for upper extremities sitting in chairs. There is a large activity room in the basement but many have never seen it—elevator is available, easy access, good lighting. My personal wish is that we might be encouraged to utilize any work habits and garden knowledge that we developed before coming here. We would take pride in the results, providing plants and seeds, even if we developed a hodge-podge! I get a guilty feeling just picking off dead flowers . . . maybe next year (Anonymous, 1990).

Clearly, future research needs to include women's work in energy estimates and examine this activity link to health. Only recently have women's activities as homemakers been accounted for (Cauley, LaPorte, Black-Sandler, Schramm, & Kriska, 1987; Kolanowski & Gunter, 1988). It appears that most occupational studies, linking life occupation to mortality and health outcomes, have been done on all-male samples. In recent years, physical energy output in employment settings has altered so dramatically that research interest in male occupational physical activity has waned. However, for many women, the impact of domestic labor continues lifelong, and the changing leisure time patterns of women are worthy of study, particularly in view of women's extra longevity. Exercise physiologists may eventually find that mild and moderate forms of domestic physical activity over the life course may contribute to added years of functional independence, improved quality of life, or even added years of life.

Perhaps most important of all, older people who move to seniors' lodges report that they have to give up their favorite walking companion—their dog. So far, the research literature has neglected the role of "man's best friend," or in a woman's case, a reliable walking companion and protector on the streets. Many widowed or single women have found their canine pet to be the perfect type of social support and environmental cue for regular physical activity. Owning a dog of any size or breed requires that the dog be exercised every day. Older individuals who own dogs are therefore reminded to get out for a daily walk. For many people, this is just the incentive and support they need to obtain reliable walking exercise, and furthermore, a dog may provide the older person with some sense of personal security in public spaces.

The Significance of Being a Turn-of-the-Century Tomboy

Recent research has opened a treasure trove of questions about the early activity and socialization experiences of today's elders, and it is today's oldest survivors who hold the keys to that historical knowledge. Significant advances in the physical liberation of young females took place around the turn of the century. The bicycle craze of the 1890s provided many young women and girls with new opportunities for transportation and physical challenge that forced an alteration of the restrictive fashion of the day. By the 1920s, women in North America were prominent in sports such as golf, competitive ice skating, and tennis. Further research is urgently needed to learn about the sporting experiences of women at this time as reported by them.

Many older women are quick to point out that they were as active as was tolerated for girls of their day, and that they were often called "tomboys" back then. Despite the tomboy label, their active nature was not easily curtailed and therefore vigorous activity must have been tolerated at some level by their childhood family and community. Now at the other end of the life spectrum, these women still seem to revel in the memory of this deviant behavior, which in some way continues to provide them with rewards.

For the self-proclaimed "tomboys," lifelong advantages appear to have been acquired through their exuberant involvement in their early physical exploits. For example, the consequences of certain past behaviors may have informed them as to what they must do to gain beneficial outcomes from activity and how to avoid punishing ones. Women, who 50, 60, and 70 years later, recall being a tomboy, provide this admission with little embarrassment, and usually a great deal of pride. Bandura and Walters (1963) suggested decades ago that the acquisition of physical skill requires more than genetic predisposition.

> Because proficiency in physical skills is often dependent on an early commencement of training, which must then continue over a lengthy period of time, persons not infrequently find that lack of opportunities or guidance during their childhood and adolescent years has, in effect, imposed a life-time barrier to their legitimately acquiring possessions and status, or participating in activities that for other persons are evident sources of enjoyment and means for obtaining additional social and material rewards. Thus, both genetic and early-experience factors may create conditions under which persons are tempted to acquire socially acceptable rewards by socially unacceptable means (Bandura & Walters, 1963).

Exploration of the tomboy theme in future research will require some creative approaches, especially in finding ways to encourage women to give 'voice' to their early childhood experiences in sport and physical activity.

Chapter 15

Policy Implications

IMPLICATIONS FOR BETTER AGING

Contemporary research has provided important information for social progress and professional practice. Motivation to live a long and healthy life is a universal goal of almost every aging adult; yet few of these adults are prepared to mobilize their bodies toward that end. The sedentary lifestyle adopted by most North Americans has lead to enormous obesity problems and soon will lead to a health crisis of profound proportion. Unbelievably, Canadians and Americans are shortening their lives and virtually guaranteeing a poor aging outcome by their inactivity. Akin to the risk level of smoking, physical *inactivity* doubles one's health risks! This book has tried to clarify the motivational barriers we all face in staying active over the life course.

Evidence is accumulating that many of the optimally active people are not even exercising for health reasons. Rather they are active for social and personal reasons that need further study. Aside from the pleasure and self-satisfaction that is derived from moving skillfully in one's environment, and the pleasure obtained from being in a physically stimulating environment, the core reasons for engaging in late-life physical activity need clarification. One area that has emerged in current research is that many older people are "afraid" of exercise. They perceive a host of risks and problems accompanying the exerting aspects of active living; ironically the facts suggest that most of the very same issues could be resolved with increased physical activity.

Some older women are more motivated for reasons of beauty rather than health; aging men are often only provoked to exercise when a serious health condition arises.

The two key factors leading to a better aging experience through active living are feeling confident and capable of moving the body in moderate physical activity, and finding community, family, and professional support to be more active. This final chapter explores how these factors implicate social and health policy.

CREATING SOCIAL SUPPORT FOR PHYSICAL ACTIVITY

Evidence is rapidly accumulating that social support is perhaps the most significant force in assisting individuals to initiate activity, to adhere to activity once started, and to increase enjoyment of the activity experience. Although it has been suggested that health educators and fitness leaders should assist individuals in seeking and recognizing sources of social support for more physically active lifestyles (Blair et al., 1980), it is becoming apparent that older adults, especially women, may be most in need of a helping hand in this regard. This means that over their entire life course, incentives and opportunities need to be created for girls and women to enjoy the broad health and social benefits of leisure time physical activity and sport pursuits. In contemporary society, females lack a number of resources to do this; they lack social power in domestic relations to access adequate leisure time for themselves; they lack financial resources to do the things they would most enjoy; and they lack the skills to feel confident and be competent in skillful physical activity.

Social support for a more physically active lifestyle may be the most powerful intervention or source of motivation for people over the age of 70. Older women, in particular, will be more active if they are encouraged from multiple sources: their spouse or immediate family, at least one exercise companion, friends who are active, and advocacy support to be more active by their primary physician. Our current understanding suggests that older adults easily get caught up in the social dynamics or momentum of an active community. In a sedentary community, on the other hand, people may easily feel disempowered by the surrounding lethargy and passive social activities available to them.

Communities may be able to rapidly shed the stereotypes of old age by highlighting local groups and individuals who are ordinary seniors in most respects, but who are authentic role models for healthy lifestyles and physical activity involvement. More attention could be placed on the "come-back" stories of older individuals—those who have rehabilitated themselves through physical activity after a debilitating illness, or of individuals who were former exercise skeptics, but are now keen advocates of physical activity. People like these are found in most communities. Added to this strategy for setting new norms for elderly living, is a need for more leadership from seniors themselves, to develop the kinds of programs, and to lead their peers in the physical activities that they most enjoy. Seniors, although reluctant to spend money on their own recreation, need to explore their attitudes about the expected value of physical leisure to their well-being and compare recreation fees to the costs of medications or treatment which might be avoided altogether.

To promote broader and more vigorous physical activity participation at all ages, the input and advocacy of physicians is essential (Allen & Allen, 1986). But practitioners are advised to team up with professionals outside of traditional medicine (e.g., recreationists, homeopathic healers, fitness leaders, environmental planners, city developers, social workers, engineers) to create community partnerships for the development of holistic strategies for health promotion. Physicians could also be more willing and able to talk to patients about the central place of appropriate exercise for their health, to be more optimistic about the ability of older adults to become more active, and to specifically identify who and where in the community older adults can get the exercise supervision or help they need to initiate or resume activity. Physical activity leaders and community recreation programmers can assist by informing local physicians about the nature and quality of their activity programs.

Walking is recommended as the ideal form of mild to moderate exercise (Monahan, 1987) and is the favorite mode of exercise for women over the age of 70. This finding is not surprising, and it is not new. But little research has yet focused specifically on the determinants and barriers to walking in adults. One study has found that people become more cautious in pedestrian behavior with age (Harrel, 1991).

Although brisk walking may be adequate aerobic exercise for the unfit, it may not be suitable or effective for more fit, or the very unfit, or obese populations of older adults. Walking is also not the exercise panacea to full fitness. Walking makes no contribution to upper body strength, nor to most joints for increased flexibility. Walking may be adequate movement to maintain one's balance and proprioception, but no scientific evidence exists to demonstrate that.

Research is needed that could identify the specific benefits of various intensities of walking, at various frequencies, at various duration in different populations of adults. Research is needed that could inform the public about the specific benefits about specific walking regimens and how best to develop the social support systems to ensure that this form of exercise is as enjoyable as possible. A good example of a supportive environment for walking all-year around is now seen in the larger shopping malls, where groups of adults meet regularly walk for fitness. Notwithstanding its low-risk, low-cost prospects for participation, walking may be the most compatible mode for conversation with companions, and thereby create and strengthen opportunities for further social support and personal enjoyment (Kasper, 1990).

Future research will need to tease out which types of social cues motivate adults best for increasing or sustaining participation in exercise settings. Until such time as more is known about the specific nature of social support, adult educators should ensure that there are social rewards and reinforcements in their exercise programs by fostering social networks and enhancing self-confidence as the MAIN objectives of physical activity participation for aging women.

INCREASING SELF-EFFICACY AND INCENTIVE FOR PHYSICAL ACTIVITY

There has been some debate on whether efficacy perceptions involving physically skilled behavior can be easily altered by simply increasing people's knowledge and

incentives to act. Kirsch (1985) discussed possible conceptual confusion in the definition of self-efficacy and outcome expectations in that both are related to expectancy
theory. In comparing self-efficacy to approach a live snake, and self-efficacy to accurately toss a wad of paper into a wastebasket, Kirsch found that snake phobia was
easy to alter by adding a five dollar incentive. However, he found that it was difficult,
even with a million dollar incentive, to increase people's confidence to toss a wad of
paper accurately.

This finding raises the possibility that increasing self-efficacy for highly skilled
physical tasks, such as that found in sport settings, may be extremely difficult in the
adult population. Therefore, more casual and less skilled forms of health-promoting
exercise may be important to certain social groups who have traditionally lacked the
opportunity to acquire the necessary skills in advance of adulthood.

IMPLICATIONS FOR PROFESSIONAL PRACTICE

To capitalize on the finding that perceived efficacy in exercise settings is a key determinant for older adult participation, educators in health and activity counselling must
find ways to improve the initial personal confidence of the participants. Because just
being more active has been associated with efficacy estimates, educators should intro-
duce adults to low skilled activity first, and then *progressively* challenge participants
into higher skilled activity.

Higher efficacy estimates are known to accompany higher levels of experience
and performance, but only if the individual perceives success. Thus individuals must
be given latitude to set personal goals and pursue these at a *self-paced rate* so that
success is ensured. New learners in physical activity settings have little past experience on which to base present efficacy. Thus former athletes or older adults with
previous skills, may need to be challenged at a faster pace than those who are newcomers to sport and physical activity settings.

Contemporary literature suggests that the activity and health habits of children are
in crisis—North American children in the last part of the 20th century are among the
least physically active in history. Yet current understanding holds that early experience and skill in physical activity and sport are important to lifelong health and
lifestyle skills. Experiencing early mastery of vigorous and adventurous activities
provides first-hand knowledge of the benefits, and increases the prospects that individuals will return to healthy levels of physical activity at various points over their life
course (O'Brien Cousins & Keating, 1995). Particularly for women, many of whom
can be expected to have activity patterns disrupted with marriage, relocation, child-
bearing, childrearing, and changing work patterns, the enhancement of their ability
to keep reentering activity settings in adulthood will be important. Examination of
the life stages and individual circumstances that support exercise reentry would be
valuable in future research.

Some cultures outside of North America are apparently able to accomplish successful and lifelong lasting experiences in female physical activity, exercise, and sport
settings. The physical activity experiences in present-day school curricula need to be
examined and culturally compared to those of Northern Europe, at least for girls.

Mandatory, high-quality, and daily physical education may be the common feature of Northern European countries that explains why so many active older adults have a direct European heritage. More studies examining the determinants of successful participation for people at all ages is warranted.

The finding that impressionable beliefs, more than poor health and old age, are primary barriers to physical activity in one's older years suggests that adult educators, health professionals, and activity leaders have the potential to influence sedentary older adults who wish they were more active. Exercise leaders of older adults should seek information about what the participants actually value as expected outcomes of the exercise participation. Then they must strive to create the kind of program that will lead to these outcomes. Powerful self-rated evaluation tools are being designed by Dr. Anita Myers at the University of Waterloo. These tools will allow gains made in improving sleep, appetite, and feelings of vitality to be assessed as quality of life outcomes of more active living.

Ultimately, leaders will want to find out which aspects of exercise increases and decreases anxiety in participants, and which aspects of the exercise environment interfere with their participation. Current findings suggest that older adults may need more specific knowledge about the kinds of benefits to expect from various activities, and how these benefits may outweigh the expected risks. The kind of detail and specificity seen in nutrition counselling may well need to apply to exercise counseling.

Although activity levels appear to be improving at all ages, older men and women persist in underestimating their physical abilities and limiting their activity choices to a few involvements that are deemed to be socially acceptable and age-appropriate. Social incentives need to be explored that would challenge the self-fulfilling prophecy of decrepitude and ultimately empower older people to venture into less passive activities for which they might find new opportunities and new skills to learn. Unravelling ageism and sexism in everyday settings of exercise and sport will require innovation, intergenerational cooperation, and exceptional levels of social support.

To enact more variety in adult programming, and to provide opportunities for invigorating physical activity at all ages, society must be willing to share its sport and recreation resources with its oldest taxpayers, and allow them moments of priority to enjoy these facilities as full participants, rather than as spectators. This means that administrators of sport facilities and community centers must be willing to share their limited resources and expertise by providing the best of support staff, including elite coaches and fitness leaders, to address the challenges of creating the richest experiences possible for citizens at their oldest life stage.

References

Abdellah, F. G. (1985). The aged woman and the future of health care delivery. In M. R. Haug, A. B. Ford, & M. Sheafor (Eds.), *The physical and mental health of aged women* (pp. 254–263). New York: Springer.

Abeles, R. P., Gift, H. C., & Ory, M. G. (Eds.). (1994). *Aging and quality of life.* New York: Springer.

Abrams, M. (1988). Use of time by the elderly in Great Britain, In K. Altergott (Ed.). *Daily life in later life* (pp. 23–41). Newbury Park: Sage.

Active Living. (1994). Collingwood, ON: The Fitness Report. p. 157.

Adams, G. M., & de Vries, H. A. (1973). Physiological effects of an exercise training regimen upon women aged 52 to 79. *Journal of Gerontology, 28,* 50–55.

Ajzen, I. (1985). From intentions to actions: A theory of planned behavior. In J. Kuhl & J. Beckman (Eds.). *Action-control: From cognition to behavior* (pp. 11–39). Heidelberg: Springer.

Ajzen, I., & Fishbein, M. (1980). *Understanding attitudes and predicting social behavior.* Englewood Cliffs, NJ: Prentice-Hall.

Ajzen, I., & Madden, T. J. (1986). Prediction of goal-directed behavior: Attitudes, intentions, and perceived behavioral control. *Journal of Experimental Social Psychology, 22,* 453–474.

Alberta Centre for Well-Being. (1995). Assessing the stages of physical activity behaviour of Albertans. *Research Update, 3*(1), 1.

Aldana, S., & Stone, W. (1991). Changing physical activity preferences of American adults. *Journal of Physical Education, Recreation & Dance, 62*(4), 67–71, 76.

Alderson, M., & Yasin, S. (1966). Measuring habitual leisure time activity: A questionnaire method suitable for epidemiologic studies. In K. Evany & K. Lange-Anderson (Eds.). *Physical activity in health and disease* (pp. 215–221). Baltimore: Williams & Wilkins.

Alexander, M. J., Ready, A. E., & Fougere-Mailey, C. (1985). The fitness levels of females in various age groups. *CAHPER Journal, March/April,* 8–12.

Allen, J. & Allen, R. F. (1986). From short term compliance to long term freedon: Culture-based health promotion by health professionals. *American Journal of Health Promotion, 1*(1), 39–47.

Andrew, G. M., Oldridge, N. B., Parker, J. O., Cunningham, D. A., Rechnitzer, P. A., Jones, N. L., Buck, C., Kavanagh, T., Shephard, R. J., Sutton, J., & McDonald, W. (1981). Reasons for dropout from exercise programs in post-coronary patients. *Medicine & Science in Sports & Exercise, 13*(3), 164–168.

Arfken, C. L., Lach, H. W., McGee, S., Birge, S. J., & Miller, J. P. (1994). Visual acuity, visual disabilities and falling in the elderly. *Journal of Aging & Health, 6*(1), 38–50.

Aronow, W. S., & Ahn, C. (1994). Correlation of serum lipids with the presence or absence of coronary artery disease in 1,793 men and women age >62 years. *American Journal of Cardiology, 73*, 703–708.

Astrand, P. O. (1986). Exercise physiology of the mature athlete. In J. R. Suton & R. M. Brock (Eds.), *Sports Medicine for the Mature Athlete* (pp. 3–13). Indianapolis, IN: Benchmark.

Atkins, C. J., Kaplan, R. M., Reinsch, S., & Lofback, K. (1984). Behavioral exercise programs in the management of chronic obstructive pulmonary disease. *Journal of Consulting & Clinical Psychology, 52*, 591–603.

Avlund, K., Schroll, M., Davidsen, M., Levborg, B., & Rantanen, T. (1994). Maximal isometric muscle strength and functional ability in daily activities among 75-year-old men and women. *Scandinavian Journal of Medicine & Sport Science, 4,* 32–40.

Baecke, J. A. H., Burema, J., & Frijters, J. E. R. (1982). A short questionnaire for the measurement of habitual physical activity in epidemiological studies. *American Journal of Clinical Nutrition, 36,* 936–942.

Bain, L. L., Wilson, T., & Chaikland, E. (1989). Participant perceptions of exercise programs for overweight women, *Research Quarterly for Exercise & Sport, 60*(2), 134–143.

Bandura, A. (1977a). Self-efficacy: Toward a unifying theory of behavioral change. *Psychological Review, 84,* 191–215.

Bandura, A. (1977b). *Social learning theory.* Englewood Cliffs, NJ: Prentice-Hall.

Bandura, A. (1986). *Social foundations of thought and action.* Englewood Cliffs, N.J.: Prentice-Hall.

Bandura, A. (1989). Human agency in Social Cognitive Theory. *The American Psychologist, 44*(9), 1175–1184.

Bandura, A. (1995). Moving into forward gear in health promotion and disease prevention. Keynote address at the Annual Meeting of the Society of Behavioral Medicine, March 23, San Diego.

Bandura, A., (1997). *Self-efficacy: The exercise of control.* New York: W. H. Freeman & Company.

Bandura, A., Adams, N. E., & Beyer, J. (1997). Cognitive processes mediating behavioral change. *Journal of Personality and Social Psychology, 35,* 125–139.

Bandura, A. & Cervone, D. (1983). Self-evaluative and self-efficacy mechanisms governing the motivational effects of goal systems. *Journal of Personality & Social Psychology, 45*(5), 1017–1028.

Bandura, A., & Cervone, D. (1986). Differential engagement of self-reactive influences in cognitive motivation. *Organizational Behaviours & Human Decision Processes, 38,* 92–113.

Bandura, A. & Walters, R. H. (1963). *Social learning and personality development.* Toronto: Holt, Rinehart & Winston, Inc.

Baranowski, T. (1988). Validity and reliability of self-report measures of physical activity: An information-processing perspective. *Research Quarterly for Exercise & Sport, 59*(4), 314–327.

Barling J. & Abel, M. (1983). Self-efficacy beliefs and tennis performance. *Cognitive Therapy & Research, 7*(3), 265–272.

Barnard, R. J. (1991). Effects of lifestyle modification on serum lipids. *Archives of Internal Medicine, 151*(7), 1389–1394.

Barnard, R. J., Ugianskis, E. J., Martin, D. A., & Inkeles, S. B. (1992). Role of diet and exercise in the management of hyperinsulihenia and associated artherioschlerotic risk factors. *The American Journal of Cardiology, 69*(Feb. 15), 440–444.

Bar-Or, O. (1994). Childhood and adolescent physical activity and fitness and adult risk profile. In C. Bouchard, R. J. Shephard, & T. Stephens (Eds.), *Physical Activity, Fitness and Health* (pp. 931–942).

Barris, R. (1987). Activity: The interface between person and environment. *Physical & Occupational Therapy in Geriatrics, 5*(2), 39–49.

Barry, A. J., Daly, J. W., Pruett, E. D. R., Steinmetz, J. R., Page, H. F., Birkhead, N. C., & Rodahl, K. (1966). The effects of physical conditioning on older individuals. I. Work capacity, circulatory-respiratory function, and work electrocardiogram. *Journal of Gerontology, 21*(1), 182–191.

Barry, H. C., Rich, B. S. E., & Carlson, R. T. (1993). How exercise can benefit older patients: A practical approach. *The Physician & Sports Medicine, 21*(2), 124–140.

Bashore, T. R. (1989). Age, physical fitness and mental processing speed. *Annual Review of Gerontology & Geriatrics, 9*, 120–144.

Bashore, T. R., Martinerie, J. M., Weiser, P. C., Greenspan, L. W., & Heffley, E. F. (1988). Preservation of mental processing speed in aerobically fit older men. *Psycho–Physiology, 25*, 433–434.

Baylor, A. M., & Spirduso, W. W. (1988). Systematic aerobic exercise and components of reaction time in older women. *Journal of Gerontology, 43*(5), 121–126.

Becker, M. H. (1974). The health belief model and personal health behavior. *Health Education Monographs, 2*, 324–508.

Belloc, N. B., & Breslow, L. (1972). Relationships of physical health status and health practices. *Preventive Medicine, 11*, 409–421.

Berger, B. G. (1989). The role of physical activity in the life quality of older adults. In W. W. Spirduso & H. M. Eckert (Eds.), *Physical activity and aging* (pp. 42–58). Champaign, IL: Human Kinetics Books.

Beverly, M. C., Rider, T. A., Evans, M. J., & Smith, R. (1987). Local bone mineral response to brief exercise that stresses the skeleton. *Journal of the American Medical Association, 257*, 3115–3117.

Biddle, S., & Smith, R. A. (1992). Motivating adults for physical activity: Towards a healthier present. *JOPERD, 62*(7), 39–43.

Binder, E. F., Brown, M., Craft, S., Schechtman, K. B., & Birge, S. J. (1994). Effects of a group exercise program on risk factors for falls in frail older adults. *Journal of Aging & Physical Activity, 3*, 383–395.

Blair, S. N. (1984). How to assess exercise habits and physical fitness. In J. D. Matarazzo, S. M. Weiss, J. A. Herd, & N. E. Miller (Eds.), *Behavioral health: A handbook for health enhancement and disease prevention* (pp. 424–427). New York: John Wiley & Sons.

Blair, S. N., Brill, P. A. & Kohl, H. W., III. (1989). Physical activity patterns in older individuals. In W. W. Spirduso & H. M. Eckert (Eds.), *Physical activity and aging* (pp. 120–139). Champaign, IL: Human Kinetics Books.

Blair, S. N., Haskell, W. L., Ho, P., Paffenbarger, R. S., Jr., Vranizan, K. M., Farquhar, J. W., & Wood, P. D. (1985). Assessment of habitual physical activity by a seven-day recall in a community survey and controlled experiments. *American Journal of Epidemiology, 122*(5), 794–804.

Blair, S. N., Kohl, H., III, Paffenbarger, R., Clark, D., Cooper, K., & Gibbons, L. (1989). Physical fitness and all-causes mortality: A prospective study of healthy men and women. *Journal of the American Medical Association, 262*, 2395–2401.

Blair, S. N., Kohl, H., III, Pate, R. R., Blair, A., Howe, H. G., Rosenberg, M., & Parker, G. M. (1980). Leisure time physical activity as an intervening variable in research. *Health Education*, Jan–Feb, 8–11.

Blair, S. N., Kohl, H., III, Gordon, N. F., & Paffenbarger, R. (1992). How much physical activity is good for health? *Annual Reviews of Public Health, 13*, 99–126.

Blazer, D. G. (1982). Social support and mortality in an elderly community population. *American Journal of Epidemiology, 115*(5), 684–694.

Block, J. E., Smith, R., Friedlander, A., & Genant, H. K. (1989). Preventing osteoporosis with exercise: A review with emphasis on methodology. *Medical Hypotheses, 30*, 9–19.

Blumenthal, H. T. (1983). *Handbook of diseases of aging*. Toronto: Van Nostrand Reinhold.

Blumenthal, J. A., Emery, C. F., Madden, D. J., George, L. K., Coleman, R. E., Riddle, M. W., McKee, P. C., Reasoner, J., & Sanders Williams, R. (1989). Cardiovascular and behavioral effects of aerobic exercise training in healthy older men and women. *Journal of Gerontology: Medical Sciences, 44*(5), 147–157.

Blumenthal, J. A., Emery, C. F., Madden, D. J., Schniebolk, S., Walsh-Riddle, M., George, L. K.,

McKee, D. C., Higginbotham, M. B., Cobb, F. R., & Coleman, R. E. (1991). Long-term effects of exercise on psychological functioning in older men and women. *Journal of Gerontology: Psychological Sciences, 46*(6), 352–361.

Board of Education. (1909). *The syllabus of physical exercises for the public elementary school.* London: Eyre & Spottiswoode, Ltd.

Bokovoy, J. & Blair, S. (1994). Aging and exercise: A health perspective. *Journal of Aging & Physical Activity, 2,* 243–260.

Bolla-Wilson, K., & Bleeker, M. L. (1989). Absence of depression in elderly adults. *Journal of Gerontology, 44*(2), 53–55.

Bolotin, N. (1980). *Klondike lost: A decade of photographs.* Anchorage, AL: Alaska Northwest Pub. Co.

Bolotin, N. (1987). *A Klondike scrapbook.* San Francisco: Chronicle Books.

Bonds, A. G. (1980). The relationship between self-concept and locus of control and patterns of eating, exercise and social participation in older adults. *Dissertation Abstracts International, 41*(4), 1397A.

Bonner, A., & O'Brien Cousins, S. (1996). Exercise and alzheimer's disease: Benefits and barriers. *Activities, Adaptation, & Aging, 20*(4), 21–34.

Borchelt, M. F., & Steinhagen-Thiesen, E. (1992). Physical performance and sensory function as determinants of independence in activities of daily living in the old and very old. *Physiopathological Processes of Aging, 673,* 350–361.

Borg, G. A. (1970). Perceived exertion as an indicator of somatic stress. *Scandinavian Journal of Rehabilitation Medicine, 2,* 92–98.

Borg, G., Hassmen, P., & Lagerstrom, M. (1987). Perceived exertion related to heart rate and blood lactate during arm and leg exercise. *European Journal of Applied Psychology, 56,* 679–685.

Bortz, W. M. (1980). Effect of exercise on aging: Effect of aging on exercise. *Journal of the American Geriatrics Society, 28,* 49–51.

Bortz, W. M. (1982). Disuse and aging. *Journal of the American Medical Association, 248,* 1203–1208.

Bouchard, C., Shephard, R. J., & Stephens, T., Eds. (1994). *Physical activity, fitness and health: International proceedings and concensus statement.* Champaign, IL: Human Kinetics.

Bouchard, C., Shephard, R. J., Stephens, T., Sutton, J. R., & McPherson, B. D. (Eds.). (1990). *Exercise, fitness and health: consensus of current knowledge.* Champaign, IL: Human Kinetics Books.

Bourliere, F. (1973). Ecology of human senescence. In J. C. Brocklehurst (Ed.), *Textbook of geriatric medicine and gerontology* (pp. 60–74). London: Churchill Livingstone.

Boyle, E. S., & Sielski, K. A. (1981). Correlates of health locus of control in an older, disabled group. *Journal of Psychology, 109*(1), 87–91.

Branch, L. G., & Jette, A. M. (1984). Personal health practices and mortality among the elderly. *American Journal of Public Health, 74,* 1126–1129.

Branigan, K. (1995). Physician advocacy of exercise for older adults. Master's thesis. Faculty of Physical Education and Recreation, The University of Alberta, Edmonton, Alberta.

Branigan, K., & O'Brien Cousins, S. (1995). Older women and beliefs about exercise risk: What has motherhood got to do with it? *The Journal of Women & Aging, 7*(4), 47–66.

Brody, E. B., Hatfield, B. D., & Spalding, T. W. (1988). Generalization of self-efficacy to a continuum of stressors upon mastery of a high-risk sport skill. *Journal of Sport & Exercise Psychology, 10,* 32–44.

Brooks, C. (1988). A causal modeling analysis of sociodemographics and moderate to vigorous physical activity behavior of American adults. *Research Quarterly for Exercise and Sport, 59*(4), 328–338.

Brooks, C. (1987). Leisure time physical activity assessment of American adults through an analysis of time diaries collected in 1981. *American Journal of Public Health, 77,* 455–460.

Brooks, J. D. (1993). Exercise: It adds life to our years, so why don't more people do it? Poster presentation, Gerontological Society of America Annual Scientific Meeting, New Orleans.

Brown, M., & Holloszy, J. O. (1991). Effects of a low intensity exercise program on selected physical performance characteristics of 60- to 71-year-olds. *Aging, 3,* 129–139.

Bruce, R. A. (1984). Exercise, functional aerobic capacity, and aging—Another viewpoint. *Medicine & Science in Sports and Exercise, 16*(1), 8–13.

Bruce, R. A., & McDonough, J. (1969). Stress testing in screening for cardiovascular disease. *Bulletin of the New York Academy of Medicine, 45,* 1288–1305.

Buchner, D. M., Beresford, S. A., Larson, E. B., LaCroix, A. Z., & Wagner, E. H. (1992). Effects of physical activity on health status in older adults II. Intervention studies. *Annual Review of Public Health, 13,* 469–488.

Burckhardt, C. S. (1988). Quality of life for women with arthritis. *Health Care for Women International, 9,* 229–238.

Buskirk, E. R., Harris, D., Mendes, J., & Skinner, J. (1971). Comparison of two assessments of physical activity and a survey method for calorie intake. *American Journal of Clinical Nutrition, 24,* 1119.

Butler, R. H. (1968). The facade of chronological age. In B. L. Neugarten (Ed.), *Middle age and aging* (pp. 235–246). Chicago: University of Chicago Press.

Butler, R. M. (1988). What is 'successful' aging? *Geriatrics, 43*(5), 11–12.

Butterworth, D. E., Nieman, D. C., Perkins, R., Warren, B. J., & Dotson, R. G. (1993). Exercise training and nutrient intake in elderly women. *Journal of the American Dietetic Association, 93,* 653–657.

Calnan, M. (1985). Patterns of preventive behavior: A study of women in middle age. *Social Science in Medicine, 20*(3), 263–268.

Calnan, M. (1988). The health locus of control: An empirical test. *Health Promotion, 2*(4), 323–329.

Calnan, M., & Johnson, B. (1985). Health, health risks and inequalities: An exploratory study of women's perceptions. *Sociology of Health & Illness, 17*(1), 55–75.

Campbell, A. J., Borrie, M. J., & Spears, G. F. (1989). Risk factors for falls in a community-based prospective study of people 70 years and older. *Journal of Gerontology, 44,* M112–M117.

Campbell, A. J., Borrie, M. J., Spears, G. F., Jackson, S. L., Brown, J. S., & Fitzgerald, J. L. (1990). Circumstances and consequences of falls experienced by a community population 70 years and over during a prospective study. *Age & Ageing, 19,* 136–141.

Campbell, A. J., Spears, G. F. S., Borrie, M. J., & Fitzgerald, J. L. (1988). Falls, elderly women and the cold. *Gerontology, 34,* 205–208.

Canada Fitness Survey. (1983). *Fitness and lifestyle in Canada.* Ottawa: Government of Canada, Fitness Canada.

Cantu, R. C. (1980). *Toward fitness: Guided exercise for those with health problems.* New York: Human Sciences Press.

Cantu, R. C. (1982). *Diabetes and exercise: A practical, positive way to control diabetes.* Ithaca, NY: Movement Publishers.

Carlson, B. J., & Petti, K. (1989). Health locus of control and participation in physical activity. *American Journal of Health Promotion, 3*(3), 32–37.

Carron, A. V., Widmeyer, W. M., & Brawley, L. R. (1988). Group cohesion and individual adherence to physical activity. *Journal of Sport & Exercise Psychology, 10,* 127–138.

Carter, W. B., Elward, K., Malmgren, J., Martin, M. L., & Larson, E. (1991). Participation of older adults in health programs and research: A critical review of the literature. *The Gerontologist, 31*(5), 584–592.

Cassel, J. (1976). The contribution of the social environment to host resistance. *American Journal of Epidemiology, 104,* 107–123.

Cauley, J. A., LaPorte, R. E., Black-Sandler, R. B., Schramm, M. M., & Kriska, A. M. (1987). Comparison of methods to measure physical activity in post menopausal women. *American Journal of Clinical Nutrition, 45,* 14–22.

Canadian Fitness and Lifestyle Research Institute (CFLRI). (1995). Active living enhances health. *The research file.* Reference No. 95–08.

Charette, A. (1988). *Technical Report Series: Special study on adults with an activity limitation.* Health Promotion Studies Unit, Ottawa: Health & Welfare Canada.

Chen, M. K., Calderone, G .E., & Pellarin, M. L. (1987). The validity of an index of leisure-time physical activity. *Social Indicators Research, 19,* 357–365.

Chodzko-Zajko, W. J. (1991). Physical fitness, cognitive performance, and aging. *Medicine & Science in Sports & Exercise, 23*(7), 868–872.

Chodzko–Zajko, W. J., Schuler, P., Solomon, J., Heinl, B., & Ellis, N. R. (1992). The influence of physical fitness on automatic and effortful memory changes in aging. *International Journal of Aging & Human Development, 35,* 265–285.

Choosing wellness. (1988). Victoria, B.C.: British Columbia Ministry of Health.

Christenson, H., & MacKinnon, A. (1993). The association between mental, social and physical activity and cognitive performance in young and old subjects. *Age & Ageing, 22,* 175–182.

Cinque, C. (1990). Women's strength: lifting the limits of aging? *The Physician & Sports Medicine,18* (8), 123–127.

Clark, B. A., Wade, M. G., Massey, B. H., & Van Dyke, R. (1975). Response of institutionalized geriatric mental patients to a twelve-week program of regular physical activity. *Journal of Gerontology, 30*(5), 565–573.

Clark, N. M., Janz, N. K., Becker, M. H., Schork, M. A., Wheeler, J., Liang, J., Dodge, J. A., Keteyian, S., Rhoads, K. L., & Santinga, J. T. (1992). Impact of self-management education on the functional health status of older adults with heart disease. *The Gerontologist, 2*(4), 438–443.

Clarkson, P. M. (1978). The effect of age and activity level on simple and choice fractionated response time. *European Journal of Applied Physiology & Occupational Therapy, 60,* 183–186.

Clarkson-Smith, L., & Hartley, A. A. (1990). Relationships between physical exercise and cognitive abilities. *Psychology & Aging, 5,* 437–446.

Cobb, S. (1976). Social support as a moderator of life stress. *Psychosomatic Medicine, 3B*(5), 300–314.

Cockburn, J., Smith, P. T., & Wade, D. T. (1990). Influence of cognitive function on social, domestic, and leisure activities of community-dwelling older people. *International Disability Studies, 72,* 1780–1786.

Coggan, A. R., Spina, R. J., Rogers, M. A., King, D. S., Brown, M., Nemeth, P. M., & Holloszy, J. O. (1990). Histochemical and enzymatic characteristics of skeletal muscle in master athletes. *Journal of Applied Physiology, 68,* 1896–1901.

Colsher, P. L. & Wallace, R. B. (1989). Data quality and age: Health and psychobehavioral correlates of item nonresponse and inconsistent responses. *Journal of Gerontology, 44*(2), 45–52.

Connell, B. R. (1993). *Patterns of naturally occurring falls among frail nursing home residents.* Poster presentation at the 46th Gerontological Society of America Annual Scientific Meetings, New Orleans, November.

Conrad, C. C. (1976). When you're young at heart. *Aging, 258,* 11–13.

Cook, P. J., Exton-Smith, A. N., Brocklehurst, J. C., & Lemper-Barber, S. M. (1982). Fractured femurs, falls and bone disorders. *Journal of the Royal College of Physicians,* 45–49.

Cropley, A. J. (1977). *Lifelong education: A psychological analysis.* Oxford: Pergamon.

Cruikshank, J. (1921). *Figure skating for women.* New York: American Sports Co.

Csizma, K. A., Wittig, A. F., & Schurr, K. T. (1988). Sport stereotypes and gender. *Journal of Sport & Exercise Psychology, 10,* 62–74.

Cumming, E. & Henry, W. (1961). *Growing old: The process of disengagement.* New York: Basic Books.

Curtis, J. E. & White, P. G. (1984). Age and sport participation: Decline in participation or increased specialization with age? In N. Theberge & P. Donnelly (Eds.), *Sport and the sociological imagination* (pp. 273–293). Fort Worth, TX: Texas Christian University.

Danielson, M. E., Cauley, J. A., & Rohay, J. M. (1993). Physical activity and its association with plasma lipids and lipoproteins in elderly women. *Annals of Epidemiology, 3,* 351–357.

Danielson, R. R., & Wanzel, R. S. (1977). Exercise objectives of fitness program dropouts. In D. M. Landers & R. W. Christina (Eds.), *Psychology of motor behavior and sport.* Champaign, IL: Human Kinetics.

Danzig, A. (1928). Helen Wills is queen of her tennis world. *The New York Times Magazine,* September 9, 6.

Davidson, A. H., & Sedgewick, S. W. (1978). Fitness program—A reappraisal of women's needs. In Commonwealth Department of Health (Ed.), *Women's health in a changing society,* Volume 2. Canberra: Australia Government Publishing Service.

Davidson, D. M. (1986). Cardiovascular risk reduction in postmenopausal women. *Journal of Nutrition for the Elderly, 5*(4), 3–10.

Davis-Berman, J. (1989). Physical self-efficacy and depressive symptomatology in older women: A group treatment approach. *Journal of Women & Aging, 1*(4), 29–40.

de Beauvoir, S. (1972). *The coming of age*. New York: G. P. Putnam's Sons.

Del Rey, P. (1982). Physical activity as a deterrent to the aging process: Overview of a motor learning study on older adults. *Psycho-Physiology, 17*, 3–4.

DeLorey, C. (1989). Women at mid-life: Women's perceptions, physician's perceptions. *Journal of Women and Aging, 1*(4), 57–69.

Denney, D. R., & Denney, N. W. (1973). The use of classification for problem solving: A comparison of middle and old age. *Developmental Psychology, 9*, 275.

Dermody, E. W., Saxon, S. V., & Scheer, L. E. (1986). *Successful aging*. Clearwater, FL: Morton Plant Hospital Foundation.

Desharnais, Bouillon J., & Godin, G. (1986). Self-efficacy and outcome expectations as determinants of exercise adherence. *Psychological Reports, 59*, 1155–1159.

DeVries, H. A. (1970). Physiological effects of an exercise training program upon men aged 50–88. *Journal of Gerontology, 25*(4), 325–335.

DeVries, H. A. (1975). Physiology of exercise and aging. *Aging: Scientific perspective and social forces*. New York: Van Nostrand.

DeVries, H. A. (1979). Tips on prescribing exercise regimens for your older patient. *Geriatrics, 34*, 75–81.

DeVries, H. A. (1981). Tranquilizer effects of exercise: A critical review. *The Physician & Sports Medicine, 9*, 46–53.

DeVries, H. A., & Adams, G. M. (1972). Comparison of female exercise responses in old and young men. *Journal of Gerontology, 27*, 344–348.

Dishman, R. K. (1986). Exercise compliance: A new view for public health. *The Physician & Sports Medicine, 14*(5), 127–142.

Dishman, R. K. (1990). Determinants of participation in physical activity. In C. Bouchard, R. J. Shephard, T. Stephens, J. R. Sutton, & B. D. McPherson (Eds.), *Exercise, fitness and health: Consensus of current knowledge* (pp. 75–101). Champaign, IL: Human Kinetics Books.

Dishman, R. K., & Dunn, A. L. (1988). Exercise adherence in children and youth: Implications for adulthood. In R. K. Dishman (Ed.), *Exercise adherence: Its impact on public health* (pp. 155–200). Champaign, IL.: Human Kinetics Pub.

Dishman, R. K., & Gettman, L. R. (1980). Psychobiologic influences on exercise adherence. *Journal of Sport Psychology, 2*, 295–310.

Dishman, R. K., & Ickes, W. (1981). Self motivation and adherence to therapeutic exercise. *Journal of Behavioral Medicine, 4*, 421–438.

Dishman, R. K., & Steinhardt, M. (1990). Health locus of control predicts free-living but not supervised, physical activity: A test of exercise specific control and outcome-expectancy hypotheses. *Research Quarterly for Exercise and Sport, 61*(4), 383–394.

Donahue, R. P., Abbott, R. D., Reed, D. M., & Yano, K. (1988). Physical activity and coronary heart disease in middle-aged and elderly men: The Honolulu Heart Study. *American Journal of Public Health, 78*, 683–685.

Dowell, J. R., Bolter, C. P., Flett, R. A., & Kammann, R. (1988). Psychological well-being and its relationship to fitness and activity levels. *Journal of Human Movement Studies, 14*, 39–45.

Drinkwater, B. L. (1988). Exercise and aging: The female master's athlete. In J. L. Puhl, C. H. Brown & R. O. Voy (Eds.), *Sport science perspectives for women* (pp. 161–169). Champaign, IL: Human Kinetics.

Droller, H. (1955). Falls among elderly people living at home. *Geriatrics, 10*, 239–245.

Duda, J. L., & Tappe, M. K. (1989). Personal investment in exercise among middle-aged older adults. *Perceptual Motor Skills, 66*(2), 543–549.

Duffy, M. E., & MacDonald, E. (1990). Determinants of functional health of older persons. *The Gerontologist, 30*, 503–509.

Dummer, G. H., Clarke, D. H., Vaccaro, P., Vander Velden, L., Goldfarb, A. H., & Sockler, J. M. (1985). Age-related differences in muscular strength and muscular endurance among female master's swimmers. *Research Quarterly for Exercise & Sport, 56*(2), 97–102.

Dunbar, C. C., Robertson, R. J., Baun, R., Blandin, M. F., Metz, K., Burdett, R., & Goss, F. L. (1992). The validity of regulating exercise intensity by ratings of perceived exertion. *Medicine & Science in Sport & Exercise, 24*(1), 94–99.

Duncan, P. W., Chandler, J., Studenski, S., Hughes, M., & Prescott, B. (1993). How do physiological components of balance affect mobility in elderly men? *Archives of Physical Medicine & Rehabilitation, 74,* 1343–1349.

Durak, E. (1989). Exercise for specific populations: Diabetes mellitus. *Sports Training, Medicine, & Rehabilitation,* 175–180.

Dustman, R. E., Emmerson, R. Y., & Shearer, D. E. (1990). Aerobic fitness may contribute to CNS health: Electrophysiological, visual and neurocognitive evidence. *Journal of Neuropsychology Research, 44,* 241–254.

Dustman, R. E., Ruhling, R. O., Russell, E. M., Shearer, D. E., Bonekat, H. W., Shigeoka, J. W., Wood, J. S., & Bradford, D. C. (1984). Aerobic exercise training and improved neuropsychological function of older individuals. *Neurobiological Aging, 5,* 35–42.

Dzewaltowski, D. A. (1989a). A social cognitive theory of older adult exercise motivation. In A. C. Ostrow (Ed.), *Aging and motor behaviour* (pp. 257–281). Indianapolis, IN: Benchmark.

Dzewaltowski, D. A. (1989b). Toward a model of exercise motivation. *Journal of Sport & Exercise Psychology, 11,* 251–269.

Dzewaltowski, D. A., Noble, J. M., & Shaw, J. M. (1990). Physical activity participation: Social Cognitive Theory versus the Theories of Reasoned Action and Planned Behavior. *Journal of Sport & Exercise Psychology, 12,* 388–405.

Eckert, H. M. (1986). Social motivation for sport in retirement. In International Association of Physical Education and Sport for Girls and Women, Physical Education, Recreation and Sport (Ed.), *Lifelong participation* (pp. 299–307). London: Milton-under-Wynchwood.

Edington, D. W., Cosmas, A. C., & McCafferty, W. B. (1972). Exercise and longevity: Evidence for a threshold age. *Journal of Gerontology, 27*(3), 341–343.

Edwards, L. R., & Hill, K. (1982). The women's movement and women's fitness. *JOPERD, 53*(3), 38–40.

Edwards, P. (1993). *Walking—The activity of a lifetime.* Toronto, ON: ParticipACTION.

Ehsani, A. A., Ogawa, T., Miller, T. R., Spina, R. J., & Jilka, S. M. (1991). Exercise training improves left ventricular systolic function in older men. *Circulation, 83,* 96–103.

Eichner, E. R. (1987). Exercise, lymphokines, calories and cancer. *The Physician & Sports Medicine, 15*(6), 109–115.

Eisdorfer, C., & Wilkie, F. (1977). Stress, disease, aging and behaviour. *The psychology of aging.* New York: Van Nostrand Reinhold.

Ellert, G. (1985). *Arthritis and exercise: A user's guide to fitness and independence.* Winnipeg: Hignell (Arthritis Society).

Emery, C. F. (1991). Effects of age on physiological and psychological functioning among COPD patients in an exercise program. *Journal of Aging & Health, 6,* 3–16.

Emery, C. F., & Gatz, M. (1990). Psychological and cognitive effects of an exercise program for community-residing older adults. *The Gerontologist, 30,* 184–188.

Emes, C. G. (1979). The effects of a regular program of light exercise on seniors. *Journal of Sports Medicine & Physical Fitness, 19,* 185–189.

Engel, G. L. (1980). The clinical application of the biopsychosocial model. *American Journal of Psychiatry, 137*(5), 535–544.

Epstein, L., Wing, R .R., & Thompson, J. K. (1978). The relationship between exercise intensity, caloric intake and weight. *Addictive Behaviors, 3,* 185–190.

Era, P., Jokela, J., & Heikkinen, E. (1986). Reaction time and movement times in men of different ages: A population study. *Perceptual & Motor Skills, 63,* 111–130.

Era, P., Rantanen, T., Avlund, K., Gause-Nilsson, I., Heikkinen, E., Schroll, M., Steen, B., & Suominen, H. (1994). Maximal isometric muscle strength and anthropometry in 75-year-old men and women in three Nordic localities. *Scandinavian Journal of Medicine, Science & Sports, 4,* 26–31.

Eriksson, B. G., Mellstrom, D., & Svanborg, A. (1987). Medical-social intervention in a 7-year-old Swedish population. *Comprehensive Gerontological Clinics, 1,* 49–56.

Esdaile, J. M., & Wilkins, K. (1987). Social support and social networks as promoters of physical and psychological well-being in arthritic and rheumatic disorders. *Health Services and Promotion Branch Working Paper No. HSPB 88–15.* Ottawa: Health and Welfare Canada.

Espenshade, A. S. (1969). Role of exercise in the well-being of women 35 to 80 years of age. *Journal of Gerontology, 24,* 86–89.

Evans, R. G., Barer, M. L., & Marmor, T. R. (1995). *Why are some people healthy and others are not?* New York: Aldine de Gryter.

Evans, W. A. (1913). Human efficiency. *The Public Health Journal, March,* 138–141.

Evans, W. J., & Meredith, C. N. (1989). Exercise and nutrition in the elderly. In H. N. Munro & D. E. Danford (Eds.), *Nutrition, aging and the elderly* (pp. 89–125). New York: Plenum.

Evers, H. (1985). The frail elderly woman: Emergent questions in aging and women's health. In E. Lewin & V. Olsen (Eds.), *Women, health and healing: Toward a new perspective.* New York: Tavistock.

Ewart, C. K., Stewart, K. J., Gillilan, R. E., Keleman, M. H. (1986a). Self-efficacy mediates strength gain during circuit weight-training in men with coronary artery disease. *Medicine & Science in Sports & Exercise, 18,* 531–540.

Ewart, C. K., Stewart, K. J., Gillilan, R. E., Keleman, M. H., Valenti, S. A., Manley, J. D., & Keleman, M. D. (1986b). Usefulness of self-efficacy in predicting overexertion during programmed exercise in coronary artery disease. *American Journal of Cardiology, 57,* 557–561.

Ewart, C. K., & Taylor, C. B. (1985). The effects of early postmyocardial infraction exercise testing on subsequent quality of life. *Quality of Life and Cardiovascular Care, 1*(March–April), 162–175.

Ewart, C. K., Taylor, C. B., Reese, L. B., & DeBusk, R. F. (1983). Effects of early postmyocardial infarction exercise testing on self-perception and subsequent physical activity. *American Journal of Cardiology, 57,* 1076–1080.

Fedorak, S. A., & Griffin, C. (1986). Developing a self-advocacy program for seniors: The essential component of health promotion. *Canadian Journal on Aging, 5*(4), 269–277.

Feel Better. (1980). Blue Cross/Blue Shield.

Feit, E. M., & Berenter, R. (1993). Lower extremity injuries. Prevalence, etiology and mechanism. *Journal of the American Podiatric Medical Association, 83,* 509–514.

Feltz, D. H. (1988). Gender differences in the causal elements of self-efficacy on a high avoidance motor task. *Journal of Sport & Exercise Psychology, 10,* 151–166.

Fiatarone, M. A., & Evans, W. J. (1990). Exercise in the oldest-old. *Topics in Geriatric Rehabilitation, 5,* 63–77.

Fiatarone, M., Marks, E., Ryan, N., Meredith, C., Lipsita, L., & Evans, W. (1990). High-intensity strength training in nonagenarians. *Journal of the American Medical Association, 263,* 3029–3034.

Fiatarone, M. A., Morley, J. E., Bloom, E. T., Benton, D., Solomon, G. T., & Makinodan, M. (1989). The effect of exercise on natural killer cell activity in young and old subjects. *Journal of Gerontology, 44*(2), 37–45.

Fiatarone, M. A., O'Neill, E. F., Ryan, N. D., Clements, K. M., Solares, G. R., Nelson, M. E., Roberts, S. B., Kehayias, J. J., Lipsitz, L. A., & Evans, W. J. (1994). Exercise training and nutritional supplementation for physical frailty in very elderly people. *New England Journal of Medicine, 330,* 1760–1885.

Fishbein, M. & Ajzen, I. (1975). *Belief, attitude, intention and behaviour: An introduction to theory and research.* Reading, MA: Addison-Wesley.

Fitness and aging. (1982). A report by the Canada Fitness Survey. Ottawa: Government of Canada.

Fitness & Amateur Sport: Women's Program. (1984). *Changing times: Women and physical activity.* Ottawa: Fitness Canada.

Fitness Canada Women's Program (1990). *Physical activity and women with disabilities: A national survey.* Ottawa: Fitness Canada Women's Program.

Fleming, B. E., & Pendergast, D. R. (1993). Physical condition, activity pattern, and environment as factors in falls by adult care facility residents. *Archives of Physical Medicine & Rehabilitation, 74,* 627–630.

Fletcher, S. & Stone, L. O. (1982). *The living arrangement of Canada's older women.* Ottawa: Statistics Canada, Ministry of Supply & Services.

Fletcher, G., Blair, S. N., & Blumenthal, J. A. (1994). A. H. A. Medical/Scientific Statement: Statement on exercise. Benefits and recommendations for physical activity programs for all Americans. A statement for health professionals by the committee on exercise and cardiac rehabilitation of the Council on Clinical Cardiology, American Heart Association. *Circulation, 86,* 340–344.

Foster, V. L., Hume, G. J. E., Byrnes, W. C., Dickinson, A. L., & Chatfield, S. J. (1989). Endurance training for elderly women: Moderate vs low intensity. *Journal of Gerontology, 44*(6), M184–188.

Frekany, G. A., & Leslie, D. K. (1975). Effects of an exercise program on selected flexibility measures of senior citizens. *The Gerontologist, 4,* 182–183.

Friedman, R., & Tappen, R. M. (1991). The effect of planned walking on communication in Alzheimer's disease. *Journal of the American Geriatric Society, 39,* 650–654.

Gandee, R. N., Campbell, T. A., Knierim, H., Cosky, A. C., Leslie, D. K., Ziegler, R. G., & Snodgrass, J. E. (1989). Senior Olympic Games: Opportunities for older adults. *JOPERD, March,* 72–76.

Gardner, A. W., & Poehlman, E. T. (1993). Physical activity is a significant predictor of body density in women. *The American Journal of Clinical Nutrition, 57,* 8–14.

Gee, E., & Kimball, M. (1987). *Women and aging.* Vancouver, BC: Butterworth.

Gee, E. (1986a). Historical change in the family life course of Canadian men and women. In V. W. Marshall (Eds.), *Aging in Canada: Social Perspectives* (pp. 265–287). Markham, ON: Fitzhenry & Whiteside.

Gee, E. (1986b). The life course of Canadian women: An historical and demographic analysis. *Social Indicators Research, 18,* 263–283.

General Social Survey. (1987). *Health and social support, 1985.* Ottawa, Statistics Canada: Minister of Supply & Services Canada.

Gerhardsson, D., Verdier, M., Steineck, G., Hagman, U., Rieger, A., & Norell, S. E. (1990). Physical activity and colon cancer: A case referent study in Stockholm. *International Journal of Cancer, 46,* 985–989.

Gilman, C. (1911). *The man-made world of our androcentric culture.* New York: Johnson Reprint.

Gintner, G. G., Rectanus, E. F., Achord, K., & Parker, B. (1987). Parental history of hypertension and screening attendance: Effects of wellness appeal versus threat appeal. *Health Psychology, 6*(5), 431–444.

Godin, G. (1982). Untitled questionnaire sent in personal correspondence. Toronto: School of Physical and Health Education, University of Toronto.

Godin, G., & Shephard, R. J. (1985). A simple method to assess exercise behaviour in the community. *Canadian Journal of Applied Sport Science, 10,* 141–148.

Godin, G., & Shephard, R. J. (1986). Importance of type of attitude to the study of exercise behaviour. *Psychological Reports, 58,* 991–1000.

Godin, G., & Shephard, R. J. (1987). Psychosocial factors influencing intentions to exercise in a group of individuals ranging in age from 45 to 74 years of age. In M. E. Berridge & G. R. Ward (Eds.), *International perspectives on adapted physical activity* (pp. 243–249). Champaign, IL: Human Kinetics Books.

Godin, G., Jobin, J., & Bouillon, J. (1986). Assessment of leisure time exercise behaviour by self-report: A concurrent validity study. *Canadian Journal of Public Health, 77*(5), 359–362.

Godin, G., Shephard, R. J., & Colantino, A. (1986). The cognitive profile of those who intend to exercise but do not. *Public Health Reports, 101*(5), 521–526.

Godin, G., Valois, P., Shephard, R. J., & Desharnais, R. (1987). Prediction of leisure-time exercise behavior: A path analysis (LISREL V) model. *Journal of Behavioral Medicine, 10*(2), 145–158.

Goforth, D., & James, F. (1985). Exercise training in noncoronary heart disease. In N. K. Wenger, (Eds.), *Exercise and the heart, 15*(2). Philadelphia: F. A. Davis Co.

Golini, A. & Lori, A. (1990). Aging of the population: Demographic and social changes. *Aging, 2*(4), 319–336.

Gottlieb, B. H., & Baker, J. A. (1986). The relative influence of health beliefs, parental and peer behaviors and exercise program participation on smoking, alcohol use and physical activity. *Social Science and Medicine, 22,* 915–927.

Gottlieb, S. O., & Gerstenblith, G. (1988). Silent myocardial ischemia in the elderly: Current concepts. *Geriatrics, 43*(4), 29–34.

Graham, D. F., Graham, I., & MacLean, M. J. (1991). Going to the mall: A leisure activity of urban elderly people. *Canadian Journal on Aging, 10*(4), 345–358.

Grand, A., Grosclaude, P., Bocquet, J., Pous, J., & Albarede, J. L. (1990). Disability, psychosocial factors and mortality among the elderly in a rural French sample. *Journal of Clinical Epidemiology, 43*, 773–782.

Grau, L. (1988). Mental health and older women. *Women & Health, 14*(3–4), 75–91.

Gray, J. A. (1987). Exercise and aging. In D. Macleod, R. Maughan, M. Nimmo, T. Reilly, & C. Williams (Eds)., *Exercise: Benefits, limits and adaptations.* New York: E. & F. Spon.

Greendale, G. A., Hirsch, S. H., & Hahn, T. J. (1993). The effect of a weighted vest on perceived health status and bone density in older persons. *Quality of Life Research, 2*, 141–152.

Greendorfer, S. L. (1983). Shaping the female athlete: The impact of the family. In M. Boutilier & L. San Giovanni (Eds.), *The sporting woman* (pp. 135–155). Champaign, IL: Human Kinetics.

Griffin, N. S., Keogh, J. F., & Maybee, R. (1984). Performer perceptions of movement confidence. *Journal of Sport Psychology, 6*, 395–407.

Griffin, N. S. (1982). Gymnastics is a girl's thing. Student participation and interaction patterns in a middle school gymnastics unit. In T. J. Templin & J. K. Olson (Eds.), *Teaching in physical education* (pp. 71–85). Champaign, IL: Human Kinetics.

Griffin, N. S., & Trinder, J. (1978). Measurement of movement confidence with a stunt movement confidence inventory. *Journal of Sport & Exercise Psychology, 11*, 26–40.

Gross, L., Sallis, J., Buono, M., Roby, J. & Nelson, J. (1990). Reliability of interviewers using the seven-day physical activity recall. *Research Quarterly for Exercise and Sport, 61*(4), 321–325.

Gueldner, S. H., & Spradley J. (1988). Outdoor walking lowers fatigue. *Journal of Gerontological Nursing, 14*(10), 6–12.

Gutin, B., & Kasper, M. J. (1992). Can vigorous exercise play a role in osteoporosis prevention? A review. *Osteoporosis International, 2*, 55–69.

Guttman, A. (1988). *A whole new ball game.* Chapel Hill: University of North Carolina.

Haefner, D. P., & Kirscht, J. B. (1970). Motivational and behavioral effects of modifying beliefs. *Public Health Reports, 85*, 478–484.

Hagberg, J., Graxes, J., Limacher, M., Woods, D., Leggett, S., Cononie, C., Gruber, J., & Pollock, M. (1989). Cardiovascular responses of 70–79-year-old men and women with essential hypertension. In American Academy of Physical Education papers No. 22 (Ed.), *Physical activity and aging* (pp. 186–193). Champaign, IL: Human Kinetics.

Hallinen, C. J., & Schuler, P. B. (1993). Body-shape perceptions of elderly women exercisers and nonexercisers. *Perceptual & Motor Skills, 77*, 451–456.

Hamdorf, P. A., Withers, R. T., Penhall, R. K., & Haslam, M. V. (1992). Physical training effects on the fitness and habitual activity patterns of elderly women. *Archives of Physical Medicine & Rehabilitation, 73*, 473–477.

Harcom, T. M., Lampman, R. M., Banwell, B. F., & Castor, C. W. (1985). Therapeutic value of graded aerobic exercise training in rheumatoid arthritis. *Arthritis & Rheumatism, 28*(1), 32–39.

Harmond, R. (1984). Progress and flight: an interpretation of the American cycle craze of the 1890s. In S. A. Reiss (Ed.), *The American sporting experience.* (pp. 190–211). New York: Leisure Press.

Harrel, W. A. (1991). Precautionary street crossing by pedestrians. *International Journal of Aging & Human Development, 32*(1), 65–80.

Hart, B. A. (1986). Fractionated myostatic reflex times in women by activity level and age. *Journal of Gerontology, 41*, 361–367.

Haskell, W. L., Taylor, H. L., Wood, P. D., Schrott, H., & Heiss, G. (1980). Strenuous physical activity, treadmill exercise test performance and plasma high density lipoprotein cholesterol. *Circulation, 62*(Suppl. IV), 53–61.

Haskell, W. L. (1984). Overview: Health benefits of exercise. In J. D. Matarazzo, S. M. Weiss, J. A. Herd, & N. E. Miller (Eds.), *Behavioral health* (pp. 409–423). John Wiley & Sons.

Hassmen, P., Ceci, R., & Backman, L. (1992). Exercise for older women: A training method and its influences on physical and cognitive performance. *European Journal of Applied Physiology, 64*, 460–466.

Hatori, M., Hasegawa, A., Adachi, H., Shinozaki, A., Hayashi, R., Okano, H. Minunuma, H., & Murata, K. (1993). The effects of walking at the anaerobic threshold level on vertebral bone loss in postmenopausal women. *Calcified Tissue International, 52*, 411–414.

Haug, M. R., Ford, A. B., & Sheafor, M. (Eds.). (1985). *The physical and mental health of aged women.* New York: Springer.

Hauge, A. (1973). The influence of the family on female sports participation. In D. V. Harris (Ed.), *DGWS research reports: Women in sport.* Washington, DC: AAHPER Press.

Hawkins, H. L., Kramer, A. F., & Capaldi, D. (1992). Aging, exercise, and attention. *Psychology and Aging, 7,* 643–653.

Havighurst, R. (1963). Successful aging. In R. Williams, C. Tibbits, & W. Donahue (Eds.), *Processes of aging.* New York: Atherton.

Health Canada. (1993). Copy writing by Peggy Edwards. *Walking—The activity of a lifetime.* Ottawa, ON: Health Canada.

Health & Welfare Canada. (1989). *The active health report on seniors.* Ottawa: Minister of Supply & Services.

Heathcote, J. (1894). *Tennis.* London: Longmans, Green & Co.

Heckler, M. M. (1984). Health, make it last a lifetime. *Public Health Reports, 99*(3), 221.

Heinzelman, F., & Bagley, R. W. (1970). Response to physical activity programs and their effects on health behavior. *Public Health Reports, 85,* 905–911.

Heisch, A. (1988). Sporting chances. *The Women's Review of Books, 6*(1), 1, 3, 4.

Heislein, D. M., Harris, B. A., & Jette, A. (1994). A strength training study for postmenopausal women: A pilot study. *Archives of Physical Medicine & Rehabilitation, 75,* 198–204.

Hein, H. O., Suadicani, P., Sorensen, H., & Gyntelberg, F. (1994). Changes in physical activity level and risk of ischemic heart disease: A six-year follow-up in the Copenhagen male study. *Scandinavian Journal of Medicine, Science & Sports, 4,* 57–64.

Heitmann, H. M. (1982). Older adult physical education: Research implications for instruction. *Quest, 34*(1), 34–42.

Henderson, K. A., Bialeschki, M. D., Shaw, S. M., & Freysinger, V. J. (1990). *A leisure of one's own: A feminist perspective on women's leisure.* State College, PA: Venture Press.

Hofstetter, C., Hovell, M., Macera, C., Sallis, J., Spry, V., Barrington, E., Callender, L., Hackley, M., & Rauh, M. (1991). Illness, injury and correlcates of aerobic exercise and walking: A community study. *Research Quarterly for Exercise & Sport, 62*(1), 1–9.

Hogan, P. I., & Santomier, J. P. (1984). Effect of mastering swim skills on older adults' self-efficacy. *Research Quarterly for Exercise & Sport, 55*(3), 294–296.

Holohan, C. J., & Moos, R. H. (1981). Social support and psychological distress: A longitudinal analysis. *Journal of Abnormal Psychology, 4,* 365–370.

Hopkins, D., Murrah, B., Hoeger, W., & Rhodes, R. (1990). Effects of low-impact aerobic dance on the functional fitness of elderly women. *The Gerontologist, 30*(2), 189–192.

Hornbrook, M. C., Wingfield, D. J., Stevens, V. J. et al. (1991). Falls among older persons: antecedents and consequences. In R. Weindruch, E.C. Hadley, & M. G. Ory (Eds.), *Reducing frailty and falls in older persons.* Springfield, IL: Charles C. Thomas.

Horowitz, S. M., Blackburn, R. T., Edington, D. W., & Berlin, J. A. (1987). Predicting fitness parameters from the health risk appraisal. *Health Education,* Oct/Nov, 14–16.

Howze, E. J., DiGilio, D. A., Bennett, J. P., & Smith, M. (1983). Health education and physical fitness. In B. D. McPherson (Ed.), *Sport and Aging* (pp. 153–156). Champaign, IL: Human Kinetics.

Hu, M., & Woollacott, M. H. (1994). Multisensory training of standing balance in older adults: II. Kinematic and electromyographic postural responses. *Journal of Gerontology: Medical Sciences, 49*(2), M62–M71.

Ishii-Kuntz, M. (1990). Formal activities for elderly women: Determinants of participation in voluntary and senior center activities. *Journal of Women and Aging, 2*(1), 79–97.

Janz, N. K., & Becker, M. H. (1984). The health belief model: A decade later. *Health Education Quarterly, 11*(1), 1–47.

Jedrychowski, W., Mroz, E., Bojanczyk, M., & Jedrychowska, I. (1991). Excessive weight and hypertension in the elderly: The results of the community study. *Archives of Gerontology & Geriatrics, 13* 61–69.

Jette, A., Cummings, K. M., Brock, B. M., Phelps, M. C., & Naessens, J. (1981). The structure and reliability of health belief indices. *Health Services Research, 16,* 81–98.

Johannessen, S., Holly, R. G., Lui, H., & Amsterdam, E. A. (1986). High-frequency, moderate-intensity training in sedentary middle-aged women. *The Physician & Sports Medicine, 14*(5), 99–102.

Johnson, T. E. (1988). Genetic specification of the life span: Processes, problems and potentials. *Journal of Gerontology: Biological Sciences, 43*(4), B87–92.

Johnston, S. (1997). *Physical activity and exercise programs for adults 55+ in Edmonton: P. E. P. Directory.* Edmonton, AB: University of Alberta, A.C.F.W.B. and Alberta Community Development.

Jokl, E. (1985). Keynote speech. Physical activity, aging and sport conference. Albany, New York.

Kahn, S. E., Larson, V. G., Beard, J. C., Cain, K. C., Fellingham, G. W., Schwartz, R. S., Veith, R. C., Stratton, J. R., Cerqueira, M. D., & Abrass, I. B. (1990). Effect of exercise on insulin action, glucose tolerance, and insulin secretion in aging. *American Journal of Physiology, 258,* E937–943.

Kallinen, M., & Allen, M. (1994). Sports-related injuries in elderly men still active in sports. *British Journal of Sports Medicine, 28,* 52–55.

Kaplan, G. A., Seeman, T. E., Cohen, R. D., Knudsen, L. P., & Guralnik, J. (1987). Mortality among the elderly in the Alameda County Study: Behavioral and demographic risk factors. *American Journal of Public Health, 77,* 307–312.

Kaplan, G. A., Strawbridge, W. J., Camacho, T., & Cohen, R. D. (1993). Factors associated with change in physical functioning in the elderly.: A six-year prospective study. *Journal of Aging & Health, 5,* 140–153.

Kaplan, R. M., Atkins, C. J., & Reinsch, S. (1984). Specific efficacy expectations mediate exercise compliance in patients with COPD. *Health Psychology, 3*(3), 223–242.

Karl, C. A. (1982). The effect of an exercise program on self-care activities for the institutionalized elderly. *Journal of Gerontological Nursing, 8,* 282–283.

Karvonen, M. J., Klemola, H., Virkajarvi, J., & Kellonen, A. (1974). Longevity of endurance skiers. *Medicine & Science in Sports, 6*(1), 49–51.

Kasch, F. W., Boyer, J. L., Van Camp, S. P., Verity, L. S., & Wallace, J. P. (1990). The effect of physical activity and inactivity on aerobic power in older men (a longitudinal study). *The Physician & Sports Medicine, 18,* 73–77, 80, 83.

Kasper, M. J. (1990). Emphasis on cardiovascular fitness as a barrier toward mobilizing the sedentary individual. *Health Education, 21*(40), 41–45.

Kavanagh, T., & Shephard, R. J. (1978). The effects of continued training on the aging process. *Annals of the New York Academy of Sciences,* 656–670.

Keim, R. J., Cook, M., & Martini, D. (1992). Balance rehabilitation therapy. *Laryngoscope, 102*(11), 1302–1307.

Kelly, J. R. (Ed.) (1987). The resource of leisure. *Peoria Winter* (pp. 109–126). Lexington, MA: Lexington Books, D. C. Heath & Co.

Kerr, R., & Normand, R. (1992). Independent living and psychomotor performance. *Canadian Journal on Aging, 11,* 92–100.

Kesler, M. S., Denney, N. W., & Whitely, S. E. (1976). Factors influencing problem solving in middle-aged and elderly adults. *Human Development, 19,* 310.

Kilbom, A. (1971). Effect on women of physical training with low intensities. *Scandinavian Journal of Clinical Laboratory Investigations, 24,* 315–322.

Kilborn, P. T. (1990). Tales from the digital treadmill. *New York Times,* June 3.

King, A. C., Taylor, C. B., Haskell, W. L., & DeBusk, R. F. (1989). Influence of regular aerobic exercise on psychological health: A randomized controlled trial of healthy middle-aged adults. *Health Psychology, 8,* 305–324.

Kirsch, I. (1985). Self-efficacy and expectancy: Old wine with new labels. *Journal of Personality & Social Psychology, 49*(3), 824–830.

Kirscht, J. P. (1974). Research related to the modification of health beliefs. *Health Education Monographs, 2*(4), 455–473.

Kirwan, J. P., Kohrt, W. M., Wojta, D. M., Bourey, R. E., & Holloszy, J. O. (1993). Endurance exercise training reduces glucose-stimulated insulin levels in 60- to 70-year-old men and women. *Journal of Gerontology: Medical Sciences, 48,* M84–M90.

Kist-Kline, G., & Lipnickey, S. C. (1989). Health locus of control: Implications for the health professional. *Health Values, 13*(5), 38–47.

Kleiber, D. A., & Hemmer, S. (1981). Sex differences in the relationship of locus of control and recreational sport participation. *Sex Roles, 7,* 801–810.

Kohl, H., Blair, S., Paffenbarger, R., Macera, C., & Kronenfeld, J. (1988). A mail survey of physical activity habits as related to measured physical fitness. *American Journal of Epidemiology, 127,* 1228–1239.

Kohl, H. W., Gordon, N. F., Villegras, J. A., & Blair, S. N. (1992). Cardiorespiratory fitness, glycemic status, and mortality risk in men. *Diabetes Care, 15,* 184–192.

Kohrt, W. M., Malley, M. T., Dalsky, G. P., & Holloszy, J. O. (1992). Body composition of healthy sedentary and trained, young and older men and women. *Medicine & Science in Sports, 24,* 832–837.

Kohrt, W. M., Obert, K. A., & Holloszy, J. O. (1992). Exercise training improves fat distribution patterns in 60- to 70-year-old men and women. *Journal of Gerontology: Medical Sciences, 47*(4), M99–M105.

Koiso, T., & Ohsawa, S. (1992). Analysis of survival rates of sportsmen utilizing Cutler-Ederer method. *Journal of Human Ergology, 21,* 135–151.

Kolanowski, A. M., & Gunter, L. M. (1988). Do retired career women exercise? *Geriatric Nursing, 9*(6), 350–352.

Konradsen, L., Hansen, E. M., & Sondergaard, L. (1990). Long-distance running and osteoarthrosis. *The American Journal of Sports Medicine, 18,* 379–381.

Koplan, J. P., Siscovick, D. S., & Goldbaum, G. M. (1985). The risks of exercise: A public health view of injuries and hazards. *Public Health Reports, 100,* 189–195.

Krall, E. A., & Dawson-Hughes, B. (1994). Walking is related to bone density and rates of bone loss. *American Journal of Medicine, 96,* 20–26.

Kriska, A. M., Bayles, C., Cauley, J. A., LaPorte, R. E., Sandler, R. B., & Pambianco, G. (1986). A randomized exercise trial in older women: Increased activity over two years and the factors associated with compliance. *Medicine & Science in Sports & Exercise, 18,* 557–562.

Kroll, W., & Clarkson, P. M. (1978). Age, isometric knee extension strength, and fractionated resisted response time. *Experimental Aging Research, 4,* 389–409.

Kuypers, J. A., & Bengston, V. L. (1973). Social breakdown and competence: A model of normal aging. *Human Development, 16,* 181–201.

Labonte, R., & Penfold, S. (1981). Canadian perspectives in health promotion: A critique. *Health Education,* April, 4–9.

LaCroix, A. Z., Guralnik, J. M., Berkman, L. F., Wallace, R. B., & Satterfield, S. (1993). Maintaining mobility in later life. II. Smoking, alcohol consumption, physical activity, and body mass index. *American Journal of Epidemiology, 137,* 858–869.

Laffrey, S. C., & Isenberg, M. (1983). The relationship of internal locus of control, value placed on health, perceived importance of exercise, and participation in physical activity during leisure. *International Journal of Nursing Studies, 20*(3), 187–196.

Langlie, J. K. (1977). Social networks, health beliefs and preventive health behaviour. *Journal of Health & Social Behaviour, 18,* 244–260.

LaPorte, R. E., Black-Sandler, R., Cauley, J. A., Link, M., Bayles C., & Marks, B. (1983). The assessment of physical activity in older women: Analysis of the interrelationship and reliability of activity monitoring, activity surveys, and caloric intake. *Journal of Gerontology, 38*(4), 394–397.

LaPorte, R. E., Kuller, L. H., & Kupper, D. J. (1979). An objective measure of physical activity for epidemiologic research. *American Journal of Epidemiology, 109*(2), 158–168.

LaPorte, R. E., Montoye, H. J., & Casperson, C. J. (1985). Assessment of physical activity in epidemiologic research: Problems and prospects. *Public Health Reports, 100* (March/April), 131–146.

Lau, E. M., Woo, J., Leung, P. C., Swaminathan, R., & Leung, D. (1992). The effects of calcium supplementation and exercise on bone density in elderly Chinese women. *Osteoporosis International, 2,* 168–173.

Lee, C. (1991). Women and aerobic exercise: directions for research development. *Annals of Behavioral Medicine, 13*(3), 133–140.

Lee, D. J., & Markides, K. S. (1990). Activity and mortality among aged persons over an eight-year period. *Journal of Gerontology, 45*(1), 539–542.

Lewin, E., & Olsen, V. (Eds.). (1985). *Women, health and healing: Toward a new perspective*. New York: Tavistock.

Lewis, C. (1984). Arthritis and exercise. In L. Biegel (Ed.), *Physical fitness and the older person* (pp. 129–149). Rockville, MD: Aspen Systems.

Levi, F., LaVecchia, C., Negri, E., & Franceschi, S. (1993). Selected physical activities and the risk of endometrial cancer. *British Journal of Cancer, 67*, 846–851.

Levy, S. M., Derogatis, L. R., Gallagher, D., & Gatz, M. (1980). Intervention with older adults and the evaluation of outcome. In L. W. Poon (Ed.), *Aging in the 1980s: Psychological issues* (pp. 41–61). Washington, DC: American Psychological Association.

Lichenstein, M. J., Shields, S. L., Shiavi, R. G., & Berger, M. C. (1989). Exercise and balance in aged women: A pilot controlled clinical trial. *Archives of Physical Medicine & Rehabilitation, 70*, 138–143.

Lindsay-Reid, E., & Osborn, R. W. (1980). Readiness for exercise adoption. *Social Science & Medicine, 14A*, 139–146.

Linstead, K. D., Tonstad, S., & Kuzma, J. W. (1991). Self-report of physical activity and patterns of mortality in Seventh Day Adventist men. *Journal of Clinical Epidemiology, 44*, 355–364.

Long, B. C., & Haney, C. J. (1986). Enhancing physical activity in sedentary women: Information, locus of control and attitudes. *Journal of Sport Psychology, 8*, 8024.

Lord, S. R., & Castell, S. (1994). Physical activity program for older persons: Effects on balance, strength, neuromuscular control, and reaction time. *Archives of Physical Medicine & Rehabilitation, 75*, 648–652.

Lord, S. R., Caplan, G. A., & Ward, J. A. (1993). Balance, reaction time, and muscle strength in exercising and nonexercising older women: A pilot study. *Archives of Physical Medicine & Rehabilitation, 74*, 837–839.

Lucas, J. A., & Smith, R. A. (1978). *Saga of American sport*. Philadelphia: Lee & Febiger.

Lumpkin, J. R. (1985). Health versus activity in elderly persons' locus of control. *Perceptual Motor Skills, 60*(1), 288.

Lupinacci, N. S., Rikli, R. E., Jones, C., & Ross, D. (1993). Age and physical activity effects on reaction time and digit symbol substitution performance in cognitively active adults. *Research Quarterly in Exercise & Sport, 64*, 144–150.

Lutter, J. M., Merrick, S., Steffen, L., Jones, C., & Slavin, J. (1985). Physical activity through the life span: Long-term effects of an active lifestyle. *Melpomene Institute Report, 4*(1), 4–8.

Lynn, R., Phelan, J., & Kiker, V. (1969). Beliefs in internal-external control of reinforcement and participation in group and individual sports. *Perceptual Motor Skills, 29*, 551–553.

MacFadden, B. (1903). Health made and preserved by daily exercise. *Cosmopolitan, 34*, 707–712.

MacRae, P. G. (1989). Physical activity and central nervous system integrity. In W. W. Spirduso & H. M. Eckert (Eds.), *Physical activity and aging* (pp. 69–77). Champaign, IL: Human Kinetics Books.

MacRae, P. G., Feltner, M. E., & Reinsch, S. (1994). A one-year exercise program for older women: Effects on falls, injuries, and physical performance. *Journal of Aging & Physical Activity, 2*, 127–142.

Maddux, J. E. (1993). Social cognitive models of health and exercise behavior: An introduction and review of conceptual issues. *Journal of Applied Sport Psychology, 5*, 116–140.

Manchester, D., Woollacott, M., Zederbauer-Hylton, N., & Marin, O. (1989). Visual, vestibular and somatosensory contributions to balance control in the older adult. *Journal of Gerontology, 44*(4), M118–127.

Marcus, B. H., Rakowski, W., Simkin, L. R., & Taylor, E. R. (1992). Exercise behavior among older adults. *Rhode Island Medicine, 76*, 31–34.

Marcus, B. H., Selby, V. C., Niaura, R. S., & Rossi, J. S. (1992). Self-efficacy and the stages of exercise behaviour change. *Research Quarterly for Exercise and Sport, 63*(1), 60–66.

Marti, B., Pekkanen, J., Nissinen, A., Ketola, A., Kivela, S., Punsar, S., & Karvonen, M. J. (1989). Association of physical activity with coronary risk factors and physical ability: Twenty-year follow-up of a cohort of Finnish men. *Age & Ageing, 18*, 103–109.

Martin, D., & Notelvitz, M. (1993). Effects of aerobic training on bone mineral density of postmenopausal women. *Journal of Bone & Mineral Research, 8*, 931–936.

Martin, J. E., Dubbert, P. M., Katell, A. D., Thompson, J. K., Raczynski, J. R., Lake, M., Smith, P. O., Webster, J. S., Sikora, T., & Cohen, R. E. (1984). Behavioral control of exercise in sedentary adults: Studies 1 through 6. *Journal of Consulting & Clinical Psychology, 52*(5), 795–811.

Mattiason-Nilo, I., Sonn, U., Johannesson, K., Gosman-Hedstrom, G., Persson, G. B., & Grimby, G. (1990). Domestic activities and walking in the elderly: Evaluation from a 30-hour heart rate recording. *Aging, 2,* 191–198.

McAuley, E., & Courneya, K. S. (1992). Self-efficacy relationships with affective and exertion responses to exercise. *Journal of Applied Social Psychology, 22,* 312–326.

McAuley, E., Courneya, K. S., & Lettunich, J. (1991). Effects of acute and long-term exercise on self-efficacy responses in sedentary, middle-aged males and females. *The Gerontologist, 31*(4), 534–542.

McAuley, E. & Gill, D. (1983). Reliability and validity of the physical self-efficacy scale in a competitive sport setting. *Journal of Sport Psychology, 5,* 410–418.

McCready, M., & Long, B. C. (1985). Locus of control, attitudes toward physical activity and exercise adherence. *Journal of Sport Psychology, 7,* 346–359.

McCrone, K. E. (1988). *Playing the game: Sport and the physical emancipation of English women, 1870–1914.* Lexington, KY: University Press of Kentucky.

McGinnis, J. M. (1992). The public health burden of a sedentary lifestyle. *Medicine & Science in Sports & Exercise, 24*(6), S196–S200.

McKelvie, R. S. (1986). Special cardiovascular precautions for the masters athlete. In J. R. Sutton & R. M. Brock (Eds.), *Sports medicine for the mature athlete* (pp. 113–122). Indianapolis, IN: Benchmark.

McMurdo, M. E., & Rennie, L. (1993). A controlled trial of exercise by residents of the people's homes. *Age & Ageing, 22,* 11–15.

McPherson, B. D. (1982). Leisure life-styles and physical activity in the later years of the life cycle. *Recreation Research Review, 9*(4), 5–14.

McPherson, B. D. (1994). Sociocultural perspectives on aging and physical activity. *Journal of Aging and Physical Activity, 2,* 329–353.

McPherson, B. D. (Ed.). (1986). Sport, health, well-being, and aging: Some conceptual and methodological issues and questions for sport scientists. *Sport and aging* (pp. 1–10). Champaign, IL: Human Kinetics Books.

McPherson, B. D., Curtis, J. E., & Loy, J. W. (1989). *The social significance of sport.* Champaign, IL: Human Kinetics.

Meddaugh, D. I. (1987). Exercise-to-music for the abusive patient. In T. L. Brink (Ed.), *The elderly uncooperative patient* (pp. 147–153). New York: Haworth.

Mellemgaard, A., Engholm, G., Mclaughlin, J. K., & Olsen, J. H. (1994). Risk factors for renal-cell carcinoma in Denmark, III. Role of weight, physical activity and reproductive factors. *International Journal of Cancer, 56,* 66–71.

Meredith, C. N., Frontera, W. R., Fisher, E. C., Hughes, V. A., Herland, J. C., Edwards, J., & Evans, W. J. (1989). Peripheral effects of endurance training in young and old subjects. *Journal of Applied Physiology, 66*(6), 2844–2849.

Meusel, H. (1991). Sport activity—healthy development—successful aging. *International Journal of Physical Education, 28*(2), 10–17.

Milde, F. K. (1988). Impaired physical mobility. *Journal of Gerontological Nursing, 14*(3), 20–24.

Mihevic, P. M. (1991). Sensory cues for perceived exertion: A review. *Medicine & Science in Sports & Exercise, 13*(3), 150–163.

Miller, B. (1990). Gender differences in spouse caregiver strain: Socialization and role expectations. *Journal of Marriage & the Family, 52,* 311–322.

Miller, B., & Cafasso, L. (1992). Gender differences in caregiving: Fact or artifact? *The Gerontologist, 32*(4), 498–507.

Miller, N. H., Haskell, W. L., Berra, K., & DeBusk, R. F. (1984). Home versus group exercise training for increasing functional capacity after myocardial infarction. *Circulation, 70*(4), 645–659.

Minor, M. A., & Brown, J. D. (1993). Exercise maintenance of persons with arthritis after participation in a class experience. *Health Education Quarterly, 20,* 83–95.

Minor, M. A., Hewett, J. E., Webel, R., Anderson, S. K., & Kay, D. R. (1989). Efficacy of physical conditioning exercise in patients with rheumatoid arthritis and osteoarthritis. *Arthritis & Rheumatism, 32*(11), 1396–1405.

Mirowski, J., & Ross, C.E. (1990). Control or defence? Depression and the sense of control over good and bad outcomes. *Journal of Health & Social Behaviour, 31*, March, 71–86.

Mishler, E. G., Amarasingham, L. R., Osherson, S. D., Hauser, S. T., Waxler, N. E., & Liem, R. (1981). *Social contexts of health, illness and patient care*. London: Cambridge University Press.

Misner, J. E., Massey, B. H., Bemben, M., Going, S., & Patrick, J. (1992). Long-term effects of exercise on the range of motion of aging women. *Journal of Orthopaedic & Sports Physical Therapy, 16*, 37–42.

Mittleman, K., Crawford, S., Holliday, S., Gutman, G., & Bhaktan, G. (1989). The older cyclist: Anthropometric, physiological and psychological changes observed during a trans-Canada cycle tour. *Canadian Journal of Aging, 8*(2), 144–156.

Mobily, K. E., Lemke, J. H., Drube, G. A., Wallace, R. B., Leslie, D. K., & Weissinger, E. (1987). Relationship between exercise attitudes and participation among the rural elderly. *Adapted Physical Activity Quarterly, 4*, 30–50.

Molloy, D. W., Delaquerriere Richardson, L., & Crilly, R. G. (1988). The effects of a three-month exercise programme on neuropsychological function in elderly institutionalized women: A randomized controlled trial. *Age & Ageing, 17*, 303–310.

Monahan, T. (1986). Should women go easy on exercise? *The Physician & Sports Medicine, 14*(12), 188–197.

Monahan, T. (1987). Is "activity" as good as exercise? *The Physician & Sports Medicine, 15*(10), 181–186.

Monahan, T. (1988). Perceived exertion: An old exercise tool finds new applications. *The Physician & Sports Medicine, 16*(10), 174–179.

Moore, S. L. (1980). A study of perceived locus of control in college women athletes in team and individual spots. *Dissertation Abstracts International, 41*, 3479A.

Morey, M. C., Cowper, P., Feussner, J. R., DisPasquale, R. C., Crowly, G., Kitzman, D. W., & Sullivan, R. J. (1989). Evaluation of a supervised exercise program in a geriatric population. *Journal of the American Geriatric Society, 37*, 348–354.

Morrow, D., Keyes, M., Simpson, W., Cosentino, F., & Lappage, R. (1989). *A Concise History of Sport in Canada*. Toronto, ON: Oxford University Press.

Mummery, K. (1995). The case for incorporating physical activity into one's lifestyle. *Research Update, 2*(1), 1.

Munnings, F. (1988). Exercise and estrogen in women's health: Getting a clearer picture. *The Physician & Sports Medicine, 16*(5), 152–161.

Murray, J. (1982). *Strong-minded women: And other lost voices from nineteenth century England*. New York: Pantheon.

Myers, A. M., & Huddy, L. (1985). Evaluating physical capabilities in the elderly: The relationship between ADL self-assessments and basic abilities. *Canadian Journal on Aging, 4*(4), 189–200.

Myers, A. M., Gray, E., Tudor-Locke, C., Ecclestone, N. A., O'Brien Cousins, S., & Petrella, R. (in press). The vigor scale: A new measure of psycho–physical outcomes of physical activity. *Journal of Aging & Physical Activity*.

Nachitall, L. E., & Nachitall, L. B. (1990). Protecting older women from their growing risk of cardiac disease. *Geriatrics, 45*(5), 24–34.

National Advisory Council on Aging. (1991). *Information Communique*, Precis No. 1, 1.

National Advisory Council on Aging. (1993). *Aging Vignette*, Nos. 2, 4, 12, 13, 14, 15, 16, 17.

National Center for Health Statistics. (1994). *Health United States, 1993*. Washington, DC: Government Printing Office.

National Film Board of Canada. (1990). Age is no barrier. Video production. Government of Canada.

Nelson, E. A., & Dannefer, D. (1992). Aged heterogeneity: Fact or fiction? The fate of diversity in gerontological research. *The Gerontologist, 32*(1), 17–23.

Nelson, M. E., Fisher, E. C., Dilmanian, F. A., Dallal, G. E., & Evans, W. J. (1991). A 1-Y walking program and increased dietary calcium in postmenopausal women: Effects on bone. *American Journal of Clinical Nutrition, 53*, 1304–1311.

Nelson, M. E., Fiatarone, M. A., Morgani, C. M., Trice, I., Greenberg, R. A., & Evans, W. J. (1994). Effects of high-intensity strength training on multiple risk factors for osteoporotic fractures: A randomized control trial. *Journal of the American Medical Association, 272*(24), 1909–1914.

Nevitt, M. C., Cummings, S. R., & Hudes, E. S. (1991). Risk factors for injurious falls: A prospective study. *Journal of Gerontology: Medical Sciences, 46*(5), M164–170.

Nickerson, E. (1987). *Gold: A women's history*. Jefferson, NC: McFarland & Co.

Nieman, D. C., Pover, N. K., Segebartt, K. S., Arabatzis, K., Johnson, M., & Dietrich, S. J. (1990). Hematological, anthropometric, and metabolic comparisons between active and inactive elderly women. *Annals of Sports Medicine, 5*, 2–8.

Nieman, D. C., Warren, B. J., O'Donnell, K. A., Dotson, R. G., Butterworth, D. E., & Henson, D. A. (1993). Physical activity and serum lipids and lipoproteins in elderly women. *Journal of the American Geriatric Society, 41*, 1339–1344.

Norman, R. (1985). Health behavior—the implications of research. *Health Promotion, 24*(2), 2–5.

Normand, R., Kerr, R., & Metivier, G. (1987). Exercise, aging and fine motor performance: An assessment. *The Journal of Sports Medicine & Physical Fitness, 27*, 488–496.

Novak, M. (1993). *Aging and society: A Canadian perspective*. Scarborough, ON: Nelson Canada.

Novak, M. (1994). Access to active living for seniors. *Access to Active Living Proceedings*, 10th Commonwealth oand International Scientific Congress, August 10–14, 1994. University of Victoria, Victoria, British Columbia, Canada.

Nowlin, J. B. (1985). Successful aging. In E. Palmore (Ed.), *Normal aging III* (pp. 36–43). Durham, NC: Duke University Press.

O'Brien, S., & Conger, P. R. (1988). Physical fitness of women participating in the Alberta Seniors Games. Unpublished paper, Department of Physical Education & Sport Studies, The University of Alberta, Edmonton, Alberta, T6G 2H9.

O'Brien, S., & Vertinsky, P. (1991). Unfit survivors: Exercise as a resource for aging women. *The Gerontologist, 31*(3), 347–357.

O'Brien Cousins, S. (1993). The determinants of late life exercise among women over age 70. Doctoral dissertation, Faculty of Education, The University of British Columbia, Vancouver, B.C.

O'Brien Cousins, S. (1994) Social support and late life exercise. In A. C Quinney, A. E. Wall, & L. Gauvin (Eds.), *Toward active living* (pp. 247–253). Champaign, IL: Human Kinetics Publishers.

O'Brien Cousins, S. (1995a). Social support among elderly women in Canada. *Health Promotion International, 10*(4), 273–282.

O'Brien Cousins, S. (1995b). Anticipated exertion for exercise activities among women over age 70. *Canadian Women Studies Journal, 15*(4), 73–77.

O'Brien Cousins, S. (1995c). The life situational determinants of exercise in women over age 70. In S. Harris, E. Heikkinen, & W. S. Harris (Eds.), *Physical Activity, Aging and Sports Volume IV*. (pp. 259–277). Albany, New York: Center for the Study of Aging.

O'Brien Cousins, S. (1996). Exercise cognition among elderly women. *Journal of Applied Sport Psychology, 8*(2), 131–145.

O'Brien Cousins, S. (1997a). An older adult exercise inventory: Reliability and validity in adults over age 70. *Journal of Sport Behavior, 19*(4), 288–306.

O'Brien Cousins, S. (1997b). Elderly tomboys? Self-efficacy for physical activity may originate in childhood. *Journal of Aging & Physical Activity, 5*, 229–243.

O'Brien Cousins, S. (1997c). Validity and reliability of self-reported health of persons aged 70 and older. *Health Care for Women International, 18*, 165–174.

O'Brien Cousins, S., Bell, G., Harber, V., Horne, T., Wankel, L. M., Vergeer, I., Branigan, K., Clamp, T., Cushing, J., & Horne, L. (1995). *Active living among older Canadians: A review and critical analysis of health benefits and outcomes*. A report submitted to the Active Living Coordinating Centre for Older Adults, Health Canada. Ottawa, ON: The Canadian Fitness and Lifestyle Research Institute.

O'Brien Cousins, S., & Burgess, A. C. (1992). Perspectives on older adults in sport and physical activity. *Educational Gerontology, 18*, 461–481.

O'Brien Cousins, S,. & Horne, T. (in press). *Active living among older adults: Health benefits and outcomes*. Washington, DC: Taylor & Francis Publishers.

O'Brien Cousins, S., & Keating, N. (1995). Life cycle patterns of physical activity among sedentary and active older women. *Journal of Aging & Physical Activity 3*, 340–359.

O'Brien Cousins, S., & Vertinsky, P. A. (1995). Recapturing the physical activity experiences of the old: A study of three women. *International Journal of Aging & Human Development, 3*, 146–162.

O'Connell, J., & Price, J. (1982). Health locus of control of physical fitness program participants. *Perceptual Motor Skills, 25*, 925–926.

O'Donnell, D. E., Webb, K. A., & McGuire, M. A. (1993). Older patients with COPD: Benefits of exercise training. *Geriatrics, 48*, 60–66.

O'Hagan, C. M., Smith, D. M., Dae, M. W., Haskell, W. L., & Gortner, S. R. (1994). Exercise classes in rest homes: Effect on physical function. *New Zealand Medical Journal, 107*(971), 39–40.

Okun, M. A. (1976). Adult age and cautiousness in decision: A review of the literature. *Human Development, 19*, 220.

O'Loughlin, J. L., Robitaille, Y., Boivin, J. F., & Suissa, S. (1993). Incidence of and risk factors for falls and injurious falls among the community dwelling elderly. *American Journal of Epidemiology, 137*, 342–354.

Olshansky, S. J., Carnes, B. A., & Cassel, C. K. (1993). The aging of the human species. *Scientific American, 268*(4), 46–52.

Orban, W. A. R. (1994). Active living for older adults: A model for optimal living. In H. A. Quinney, L. Gauvin, & A. E. Wall (Eds.), *Toward Active Living.* (pp. 153–161). Champaign, IL: Human Kinetics.

Osis, M. (1986). Insomnia in the elderly. *Gerontion, May/June, 8–11.*

Ostrow, A. C. (1989). *Aging and motor behavior.* Indianapolis: Benchmark.

Oyster, N., Morton, M., & Linnell, S. (1984). Physical activity and osteoporosis in post-menopausal women. *Medicine and Science in Sports & Exercise, 16*(1), 44–50.

Paffenbarger, R. S., & Hale, W. E. (1975). Work activity and coronary heart mortality. *New England Journal of Medicine, 292*, 545–550.

Paffenbarger, R. S., Hyde, R. T., Wing, A. L., & Hsied, C. (1986). Physical activity, all-cause mortality and longevity of college alumni. *New England Journal of Medicine, 314*(10), 605–513.

Paffenbarger, R. S., Wing, A. L., & Hyde, R. T. (1978). Physical activity as an index of heart attack risk in college alumni. *American Journal of Epidemiology, 108*, 161–175.

Page, R. C. L., Harnden, K. E., Walravens, N. K. N., Onslow, C., Sutton, P., Levy, J. C., Hockaday, D. T., & Turner, R. C. (1993). 'Healthy living' and sulphonylurea therapy have different effects on glucose tolerance and risk factors for vascular disease in subjects with impaired glucose tolerance. *Quarterly Journal of Medicine, 86*, 145–154.

Paige, J. (1987). A life time of activity: Observations on osteoporosis study participants. *Melpomene Report, 6*(1), 9–11.

Palmore, E. B. (1989). Exercise and longevity: A review of the epidemiologic evidence. In R. Harris & S. Harris (Eds.), *Scientific and medical research: Physical activity, aging, and sports* (pp. 151–156). Albany, NY: Center for the Study of Aging.

Palmore, E. B. (1990). *Ageism: Negative and positive.* New York: Springer.

Panton, L. B., Graves, J. E., Pollock, M. L., Hagberg, J. M., & Chen, W. (1990). Effect of aerobic and resistance training on fractionated reaction time and speed of movement. *Journal of Gerontology, 45*(1), M26–M31.

Passmore, R., & Durnin, J. V. G. A. (1955). Human energy expenditure. *Physiology Reviews, 35*, 801–840.

Pate, R. R., Pratt, M., Blair, S. N., Haskell, W. L., Macera, C. A., Bouchard, C., Bucher, D., Ettinger, W., Heath, G. W., King, A. C., Kriska, A., Leon, A. S., Marcus, B. H., Morris, J., Paffenbarger, R. S., Jr., Patrick, K., Pollock, M. L., Rippe, J. M., Sallis, J., & Wilmore, J. H. (1995). Physical activity and public health. *Journal of the American Medical Association, 273*(5), 402–407.

Patrick, K., Sallis, J. F., Long, B., Calfas, K. J., Wooten, W., Heath, G., & Pratt, M. (1994). A new tool for encouraging activity: Project PACE. *The Physician & Sports Medicine, 22*(11), 45–55.

Pelletier, K. R. (1993). A review and analysis of the health and cost-effective outcome studies of comprehensive health promotion and disease prevention programs at the worksite: 1991–1993 update. *American Journal of Health Promotion, 8*(1), 50–62.

Pemberton, C. L., & McSwegin, P. J. (1993). Sedentary living: A health hazard. *Journal of Physical Education, Recreation & Dance, 64*(5), 27–31.

Perri, S., II, & Templer, D. I. (1984–85). The effects of an aerobic exercise program on psychological variables in older adults. *International Journal of Aging & Human Development, 20*(3), 167–172.

Perusse, L., LeBlanc, C., & Bouchard, C. (1988). Familial resemblance in lifestyle components: Results from the Canada Fitness Survey. *Canadian Journal of Public Health, 79*, 201–205.

Peterson, S. E., Peterson, M. O., Raymond, G., Gilligan, C., Checovich, M. M., & Smith, E. L. (1993). Muscular strength and bone density with weight training in middle-aged women. *Medicine & Science in Sports & Exercise, 23*(4), 499–504.

Pfeiffer, E. (1973). *Successful aging: A conference report.* Duke University Campus, June 7–9, 1973, Durham, NC: Older Americans Resources and Services Program of the Duke University Center for the Study of Aging and Human Development.

Pilisuk, M. & Minkler, M. (1985). Social support: Economics and political considerations. *Social Policy, 15*(3), 6–11.

Posner, J. (1980). Old and female: The double whammy. In V. W. Marshall (Ed.), *Aging in Canada: Social perspectives* (pp. 80–87). Toronto: Fitzhenry & Whiteside.

Posner, M. (1991). The death of leisure. *The Globe and Mail,* May 25.

Powell, K. E., Spain, K. G., Christenson, G. M., & Mollenkamp, M. P. (1986). The status of the 1990 objective for physical fitness and exercise. *Public Health Reports, 101*, 15–21.

Powell, K., Thompson, P., Casperson, C., & Kendrick, J. (1987). Physical activity and the incidence of coronary heart disease. *Annual Review of Public Health, 8*, 253–287.

Powell, R. R. (1974). Psychological effects of exercise therapy upon institutionalized geriatric mental patients. *Journal of Gerontology, 29*, 157–161.

Prado, C. G. (1986). *Rethinking how we age: A new view of the aging mind.* London: Greenwood Press.

Prudham, D., & Evans, J. G. (1981). Factors associated with falls in the elderly: A community study. *Age & Ageing, 10*, 141–146.

Public Health Service. (1990). *Healthy people 2000: National health promotion and disease prevention objectives.* Washington, DC: U.S. Department of Health & Human Services, DHHS pub. no. (PHS) 91-50212.

Puggaard, L., Pedersen, H. P., Sandager, E., & Klitgaard, H. (1994). Physical conditioning in elderly people. *Scandinavian Journal of Medicine, Science & Sports, 4*, 47–56.

Pukkala, E., Poskiparta, M., Apter, D., & Vihko, V, (1993). Life-long physical activity and cancer risk among Finnish female teachers. *European Journal of Cancer Prevention, 2*, 369–376.

Pyka, G., Lindenberger, E., Charette, S., & Marcus, R. (1994). Muscle strength and fiber adaptations to a year-long resistance training program in elderly men and women. *Journal of Gerontology, 49*(1), M22–M27.

Quinlan, A. (1988). The picture of health for midlife and older women in America. *Women & Health, 14*(3–4), 57–73.

Quinn, T. J., Sprague, H. A., Van Huss, W. D., & Olson, H. W. (1990). Caloric expenditure, life status, and disease in former male athletes and non-athletes. *Medicine & Science in Sports, 22*, 742–750.

Ragosta, M., Crabtree, J., Sturner, W. Q., & Thompson, P. D. (1984). Death during recreational exercise in the state of Rhode Island. *Medicine & Science in Sports & Exercise, 16*(4), 339–342.

Rakowski, W. (1984). Health psychology and late life: The differentiation of health and illness for the study of health-related behaviors. *Research on Aging, 6*, 593–620.

Rakowski, W., & Mor, V. (1992). The association of physical activity with mortality among older adults in the Longitudinal Study of Aging (1984–1988). *Journal of Gerontology: Medical Sciences, 47*(4), M122–M129.

Rantanen, T., Era, P., Kauppinen, M., & Heikkinen, E. (1994). Maximal isometric muscle strength and socio-economic status, health, and physical activity in 75-year-old persons. *Journal of Aging & Physical Activity, 2*, 206–220.

Rehm, J., Fichter, M. M., & Elton, M. (1993). Effects on mortality of alcohol consumption, smoking, physical activity, and close personal relationships. *Addiction, 88*, 101–112.

Reiff, G. G., Montoye, H. J., Remington, R. D., Napier, J. A., Metzner, H. L., & Epstein, F. H. (1967).

Assessment of physical activity by questionnaire and interview. In M. J. Karvonnen & A. J. Barry (Eds.), *Physical activity and the heart* (pp. 336–371). Springfield, IL: Charles C. Thomas.

Reinsch, S., MacRae, P., Lachenbruch, P. A., & Tobis, J. S. (1992). Attempts to prevent falls and injury: A prospective community study. *The Gerontologist, 32*(4), 450–456.

Rejeski, W. J. (1981).The perception of exertion: A social psychophysiological integration. *Journal of Social Psychology, 4,* 305–320.

Reuben, D. B., Siu, A. L., & Kimpau, S. (1992). The predictive validity of self-report and performance-based measures of function and health. *Journal of Gerontology: Medical Sciences, 47*(4), M106–M110.

Richardson, P., & Rosenberg, B. (1989). The effects of age on physiological and psychological responses to a training and detraining program in females. In A. C. Ostrow (Ed.), *Aging and motor behavior* (pp. 159–172). Indianapolis, IN: Benchmark Press.

Riddle, P. K. (1980). Attitudes, beliefs, behavioral intentions, and behaviors of women and men toward regular jogging. *Research Quarterly for Exercise & Sport, 51,* 663–674.

Ridley, J. C., Bachrach, C. A., & Dawson, D. A. (1979). Recall and reliability of interview data from older women. *Journal of Gerontology, 34,* 99–105.

Rikli, R., & Edwards, D. (1991). Effects of a three-year exercise program on motor function and cognitive processing speed in older women. *Research Quarterly for Exercise & Sport, 62*(3), 243–249.

Rikli, R. E., & McManis, B. G. (1990). Effects of exercise on bone mineral content in postmenopausal women. *Research Quarterly for Exercise & Sport, 61*(3), 243–249.

Robinson, K. (1988). Older women who are caregivers. *Health Care for Women International, 9,* 239–249.

Robson, E. (1995). *Steady as you go.* Capital Health Authority (Edmonton Board of Health). Edmonton, Alberta.

Rodin, J. (1986). Aging and health: Effect of the sense of control. *Science, 233,* 1271–1276.

Rogers, M. A. (1989). Acute effects of exercise on glucose tolerance in non-insulin dependent diabetics. *Medicine & Science in Sports & Exercise,* 362–368.

Rogers, R. L., Meyer, J. S., & Mortel, K. F. (1990). After reaching retirement age physical activity sustains cerebral perfusion and cognition. *Journal of the American Geriatric Society, 38,* 123–128.

Rooney, E. M. (1993). Exercise for older patients: Why it's worth your effort. *Geriatrics,* 48, 68, 71–74, 77.

Rosenstock, I. M. (1974). The health belief model and preventive health behavior. *Health Education Monographs, 2*(4), 354–386.

Rosenstock, I. M., Strecher, V. J., & Becker, M. H. (1988). Social learning theory and the health belief model. *Health Education Quarterly, 15*(2), 175–183.

Rotter, J. B. (1954). *Social learning and clinical psychology.* Englewood Cliffs, NJ: Prentice-Hall.

Rotter, J. B. (1966). Generalized expectancies for internal versus external control of reinforcement. *Psychological Monographs, 80* (1 Whole no. 609).

Rowe, J. W., & Kahn, R. L. (1987). Human aging: Usual and successful. *Science, 237*(4811), 143–149.

Rudman, W. J. (1986a). Sport as a part of successful aging. *American Behavioral Scientist, 29*(4), 453–470.

Rudman, W. J. (1986b). Life course socioeconomic transitions and sport involvement: a theory of restricted opportunity. In B. D. McPherson (Ed.), *Sport and Aging* (pp. 25–35). Champaign, IL: Human Kinetics.

Rutherford, O. M., & Jones, D. A. (1992). The relationship of muscle and bone loss and activity levels with age in women. *Age & Ageing, 21,* 286–283.

Ryckman, R., Robbins, M., Thornton, B., & Cantrell, P. (1982). Development and validation of a physical self-efficacy scale. *Journal of Personality & Social Psychology, 42,* 891–900.

Sallis, J. F. (1994). Influences on physical activity on children, adolescents and adults or determinants of active living. *Research Activities and Fitness Research Digest, 1*(7), 1–8.

Sallis, J. F., Haskell, W. L., Wood, P. D., Fortman, S. P., Rogers, T., Blair, S. N., & Paffenbarger, R. S., Jr. (1985). Physical activity assessment methodology in the Five City project. *American Journal of Epidemiology, 121*(1), 91–106.

Sallis, J. F., & Hovell, M. F. (1990). Determinants of exercise behavior. *Exercise & Sport Science Reviews, 18,* 307–330.

Sandvik, L., Erikssen, J., Thaulow, E., Erikksen, G., Mundal, R., & Rodahl, K. (1993). Physical fitness as a predictor of mortality among healthy, middle-aged Norwegian men. *New England Journal of Medicine, 328,* 533–537.

Satariano, W. A., Ragheb, N. E., Branch, L. G., & Swanson, G. M. (1990). Difficulties in physical functioning reported by middle-aged and elderly women with breast cancer: A case-control comparison. *Journal of Gerontology, 45,* M3–M11.

Sauvage, L. R., Jr., Myklebust, B. M., Crow-Pan, J., Novak, S., Millington, P., Hoffman, M. D., Hartz, A. J., & Rudman, D. (1992). A clinical trial of strengthening and aerobic exercise to improve gait and balance in elderly nursing home residents. *American Journal of Physical Medicine and Rehabilitation, 71*(6), 333–342.

Schaberg, G., Ballard, J. E., McKeown, B. C., & Zinkgraf, S. A. (1990). Body composition alterations consequent to an exercise program for pre- and postmenopausal women. *The Journal of Sports Medicine & Physical Fitness, 30,* 461–433.

Schick, F. L. (Ed.). (1986). *Statistical handbook on aging Americans.* Oryx Press.

Schneider, S. H., Amorosa, L. F., Clemow, L., Khachadurian, A. V., & Ruderman, N. B. (1992). Ten-year experience with an exercise -based outpatient life-style modification program in the treatment of diabetes mellitus. *Diabetes Care, 15,* 1800–1809.

Schulz, R. (1980). Aging and control. In J. Garber & M. Seligman (Eds.), *Learned helplessness: Theory and applications* (pp. 261–277). Toronto: Academic.

Schunk, D. H., & Carbonari, J. P. (1984). Self-efficacy models. In J. D. Matarazo, S. M. Weiss, J. A. Herd, & N. E. Miller, (Eds.), *Behavioral Health* (pp. 231–246). New York: John Wiley & Sons.

Seals, D. R., Hagberg, J. M., Hurley, F. B., Ehsani, A. A., & Holloszy, J. O. (1984). Endurance training in older men and women. I. Cardiovascular responses to exercise. *Journal of Applied Physiology, 57,* 1024–1029.

Sedgwick, A. W., Taplin, R. E., Davidson, A., & Thomas, D. W. (1988). Effects of physical activity on risk factors for coronary heart disease in previously sedentary women: A five-year longitudinal study. *Australia & New Zealand Journal of Medicine 18,* 600–605.

Segall, A., & Chappell, N. L. (1989). Health care beliefs and the use of medical and social services by the elderly. In *Aging and health: Linking research and public policy* (pp. 129–141). Chelsea, MI: Lewis Publications, Inc.

Sharpe, P. A., & O'Connell, C. M. (1992). Exercise beliefs and behaviors among older employees: A health promotion trial. *The Gerontologist, 32*(40), 444–449.

Shay, K. A., & Roth, D. L. (1992). Association between aerobic fitness and visuospatial performance in healthy older adults. *Psychology & Aging, 7,* 15–24.

Shea, E. J. (1986). *Swimming for seniors.* Champaign, IL: Leisure Press.

Shephard, R. J. (1978). *Physical activity and aging.* Chicago, IL: Yearbook Medical Publishers.

Shephard, R. J. (1984). Can we identify those for whom exercise is hazardous? *Sports Medicine, 1,* 75–86.

Shephard, R. J. (1986a). Physical training for the elderly. *Clinics in Sports Medicine, 5*(3), 515–533.

Shephard, R. J. (1986b). Physical activity and aging in a post-industrial society. In B. D. McPherson (Ed.), *Sport and aging* (pp 37–44). Champaign, IL: Human Kinetics.

Shephard, R. J. (1986c). Fitness of a nation: Lessons from the Canada Fitness Survey. *Medicine & Sport Science, 22,* 134–179.

Shephard, R. J. (1992). Does exercise reduce all-cancer death rates? *British Journal of Sports Medicine, 26,* 125–128.

Shephard, R. J. (1997). *Aging, Physical Activity and Health.* Champaign, IL: Human Kinetics.

Shephard, R. J., Corey, P., & Cox, M. (1982). Health hazard appraisal—The influence of an employee fitness program. *Canadian Journal of Public Health, 73,* 183–187.

Shephard, R. J., & Montelpare, W. M. (1988). Geriatric benefits of exercise as an adult. *Journal of Gerontology, 43,* M86–M90.

Shivers, J. S. (1991). Physical recreational experience in successful aging. *Physical activity and sports for healthy aging: Program and abstracts, Abstract No. 84,* p. 58.

Shu, X. O., Hatch, M. C., Zheng, W., Gao, Y. T., & Brinton, L. A. (1993). Physical activity and risk of endometrial cancer. *Epidemiology, 4*, 342–349.

Siconolfi, S. F., Lasater, T. M., Snow, R. C. K., & Carleton, R. A. (1985). Self-reported physical activity compared with maximal oxygen uptake. *American Journal of Epidemiology, 122*(1), 101–105.

Sidney, K. H., & Shephard, R. J. (1976). Attitudes towards health and physical activity in the elderly: Effects of a physical training program. *Medicine & Science in Sports, 8*(4), 246–252.

Sidney, K. H., & Shephard, R. J. (1978). Frequency and intensity of exercise training for elderly subjects. *Medicine & Science in Sports & Exercise, 10*(2), 125–131.

Sidney, K. H., Shephard, R. J., & Harrison, J. E. (1977). Endurance training and body composition of the elderly. *The American Journal of Clinical Nutrition, 30*, 326–333.

Sinaki, M., & Grubbs, N. C. (1989). Back strengthening exercises: quantitative evaluation of their efficacy for women aged 40 to 65 years. *Archives of Physical Medicine & Rehabilitation, 70*, 16–20.

Singh, R. B., Singh, N. K., Rastogi, S. S., Mani, U. V., & Niaz, M. A. (1993). Effects of diet and lifestyle changes on atherosclerotic risk factors after 24 weeks on the Indian Diet Heart Study. *The American Journal of Cardiology, 71*, 1283–1288.

Siscovick, D. S., Laporte, R. E., & Newman, J. M. (1985). The disease-specific benefits and risks of physical activity and exercise. *Public Health Reports, 100*, 180–188.

Skinner, H. A., Palmer, W., Sanchez-Craig, M., & McIntosh, M. (1987). Reliability of a lifestyle assessment using microcomputers. *Canadian Journal of Public Health, 78*(Sept/Oct), 329–334.

Slattery, M. L., Schumacher, M. C., Smith, K. R., West, D. W., & Abd-Elghany, N. (1990). Physical activity, diet and risk of colon cancer in Utah. *American Journal of Epidemiology, 13*, 567–570.

Slovic, P. (1986). Informing and educating the public about risk. *Risk Analysis, 6*, 403–415.

Smith, E. L. (1981). Age: The interaction of nature and nurture. In E. L. Smith & R. C. Serfass (Ed.), *Exercise and aging: The scientific basis* (pp. 11–18). Hillside, NJ: Enslow.

Smith, E. L., Reddan, W., & Smith, P. E. (1981). Physical activity and calcium modalities for bone mineral increase in aged women. *Medicine & Science in Sports & Exercise, 13*(1), 60–64.

Smith, L. K. (1988). Cardiac disorders: A guide to assessing risk in the elderly. *Geriatrics, 43*(7), 33–38.

Smith, R. A. (1984). The rise of basketball for women in colleges. In S. A. Reiss (Ed.), *The American sporting experience* (pp. 239–253). New York: Leisure Press.

Snow-Harter, C. (1987). Biochemical changes in postmenopausal women following a muscle fitness program. *The Physician & Sports Medicine, 15*(8), 90–96.

Snyder, E. E., & Spreitzer, E. (1973). Family influence and involvement in sports. *The Research Quarterly, 44*(2), 249–255.

Sonstroem, R. J., & Walker, M. I. (1973). Relationship of attitudes and locus of control to exercise and physical fitness. *Perceptual & Motor Skills, 36*, 1031–1034.

Sorock, G. S., Bush, T. L., Golden, A. L., Fried L. P., Breur, B., & Hale, W. E. (1986). Physical activity and fracture risk in a free-living elderly cohort. *Journal of Gerontology, 43*, M134–M139.

Sources: Information for seniors and seniors' organizations in British Columbia. (1991). Profile of Seniors in B.C. Vancouver, B.C.: Seniors' Resources and Research Society of B.C.

Spacapan, S., & Oskamp, S. (1989). *The social psychology of health.* Newbury Park, CA: Sage.

Speechly, M., & Tinetti, M. (1991). Falls and injuries in frail and vigorous community elderly persons. *Journal of the American Geriatric Society, 39*, 46–52.

Spina, R. J., Ogawa, T., Miller, T. R., Kohrt, W. M., & Ehsani, A. A. (1993). Effect of exercise training on left ventricular performance in older women free of cardiopulmonary disease. *The American Journal of Cardiology, 71*, 99–104.

Spirduso, W. W. (1975). Reaction and movement time as a function of age and physical activity level. *Journal of Gerontology, 30*, 435–440.

Spirduso, W. W. (1980). Physical fitness, aging and psychomotor speed: A review. *Journal of Gerontology, 35*(6), 850–865.

Spirduso, W. W. (1986). Physical activity and the prevention of premature aging. In V. Seefeldt (Ed.), *Physical activity and well-being* (pp. 146–160). Reston, VA: AAHPERD.

Spirduso, W. W., & Clifford, P. (1978). Replication of age and physical activity effects on reaction and movement time. *Journal of Gerontology, 33*, 26–30.

Spirduso, W. W., & MacRae, P. G. (1991). Physical exercise and the quality of life in the frail elderly.

In J. E. Lubben, J. C. Rowe, & D. E. Deutchman (Eds.), *The concept and measurement of quality of life in the frail elderly* (pp. 226–255). New York: Academic Press.

Spreitzer, E., & Snyder, E. E. (1976). Socialization into sport: An exploratory path analysis. *Research Quarterly, 47*(2), 238–245.

Spreitzer, E., & Snyder, E. E. (1983). Correlates of participation in adult recreational sports. *Journal of Leisure Research, 15*(1), 27–38.

Stacey, C., Kozma, A., & Stones, M. J. (1985). Simple cognitive and behavioural changes resulting from improved physical fitness in persons over 50 years of age. *Canadian Journal of Aging, 4*(2), 67–74.

Stamford, B. A., Hambacher, W., & Fallica, A. (1974). Effects of daily physical exercise on the psychiatric state of institutionalized geriatric mental patients. *Research Quarterly, 45*, 34–41.

Starischka, S. & Bohmer, D. (1986). Diagnosis and optimization of selected components of physical fitness in elderly sport participants. In B. D. McPherson (Ed.), *Sport and aging* (pp. 125–136). Champaign, IL: Human Kinetics.

Statistics Canada. (1984). *The elderly in Canada, 1981 census.* Ottawa, ON: Ministry of Supply & Services.

Statistics Canada. (1986). *Women in Canada: A statistical report.* Ottawa: Minister of Supply & Services.

Statistics Canada. (1988). Disabled Canadians. *The Daily*, May 31, p. 2.

Statistics Canada. (1990). *Women in Canada: A statistical report.* Ottawa, ON: Minister of Supply & Services.

Statistics Canada. (1992). *Aging and Independence.* Ottowa, Ontario: Government of Canada.

Steinhardt, M. A., & Carrier, K. M. (1989). Early and continued participation in a work-site health and fitness program. *Research Quarterly for Exercise & Sport, 60*(2), 117–126.

Stenstrom, C. H. (1994). Radiologically observed progression of joint destruction and its relationship with demographic factors, disease severity, and exercise frequency in patients with rheumatoid arthritis. *Physical Therapy, 74*, 32–39.

Stephens, T. (1988). Physical activity and mental health in the United States and Canada: Evidence from four population surveys. *Preventive Medicine, 17*, 35–47.

Stephens, T. (1992). Leisure time physical activity. Chapter 10 in *Health Promotion Survey.* Ottawa, ON: Minister of Supply & Social Services.

Stephens, T., & Caspersen, C. J. (1994). The demography of physical activity. In C. Bouchard, R. J. Shephard, & T. Stephens (Eds.). *Physical Activity, Fitness and Health.* (pp. 204–213). Champaign, IL: Human Kinetics.

Stephens, T., & Craig, C. L. (1990). *The well-being of Canadians: Highlights of the 1988 Campbell's Survey.* Ottawa: Canadian Fitness and Lifestyle Research Institute.

Stephens, T., Craig, C. L., & Ferris, B. F. (1986). Adult physical fitness in Canada: Findings from the Canada Fitness Survey I. *Canadian Journal of Public Health, 77*(4), 285–290.

Stephens, T., Jacobs, D. R., Jr., & White, C. C. (1985). The descriptive epidemiology of leisure-time physical activity. *Public Health Reports, 100*, 147–158.

Stewart, A. L., & King, A. C. (1991). Evaluating the efficacy of physical activity for influencing quality-of-life outcomes in older adults. *Annals of Behavioral Medicine, 13*(3), 108–116.

Stone, L. O., & Fletcher, S. (1980). *A profile of Canada's older population.* Montreal, PQ: The Institute for Research on Public Policy.

Stone, L. O., & Frenken, H. (1988). *Canada's seniors.* Ottawa, ON: Minster of Supply and Services, Canada.

Stones, M. J., & Dawe, D. (1993). Acute exercise facilities semantically cued memory in nursing home residents. *Journal of the American Geriatric Society, 41*, 531–534.

Stones, M. J., & Kozma, A. (1988). Physical activity, age, and cognitive/motor performance. In M. L. Howe & C. J. Brainerd (Eds.), *Cognitive development in adulthood, progress in cognitive development research* (pp. 273–321).

Stones, M. J., & Kozma, A. (1989). Age, exercise, and coding performance. *Psychology & Aging, 4*, 190–194.

Sturgeon, S. R., Brinton, L. A., Berman, M. L., Mortel, R., Twiggs, L. B., Barrett, R. J., & Wilbanks, G. D. (1993). Past and present physical activity and endometrial cancer risk. *British Journal of Cancer, 68*, 584–589.

Suominen, H., Heikkinen, E., & Parkatti, T. (1977). Effect of eight weeks' physical training on muscle and connective tissue of the M. vastus lateralis in 69-year-old men and women. *Journal of Gerontology, 32,* 33–37.

Suominen, H., & Rahkila, P. (1991). Bone mineral density of the calcaneus in 70- to 81-year old male athletes and a population sample. *Medicine & Science in Sports, 23,* 1227–1233.

Svanstrom, L. (1990). Simply osteoporosis—Or multifactorial genesis for the increasing incidence of fall injuries in the elderly? *Scandinavian Journal of Social Medicine, 18,* 165–169.

Swerts, P. M. J., Kretzers, L. M. J., Terpstra-Lindeman, E., Verstappen, F. T. J., & Wouters, E. F. M. (1990). Exercise reconditioning in the rehabilitation of patients with chronic obstructive disease: A short- and long-term analysis. *Archives of Physical Medicine & Rehabilitation, 71,* 570–573.

Tabachnick, B. G. & Fidell, L. S. (1989). *Using multivariate statistics.* New York: Harper & Row.

Tait, J. R., & Dobash, R. E. (1986). Sporting women: The social network of reasons for participation. In J. A. Mangan & R. B. Small (Eds.), *Sport, culture society: International historical and sociological perspectives* (pp. 262–269). New York: E. & F.N. Spon.

Takala, P. (1991). The meaning of physical activity during old age. *Physical activity and sports for healthy aging: Program and abstracts, Abstract No. 87,* p. 59.

Takeshima, N., Tanaka, K., Kobayashi, F., Watanabe, T., & Kaot, T. (1993). Effects of aerobic exercise conditioning at intensities corresponding to lactate threshold in the elderly. *European Journal of Applied Physiology, 67,* 138–143.

Taylor, C. B., Coffey, T., Berra, K., Iaffaldano, R., Casey, D. & Haskell, W. L. (1984). Seven day activity and self-report compared to a direct measure of physical activity. *American Journal of Epidemiology, 120*(6), 818–824.

Taylor, H. L., Jacobs, D. R., Schucker, B., Kinedsen, J., Leon, A. S., & Debacker, G. (1978). A questionnaire for the assessment of leisure time physical activities. *Journal of Chronic Diseases, 31,* 741–755.

Teague, M. L. (1987, 1992). *Health Promotion: Achieving high-level wellness in the later years.* Indianapolis, IN: Benchmark.

Teague, M. L., & Hunnicutt, B. K. (1989). An analysis of the 1990 Public Health Service physical fitness and exercise objectives for older Americans. *Health Values, 13*(4), 15–23.

Thomas, S. P. (1984). The holistic philosophy and perspective of selected health educators. *Health Education, 15*(1), 16–20.

Thomas, S. P. (1990). Predictors of health status in mid-life women: Implications for later adulthood. *Journal of Women & Aging, 2*(1), 49–77.

Ting, A. J. (1991). Running and the older athlete. *Clinics in Geriatric Medicine, 10,* 319–325.

Tinetti, M. E., Speechly, M., & Ginter, S. F. (1988). Risk factors for falls among elderly persons living in the community. *New England Journal of Medicine, 319,* 1701–1707.

Tinsley, H. E. A., Teaff, J. D., Colbs, S. L., & Kaufman, N. (1985). A system of classifying laisure activities in terms of the psychological benefits of participation reported by older persons. *Journal of Gerontology, 40*(2), 172–178.

Tirrell, B. E., & Hart, L. K. (1980). The relationship of health beliefs and knowledge to exercise compliance in patients after coronary bypass. *Heart & Lung, 9,* 487–493.

Tonino, R. P., & Driscoll, P. A. (1988). Reliability of maximal and submaximal parameters of treadmill testing for the measurement of physical training in older persons. *Journal of Gerontology, 43,* M101–M104.

Topper, A. K., Maki, B. E., & Holliday, P. J. (1993). Are activity-based assessments of balance and gait in the elderly predictive of risk of falling and/or type of fall? *Journal of the American Geriatric Society, 41,* 479–487.

Toshima, M. T., Kaplan, R. M., & Ries, A. L. (1990). Experimental evaluation of rehabilitation in chronic obstructive pulmonary disease: Short-term effects on exercise endurance and health status. *Health Psychology, 9,* 237–252.

Toward a better age. (1990). Report of the British Columbia Task Force on Issues of Concern to Seniors. Victoria, BC: Ministry of Health and Ministry of Seniors.

Traugott, M. W., & Katosk, J. P. (1979). Response validity in surveys of voting behavior. *Public Opinion Quarterly, 43,* 359.

Tucker, L. A., & Mortell, R. (1993). Comparison of the effects of walking and weight training programs on body image in middle-aged women: An experimental study. *American Journal of Health Promotion, 8,* 34–42.

Tupper, E. S. (1888). As we at tennis played. *Outing, 12,* 347.

University of Victoria Centre on Aging Newsletter. (1993). January.

United Nations Office at Vienna. (1990). United States: Statistics on older women. *Bulletin on Aging, 1,* 5.

United Nations Office at Vienna (1991). Aging: Individuals and populations. *Bulletin on Aging, 1,* 1.

Upton, S. J., Hagan, R. D., Rosentswieg, J., & Gettman, L. R. (1983). Comparison of physiological profiles of middle-aged women distance runners and sedentary women. *Research Quarterly for Exercise and Sport, 54*(1), 83–87.

U.S. Bureau of the Census. (1975). *Historical statistics of the United States: Colonial times to 1970.* U.S. Department of Commerce.

U.S. Department of Health and Human Services. (1991) *Monthly Vital Statistics Report, 40*(1), 14, May 16.

U.S. Department of Health and Human Services, National Center for Health Statistics. (1994a). *Health United States, 1993.* Washington, DC: Government Printing Office.

U.S. Department of Health & Human Services. (1994b). *Healthy People 2000 Review, 1993.* Rockville, MD: U.S. Government Printing Office.

U.S. Department of Health and Human Services. (1994c) *Health: United States, 1993.* Hyattsville, MD: U.S. Department of Health and Human Services.

U.S. Department of Health and Human Services. (1995) *Health: United States 1994.* Hyattsville, MD: U.S. Department of Health and Human Services.

U.S. Department of Health and Human Services. (1996). *Physical activity and health: A report of the Surgeon General.* Centers for Disease Control and Prevention.

Vaccaro, P., Dummer G. M., & Clarke, D. H. (1981). Physiological characteristics of female master's swimmers. *The Physician & Sports Medicine, 9*(12), 75–78.

Vaccaro, P., Ostrove, S. M., Vandervelden, L., Goldfarb, A. H., & Clarke, D. H. (1984). Body composition and physiological responses of masters female swimmers 20 to 70 years of age. *Research Quarterly for Exercise & Sport, 55*(3), 278–284.

Verbrugge, L. M. (1990a). Knowledge and power: Health and physical education for women in America. In R. D. Apple (Ed.), *Women, health, and medicine in America: A historical handbook* (pp. 369–390). New York & London: Garland Publishing Inc.

Verbrugge, L. M. (1990b). Pathways of health and death. In R.D. Apple (Ed.), *Women, health, and medicine in America: A historical handbook.* New York: Garland Publishing.

Verbrugge, L. M. (1994).

Verbrugge, L. M., & Wingard, D. L. (1987). Sex differentials in health and mortality. *Women & Health, 12*(2), 103–145.

Vertinsky, P. A. (1987). Exercise, physical capability, and the eternally wounded woman in late nineteenth century North America. *Journal of Sport History, 14*(1), 7–13.

Vertinsky, P. A. (1988a). Of no use without health: Late nineteenth century medical prescriptions for female exercise throughout the life span. *Women & Health, 14*(1), 89–115.

Vertinsky, P. A. (1988b). Escape from freedom: G. Stanley Hall's totalitarian views on female health and physical education. *International Journal of History & Sport, 5*(1), 69–95.

Vertinsky, P. A. (1989). Feminist Charlotte Perkins Gilman's pursuit of health and physical fitness as a strategy for emancipation. *Journal of Sport History, 16*(1), 5–26.

Vertinsky, P. A. (1990). *The eternally wounded woman.* Manchester: Manchester University Press.

Vertinsky, P. A. (1991). Priorities and policy directions in health promotion: Elderly women and exercise: Benefits, barriers and risks. Unpublished paper presented at the Faculty of Health Sciences, McGill University, Montreal, November, 1991.

Vertinsky, P. A. (1992). Reclaiming space, revisioning the body: The quest for gender sensitive physical education. *Quest, 44,* 373–396.

Vertinsky, P. A. (1994). The social construction of the gendered body: Exercise and the exercise of power. *The International Journal of the History of Sport, 11,* 147–171.

Vetter, N. J., & Lewis, P. A. (1992). Home accidents in elderly people [letter]. *British Medical Journal, 305,* 312.

Voorips, L. E., Lemmick, K. A., Van Heuvelen, M. J. G., Bult, P., & Van Staveren, W. A. (1993). The physical condition of elderly women differing in habitual physical activity. *Medicine & Science in Sports, 25*, 1152–1157.

Wakat, D., & Odom, S. (1982). The older woman: Increased psychosocial benefits from physical activity. *Journal of Physical Education, Recreation & Dance, 53*(3), 34–35.

Wallberg-Henriksson, H. (1989). Acute exercise: Fuel homeostasis and glucose transport in insulin dependent diabetes mellitus. *Medicine & Science in Sports & Exercise*, 356–360.

Waldron, I. (1976). Why do women live longer than men? *Social Science & Medicine, 10*, 349–362.

Waller, K. V., & Bates, R. C. (1992). Health locus of control and self-efficacy beliefs in a healthy elderly sample. *American Journal of Health Promotion, 6*(4), 302–309.

Waller, B. (1985). Exercise-related sudden death in young (age 0–30 years) and old (age 30+ years). conditioned subjects. In N. K. Wenger (Eds.), *Exercise and the heart* (pp. 9–75). Philadelphia: F.A. Davis Co.

Wallston, K. A. & Wallston, B. S. (1978). Health locus of control. *Health Education Monographs, 6*(1), 100–105.

Wankel, L. M. (1984). Decision-making and social-support strategies for increasing exercise involvement. *Journal of Cardiac Rehabilitation, 4*, 124–152.

Washburn, R. A., Jette, A. M., & Janney C. A. (1990). Using age-neutral physical activity questionnaires in research with the elderly. *Journal of Aging & Health, 2*, 341–356.

Waterbor, J., Cole, P., Delzell, E., & Andjelkovich, D. (1988). The mortality experience of major league baseball players. *New England Journal of Medicine, 318*(19), 1278–1280.

Weaver, T. E., & Narsavage, G. L. (1992). Physiological and psychological variables related to functional status in chronic obstructive pulmonary disease.*Nursing Research 41*, 286–291.

Webb, G. D., Poehlman, E. T., & Tonino, R. P. (1993). Dissociation of changes in metabolic rate and blood pressure with erythrocyte Na-K pump activity in older men after endurance training. *Journal of Gerontology: Medical Sciences, 48*(2), M47–M52.

Weber, F., Barnard, R. J., & Roy, D. (1983). Effects of a high-complex-carbohydrate, low-fat diet and daily exercise on individuals 70 years of age and older. *Journal of Gerontology, 38*(2), 155–161.

Webster, J. A. (1988). Key to healthy aging: Exercise. *Journal of Gerontological Nursing, 14*(12), 8–15.

Wechsler, H., Levine, S., Idelson, R. K., Rohman, M., & Taylor, J. O. (1983). The physician's role in health promotion—A survey of primary-care physicians. *New England Journal of Medicine, 308*, 97–100.

Weiner, D. K., Bongiorni, D. R., Studenski, S. A., Duncan, P. W., & Kochersberger, G. G. (1993). Does functional reach improve with rehabilitation? *Archives of Physical Medicine & Rehabilitation, 74*, 796–800.

Weinstein, N. D. (1984). Why it won't happen to me: Perceptions of risk factors and susceptibility. *Health Psychology, 3*(5), 431–457.

Weinstein, N. D. (1988). The precaution adoption process. *Health Psychology, 7*(4), 355–386.

Whitehurst, M., & Menendez, E. (1991). Endurance training in older women: Lipid and lipoprotein responses. *The Physician & Sports Medicine, 19*, 95–104.

Wilkins, R., & Adams, O. B. (1983). Health expectancy in Canada, late 1970s: Demographic, regional, and social dimensions. *American Journal of Health Promotion, 73*(9), 1073–1080.

Williams, M. (1987). Type II Diabetes: A new emphasis for prevention and management? *ACHPER National Journal*, 13–15.

Wilmore, J. H., Miller, H. L., & Pollock, M.L. (1974). Body composition and physiological characteristics of active endurance athletes in their eighth decade of life. *Medicine & Science in Sports, 6*(1), 44–48.

Wilson, P. W. F., Paffenbarger, R. S., Morris, J. N., & Havlik, R. J. (1986). Assessment methods for physical activity and physical fitness in population studies: Report of a NHLBI workshop. *American Heart Journal, 111*(6), 1177–1192.

Winborn, M. D., Meyers, A. W., & Mulling, C. (1988). The effects of gender and experience on perceived exertion. *Journal of Sport & Exercise Physiology, 10*, 22–31.

Woodward, N. J. & Wallston, B. S. (1987). Age and health care beliefs: Self-efficacy as a mediator of low desire for control. *Psychology & Aging, 2*(2), 3–8.

Work, J. A. (1989). Strength training: A bridge to independence for the elderly. *The Physician & Sports Medicine, 17*(11), 134–140.

World Health Organization (WHO). (1992). *Health of the elderly: A concern for all.*

Wurtele, S. K., & Maddux, J. E. (1987). Relative contributions of protection motivation theory components in predicting exercise intentions and behavior. *Health Psychology, 6*(5), 453–466.

Yasin, S., Alderson, M. R., Marr, J. W., Pattison, D. C., & Morris, J. N. (1967). Assessment of habitual physical activity apart from occupation. *British Journal of Preventive Social Medicine, 21*, 163–169.

Young, C., Blondin, J., Tensuan, R., & Fryer, J. (1963). Body composition studies of "older" women thirty to seventy years of age. *Annals of the New York Academy of Sciences, 110*, 589–607.

Zinberg, N. E., & Kaufman, I. (1963). *Normal psychology of the aging process.* New York: International Universities Press.

Index